A Military Pilot's Exciting Life and Visit from the Hereafter

LT. COL. KENNETH HAWK SLAKER

www.ivyhousebooks.com

PUBLISHED BY IVY HOUSE PUBLISHING GROUP
5122 Bur Oak Circle, Raleigh, NC 27612
United States of America
919-782-0281
www.ivyhousebooks.com

ISBN13: 978-1-57197-489-1
Library of Congress Control Number: 2007943789

© 2008 Lt. Col. Kenneth Hawk Slaker
All rights reserved, which includes the right to reproduce this book or portions thereof in any form whatsoever except as provided by the U.S. Copyright Law.

Printed in the United States of America

*Dedicated to Charles Lindbergh, who influenced
my life more than any other man.*

TABLE OF CONTENTS

Chapter 1: A Farm Boy Grows Up 1
Chapter 2: Reaching for the Silver Wings 7
Chapter 3: Learning to Fly the B-17 15
Chapter 4: Piloting the B-17 in Combat 31
Chapter 5: Stateside War Years, 1943-45 59
Chapter 6: Army Reserve Pilot Goes to College 97
Chapter 7: Escape Through Russia's Iron Curtain 109
Chapter 8: Classified Mission With Charles Lindbergh 135
Chapter 9: Two Lives Saved and a Love Lost 143
Chapter 10: Washburn University AFROTC 157
Chapter 11: Chasing Weather to the North Pole 173
Chapter 12: Love's Third Charm in Alaska 183
Chapter 13: Saving Lives in Alaska 189
Chapter 14: Chief Transport Control, Continental Div. MATS 199
Chapter 15: Air Force Pilot Studies for His MBA 211
Chapter 16: Becoming a Jet Pilot 221
Chapter 17: A Management Engineering Pilot 229
Chapter 18: Chief of Nuclear Missile War Plans 241
Chapter 19: Professor of Aerospace Studies at UNC 265
Chapter 20: Boeing Hires A Management Engineer 277
Chapter 21: A New Career 285
Chapter 22: A Visit From the Hereafter 309
Bibliography 315

List of Illustrations

Slaker on His 21st Birthday 8
Slaker & O'Hoppe at Their Pup Tent in North Africa 20
Officer Crew of the *Elaine* 32
Thank You Letter from the U.S. Treasury 63
Slaker Receiving Air Medal with Three Oak Leaf Clusters 69
Slaker in Front of His New B-24 72
Thank You Letter from Radio Station WOW 74
Lincoln Army Air Field 77
Certificate of Completion of Long Range Cruise Control Course 86
Slaker Appointed as a Regular Army Officer. 101
A Commendation from the Surgeon General 102
Slaker in Front of Air Mileage Computer 104
Congratulations Letter for Commission into Regular Air Force. 105-106
Certificate of Completion for Post Engineer Course 107
Lincoln Star News Article About Slaker's Escape from Russia 128
Congratulations Letter from Edwin G. Hill 130
Rudolph Schnabel, Savior of Slaker's Life 134
Letter of Commendation and Appreciation 154
Letter of Commendation and Appreciation 155
Slaker's 30th Birthday, 14 April 1950 156
Diploma (BA) from Washburn University of Topeka 172
Diploma from Arctic Indoctrination School in Alaska 177
Lee Ann Stanislaus, Lackland AFB, San Antonio, Texas, 1960 179
Commendation for H-19 Deliveries to Alaska 197
MATS Letter Order 224 207
Appreciation Letter from Commander Randolph AFB 223
Article from San Antonio's *The Light* About Randolph Air Base Open House . . . 225
Commendation Letter from 3510th Flying Training Wing 226

University of California MBA Degree. 233

Personal Letter from Colonel Boys, Commander 235

Newspaper Welcomes Slaker to Missile Wing. 243

Slaker Sworn into the Daedalian Society 245

Test Firing of the Mace Nuclear Missile 251

Stars and Stripes with Headline About President Kennedy's Death 257

Baby New Year's 1964 258

West Berliner Article About Slaker's Escape from Russia 267

Performance of Duty Letter from Keesler Technical Training Center 269

Congratulations Letter from the Department of the Air Force 271

Certificate from Arnold Air Society 274

Certificate from the 301st Veteran's Association 275

Note of Thanks from Sales Analysis Class at Boeing Aerospace Center. 280

Letter of Appreciation for Slaker's Motivation Presentation 282

Certificate of Outstanding Performance from Boeing. 284

Welcome Letter from the Mayor of Seattle. 287

Corporate License to Algo Diferente, Inc. 289

New Vacation Home in Puerto Vallarta, Mexico. 299

Slaker Commissioned a Washington State General. 300

Appreciation of Slaker's Service as Vice President General for the Sons of the State of Washington Certificate for Contributions to State Seal 303

American Revolution 306

Record of the Pacific District Meeting of the SAR at Anchorage, Alaska. 307

Graduation, Jet Aircraft Flying School, Randolph Air Base, Texas, 1959 313

Chapter 1
A Farm Boy Grows Up

Dr. Keeler, the country doctor that delivered my mother into this world on January 1, 1900, also brought me into the family in April 1920. He was the only doctor in this small country town of Elderton, with a population of about 700. It is located midway between Kittanning, the county seat of Armstrong County, and Indiana, the seat of Indiana County, Pennsylvania. My mother, Rosanna Ruth Hawk, was the daughter of James Gaily Hawk, whose fourth great-grandfather, George Haag (Hawk), arrived at Philadelphia on September 7, 1748 from Reutlingen, Germany. Rosanna's mother was Anna Maude Craft, born in 1875 at Elderton, Pennsylvania.

My father, Kenneth Waverly Slaeker, was born in Beaver Falls, Pennsylvania on the 18th of June, 1900. His father was Ferdinand Schleicher, who arrived in New York City on the 9th of June 1866, from Germany. He married Elizabeth Heckman of Apollo, Pennsylvania in 1893. After son Kenneth was born, the family moved to Milwaukee, Wisconsin. In 1912 the family moved to Montana where they homesteaded at Lavina. When son Kenneth was seventeen years old, he became bored working as a waiter in the family hotel and departed to visit relatives in western Pennsylvania. He became employed at the large steel mill located at Vandergrift, Pennsylvania.

Rosanna Hawk moved to Vandergrift in 1918 to work at a local store. Kenneth met and dated her, which became a steady relationship. She became pregnant and Kenneth refused to marry her. She returned to the Hawk family home in Elderton, and when the family learned of her pregnancy, her oldest brother, Leslie Hawk, a big muscular oil field driller, decided that his sister's child was not going to be born out of wedlock. In January 1920, he put his sister in his new Ford auto and drove the dirt road to Vandergrift. He found Kenneth and convinced him that he was going to marry his sister Rosanna. He drove them to the courthouse in Butler, Pennsylvania, where the Judge married Kenneth and Rosanna on January 31, 1920.

Kenneth refused to have his new wife live with him and she returned to Elderton. I was born in the Hawk house early in the morning of April 14th. My dad then filed for an annulment of the marriage based on the fact that both he and Rosanna had lied about their ages. The law required approval by the parents for the children to marry if they were not twenty-one. The judge denied the annulment and told Kenneth that he had a good wife, a new son, and a good job and to get back to work and raise his family. Again he refused to live with Rosanna, and she returned to Elderton. When he heard that his son was very ill with the flu, he started visiting my mother. My uncle Leslie told me in later years that my dad was really pissed off when he found out that my mother had named me after him.

When I was one year old there was a flu epidemic in the area and many suffered from it, including me. There were fatalities, and Dr. Keeler was doing everything he could to stop it from spreading. I came down with it and Dr. Keeler gave me a shot in the back, which my mother said really made me sick. Years later, Mother told me that it was her mother that had saved me. She died about three months after I was born and just before her last breath, she told my mother that with God's help she was going to look after young Kenneth for the rest of his life. My Guardian Angel!

My dad had been informed of my severe illness and, for the first time since their marriage, my dad came to Elderton to visit my mother and me. His visits became more frequent and my mother became pregnant again. My brother was born on March 26, 1922 and was named James after our grandfather. My dad visited us often but made no effort to have us join him in Vandergrift.

My grandfather, James Gaily Hawk, was like a father to me. He was always close by, for the general store that he owned and operated was next door to the Hawk brick mansion. My constant companion was the family collie named Fanny. In the third year of my life, my father finally decided to have us join him in Vandergrift. I have a clear memory of his arriving in a sedan with plastic curtains for windows and driving us to our new home. It was an apartment located above a five-and-dime store on the town's main street.

The apartment above us was occupied by a family named Means, and their daughter became our sitter. One day when the daughter was meant to watch us, mother gave me a nickel to get an ice cream cone while she went shopping. Not happy with my dad, I went across the street where the streetcar tracks terminated and boarded the streetcar with my nickel. People on the streetcar were very nice to me and one man gave me a sandwich out of his dinner bucket. When we got to the end of the line in Leechburg, I was the only passenger left in the car. The conductor became concerned, and I would not answer any of his questions, so he called the police. They told the conductor that they had a call from the Vandergrift police of a missing child and that the boy's mother was at the station and very distraught. A policeman got into the streetcar with me and delivered me to the Vandergrift police. My dear mother cried and hugged and kissed me and we walked to the apartment. My father was there and he gave me one hell of a licking. I never forgot that reception.

When I was four years old we moved to a small house in Vandergrift Heights where many of the steel workers lived. Our neighborhood consisted of Polish, American, and

Italian families, and a German family named Stoltz that moved in the same time as we did. They all had children my age, and we kids played and grew up together.

When I was six years old, my mother took me to the elementary school, which was only three blocks from our house. The school consisted of two yellow brick buildings three stories high and fairly new. Across the street behind some commercial buildings was a water pond. During recess and after school we kids tied together some boards to make a raft. When I was in third grade, I was on the raft by myself and fell into the deep water but had not yet learned to swim. As I struggled and shouted for help, a man walking nearby saw that I was in trouble and rescued me from the pond. Again I got the usual licking from my father for being on the raft. This time he was right. Years later when I was in high school, my mother told me that just before her mother died, she had said that with God's help, she was going to watch over me all my life. Then I knew that my grandmother steered that man who saved me from drowning to the pond.

The summer after I had turned nine years old, we kids were playing kick the can and Richard Martin, a playmate, was chasing me when I ran directly in front of a Nash sedan that ran over my lower chest and abdomen. I remember women yelling to the driver to back up. Fortunately, a man across the street came running and shouting to the driver not to back up. He lifted me from behind the right front wheel and carried me to my house. The wheel had squeezed my bowels and bladder, and I was a wet and stinking mess. Dr. Stear arrived, and after examining me, said that no bones were broken but I might have internal injuries. The nearest hospital was forty miles away by dirt road to Pittsburgh. The doctor said that he would be back the next day to examine me again. I got to feeling better, and if there were internal injuries, they were healing.

The next summer just after school was out, we kids were playing catch, and I climbed over a backyard fence to keep from being tagged. I did not see the wire clothesline that caught under my chin, causing me to flip and land with my right leg twisted under me. I could not move and a neighbor called my mother, who found a neighbor that carried me home. When my father came home from work, he examined my leg and said that my right leg bone was cracked and I did not need a doctor. He wrapped my leg, and I spent the summer crawling around until school started. With the help of a cane, I limped to school for a month. The rest of my life, when I have stood erect, my right foot—instead of pointing straight ahead—points ten degrees to the right. *Thanks a lot, Dad.*

I was ten years old when my life's goal was established. I was learning to read, and at the city library I saw a book titled *WE*. I read about Charles Lindbergh flying solo to Paris, and the seed for my life's career was planted. I started making model airplanes at my grandfather's farm during the summer since my dad thought I was crazy and would not allow this at home. A flight strip with a hangar was constructed about a mile from Vandergrift. The local newspaper stated that on a certain future date the big Ford tri-motored airplane would be at the Vandergrift airport and offering rides for twenty-five cents. I borrowed enough nickels to pay for my flight and was really excited when the engines roared and we rolled down the grass runway. I cannot describe the thrill of being up in the sky, looking down at the houses and the steel mill by the river. When we approached the airfield for a landing, watching the ground rushing up at us was scary. There was no doubt in my mind that my life's goal was to become a pilot.

My mother was a strong Christian, and when I was fourteen years old, she had me attend Sunday School and church at St. Paul's Lutheran Church, which was only four blocks from our house. I had always gone to the Presbyterian church with my grandfather, but with his demise and sale of the farm, my trips to Elderton would be few. I seldom missed a Sunday at church, for I had an excellent teacher of the Bible, a Mrs. Newell. When I was sixteen, she insisted that I enter the regional Lutheran Boys and Girls Bible Contest.

I had a real surprise a month later when our minister, Rev. Frank, announced in church that a member of our church, Kenneth Slaker, had tied with a girl in Ohio for the winner of the Lutheran Boys and Girls Bible Contest. A special test was being sent to each one of their ministers, who would give the test to break the tie. At a church service a few weeks later, Rev. Frank announced that he was very proud that church member Kenneth Slaker had won the bible contest. Believe it or not, the church members applauded and my Bible teacher, Mrs. Newell, was very happy. My mother also was very pleased, but my father never said a word.

As a young teenager I loved music, and when I visited my grandfather, I would play all his records on his Victrola. I really liked the piano music and when I turned fifteen, I asked my mother if I could have a piano to learn to play music. She said that we could not afford a piano due to the Depression. The following Christmas my gift was a Gibson model classical guitar. Along with it came weekly lessons by Wayne Logan, a professional guitar player contracted by my mother. He lived one mile from our residence, and I walked with my guitar in its case once each week for my lesson for two years. By the end of my junior year in high school, I had learned all the piano chords, which were the same for the guitar. I started playing with professional dance bands, but to do so, I had to join the American Federation of Musicians Union. I became a member of three local dance bands and played two or three nights with name bands when they requested a classical guitar player from the union because their permanent member was absent. No matter where or who I played with, at intermission I had to show my union card to the AFM agent. When I played out of my union area, I had to give that local five percent of my earnings. For a teenager, I was making good money.

When I was a junior in high school, I started to date an attractive sophomore. In my senior year we were going steady, which was known by our classmates and teachers. About a month before graduating from high school, my English teacher, Miss Newcome, asked me to stop by her classroom at the end of that day's classes. I had no idea as to why she wanted to see me, for I had good grades and got along with all my teachers. When I arrived at her classroom, she asked me to close the door and to sit down by her desk. I remember every word that she said: "Kenneth, I have watched you here in school for four years and I want to give you some very personal advice. You are very intelligent and a good looking young man, and there is a great future awaiting you. Do not spoil or neglect the opportunity that exists for you by getting married just after graduation and becoming another steel mill worker spending your life here in this small town. There is no doubt in my mind that you have the potential for a much better and rewarding life. This is a very personal meeting between us, and I know that you will give serious thought to my advice." She stood up and held out her hand, which I shook, and then I surprised myself by giving her a hug and thanking her. She was so sincere in meeting and talking with me that she instilled within me the encouragement and determination to become what I wanted to be: an aviation pilot. God bless that wonderful teacher.

I graduated from high school with excellent grades and was presented the cash award for the outstanding student in Mechanical Drawing. My instructor was Ted Rosenzweig, an All-American football player from Carnegie Tech University in Pittsburgh. He informed me that he could obtain a scholarship for me in Architectural Engineering at Carnegie Tech. My total cost would be $800 per year. I told my dad of my good fortune and asked if I could borrow some money from him and would work summers to pay him back. Here was my alcoholic father's reply: "Son, I put a roof over your head, clothes on your back, and food in your stomach. Now get your ass out of here and make your own way." I knew that he had the money because a couple of weeks later he purchased a new Oldsmobile. I realized he cared less about me and my future. His lack of interest in me strengthened my desire to become a success in my own chosen career.

Chapter 2
REACHING FOR THE SILVER WINGS

I never told my parents that I had started taking flying lessons at the Vandergrift airport. They had never approved of my wanting to be a pilot because they felt that it was too dangerous and that I should forget it. My flight instructor was Mr. Schade, and he said that since I was nineteen years old and making my own money, I didn't need my parents' approval. I didn't question his statement because I wanted to fly and he wanted students. The aircraft that I was learning to fly was an Aeronca Tandem Trainer. Each flying lesson was about forty-five minutes of actual flying and cost fifteen dollars a lesson. Before you could solo the aircraft, government regulations required that you had logged eight hours of dual instruction.

It was my day off at the steel mill on the 19th of November 1940, and although it was snowing lightly, I drove to the airport to visit my flight instructor. I met Joe Schade in his office and he said, "Good to see you. Let's go for a spin." He climbed into the back seat and told me to fly a rectangular pattern and land. I knew that since it was snowing we could not do any aerial work but just practice landings. To my surprise, after the first landing Mr. Schade got out of the cockpit, patted me on the shoulder, and said, "You are okay. Take off, make three landings, and then taxi to the hangar." I was so excited. Here I was alone in an airplane and I was going to fly it! As tense as I was, I made two good landings and when I got into the downwind leg for my third landing, I looked up into the snowy sky and shouted to God, "I am a pilot!" When I arrived at the hangar, Joe Schade came up to the aircraft and said to me, "Congratulations, pilot!"

I did not tell my parents that I had soloed in an airplane, but I did tell two of my school buddies, Jack Foster and Steele Stewart. Unbeknownst to me, Mr. Schade had called the local newspaper to inform them about my solo flight. When I returned from work the next afternoon, mother showed me the front page of the newspaper and there was the article about a student at the local flying school, Kenneth Slaker, making his solo flight. My mother said she would hide the paper from my father so that he would not see it. I told her that I was twenty years old and making my own money and career, and that it was time for him to get off my back. Before he came home after his daily stop at the local speakeasy for a few beers, I placed the newspaper on his favorite chair. When we sat down for supper, I knew that he had read the article about my flying, but he never said a word. His mother had told me that my dad tried to be a pilot in World War I, but didn't qualify.

14 April 1941. My 21st Birthday and still single. I own my own 1938 Buick and was working at U. S. Steel Works at Dravosburg and playing classical guitar in Buddy Galloway's and Ray Keirn's Carnegie Tech Tartans Dance Bands.

I was the last student that Mr. Schade had at the Vandergrift airport, and he moved his flying school to the Bettis Field airport at Pittsburgh. My solo and flying instruction was at Bettis Field until November 1941. In early 1940, I had been named by our local congressman to become a cadet at the Naval Academy. I reported to the Navy recruiting center in Pittsburgh for the physical examination and failed it. The maximum height at that time was 6'2," and I was 6'3." Without any hesitation, I went to the Army recruiting office to be informed of the requirements by the Army to become an aviation cadet. First you had to be at least twenty years old. Second, you had to have completed two years of college, or pass an equivalent examination given by the Army. Finally, you had to pass the flight physical exam, which was very strict. However, being 6'3" tall was not a rejecting item in passing the physical.

I had one year of postgraduate study at my high school, but no college. I knew that the best help I could get to prepare me for the college exam would be the teachers I had my senior year at Vandergrift High. I met with them and they were very pleased to spend time with me. Miss Patton made herself available for advanced mathematics, Mr. Thompson for science, and Miss Newcome for English and literature. I mention their names because it was due to their professional tutoring that I successfully passed the college examination. I had completed the first hurdle.

A few days after being notified that I had passed the college examination, I reported to the Army induction center in Pittsburgh for my flight physical. I was one of seventeen that was given a very detailed physical examination, and only four of us passed. In October I was officially notified that I was accepted as an aviation cadet and was scheduled for the December call.

My cousin, Arlene Hawk, who was a student nurse at the Tarentum Valley Hospital, got me a date with her roommate, Jane George. She was attractive, had a good personality and an eye catching figure, and we enjoyed the same activities. We began dating steadily and became intimate. She was in full agreement with me that I should seek an appointment to the Aviation Cadets and become an Army pilot. In November 1941, I was informed that I would be receiving orders to report to Maxwell Army Airfield in December for preflight training. Many of my high school classmates who were being drafted and feeling that they were going to be gone for a long time were marrying their girlfriends. I had the same feeling and asked Jane to marry me and she agreed. Jane and I, along with her parents, drove to Winchester, Virginia the last week in November, where we were secretly married. I did not tell my parents of my marriage since I was twenty one and did not need their permission to marry. I never told them until after I was in the Aviation Cadets.

I was at work on Sunday, December 7, 1941 when I heard on the radio that the Japs had bombed Pearl Harbor. At first I thought this was a commentator just joking, but when a government spokesman came on the radio describing the destruction and casualties, I was shocked that it was the horrible truth. The very next afternoon, I received a call from the Army recruiting office in Pittsburgh that I was to be there on the 18th of December to be inducted into the aviation cadet program. During the next few days I was worried that I was secretly married, which violated the requirement to be a single person. I called the recruiting office and told the sergeant of my secret marriage. He said that since we were then at war, the requirement to be single for the aviation cadet program had been waived. I sold my Buick to my buddy, Steele Stewart, and my Gibson electric guitar and all my orchestra arrangements to a fellow musician. I had always been close to my mother, and saying goodbye to her was a tearful experience. It was then that mother said I was not to be afraid of going to war, for when her mother died just three months after I was born, she told Mother that God willing, she was going to look after Kenneth all his life. *My Guardian Angel!*

I was sworn into the Army on the morning of December 18th and boarded the train for Alabama. We arrived in Atlanta, Georgia the morning of the nineteenth, and it was cold with the temperature in the thirties. I had never been south before but always thought it was always warm there. We were changing trains for Montgomery, Alabama, but there was enough time to have breakfast and go to the restroom. I was really surprised to see two signs for the men's room: one said *White*, and the other said *Colored*. This was a new experience for me, for this didn't exist in Pennsylvania. When we arrived at Montgomery, there was a commercial bus waiting to take us to Maxwell field. I boarded the bus, and since the front seats were all full, I headed for the empty seats in the rear of the bus. The driver shouted to me, "You can't sit there, those seats are for colored people." I stood in the aisle all the way to Maxwell Field. *Welcome to the real South.*

As we new cadets stepped from the bus, an Army sergeant shouted to us to get in line and stand at attention. We obeyed his command, but this being my first visit to any Army base, I glanced around to see what the area looked like. The sergeant barked at me, "Mister, do you want to buy this place? When you are at attention, you look straight ahead." I was not used to being talked to in a loud and superior tone of voice and I felt my anger rising against this smart ass. I knew that I could floor him, for I was in excellent physical shape from flopping 140-pound steel sheets for automobile tops for two years and had very strong shoulder and arm muscles. My strong desire to be a pilot helped me to restrain myself from tangling with him.

We marched to our barracks, where five of us were assigned to the same room. We became good friends during preflight but the four of them washed out at Primary Flight School. One-half of each day was spent in the classroom learning how to disassemble and assemble the rifle, studying military law, military uniform and dress, etc. The other half was on the parade field learning how to march, do exercises, and performing guard duty. The first couple of weeks I was a little homesick, especially at 9:00 P.M. when the bugler played taps. The second week in January I met a cadet that had just washed out of Primary Flight School. When I told him that I was a private pilot, he advised me not to let anyone at the Primary Flight School know that, and I would not have any trouble graduating from Primary.

I finished Preflight in the middle of January 1942 and was ordered to the Southern Aviation Training School at Decatur, Alabama. It was a civilian flight school under contract with the Army Air Corp. My instructor was Mr. Shirley Johnson, a private pilot from Minnesota. He had a good personality and was an excellent instructor. He was impressed at how well I flew the PT-17 Stearman trainer. I had logged forty-five hours when Mr. Johnson said that I didn't need any more instruction, and on our jaunt that day, he would be in the front seat with me in the back seat and to be sure and fasten the seat belt tight. We took off and headed for his girlfriend's house and gave it a buzz job. He turned and rolled the PT-17 onto its back and flew upside down over the house with both he and his girlfriend waving to each other. When we landed he got out of the cockpit, helped me out of the rear seat, and asked me not to tell anyone what he had just done—and then he laughed.

When I had logged fifty-five hours, Mr. Johnson scheduled me for my final check flight. There was only one Army pilot there, a lieutenant who gave the final check to each cadet, either approving them for Basic Flight Training or sending them back to Preflight at Maxwell Field. He briefed me on what he wanted me to do on this check ride. I had no trouble during the flight and after we landed, he shook my hand and said that I had given him an excellent ride. I felt great.

I received orders to report to Basic Flight Training at Greenville Army Airfield in Mississippi on the first day of March. My flight instructor was Lt. Kent, a good instructor, all business, no small talk or humor. Our aircraft for training was a monoplane, a BT-13, known as the Vibrator. Training here was important because we were being taught to fly by instruments only. The front cockpit had a hood that prevented you from looking out of the cockpit. This forced you to fly by instrument only. You learned to trust your flight instruments and not the seat of your pants.

After three weeks of dual instruction, Lt. Kent let me have some solo time. He said that I was not to fly under the bridge that crossed the Mississippi river from Greenville. When I was airborne, I flew to the bridge and checked for obstructions to clearance under the bridge. There were none, so I flew under the bridge. Why did I do this? Because it was there! We had classes on navigation, weather maps and sequences, flight charts, etc. The subject that gave me trouble was the Morse Code. You had to be able to send and receive fifteen words per minute. I had to attend night classes to help me pass the code test. I passed my final flight check ride and was now eligible to attend Advanced Flight School. I thanked Lt. Kent for his instruction and apologized for flying under the bridge against his order. For the first time with me, he laughed and said, "We have to tell you cadets that, but we know you are going to do it!" We shook hands and he wished me good luck and a good career. I never saw him again.

I arrived at the Advanced Flight School at Columbus Army Airfield, Mississippi on the 29th of May 1942. Cadets were assigned two to a room and my roommate was Harold Simpson from Fitchburg, Massachusetts. In the adjacent room was Pete Schirmer, from New York. The three of us became very close friends. We had two types of training aircraft, the twin-engine Cessna, plus the new all metal, twin-engine AT-9. It was a fast and hot aircraft, which was exciting to fly. My flight instructor was Lt. Heindelieder. He was a warm and friendly instructor. Our flight training was formation flying, cross-country navigation, night flying, single-engine operation, etc. Classroom subjects were navigation, radio communication, weather science, etc. It was a six-day week of training, and many nights I was asleep before taps were played.

There was a smart-ass cadet in our barracks from New York who was disrespectful of cadet customs and rules. He made snide remarks about the training program and some of the flight instructors. As a result, he alienated himself from the majority of the cadet class. I will refer to him as cadet Jones. The weekend before graduation we were given open post Saturday and Sunday. Cadet Retchin asked me to join him in a visit to a well-known girls' school in Columbus to invite two girls to have dinner and a movie with us. We introduced ourselves to the lady in charge and informed her of our proposal. She was sure that she had two ladies that would enjoy an evening with two handsome cadets. Before long she introduced us to two charming girls and we drove them to a restaurant of their choice. After an enjoyable meal, we decided to walk to the movie, and on the way we bumped into Jones. He gave us a friendly greeting and started to join us. We returned his greeting and then gave him the cold shoulder and did not introduce the girls to him. After the movie, time became of the essence for our dates since they had to be back to the dormitory no later than midnight. We drove them to their dormitory and thanked them for a great evening.

The next afternoon Simpson, Retchin, and I were in the hallway of our barracks discussing the coming graduation when cadet Jones walked up to us and said, "How did you two cadets make out with the Southern whores that I saw you with last night?" His remark about the two girls was more than I could take, and I floored him with a hard right to the jaw. Simpson then ordered Jones to get lost and then turned to me and said, "You did the right thing Ken. He asked for that."

The next morning I received a notice to report to the base commander, Colonel Mallory, at 4:00 P.M. Both cadet Jones and I reported to Colonel Mallory, who asked me why I struck cadet Jones. I repeated what Jones had said and that I hit him to defend the honor of the two reputable girls we had dined with. He then asked Jones if he had made those remarks, and he admitted that he had but in a joking manner. Colonel Mallory then said that those were no joking words and suggested that we apologize to each other, shake hands, and from then on act as officers and gentlemen. We shook hands, and the last time I ever saw him was at graduation.

The 26th of July 1942 was one of the greatest days of my life. Since I was a young child, my goal had been to become a pilot, and now I was receiving my silver pilot wings from the best pilot training school in the world, the United States Army Air Corp. None of my family members were present for the graduation due to health problems. We cadets also received a second lieutenant's commission in the U.S. Army. After the ceremony, I approached Colonel Mallory and thanked him for his treatment of me. We shook hands and it was really uplifting when he addressed me as "Lt. Slaker!"

The adjutant then pulled me aside and asked if I knew that Cadet Simpson had a special meeting with the colonel prior to his meeting with me and Cadet Jones. I replied in the negative, and the adjutant said that Cadet Simpson gave the colonel the feeling of the cadets about Jones and that he deserved the punch that he received from me. He also said that I was one of the best pilots in the Cadet Corp and would be an asset to the Air Corp. The adjutant then said, "You really have a true friend in Lt. Simpson." I thanked him and realized how lucky I was to have a buddy like Hal.

The adjutant then handed me my orders, which assigned me to Gowen Air Base to be trained as a pilot in the big B-17 bomber! *God is on my side!*

Chapter 3
LEARNING TO FLY THE B-17

The train ride from Pittsburgh to Boise took two and a half days with changes at Chicago, Denver, and Salt Lake City. The train arrived at Boise, Idaho at daybreak on the 3rd of August. I stepped out onto the station platform and beheld a beautiful scene with the sun coming up behind the state capitol building. The cool mountain breeze smelled and felt great. I immediately liked Boise. Army buses took us to base headquarters at Gowen Air Base where we signed in and received our quarters and squadron assignments. We had private rooms but common latrines and showers. I spent the afternoon unpacking and purchasing personal sundries at the base exchange. I met with Hal Simpson and Schrimer at the officers' club for dinner. All three of us were happy to be assigned to this base for B-17 training. We retired early to get a good night's sleep because we were scheduled to be at the base theatre the next morning to be welcomed by the base commander, Colonel Travis.

We were called to attention as Colonel Travis entered the theatre, and when he reached the stage, his deputy ordered us to be seated. Colonel Travis didn't verbally welcome us to the base, or even congratulate us on becoming Army pilots. Instead he opened by saying, "You are here to be trained to go to war and many of you will not come back." He rambled on and his speech was not as professional as one would expect from a full colonel.

His last remark was that for some of us that lived through the war and wanted to make it a career, the quickest way to be discharged would be to go to bed with a high-ranking officer's wife. "Many of these old timers are no longer sexy and their wives love you hard-petered second lieutenants." That terminated his welcome speech. Simpson, Schrimer, and I got together afterwards and agreed that it was not an inspiring speech to give to a group of newly graduated Army pilots.

The day's schedule then had us reporting to our squadron, where we were briefed on the week's schedule, our training program, and assigned to a flight instructor. Mine was Captain Kidd, whom I really took a liking to and became one of the best in my mind. Our flight training was in the older B-17E models since the new B-17F models were programmed for overseas combat. It was a tight schedule, flying either in the morning or afternoon, then to class. We studied and operated the new secret Sperry bombsight and learned the electrical, hydraulic, oxygen, and fuel systems of the B-17. We also trained in the Link Trainer in instrument flying and how to handle emergency situations. We were given blindfold tests in the cockpit to be able to touch by hand each cockpit instrument and gauge. I really absorbed the training and by the end of August, I was one of the top students in the squadron.

Captain Kidd came to me and asked if I would be interested in staying in the squadron as an instructor. I told him that I would be honored, and he said that he had talked to the squadron commander, who was in agreement. The catch was that I would have to be promoted to first lieutenant, and he and the squadron commander would talk to Colonel Travis to see if he would approve my promotion to first lieutenant. The next day after class I was told to report to the commander's office where I met with him and Captain Kidd. They told me that they were very disappointed in that Colonel Travis said that he could not approve promoting a second lieutenant to a first lieutenant when he had only been a lieutenant thirty days. This refusal by Colonel Travis to promote me didn't increase his popularity with me. The really negative part of this refusal of the request of the squadron commander was that he failed to support his own people working for him. The squadron had no choice but to submit my name to Personnel as a qualified first pilot for a B-17 combat crew.

A couple of days later I went to the base exchange to purchase some sundries, and what a surprise! Standing at the counter was George O'Hoppe, the roommate of mine at Primary Flight School who had failed his flight check, and was now wearing the shiny new bombardier wings. He had just graduated from bombardier's school at Victorville, California, and been assigned to Gowen Air Base for placement on a B-17 combat crew. He had not yet been assigned to a particular crew, so I took him to Personnel and they cooperated with me, and O'Hoppe became the first member of my B-17 crew.

O'Hoppe had a car, and it did not take him more than a couple of days to date a girl that worked on base. I had told O'Hoppe that when I had some free time I would go into town and go biking for the exercise. He insisted that I get a date so that the four of us could bike together. I had made friends with a young girl that worked in the base exchange, and she agreed to go biking with us. Whenever O'Hoppe and I had a free evening, we would drive into Boise and take the girls biking and to dinner. My date, Lee Smith, was living with relatives in Boise and she insisted that we meet them. We did and they made us very welcome.

Beginning September 1st, I flew as first pilot on all training flights and had a variety of copilots. I took a liking to one of them, and since he had not qualified as a first pilot, I asked him if he would like to be on my crew. He agreed and again Personnel cooperated, and my crew then had a copilot, Leo Flowers from Omaha, Nebraska.

On the 8th of September, I received a telegram from New Kensington, Pennsylvania that my wife Jane had given birth to a baby girl named Patricia Elaine. I wired flowers and congratulations.

I was having dinner at the officers' club in the middle of September and noticed a new couple sitting by themselves. I asked if I could join them and the lieutenant was very receptive. He introduced himself as Lt. James Passmore from Columbus, Georgia, and his new wife, Marion. He had just graduated from navigation school at Sacramento where he had met and romanced his new wife. She was very charming and attractive, and Passmore was a real Southern gentleman. He asked about my training here at Gowen and I brought him up to date about my combat crew. I had a gut feeling that he would really fit into my crew, so I asked him if he had been assigned to a crew. His reply was negative, so I immediately asked him if he would be interested in joining my crew. He smiled and said that he was hoping I would ask him. The next morning I went to Personnel and they were very cooperative. Passmore became the navigator on my crew. I had personally selected the officers on my crew, but the five enlisted crewmembers were assigned to my crew by Personnel at the end of September.

My three aircrew officers did get to fly with me a few times before we received orders at the end of September to report to Alamogordo Air Base, New Mexico for high altitude bombing and gunnery training. With what little free time we had from training, O'Hoppe and I continued to bike and dine with our two lady friends. They were very unhappy when we told them that we would be leaving October 1st for New Mexico. They both were at the train station to bid us goodbye. I had told Lee on our first biking date that I was married but I had developed deep feelings for her. Lee gave me an envelope and we hugged one another, which developed into a long kiss. After we got settled in our seats in the parlor car, I opened the envelope and there was a note saying that she would miss me and prayed that God would watch over me. There was a photo of her and on the back she had written: *To Ken, with love.*

Alamogordo Air Base was a big disappointment after Gowen Air Base. The buildings were temporary tar-papered and our housing was dormitory style. The food at the mess hall was below average, and we ended up buying a lot of our food in town. We were assigned to the Aynesworth Group, and the commander, Lt. Colonel Aynesworth, turned out to be highly respected by all the aircrews. The second day there we reported to the group commander at operations and I met my enlisted aircrew members for the first time. My aerial engineer was S/Sgt. John Jaranson from Thief River Falls, Minnesota. Talk about good fortune—Jaranson turned out to be a very loyal and valuable crewmember. We were briefed that all our training flights would be at night as recommended by the British. Our training aircraft were B-17Es that had been through the mill. My radio operator was Les Varner from Tennessee; waist gunner William Childers from Childress, Texas; tail gunner Frank Laky from Buffalo, New York; and ball turret gunner William Nick from Butler, Pennsylvania.

The night of October 4th we made our first flight as a complete aerial combat crew.

We climbed to 28,000 feet and made our first run over the lighted bombing range below for O'Hoppe to drop his 200-pound practice bombs. We then flew over to the mountains and the gunners fired their fifty-caliber machine guns at lighted targets. The flight the next night was a real thriller. When we had climbed to 30,000 feet, we made a run over the bombing range for O'Hoppe to drop his bombs. As I turned the B-17 around to make a second run, I noticed that the cockpit oxygen system was empty. I pointed this out to Flowers and signaled to dive. We pilots had been trained in the high altitude chambers and we knew that we had to get to a lower altitude within three minutes or we would pass out. We had no time to alert the crew, pulled the throttles back, and shoved the nose down into a red line dive. We pulled out of the red line dive at 15,000 feet, but continued to descend to a lower altitude. Flowers called the crew and told them what had happened. Jaranson, my engineer, told me that when the aircraft went into its dive, the crew, thinking that we were going to crash, tried to parachute out of the aircraft, but the pressure of the dive prevented them from getting to the fuselage door. After we had landed, I explained to the crew why we had to dive so quickly. I told them that with these old B-17Es, we probably would experience some more flight problems.

The night flight on the 8th of October was for gunnery practice only. We climbed to 15,000 feet and headed for the lighted gunnery range in the mountains. We made a pass along the range with most guns firing. I made a 180-degree turn to make a second pass on the range when a crewmember called me on the intercom that number three engine was on fire. I immediately shut the fuel off to that engine and Flowers pushed the button to feather the engine. The prop would not feather nor did the fire extinguisher do any good. I called the crew and told them that I was going to make a steep dive to 4,000 feet to see if I could blow the fire out. If not, then they were to bail out of the aircraft. When we reached 6,000 feet, we no longer could see any flame. We returned to the base on three engines, having advised the tower of our fire problem. As soon as we got the B-17 stopped on the runway with fire vehicles all around us, we wasted no time in getting out of the aircraft and watched the firemen spray the engine, which was still smoking. Laky, my tail gunner who had been a gunner in the Navy for four years, came up to me and said that he didn't want to fly in these B-17Es anymore and was going to request a transfer out of the Air Corp. The next day Jaranson talked with Laky and got him to change his mind and stay with our crew.

Near the end of the third week of flying night missions, I reported to operations and obtained the number of the B-17E that was assigned for our mission that night. While Flowers made an outside inspection of the aircraft, I entered the cockpit to check the Form One for any negative entries.

The last pilot to fly the B-17 had made two entries that would require maintenance action to correct. One of the entries really disturbed me, for it could be a threat to the safety of the crew. I contacted a line maintenance officer and showed him the write-up that I could not accept unless it was corrected. He said that it could not be worked on until the next morning but did not feel that it was a threat to flight safety. I told him that I would not accept the aircraft with that write-up and I dismissed my crew. We all went back to our barracks and had a good night's sleep.

The next morning I had a call from the chief of maintenance's office that he wanted to see me right away. I immediately went to our group commander's office and asked to see Colonel Aynesworth. I explained to him my refusal of the aircraft and why. He joined me and we went to see the chief of maintenance. The colonel asked to see the Form One and read the entries. He said that with the emergencies I already had here, he could agree with me that it was a potential threat to flight safety. The maintenance officer said that from his point of view, it was of a routine nature. The colonel then said, "You are a maintenance officer, not a pilot. Slaker is a pilot not a maintenance man. In this situation, the pilot has the authority to decide whether to fly the aircraft with this write-up, not the maintenance officer." With that, Colonel Aynesworth got up, the maintenance officer saluted him, and we departed. I had the highest respect for him and was ready to go to combat with his group.

At the end of the third week of training, we had a four-day break and we officers decided to take a bus trip to El Paso, which was about 100 miles south of our air base. Passmore's wife had come to Alamogordo and was staying in a motel in town. Marion joined us and when we got to El Paso, we had lunch at a good restaurant. We then walked across the bridge to Juarez and started window-shopping. Before long, a Mexican approached us and in English asked us if we would like to see a show. We asked what kind of a show, and he said dancing girls. The price was reasonable so we agreed to go to the show. The Mexican then said that our lady could not go with us, so Passmore said that he and Marion would meet us at the bus terminal at 4:00 P.M. for the ride back to the base. We followed the Mexican into a small store and through a door in the rear to a room with tables and chairs. He asked if we wanted a beer. O'Hoppe said yes but both Flowers and I had a Coke. Without any fanfare a woman and young girl entered the room and sat down on the carpeted floor. Both were naked. They smiled at us and then in came the Mexican with a huge dog. The dog started to lick the woman's crotch and I realized that there were no dancing girls, so it was too raw for me and I said that I was leaving. Flowers joined me but O'Hoppe stayed. He was more worldly-wise than Flowers and me, for he had served several years as an enlisted man in the Army Infantry and at twenty-eight years old, was the old man of my aircrew.

Mess hall facilities were the same as in the field of combat. We were issued metal mess kits that we used for each meal. When you were finished eating, you swished your mess kit in one of the barrels of hot water just outside the mess hall. Then you hung it up in your barracks to dry and it was ready for the next meal. Evidently, I didn't get mine clean enough to kill all the germs and came down with trench mouth. The dentist sprayed my mouth with a vile tasting orange colored liquid for three days to enable me

301st Bomb Group, 12th Air Force, North Africa, Feburary 1943. Pilot Slaker and Bombadier O'Hoppe in front of their living quarters . . . not very plush!

to eat again. Almost every day one of my crew would have diarrhea, which grounded him.

We were scheduled for a night mission on October 27th and we had no problem until I came to the base at the end of the mission and could not land because the landing gear would not come down. Jaranson checked switches and connections within the fuselage without success. The gear could be lowered manually, which Jaranson succeeded in doing.

October 28th was a very happy day for the crew. We received orders transferring my crew to Forbes Air Base, Topeka, Kansas, departing Alamogordo on November 1st. We were scheduled for one more mission on October 30th and what a surprise. It was to be a daylight bombing mission. We were informed that the Air Corp B-17s were now flying out of England to bomb during daylight hours. Our last mission here was accomplished without any emergency. *Topeka, here we come!*

Quarters at Forbes Air Base were luxurious and the food excellent, which had been lacking at Alamogordo. Colonel Aynesworth remained with us as the group commander. The aircrews really respected him and wished that he would still be the commander when we departed for combat. I asked Captain Francis, the deputy commander, if Passmore and I could rent a house while at Topeka so that our wives could have some time with us before combat, and also that I had a baby daughter that I had not yet seen. He agreed as long as it did not interfere with our training schedule.

Passmore and I contacted a real estate office in Topeka and they said they had the very house for us. We took a cab to the address that they gave us and met the real estate lady there. She said that the house—a large, attractive one—was owned by an attorney that had been called to active duty in the Army. We signed the contract for one month and I called Jane to come to Topeka. Marion Passmore was already there and Jane arrived three days later. Her mother also came to take care of the baby so that Jane would have more free time with me. The neighbors called on us and offered their service to us. We found the people of Topeka great.

Passmore and I didn't get to spend much time with our new wives because we were either on a two-day flight or could not return to Topeka due to snowstorms that closed the air base. On a flight from Florida, all the airports in the Midwest were closed due to severe snowstorms, except Sioux Falls, where we were able to make an instrument approach in heavy snow. The airport closed immediately after we had landed and we spent two days there. When I returned from this trip, Jane and I visited the Presbyterian minister to ask him to baptize our daughter before we left Topeka. He was very cooperative, and at the church service one week later, he baptized Patricia Elaine. What really impressed me was that my entire aircrew attended the baptism.

Our training here was aerial navigation at night by computing our location from the position of the stars, and during daytime the position of the sun over the Gulf of Mexico. We were a much happier crew training here for we had the newer B-17F models for training. That in itself was a morale booster for the crew, especially the pilots.

We received orders at the end of November to move to Smoky Hill Air Base at Salina, Kansas for combat readiness. The wives departed for home and on December 1st, a B-24 arrived to airlift us to Salina. It was flown by a training crew from Herrington Air Base and one week later, the same crew that had lifted us from Forbes Air Base was killed when their B-24 exploded during a training flight.

The room and board at Smoky Hill Air Base was a copy of those at Alamogordo Air Base. Dormitory style shack buildings with one coal stove in the center of the first floor was inadequate for heating comfort. The first week was spent on physical examinations, then medical shots for the overseas combat areas, then individual combat gear, pup tent, sleeping cot, and a Colt .45 pistol for every officer.

One week after our arrival at Smoky Hill, I was told to report to Colonel Aynesworth, our training group commander, and was escorted into his office. He returned my salute and asked me to be seated. One of the most exciting days of my life happened! Colonel Aynesworth got up, walked over to me, and handed me some papers and said, "Slaker, sign the top copy for it is the receipt for your new B-17F." I was speechless! What more could a pilot ask than to have his own multi engine aircraft? He then said to come on with him and take a look at my new B-17. It had just arrived from Van Nuys, California, where it had been assembled. I walked around it, speechless, just looking and looking. I saw the tail number 25727, which entered my brain's memory bank forever. My crew arrived and were just as excited as I was. We entered the B-17F and spent the rest of the day at our respective aircrew positions, already mentally airborne.

The day of receiving the B-17 was made even more exciting by receiving a letter from my buddy and cadet classmate, Hal Simpson, who had been sent to Rapid City Air Base for his crew's bombing training. He dated a girl there, and they fell in love and planned to be married that month. He asked me to get a flight to Rapid City to be his best man! I discussed this with our deputy commander, and he said that he would approve a training flight in my new B-17F to Rapid City on the wedding date. On the 13th of December, we flew the new B-17 for the first time. We made sure that all systems were working and that the new Studebaker engines, made under contract with the Wright Co., were responding to all flight settings. We completed our flight check in one and a half hours. I made the first landing in the new B-17F with a very happy aircrew on board.

A couple of days later, just before we were to make a short local flight, O'Hoppe got me aside and said that he had very sad news for me. He said that my buddy, Hal Simpson, was on a night training flight when his aircraft caught fire, got out of control, and crashed into a mountain, killing all on board. This was a terrible personal loss to me and brought tears to my eyes, which was not to be the only time. I had the name and address of the girl that Hal was going to marry and wrote a sympathy letter to her. What a terrible loss, not only to her and his family and to me, but also to the Army Air Corp.

A couple of days later Jaranson, my engineer, met me at the B-17 and asked if I had given any thought to naming the B-17. I replied in the negative, and he said that the entire crew had a meeting and decided on a name for my consideration. I told Jaranson that I would give it serious thought and what name had they come up with? He said, "Lt., we would like to name the B-17 *Elaine* after your new daughter!" This proposal almost brought tears to my eyes for the third time in one week. What a great surprise from my crew, and I told Jaranson that this name did not need my approval, that it was their B-17 they had named, not just mine. Walking back to the barracks, I thanked

God for having given me such a loyal and great crew. The next day when I walked to the B-17, there painted on its nose in big white letters was its name, *Elaine*.

A week before Christmas the group commander informed us that immediately after the holidays, we would be departing Smoky Hill Air Base for combat. We would not be given any leave time, and he could not tell us what combat area we would be assigned to. The next afternoon Jaranson came to my barracks to tell me that Varner did not show for roll call and had been listed as AWOL. I was shocked, for Varner was an excellent radio operator and an important member of our crew. He didn't tell any member of our crew where he was going or why. This could delay us from going to combat because the group commander would have to request Personnel to find us a qualified radio operator. Five days later Varner returned. He had gone home to marry his girlfriend before going to combat.

I called my mother to tell her that I could not get any leave time to get back to Vandergrift to say goodbye to her, my wife Jane, and my close friends before going to combat. My mother said not to worry about combat, for she reminded me that her mother was my Guardian Angel. I had no fear about going to combat because I really believed that God was on our side in this war.

On December 23rd we were scheduled for our first flight out of the local area to the Gulf of Mexico for night navigation training. We arrived at the Gulf at dusk, and I was to fly over the Gulf on a mag heading selected by me. Passmore was not to have access to a mag compass nor my heading. After an hour and a half, Passmore was to shoot the stars and tell me what time we would have landfall and the heading back to Smoky Hill. Passmore did well with landfall site and time. I called Flight Service to give a position report, and they said that they had a message for me. Smoky Hill Air Base was closed due to a severe winter snowstorm, and I was to land at DeRidder Air Base, Louisiana. I talked to Colonel Aynesworth the next morning, and he said that Smoky Hill was still closed and for me to fly over the Gulf of Mexico so Passmore could practice sun shots. I was to go to Orlando Air Base and spend Christmas day there since the winter storm was spreading over the entire Midwest and would not reach Orlando.

I flew over the Gulf of Mexico for a couple of hours and then asked Passmore for a heading to Orlando. As we approached Florida, it had huge cumulus clouds built up to 60,000 feet, so I would have to penetrate the thunderstorm clouds at a low altitude. Flight control gave me permission for an instrument approach to the air base and on the letdown, we had severe turbulence and hail. I was worried about damage to the *Elaine*, but we landed intact. *Elaine* had passed her first test in severe weather and I was proud of her.

We spent Christmas day in sunny Orlando, sightseeing and dining. The Midwest severe weather kept us in Orlando another three days. On the 29th of December, we were able to get cleared to Barksdale Air Base where we spent the night. The next day we finally were cleared to Smoky Hill and arrived seven days after we had departed. We also put almost twenty-two hours in the air in our new B-17. The next day, December 31st, I was ordered to fly to Forbes Air Base to have our B-17 fuel lines modified. This being New Year's Eve, O'Hoppe and I took the bus to Kansas City for our last fling before leaving the U.S. We were able to get separate rooms at the Muelbach Hotel, and we told the manager that we were leaving for combat in Europe in two days. The manager gave us tickets to the hotel New Year's party in appreciation of fighting for our country. I never drank beer or whiskey, but O'Hoppe shamed me into having champagne. Before long I was dancing with the beautiful Kansas City girls. I really took a liking to one blond in particular and we danced most of the evening together. She really liked to dance.

She had the band play her favorite song at least three times. I still remember the title: "There Are Such Things." We enjoyed dancing with one another and during the last two dances she really turned me on. I was having a very difficult time saying no. I would not violate the Ten Commandments by asking this young lady to spend the night with me. Yes, I did. And yes, she did.

O'Hoppe and I hosted our overnight guests to a New Year's Day breakfast. They had to leave after we had eaten because they had other commitments. Maureen gave me her address and asked me for my overseas address as soon as I knew it. I complied with her request. I was uncomfortable with myself that I had broken one of the Ten Commandments, and O'Hoppe sensed my problem and said, "Kenny, what you did last night was good for you. We are at war and will be facing death everyday. Maureen could be the last woman you will have made love to in your short life. Your body has a physical need and overpowered that closed brain of yours." O'Hoppe was more mature and sophisticated than me, and more right than wrong.

O'Hoppe and I departed for Forbes Air Base to pick up our B-17, arriving there the afternoon of the 2nd of January. We received the *Elaine* the next afternoon and departed for Smoky Hill Air Base at Saling, Kansas. The rest of my aircrew was there and Lt. Passmore handed me a copy of our departure orders. We were to depart at 2:00 A.M. on the 5th of January for Morrison Air Base, West Palm Springs, Florida, where we would receive orders for North Africa. The 4th of January was spent loading the *Elaine* with floating gear, an engine changing tool kit, ten fifty-caliber machine guns, survival gear, pup tents, personnel combat gear, oxygen tanks fully charged, gasoline tanks topped off, each engine started and checked, etc. The *Elaine* was declared ready to depart Smoky Hill.

Me and my aircrew hit the sack at 7:00 P.M. with a wakeup call at 1:00 A.M. It was a clear but very cold morning and the *Elaine* was covered with frost. The de-icing truck arrived and sprayed the wings and the rudder section. Since we were loaded to the maximum weight for the B-17 type aircraft, I told my copilot and engineer that we would use the entire length of the runway to get maximum speed for takeoff. At exactly 2:00 A.M. I advanced all four throttles to their full position, released the brakes, and we rolled down the runway, getting good speed for takeoff. The weather en route was good, and seven hours later we landed at Morrison Air Base in Florida.

It was disappointing at Morrison Field to find out that our Aynesworth Group was being broken up and its aircrews being sent to existing bomb groups as replacements. Since we didn't have orders assigning us to a combat area, the ferrying group briefed us on both the northern and southern routes to the combat areas. Since it was January, the northern route to Europe was bad winter weather, so I requested the southern route to Africa.

We were really surprised when on the eighth we received orders to report to the Commander, 12th Air Force, located in North Africa. This opened up the southern route for us. Shortly after midnight on the 9th of January 1943, we took off from Morrison Field for Trinidad, a fair sized island off the northern coast of South America. None of us had ever been to South America and with very little help from radio fixes, it was now the responsibility of my navigator, Passmore, to get us there. Shortly before eight hours in the air, we sighted the coast of Venezuela. Passmore said that we were forty miles west of Trinidad, so we headed east along the coast. We had been flying around huge thunderstorms ever since we passed over Cuba, and as we approached Trinidad, a huge thunderstorm was right on top of it. We circled for thirty minutes before we could land at Waller Field. We logged a little over ten hours on this flight and all four gas gauge needles were touching the top of *E, E being empty!* It was very hot and humid, and the ground personnel suggested that we wait until morning to refuel.

The next morning at breakfast I was informed that the *Elaine* would not be ready for us until noon, which would be too late for us to take off for our next stop. A sergeant from ground personnel suggested that we get transport from the motor pool to take us to a cool waterfall pool in the mountains. This would help us get through a hot day, and the pool was isolated so we wouldn't need swimsuits, which none of the crew had anyway. We spent the entire afternoon in and out of the cool water, all nine of us in the nude. O'Hoppe was told by a crewmember that he had been elected president of our nudist camp, not because he was hung better than the rest of us, but since he was the oldest.

We took off from Waller Field on the morning of January 11th and started to follow the coastline about fifty miles out to sea. We approached huge tropical thunderstorms and I at first climbed to top them, but when I got to 30,000 feet, the tops were still another 30,000 above us. I decided to descend and penetrate them at 1,000 feet above sea level. I avoided the black centers of the storms, but we still had heavy turbulence and were on instruments most of the time. As we neared the equator, the weather improved and what a sight we saw: a yellow river at least fifty miles wide running for many miles straight out into the Atlantic Ocean. It was the mouth of the Amazon River. Our destination was Belem, which was 100 miles south of the Amazon, and we had no trouble spotting it and landed without any problem. We had no sooner arrived at our screened open-air bunks when a tropical thunderstorm hit us. It was heavy like a waterfall and lasted only fifteen minutes but left six inches of water on the ground. The water disappeared in less than an hour but now the humidity was 100 percent. We spent a hot and restless night and wasted no time the next morning in taking off for Natal, Brazil.

The briefing officer advised me to follow the coastline to Natal to avoid the heavy thunderstorms that were building up over the land area. Even so, we fought turbulence and heavy rain all the way to Natal. After seven hours of bouncing around, we arrived in Natal beaten and tired. *Elaine* had some work to be done on number three engine, which would take three days to finish. The Army Transport Command (ATC) had a detachment there and the captain in charge welcomed us. He said that Natal was an interesting city and had the best leather shops in the world. The next day we four officers went into town and shopped like tourists. We stopped at a leather shop and were so impressed by their leatherwork that a couple of us were measured for boots that would be ready for us the next day.

The next afternoon we went into town to pick up our boots. As we left the shop, O'Hoppe said, "Let's get a cab and tell him to take us to where the ladies live." I looked at O'Hoppe and asked him what ladies. He looked at me with a grin on his face and said, "The whorehouse." I had never been to one and didn't think that I should go. O'Hoppe grabbed my arm and said, "Come on Kenny, you don't have to go to bed with them. Let's have fun teasing them and they will have cold drinks for us." The primary language in Brazil is Portuguese, but English is a close second. The cab driver talked to O'Hoppe in English and pulled up in front of a modern two-story brick building. We followed O'Hoppe into a recessed entry and a mature lady answered the doorbell.

We asked if we could visit the ladies and she said yes and to go up the stairs and the ladies would greet us. An attractive young girl met us and led us onto a beautiful terrace with a view of the ocean and the city. Several young girls were on the terrace and talked with us in fairly good English. They offered us cold drinks and Passmore and I had colas. There was a short discussion period and then one of the girls spotted Passmore's wedding ring. She jumped up and said, "This man matrimonial, he know how, I take him." Passmore looked at me and I nodded my head towards the door, and he nodded his head in agreement. We got up, thanked the ladies for the drinks, left some money on the table, and departed. O'Hoppe and Flowers stayed.

The next day we were briefed on the two routes recommended by ATC to Bathurst, Africa, our next stop. There were three other B-17 crews there and they decided to fly direct to Bathurst. That could be risky because if they encountered head winds, they could run out of fuel and have to ditch in the ocean, which was in control of the German submarines. Since the winds across the south Atlantic Ocean could not be accurately forecast, I decided to be on the safe side and to dogleg it through Ascension Island.

We took off from Natal at 1:00 A.M. on the 16th of January for Ascension Island. I had been given the classified frequency and code for this date for the Ascension beacon. It was necessary to change this information daily since the Germans would transmit a false beacon and if we homed on it, we would not get to Ascension and would end up ditching in the ocean. It was a very dark night with no night horizon and the stars reflecting from the ocean. This was an invitation to vertigo, so Flowers and I spelled each other every hour. I was at the controls at the beginning of the seventh hour and it was getting daylight. Flowers was on the radio compass seeking the Ascension beacon while I was scanning the horizon looking for the island.

I called Passmore and expressed my concern that we had no contact with Ascension and only one hour of fuel in the tanks. He said that he could not establish our position at this time since the sun was just coming up and the stars could not be seen for a celestial fix. I called Varner, my radio operator, and he said that due to atmospheric conditions he could neither transmit nor receive on high frequency. I told Flowers to switch to the radio compass loop and search manually for the Ascension beacon. Fortunately, the weather was clear and we had at least twenty-mile visibility. I called Passmore and said that if we were on course we should have the island in sight. He suggested that I hold our same heading because we should see Ascension any minute.

Flowers tapped me on the shoulder and pointed to his headset. I switched to compass loop and there was a faint transmission not clear enough to identify. It was twenty-five degrees to our left and since we were thirty minutes past our ETA for Ascension and it was not in sight, I made a decision. I called Passmore and told him I was turning to a new heading twenty-five degrees to our left. He came up to the cockpit and strongly suggested that I hold the original heading. I disagreed with him and showed him that the gas tanks only had thirty minutes of fuel. I alerted the crew to prepare for a possible water landing. About twenty minutes later and with the gas gauges dancing just above the empty mark, Flowers and I spotted a dark outline on the horizon and I called Ascension tower and they answered my call. I asked for and received landing instructions and told them I was very low on fuel and wished to be cleared for a straight in approach. We were at 10,000 feet and used our altitude to set up a slow rate of descent. I had good depth perception and could see that even if we lost one or two engines that we could still make it to the runway. In my mind I thanked my Guardian Angel for helping me make and keep my decision to turn left twenty-five degrees. When we saw that we had it made, Flowers lowered the gear and flaps and the landing was normal. We braked to taxi speed and advanced power on number one engine to turn onto the taxi strip and it coughed and died! Out of gas. The ground crew towed us to the refueling area, and I told the airdrome officer that we had two crates of pineapples for the mess hall. After being shown our sleeping area, we spent the rest of the day on the sandy beach.

I did not have a discussion with Passmore about my decision not to remain on the same heading that he suggested. He knew that if we had remained on his desired heading, that we would have run out of fuel and ditched into the ocean. Our chances of survival in the south Atlantic Ocean would have been minimal, for there were very few neutral vessels since the Germans controlled this ocean area with their submarines. If they found us afloat, the *Elaine* and her crew would be gone, for they did not take prisoners. This crisis did not create friction between Passmore and me. To the contrary, he was loyal to the crew and showed his respect to me as his pilot and we became close friends.

The next morning, January 17th, we took off for Bathurst, located on the west coast of Africa, near Dakar. I was not able to wear anything except my shorts due to the severe sunburn from our afternoon on the beach. Bathurst was a British airfield with 5,500 feet of pierced steel planking for the runway. It had rained shortly before our arrival, and what a hair raising time we had landing on wet, slippery steel that was not even level. We skipped, bounced, and slid but managed to stop at the very end of the runway. We had to refuel *Elaine* from five-gallon cans, which took the rest of the day. We slept in rope hammocks stretched three feet above the ground and covered with mosquito netting.

Just before dawn we were awakened by a loud and weird chanting from black natives carrying torches. It was a scary awakening. O'Hoppe grabbed his .45 pistol and I reached for mine, and then we saw a British sergeant marching alongside of them. We then realized that these were natives on their way to work at the airfield. Further sleep was out of the question, so we had tea and rice and then received a briefing on the route to our next stop, Marrakesh, Morocco. We were to fly across the Sahara desert to 3,000-foot Mt. Atimine, then turn to our northwest heading across the Atlas Mountains to Marrakech. We were cleared to fly at 10,000 feet and when we approached the Sahara, visibility dropped to less than a half-mile due to a huge sand storm. I flew our original heading until our ETA at Mt. Atimine, and then turned to the magnetic heading for Marrakech. When we broke out of the sand storm, there in front of us were the snow-covered Atlas Mountains. We had clear skies to Marrakech, and after landing, I reported to the medical clinic for my sunburn, which was now infected. Shorts was my uniform for the day.

The doctor temporarily grounded me and assigned me to a room in a first class hotel, La Marnounia. My three officers were also given rooms there. We were very fortunate to be in this hotel, for it was blocked for the high-ranking personnel who were accompanying President Roosevelt while he was attending the conference at Casablanca with Churchill and Stalin. I was restricted to my room for three days until the infection cleared. In the meantime, the rest of my crew enjoyed casing Marrakech. On the morning of January 22nd, we were briefed on the route to our next stop, Oran, Algeria.

We arrived at Oran in the afternoon and were assigned rooms in the brick barracks built by the French when they controlled Algeria. There were no beds so we brought in our cots from *Elaine*. The rooms were large and we four officers were housed in one room. The air defense of Oran was being done by the 31st Fighter Group using British Spitfires that had replaced their P-39s in England. I knew that a cadet classmate of mine, John Lukon, was in this fighter group and looked him up. We hugged one another like long-lost brothers, for we both were from western Pennsylvania and had kept in touch after we received our Silver Wings.

Lt. Lukon informed me that the fighter group was having a Kickapoo Joy Juice party that evening and invited me and my officers to join them. The entrance fee was to bring anything alcoholic and as you entered the party room, you poured it into a ten-gallon jug. We brought two fifths of Four Roses, which we added to the mixture in the jug. The party was a blast and camaraderie ran high. My three officers and I were able to walk back to our barracks when the joy juice was gone, except Lt. O'Hoppe fell into a six-foot-deep slit trench. We laughed at him so hard that we had one hell of a time lifting him out of that trench. We finally got to our room on the top floor of the barracks. There was no heat in the room and it was cold, so we all hit the sack with our clothes on.

After we had gone to sleep, we were awakened by O'Hoppe shouting, "I'll kill those Goddamn Germans!" and he started firing his Colt .45. You could hear the bullets ricocheting off the concrete walls. Lt. Flowers pinned O'Hoppe to the floor and took his pistol. We convinced him that there were no Germans in the building and got him back to bed. The military police arrived and we told them that one of the officers had dropped his pistol, causing it to fire. We were fortunate that none of us were wounded with those bullets bouncing around the room.

There were several B-17 crews at Oran that were waiting for orders assigning us to our combat group. Finally, on the 1st of February we received our orders assigning us to the 301st Bomb Group located at Ain M'Lila, Algeria. It had just arrived there from Biskra, located on the northern edge of the Sahara Desert. We departed Oran on the 3rd of February and located the 301st on a dry lakebed, about thirty miles south of the city of Constantine. At last, after six months of training, we finally had arrived in the combat theatre. From this time on it would be a life or death situation when flying a bombing mission. Here I was, only twenty-two years old, a first pilot on a B-17 bomber, responsible for the lives of eight crewmembers. I would need God's help and hoped that my grandmother would be able to keep her promise.

Chapter 4
PILOTING THE B-17 IN COMBAT

The *Elaine* was met by Captain O'Carrol, the 419th Squadron Operations Officer, who told us we had been assigned to his squadron. He then drove me in a jeep to a large tent where I reported to the squadron commander, Captain Traylor. He was more concerned about my crew turning over any liquor we had to the supply officer than anything else. My crew turned in six bottles we still had left after selling nine bottles to the Air Corp Personnel at Ascension Island. We unloaded our pup tents from *Elaine* and erected them in the 419th Squadron area. Several of the squadron members offered to purchase our cots but they were of more good to us than their paper money called script. When it got dark, we didn't waste any time crawling into our bedrolls inside our pup tents.

About an hour later we were awakened by the roar of aircraft engines and very loud shaking noises from exploding bombs. There were no slit trenches to jump into and it was a frightening experience. The first sergeant ran through the area telling us that we were being bombed by German JU 88s. The next morning the squadron area was alive with personnel digging slit trenches. O'Hoppe and I dug ours wide enough to hold our cots and then we covered the trench with our pup tents. This would let us stay in our cots in case of future air raids.

On the 7th of February Lt. Crowell, the assistant operations officer, scheduled the *Elaine* and crew for a local flight with him as my copilot to insure that we were ready to fly a combat mission. All the guns were fired, 200-pound bombs were dropped, engines feathered, aircraft stalls made, etc. I made a couple of landings and Lt. Crowell declared us ready to fly combat missions. That evening the mission schedule for the next day was posted and the *Elaine* was on it! When a new crew was assigned to the squadron, it was policy that the squadron commander would fly the crew as its pilot for two missions. My copilot was pulled from the mission and I flew as the copilot. The *Elaine* would be leading the squadron of six B-17s on its first mission.

The mission briefing for the entire 301st Bomb Group was held in a large stone building next to our squadron area. The target to be bombed was the docks and shipping at Sousse, Tunisia. War supplies for the German General Rommel's army fighting against the British and American soldiers were being unloaded at Sousse. *Elaine*'s bomb bay held twelve 500-pound bombs, and we climbed to 24,500 feet and about ten minutes from our bomb run, we were attacked head on by General Goering's famous yellow nosed fighter aircraft *Messerschmitt*, a ME-109 fighter aircraft. We had been briefed at Alamogordo that fighter aircraft would not attack B-17s head on due to the firepower from our top turret and the ball turret under the fuselage. *Wrong!* There was a certain lateral distance in front of the B-17 nose that neither turret could cover. The German fighter pilots knew this and here they were attacking us from twelve o'clock. This area was later covered by a turret in the nose of the B-17G model.

I saw that the ME-109 coming in on us had its wings on fire, and then I realized that fire was his guns firing at us! Captain Traylor and I both ducked down behind the instrument panel which had a 3/8-inch armor plate on the backside. Fortunately none of its cannon shells or bullets hit us. Then came the black bursts of flak as we started our bomb run. We dropped our bombs and returned to our base unharmed. The 9th of February was a day of rest for our crew. The group did fly a mission since General Doolittle had arrived to fly with the 301st on a second bombing of the harbor at Sousse.

The 10th of February greeted us with snow and strong cold winds which turned to cold, heavy rain the next day. O'Hoppe's and my slit trench started to fill up with cold

Officer crew of the *Elaine*, October 1942, Alamogordo, New Mexico. L-R: Bombadier Lt. George O'Hoppe, Navigator James Passmore, Co-Pilot Leo Flowers, Pilot Kenneth Slaker.

water so we had to move to higher ground. This cold weather lasted four more days before we could see blue sky again.

February 17th. The schedule for this mission was posted late afternoon on the sixteenth with Flowers pulled and I to fly copilot with Captain Traylor, the squadron commander. General H.S. Vandenberg from the Army Air Corp arrived the morning of the seventeenth, and I was pulled from the flight and the general flew with Captain Traylor as his copilot. The *Elaine* returned safely from this bombing mission on an airfield in Sardinia, and was now one mission ahead of me.

February 22nd. I was scheduled to fly as copilot with Captain Traylor in the *Elaine* to bomb the German airfield at Gabes, Tunisia. When we arrived at the target, the airfield was obscured by thick clouds and we were unable to drop our bombs. We were given credit for this mission since we had entered the air combat zone.

February 23rd. The *Elaine* was not scheduled for the early morning mission that was accomplished by the group on a German airfield. However, shortly after the group returned from its morning mission, we were alerted and briefed for an emergency mission as quick as we could get airborne. General Rommel, who whipped the Allies, had backed up and was sitting in Kasserine Pass. Troops under the 1st Armored Division were regrouping for an attack on Rommel's Panzer Division in Kasserine Pass. Top Command in North Africa knew that our ground troops needed support in this effort and ordered the 301st Bomb Group to bomb the Pass before 1600 hours, which was the time of attack planned by the ground forces. Our armament personnel did an outstanding job loading the bomb bays of twenty-four B-17s that were empty when the alert was received at lunchtime. The *Elaine* carried twelve bundles of twenty-pound fragmentation bombs which, when exploded, burst into hundreds of pieces of jagged flak.

We took off and Captain O'Carrol, the 419th Squadron Operations Officer, replaced Flowers as my copilot. We joined the group formation and started our climb to 15,000 feet, the bombing altitude assigned for this mission. There was a solid overcast at 5,000 feet that we had to penetrate. At about 8,000 feet the temperature was below freezing and ice started forming on the windshield and side windows. I was flying formation off the left wing of the element leader, and the ice built up so fast that I no longer had outside visibility and to avoid a possible collision, I turned left thirty degrees. We had been taught this procedure during formation training at Gowen Field. I realized that this cloud cover was so thick that we would not be able to see the target and decided to descend below the overcast because I knew that we had a good 3,000-foot ceiling above the ground. I told O'Carrol my plan and he nodded his head in agreement.

We broke out of the overcast about 2,500 feet above the ground and the visibility was over ten miles. The ice had broken off the windows and I called Passmore and asked if he could give me a heading to Kasserine Pass. His voice was a high, excitable pitch when he said, "Ken, the Pass is directly ahead of us between those two mountains sticking into the overcast!" I alerted the crew to prepare for a bomb run and started to descend to a lower altitude and told O'Hoppe to drop his bundles manually, but not until we could make sure that these were Germans in the Pass. When we started getting tracers and dark bursts of cannon shells as we started to enter the Pass, they were Germans alright. Just as we entered the Pass, O'Hoppe started dropping his bombs and we could see the German markings on the tanks and other vehicles. I concentrated on flying directly over the tank column and when O'Hoppe had dropped all his bombs, I turned away from that area to avoid the artillery aimed at us.

I had the crew report to me, and not one of them had been wounded. I felt great and looked at O'Carrol and gave him the thumbs up sign, and he smiled and returned the sign. After we had landed, O'Carrol asked me to go with him to the commander's tent. When we were through briefing Captain Traylor of our successful bombing of the Pass, he congratulated us and said that as far as he knew, we were the only B-17 to actually bomb Kasserine Pass.

The *Elaine* had protected its crew from bullets and flak but she received some thirty scars in the fuselage, wings, and tail. Fortunately, none of the gas tanks were damaged. Our maintenance crew had the *Elaine* patched up and looking like new in two days. An intelligence officer is supposed to debrief each aircrew after returning from a mission but there were none there to greet us when we landed. That is most likely the reason that World War II archives do not contain the damage our B-17 did to General Rommel's Africa Korp on the 23rd of February 1943. Captain Traylor told me that whenever I completed twenty-five missions, my bombing success would support my receiving the Distinguished Flying Cross (DFC). I told him that I could not accept the DFC for this mission, for it was the award to be presented to individuals who had contributed to the progress of aviation like the Wright Brothers, Lindbergh, etc., but not for killing people.

February 26th. Three days after the Kasserine Pass mission, the *Elaine* was loaded with twelve 500-pound bombs for another mission. Captain O'Carrol was scheduled to fly as the pilot and I as his copilot. The target was a German convoy at the southern coast of Sicily. The bombing was accurate, and we destroyed the greater part of the convoy. Then we were attacked by ME-210s. Our gunners drove them off but the *Elaine* did have some damage from a cannon shell. We could not return to our base due to bad weather. I didn't know that North Africa received this much rain, but we had had rain every day for two weeks. The flying field was soggy with very thick mud in many spots. You had to keep your aircraft moving or you would get stuck in the mud. We heard that the engineers were preparing a new airfield for us on higher ground with good drainage. The rain did provide us with fresh drinking water. We put our helmets outside the tent and when they were half full, we filled our canteens with fresh water. The water provided for us by the quartermaster in large lister bags tasted like liquid chlorine. We landed at

Bone, an English airfield located on the north coast of North Africa, where we remained overnight.

When we returned to our base at Air M'Lila the next morning, we were briefed that the German Africa Korp was now in retreat due to the damage by Allied aircraft and the attack by the Allied ground forces on the 23rd of February. We had been prepared to destroy our B-17s that were mired in the mud if the German Africa Korp defeated the Allied troops. The Germans were only 100 miles away from our base on the 23rd of February. It is now history that the beginning of the end of Rommel's Africa Korp was on the 23rd of February 1943.

The bombing mission on the 28th of February was a big day for the *Elaine* crew. This was to be our first mission as a complete *Elaine* crew. Just before we boarded the *Elaine*, we were gathered in a circle and smiling, and I told them that there was no doubt in my mind that we were the best crew in the squadron. Our target that day was the docks at Cagliari, located on the island of Sardinia. During the briefing by the intelligence officer, I started munching on the dates I had bought from an Arab outside the building. One of the pilots asked if I enjoyed eating worms and suggested that I check the seeds for worms. I split open the next date and there were worms. Also the next one. And the next one. That ended my date eating in North Africa.

Elaine was carrying twelve 500-pound bombs, and the weather was clear as a bell. We reached the beginning of our bomb run without being attacked by German fighters. However, we had very heavy flak on the run from 27,000 feet and our bombs really plastered the docks. As we turned off our bomb run, we expected to be attacked by ME-109s but surprisingly, none showed. We had a quiet flight with clear weather all the way back to Ain M'Lila.

March 1st. It was the group's unwritten policy not to schedule an aircrew to fly two missions in two days' succession. The target for our second mission in two days was the docks at the city of Palermo on the island of Sicily. We took off from our muddy runway and headed north to the Mediterranean Sea. We flew just a few feet above the water to avoid radar detection by the Germans. At a predetermined point we started our climb to 25,000 feet without being attacked by German fighters. It was thirty-five degrees below zero within the aircraft with no pressurization or heat. We wore heavy sheep-lined clothing and boots. I had to keep squeezing my oxygen mask to keep it clear from the moisture in my breath. As we entered the bomb run the flak became very intense. I held the *Elaine* level so that O'Hoppe could take control of the *Elaine* with his bombsight. That was difficult for me as a pilot not to have control of the aircraft on the bomb run until the bombs were dropped. I then had control of the *Elaine* and turned left and the German ME-109s were waiting for us. Our gunners kept the fighters from entering our formation and none of their cannon shells hit the *Elaine*. We never did see any of the P-38 aircraft that were supposed to escort us after dropping our bombs. Our bombing was accurate and we returned to muddy Ain M'Lila without the loss of any aircraft.

March 4th. We received a call to report to the briefing room for an unscheduled mission briefing. Our target was a German six-ship munitions convoy coming into the harbor at Bizerte, with munitions for General Rommel's Africa Korp. The *Elaine* was loaded with twelve 500-pound bombs and full tanks of gasoline. I knew with this weight that once I left the graveled area, I would have to use full throttle to keep the *Elaine* from sinking into the mud. I gave the engines full power and released the brakes. We started out very slow but gathered speed and slid onto the muddy runway and used the entire length of the runway to get to takeoff speed. I flew 1-3 in the first element and before we reached our target, two aircraft in the second element had to abort. The third aircraft, being alone, joined another squadron. We spotted the six-ship convoy and bombed four of them out of existence. The other two were destroyed by their own munitions exploding. It was a fantastic sight to see the two ships explode from their own munitions. We were attacked by ME-109s but our P-38 escort gave us good protection.

March 7th. This was the third time our group was directed to bomb the docks at Sousse, Tunisia. This was my first bombing target when I started flying combat in February. General Rommel was receiving the majority of his war supplies from this harbor. Our bombing altitude was 24,000 feet and in spite of very heavy flak on the bomb run, our bombs hit the docks and ships in the harbor. The *Elaine* had some damage from the flak but we never saw any fighters. We returned to Ain M'Lila, this being our last mission from this location.

On the morning of the 8th of March, we packed up all our belongings and flew to a new airfield at St. Donat, located about forty miles west of Ain M'Lila, still in Algeria. It was at a higher elevation and dry, but best of all were the large four-man tents erected in the squadron area. Goodbye, pup tents! We spent the next day unpacking, hanging up our few clothes, washing underwear, etc. This move was a terrific boost to the entire squadron's morale. That evening the *Elaine* was listed on the mission schedule for the next day.

March 10th. The briefing building was a big improvement, and the briefing itself seemed more complete and professional. Our target was the German airfield at La Marsa, Tunisia. *Elaine* was loaded with the treacherous fragmentation bombs. Walking through the bomb bay frightened me just to see them hanging there. On our climb to the bombing altitude, ME-109s attacked us. Our gunners did a great job of protecting us and I saw one ME-109 go down in flames. As usual we had flak on the bomb run which damaged a couple of our aircraft, but the *Elaine* was undamaged. Although we had partial cloud cover, our bombardiers were able to put the airfield into their bombsight. Our bombs were scattered all over the airfield and as we turned off the target, I could see many fires on the airfield. The German fighters wasted no time in attacking us coming out of the flak. Again our gunners protected us and we all returned to St. Donat.

March 12th. We were told at briefing that our target was the railroad yards at Sousse because major war supplies had arrived for General Rommel and had just been off loaded from the docks onto railroad cars. No fighters appeared as we made our climb to 24,500 feet. Flak was light on the bomb run and the majority of our bombs hit the freight cars. We were ready for the attacking fighters as we turned away from the target, but to our surprise none appeared. All of our aircraft returned to St. Donat without any damage.

March 13th. The target for this mission was a German convoy approaching the harbor at Bizerte, Tunisia. *Elaine* was loaded with twelve 500-pounders. As we neared the coast, the Mediterranean Sea was completely covered with low level clouds and we were not able to locate the convoy. No fighters attacked us and we returned with our bombs. Since we had flown into the combat zone, it was classified as a combat mission. I was not going to contest this ruling but it seemed to me that if you were not attacked by fighters or flak, and did not drop your bombs, it was not a combat mission. I could go for some more of this type of combat mission.

A week of cold, rainy weather. I spent several hours writing letters although I had yet to receive any mail. Some of us pilots got together and talked about flying. The group flight surgeon scheduled the squadron personnel for a short arm inspection. We did not have any source of heat in our tent so a lot of my time was spent in the sack with clothes on to keep warm. My waist gunner, Sgt. Childers, came down with pneumonia and was transferred to a field hospital.

March 21st. Elaine was scheduled for this day's mission to bomb the German airfield at Djebel Tebega, Tunisia. Intelligence briefed us that we would not have fighter escort but could expect attacking fighters and flak over the target. No fighters appeared as we approached the airfield but flak burst all around us on the bomb run. The bombing was accurate and as we turned off the bomb run, we tightened up the formation expecting fighters, but none showed up. All twenty-four of our B-17s returned safely to St. Donat.

March 22, 1943. The *Elaine* was scheduled for the day's mission with briefing at 11:30. With briefing this late we assumed that it was another short mission, but it was a real surprise. The target was the harbor at Palermo, Sicily. To avoid detection by land radar stations, we flew on the deck around the west and north sides of Sicily. Our climb to 27,000 feet and the bomb run would be over water north of Palermo to avoid the flak batteries surrounding the harbor. We were still in our climb when we got hit hard by scores of ME-109s, 110s and 210s. Several of our group aircraft were damaged by flak and entered the bomb run with smoking engines. The huge black cloud over the target was flak, the heaviest we had ever encountered. A jagged piece of flak entered the cockpit through the metal skin of the *Elaine,* just missing my head and burying itself in the ceiling liner. I kept this nasty item for a memento. Our bomb runs normally were two minutes long to give the bombardier time to tune his bombsight to the target; however, this bomb run was over three minutes long due to strong headwinds that were not forecast. We could hear the pieces of flak falling on the *Elaine* and even though the cabin temperature was forty-five degrees below zero, I was wet with perspiration.

Finally the bomb light came on and I knew that our bombs were being dropped. As soon as the light went off, the squadron leader turned left to the open sea. The *Elaine* received a severe jolt and the flight controls were torn from my grip. Knowing that we had been hit, I asked for a crew check-in but before they could report, O'Hoppe came on the intercom and in an excited voice reported a huge, fantastic explosion in the harbor. One of our bombs had hit a munitions ship in the harbor and it was the concussion from this explosion that had given the *Elaine* a severe buffeting. As we completed our turn, we saw a huge black cloud rising above the harbor. The group leader started a gradual descent to pick up airspeed and to get out of the flak area when the fighters attacked us from all sides. My ball turret gunner called me on the intercom and said that we were trailing white smoke from number three engine. This was bad news since enemy fighters would then concentrate their attack on a B-17 that had an engine smoking or on fire. I flew a very tight formation within the squadron to take advantage of its firepower. My new waist gunner then reported on the intercom that another B-17 was on fire and spinning out of control and some of the crew had bailed out.

This was a joint mission with the 97th Bomb Group, a B-17 outfit a few miles down the road from St. Donat. I always listened on Channel C, which was for emergency use only. I heard a distress call from one of the 97th pilots that he was badly injured and was not able to bail out of his crippled aircraft. He then gave his name, and it was my close friend and classmate, Lt. Schrimer. Just a week before I had hitched a ride to the 97th Bomb Group to visit Schrimer and four of my flight school classmates: Rast, Cummings, Perkins, and Peterson. Rast was shot down and became a prisoner of war; Cummings did not live to return to the States; but Perkins and Peterson lived to return to the States.

I called Schrimer on Channel C and told him who I was and not to give up, "For even if you are injured, you can do it Schrim."

He replied, "Slaker, I have already tried but have no control of my body. Buddy, give those Nazis hell!" Then his B-17 hit the water and sank. I was really depressed, for I had lost my cadet roommate and close friend, Hal Simpson, in a B-17 crash in December, and now my other roommate from a B-17 combat mission was now in his B-17 coffin at the bottom of the Mediterranean Sea. The loss of these two classmates has haunted me all my life.

Our B-17 was no longer trailing white smoke and Jaranson, my engineer, said that flak had ruptured the glycol line to the heaters and that was the source of the white smoke. The German fighters finally departed and we arrived at St. Donat with the loss of one B-17 and several damaged from flak and cannon fire from the fighters. The gunners from our bomb group shot down six German aircraft. Our 301st Bomb Group received a commendation for the success of this mission from Lt. General Spaatz, Commander, Northwest African Air Forces.

The *Elaine* had received flak and fighter damage to number three engine, both wings, and the fuselage. Fortunately, not one of us had been injured and we were no longer green horns in this war. We had been baptized in life-threatening combat and were now veterans. My mother's words when I departed for combat came to my mind. She told me not to worry, for her mother had promised that with God's help she would watch over me all my life. I knew after getting through this dangerous Palermo mission uninjured and alive that she was my Guardian Angel.

March 24th. My crew had one day of rest while the ground maintenance crew repaired the damage to the *Elaine*. The target today was another tough one: the docks at Ferryville, Tunisia. Military supplies for Rommel's Africa Korp were currently being unloaded there and had to be destroyed. Intelligence briefed us that the target was heavily defended by German fighters and flak batteries. While climbing to our bombing altitude of 24,500 feet, we were attacked by thirty ME-109s. Our gunners shot a couple of the fighters down and were really outstanding in defending our group. Then came the heavy flak before, during, and after the bomb run. Our bombing was accurate and highly destructive. With hundreds of pieces of jagged flak hitting us for several minutes, it was a miracle that not one of our crew was wounded, even though *Elaine* had several holes from the flak. After coming off the bomb run, we got ready to defend ourselves from the fighters but to our surprise, none appeared. Our 301st Bomb Group received a Letter of Commendation from Sir Arthur Tedder, Commander in Chief of the Mediterranean Air Command, endorsed by General Doolittle.

March 31st. The *Elaine* crew had almost a week's rest before we were scheduled on the last day of March for a bombing mission on the docks at Cagliari, Sardinia. *Elaine* carried twelve 500-pound bombs, and in clear weather we climbed to our bombing altitude of 23,500 feet. On the bomb run we received light flak that did not deter us from accurate bombing. The docks were destroyed and as we turned off the target, several fighters attacked us but could not penetrate the fifty-caliber curtain established by our gunners. No aircraft were lost and there were no injuries to any aircrew member.

April 4, 1943. This mission was the first one to bomb a German airfield on the Italian mainland. We were to destroy the Capodichino airfield near Naples and would have high cover by Allied fighters. The *Elaine* was out for maintenance, so we flew a B-17 named *Alley Oop*. We flew on the deck to avoid radar detection and north of Sicily started our climb to 23,000 feet. No fighters attacked us but we had heavy flak during the bomb run. Some of our aircraft were damaged by the flak but were able to drop their bombs on the target. Our bombing was accurate and as we came off the bomb run we saw some enemy fighters but they did not attack us. All of our aircraft returned to St. Donat after our longest mission to date, seven hours and forty minutes.

April 10th. Elaine was out for maintenance for five days and was scheduled for a very exciting mission. We were to bomb the Trieste, the largest Navy cruiser in the world. It was being loaded in the harbor at Maddelena, located on the north coast of Sardinia. The *Elaine* was loaded with four 1,000-pound bombs, which were to be dropped not on the cruiser, but alongside of its hull to buckle its steel plates, which would cause it to sink. Two squadrons carried 1000-pound armor piercing bombs for direct hits on its steel decks. We planned to bomb from 16,000 feet to ensure the accuracy of our bombs. We flew on the deck up the west coast of Sardinia to the island of Corsica, then turned south towards La Maddelena. We reached our bombing altitude without a fighter attack but did have flak on the bomb run. The bombsight released our huge bombs, and O'Hoppe watched them fall and gave us a very excited call on the intercom saying that our bombs fell alongside of the cruiser as planned. The Italian cruiser, a really beautiful naval ship, sank within twenty-four hours. Photos of our bombs dropping onto the cruiser and of bubbles showing where it sank were published in *Life* magazine a few weeks later.

April 12th. After one day's rest and although the *Elaine* was out for repair, our crew was assigned to a B-17 that was available for this mission. We were awakened at 3:30 A.M., served white rice and evaporated milk for breakfast, and were in the briefing room at 5:00 A.M. Our target was a large German convoy entering the harbor at Ferryville, Tunisia. We were airborne at 6:00 A.M., and as we climbed to our bombing altitude of 15,000 feet, at least fifty ME-109s attacked us and they were fanatical, even flying through our group formation. Cannon shells were exploding within the squadrons along with hundreds of tracer bullets. Many of our aircraft were damaged, many aircrew personnel wounded, and a navigator killed. The fighters withdrew when we entered the heavy flak area, which caused additional damage to our aircraft and injuries to our aircrews. Our bombing was not very accurate due to the fierce defense by the fighters and flak. After we limped back to St. Donat, our crew assisted in helping wounded crewmembers out of their aircraft and the badly wounded into the field hospital ambulances. It was a miracle that our B-17 did not have a scratch from fighters or flak. God and my Guardian Angel went with my crew during this dangerous mission.

April 13th. This was the first time that we were scheduled to fly two days in a row. Intelligence briefed us that we would have enemy fighters and heavy flak on today's target, which was the German airfield at Castelvetrano, Sicily. I was assigned on Colonel Gormly's left wing, who was leading the group with General Spaatz, Commander 12th Air Force, as his copilot. Captain O'Carrol, the operations officer, told me that the reason I was assigned to that 1-3 position was that Flowers and I were two of the best formation flyers in the squadron.

En route we were attacked by ME-109s but our own fighters tangled with them and drove them off. The flak was heavy and one of our squadron B-17s had a direct hit, caught on fire, went into a spin, and crashed. Captain Thomas and his crew were killed. As we came off the target, fighters jumped us and our own fighters were gone. Evidently our fighters had used up their fuel fighting the ME-109s when we were inbound. Our gunners fired continuously for twenty minutes before the fighters withdrew. In spite of the tough defense by the Germans, our bombing was accurate and destroyed several score of aircraft on the field along with hangars and other facilities. The *Elaine* had several holes from flak but again, not one of our crew was wounded. After we landed, Colonel Gormly introduced me to General Spaatz, informing him that I was the pilot flying on his left wing. He thanked me for flying a tight formation and I told him that I had to protect a Pennsylvania Dutchman. He laughed and asked where I was from and when I told him near Pittsburgh, he shook my hand. We received a commendation from our top command for this very successful mission.

April 14th. This day was my birthday but this didn't carry any weight with operations, for they scheduled me for a mission the third day in a row. Our target was the German airfield at Elmas, Sardinia. *Elaine* carried twelve 500-pound bombs plus extra fifty-caliber ammunition since the target was an airfield and we would not have fighter escort. We flew on the deck until we started our climb to our bombing altitude of 21,500 feet. Sardinia was covered with towering cumulus clouds. The group leader took us through gaps between the clouds looking for the airfield, and our squadron became separated from the group. Our squadron navigator spotted the target and we started our bomb run. There was no flak and over thirty ME-109s attacked us. All hell broke loose and I could feel the constant firing of my tail gunner's fifty calibers in my rudder pedals. Finally the fighters departed and it was the first time in twenty minutes that I had taken my eyes off the element leader, for I flew a very tight formation to concentrate our defensive firepower. It was unbelievable that we didn't lose one aircraft. I turned the controls over to Flowers, grabbed a portable oxygen bottle, and went back through the bomb bay to check my gunners. Even with several holes in the *Elaine*'s fuselage, none of the crew was wounded. We were one exhausted crew when we got back to St. Donat. Armament personnel were unhappy with my gunners because they had eliminated the rifling inside the barrels from constant firing. I told them that they would feel differently if they were to have several score of ME-109s shooting at them. God and my Guardian Angel were with us that day.

April 18th. M/Sgt. Howell, chief of the ground maintenance crew for the *Elaine*, did a great job as always and had all the flak holes in the *Elaine* repaired for this day's mission to Palermo, Sicily. There was a groan from the crewmembers when the intelligence officer named the target. We had suffered a loss of personnel and aircraft on our first mission to Palermo. We would have P-38s for our escort. Another groan. We had hoped for Spitfires from Malta for cover. *Elaine* was loaded with twelve 500-pound bombs and we flew on the deck between Sardinia and Sicily until we started our climb to our bombing altitude of 29,000 feet. This altitude was selected hoping that the flak would be lighter. While still in the climb, German fighters attacked our formation. They broke off when we entered the flak area. The higher altitude paid off, for although the flak was heavy, it was not as accurate.

As soon as the bombs were released, we turned out over the ocean and the fighter aircraft were waiting for us. An ME-110 attacked us at eleven o'clock position, and I could see Passmore's tracers hitting the fighter. For every tracer in the belt, there were two armor piercing and two incinerator bullets which were tearing pieces off the fighter. As it passed underneath us it was smoking, and our ball turret operator saw it burst into flames and crash into the ocean. One of our B-17s was damaged so bad it could not maintain flight and ditched into the ocean. Several aircraft had damage and wounded crewmembers, but none of my crew was hurt. The bombing was accurate and caused much damage but at a cost to our group. When we were being debriefed by intelligence, the crew urged Passmore to put in his claim for the fighter he had shot down, but he declined. After chow we checked the mission schedule for the next day and the *Elaine* was on it. Only four more missions for me to fly, then I would have the twenty-five needed to rotate to the States.

April 19th. When the briefing officer announced that our target was the docks at Bizerte, we aircrews groaned. On our last mission to Bizerte, we lost both personnel and aircraft. This caused us to be on edge when we started our climb to bombing altitude, and our gunners had itchy fingers. We entered the bomb run without seeing one fighter but the heavy flak made up for their absence. When we turned off the target, the gunners were ready to give the fighters a hot welcome but they never showed, much to our surprise. Our bombing was accurate and some of our aircraft received flak damage, but all of our aircraft and personnel returned to St. Donat intact.

April 20th. Our target was the cargo vessels located at LaGoulette on the Gulf of Tunis. *Elaine* was loaded with twelve 500-pound bombs and as we started our climb to bombing altitude, we encountered bad weather and *Elaine*'s windows iced up. I broke formation to prevent a collision and continued to climb to 25,000 feet. The weather was worse with heavy icing so I took up the heading to take us back to St. Donat. I had to bring my bombs back to St. Donat, as did all the group aircraft.

We received good news after we landed. A C-47 from the Air Transport Command had delivered mail to our group from the States. I had not received any mail since I left the States. There were three letters and two packages for me. Two of the letters were from my wife, and one from a mutual friend. The big package was a five-pound box of chocolate candy and the small package was church envelopes for contributions. When aircrews in the squadron heard about my church envelopes, they started to call me Reverend Slaker.

On the morning of the 21st of April, a cold rain came that lasted five days. O'Hoppe went to Setif where he spent five days with a French girl that he had met. Flowers hitched a ride to Constantine where he enjoyed the good food and hot showers at the USO. Passmore wrote letters and played cards. I spent most of the time in the sack to keep warm and planning how to solve my marital problem. The letter from our mutual friend had very disturbing news for me. She said that although Jane was her friend, what my wife Jane was doing was wrong and that I should be aware of it. Jane was dating other men and having her mother take care of our daughter, Elaine, while she went out for the evening.

I realized that we did not have the strong love for one another that you should have when you get married. I decided not to say anything about this letter to Jane. It was possible that I would not survive this combat tour and the marital problem would then cease to exist. The cold rain ended on the evening of the twenty-sixth and the mission schedule posted on the twenty-seventh had *Elaine* scheduled for a mission the next day.

April 28th. The target today was the docks at Terranova, Sardinia. We would not have fighter escort, which was not unusual. As we approached the coast during our climb to bombing altitude, huge cumulus clouds had built up and the target was obscured. We made a circle looking for a break in the clouds, hoping to see the docks. We did not find them but the ME-109s found us. Our gunners did a great job in keeping the fighters from getting too close since we still had our 500-pound bombs on board. If one of them was to be exploded by a fighter cannon shell, all twelve bombs would explode, eliminating several B-17s and aircrews. Fortunately, not one of our bombs exploded and the entire group returned to St. Donat unscathed and with their bombs.

On the 1st of May, Passmore and I received orders for a five days' rest in Algiers and operations had us flown there in a B-17. Passmore already had his twenty-five missions, and I only needed one more and we would both leave for the States. We had reservations at the Hotel Elite, a first class hotel with only high-ranking officers staying there. The 12th Air Force granted permission for we two combat lieutenants to be guests there.

The next afternoon we were sitting on the veranda watching a convoy of merchant ships being brought into the harbor when there was a terrific explosion and one of the ships started to sink. A German submarine had torpedoed the ship as it entered the harbor. A ranking officer on the veranda stood up and said, "There goes our steak dinner." Besides the good food and a real bed, we enjoyed telling the headquarter-type officers of our combat experience. They were surprised that we Army pilots and aircrews were sleeping in tents and eating field rations.

They thought we were living in hotels in Constantine and Setif. Each evening there was no shortage of attractive French girls in the lounge. With Passmore and me each being married and remembering a briefing by our flight surgeon that there was a high VD rate in Algeria, we behaved ourselves.

On the 7th of May, a vehicle from our motor pool arrived to take us back to St. Donat. O'Hoppe met us there and said he had bad news for us. Since there were no replacement aircrews, the mission requirement to complete our combat tour had been extended to fifty. What a blow to our morale. The next day Eddie Rickenbacker arrived and spoke to the entire group. He complimented us on bombing results and then told us about his survival in the South Pacific. If the top command thought that by having him speak to us would help our morale, they were mistaken. The mission schedule for the next day included the *Elaine*.

May 9th. The target for the third time was Palermo—not the harbor, but a specific city block. The buildings in the area contained the top offices of the German Army. We flew on the deck until we were north of Palermo, and then climbed to our bombing altitude of 26,000 feet. We were attacked by German fighters but broke off when we entered the flak area. After we had dropped our bombs, the ME-109s attacked us again. We had P-38s for cover but the crew never saw any of them. Our bombing was accurate and destroyed the entire city block. We had some flak and cannon damage but not one of our aircrew was wounded. This was the twenty-fifth mission for both the *Elaine* and I. Jaranson painted the twenty-fifth miniature bomb on *Elaine*'s nose and our crew lined up in front of the *Elaine* for a photo.

May 11th. Although *Elaine* was out for maintenance, our crew was assigned to a backup aircraft loaded with six 1,000-pound bombs. Our target was the docks at Marsala, Sicily. Our command wanted these docks completely destroyed, so three B-17 bomb groups were launched to this target. Our group, the 301st, was the first over the target, followed by the 97th group, and following them, the newly arrived 2nd Bomb Group. We had P-38s for high cover and no fighters attacked us, but we had very heavy flak on the bomb run. When we turned off the bomb run, a huge swarm of ME-109s attacked us and the other two groups as they came off the target. This was a scary battle for our lives, and our gunners shot down several fighters but not before they had shot down two B-17s from the 97th, two B-17s from the 2nd, and two of our P-38s. We had several holes in our B-17, but not one of our crew was wounded. This was one of the toughest missions we had flown.

On our return flight from Marsala, we descended to an altitude below 10,000 feet to conserve our oxygen. We flew above the coastline of Cape Bon and watched our P-40 fighters shoot down several of the huge six-engine German transports that were evacuating their troops from the cape. The German infantry had been defeated in Tunisia and hundreds of them were on the cape waiting to be airlifted to Sicily. We could see the huge transports crashing and exploding, tossing their passengers yards away with their clothing on fire. We arrived at St. Donat a very exhausted but lucky aircrew.

May 18, 1943. The mission this day was to be an exciting one for our crew. The target was the docks at Messina, Sicily. I was flying 100 feet above the ocean, and just before we reached the combat line between Sardinia and Sicily, number three engine exploded. The front housing of the engine had been blown off and pieces of the engine scattered in all directions. The guide wheel from the end of a valve lifter rod came through the cockpit, narrowly missing copilot Flowers' head. If it had hit him, he would have been seriously injured or killed. I could not feather the propeller since the control line had been severed. The propeller was windmilling, causing a hot smoking engine and a decrease in airspeed. We were heavily loaded with maximum fuel and ammo, and I increased the RPM on the other three engines, which gave me enough airspeed to keep from ditching into the ocean.

I knew that I had to dump the bombs to gain altitude and reduce the power on the remaining three engines. I ordered Lt. O'Hoppe to check the arming pins on the bombs before we could salvo them. He came out of the bomb bay saying that all the pins were in. He entered the nose and salvoed them. *Elaine* responded immediately and started to gain altitude when a terrific explosion jarred the *Elaine* from underneath. I could not hear anything due to the ringing in my ears, but I visually checked the wings and the three engine instruments, which looked okay. We had been briefed at Alamogordo that the bombs would not explode with the safety pins in. *Wrong!* They had exploded. I managed to gain enough altitude to get over the hills and return to St. Donat.

After landing and getting out to look at the engine, the propeller fell off! We were very lucky that the fuel tank in the wing behind the engine did not catch fire or explode. Since we had not crossed the combat line, we did not receive mission credit. I was worried that we would not have an aircraft for several days and fall behind in our mission totals. But the ground maintenance crew under M/Sgt. Howell, had a new engine on the *Elaine* in twenty-four hours! Those maintenance personnel worked many continuous hours in all kinds of weather and then sweated for us to return on each mission. They were the unsung heroes of the Army Air Corp.

May 20th. Elaine was loaded with twelve 500-pound bombs to drop on the German airfield at Grosseto, located between Rome and Florence, Italy. We flew on the deck up the west coast of Sardinia, and then turned east across Corsica, where we started our climb to bombing altitude of 25,000 feet. There were no fighters to be seen but we had medium flak on the bomb run. The bombing was very accurate, and when we did a 180-degree turn to get us back over the water, we saw many fires and black smoke from the airfield. We were ready for the fighters but none showed. We had a smooth flight back to St. Donat. This was a long mission of seven hours and twenty minutes.

May 21st. At our briefing, intelligence told us the reason we were seeing less fighters was due to the destruction of German aircraft, oil refineries, and shipping by the Allied bombers from North Africa. The aircrews all cheered at that good news. Our target today was the German/Italian airfield at Sciadda, located on the southwest coast of Sicily. *Elaine*'s bomb bay was stuffed with twenty-four clusters of those deathly fragmentation bombs. If a bullet or piece of flak were to hit one and set it off, all 144 frags would explode and shred the aircraft and crew into minute pieces. This happened to one of our B-17s in a later mission. Bombing was from 24,000 feet and very accurate. This was an unusual mission—no fighters and no flak!

May 25th. Target for this date was the ferry terminal at the Straits of Messina, located on the east coast of Sicily, just six miles across the water from the toe of Italy. We flew on the deck to north of Sicily, where we started our climb to a bombing altitude of 24,000 feet. No fighters attacked us and as we neared the bomb run, we could see many ships leaving the terminal for Italian ports. They were carrying troops that had been evacuated from North Africa. Many of the ships were swamped from our bombs, which also caused great damage to the terminal. The flak was very intense and when we came off the target and out of the flak area, the fighters attacked us. We were flying off the left wing of the squadron lead aircraft, and the squadron photographer took a picture of the *Elaine* just before the bomb run showing ten bursts of flak around the *Elaine*. We had some skin damage and holes but our crew did not suffer any wounds. Again our gunners forced the fighters to keep their distance from our group. This was a long mission of seven hours and twenty-five minutes. There was no doubt in my mind then that my Guardian Angel was by my side.

May 26th. The target this day was the German airfield at Comiso, Sicily. A morale booster for the aircrews was that we would pick up Spitfire escort over Malta. We knew that the Spitfires were equal to or better than the ME-109s. At Malta the Spitfires joined us and flew in very tight formation alongside of each B-17 so that when the ME-109s showed up, they would only see the outline of our bombers. There was towering cumulus over Sicily and as we approached the coastline, from out of the cumulus clouds came the ME-109s. The Spitfires waited until the ME-109s were within firing range and then zoomed out of our bomber formation and attacked the enemy aircraft. There was no doubt that the German pilots were surprised, and we witnessed some terrific dogfights before we made our bomb run.

The flak was heavy and a shell exploded between our wing and tail, putting several large holes in the *Elaine*, but it did not interfere with flight control. When we came off the bomb run, our gunners were busy since there were more ME-109s than Spitfires and they were free to attack us. Our group did not have any aircraft loses, but the 97th lost two, the 99th lost two, and the 2nd lost one. Some of the other crewmembers were wounded, but none of my crew was wounded.

May 30th. Another long mission to central Italy. Our target was the Pomigliano airfield at Naples. We flew on the deck between Sardinia and Sicily to avoid radar and started our climb to 25,000 feet north of Sicily. No fighters greeted us but as we crossed the coast, we were welcomed by bursts of flak. Some of our aircraft were damaged by the heavy flak on the bomb run but the *Elaine* was not hit. As we turned off the bomb run and headed for the ocean, the ME-109s really gave us a battle. All of our guns were firing and I could feel Laky's guns firing from the vibrations in my rudder pedals. After the fighters departed, Laky called me on the intercom and said that a ME-109 was coming straight at our tail and that he could feel his bullets hitting it. Pieces started flying off of it and it burst into flames. This one crashed and Laky's victory was verified by other aircrew members after we landed at St. Donat. This flight was seven hours and twenty minutes long.

May 31st. The target this day was the airfield at Foggia, Italy. The *Elaine* was out for maintenance, but we received a backup B-17 which we had flown before. This would be a long flight of at least eight hours, and if we did not have enough gas to get to St. Donat, we would have to land at the British airfield at Bone. Our aircraft carried twelve 500-pound bombs and flew on the deck to north of Sicily. We started our climb to 20,000 feet and reached the target area without any fighters. The flak was heavy but our bombing was accurate. We turned west off the bomb run and crossed all of Italy without a fighter attack. When we got to the coast above Naples, the fighters hit us hard. Two ME-110s were shot down by our gunners, and several B-17s were damaged but able to stay with the group. The fighters departed and we descended to a lower altitude and decreased our airspeed to conserve gas. Just after we got past the west end of Sicily, we relaxed thinking that we were on the downside of this mission. Out of the sky came over twenty ME-109s who really gave us a tough time. A B-17 flying as a fill in with our squadron was shot down. The pilot made a beautiful water landing. We were informed later that seven of the crewmembers were rescued by the British but the two other crewmembers were killed. We had just enough fuel to get to St. Donat. With all the damage by the fighters, none of our crew was wounded. Flying time was eight hours and fifteen minutes.

Lt. Flowers, my copilot, asked to be checked out as first pilot before he finished his fifty missions. Operations gave me permission to use the Elaine for transition and formation practice the 1st and 2nd of June. I signed his checkout form that he was qualified to be a first pilot. On the 5th of June, he was given a check ride by Captain Edmonds, who agreed that Flowers was qualified to be a first pilot.

June 8th. Elaine was scheduled for this day's mission and loaded with six 1,000-pound bombs. Flowers was scheduled as pilot and I as his copilot. The target was the island of Pantelleria. The Navy was shelling the island as we approached the coastline. We climbed to our bombing altitude of 17,000 feet and just as we started our bomb run, the 2nd Bomb Group flew right over our group, dropping their bombs through our formation. It was a miracle that none of their bombs hit one or more of our B-17s, for it would have been a huge disaster. Flak was light and we had no fighter attack. We returned to St. Donat with no damages or wounded.

June 10th. Elaine was scheduled for another mission to Pantelleria with Flowers as the pilot, his first mission without me in the aircraft. His copilot was Lt. Biddlespach, a very experienced pilot and acting as a check pilot from operations. It was a milk run with no fighters and light flak. Lt. Biddlespach informed me that Flowers did very well, flew good formation, and made a good landing.

While the group was on its way to bomb Pantelleria, 12th Air Force Headquarters ordered the 301st to fly another mission that afternoon. I filled in on Lt. Biesel's crew as copilot. It was another mild run, no fighters or flak. There were so many B-17 groups, B-25s, and B-26s arriving to drop bombs that we actually got in line to drop our bombs. With the great amount of bombs dropped on this island, it is a wonder that it did not sink.

June 11th. Another mission to Pantelleria. Flowers had the *Elaine* and her crew. I had another B-17 with a mixed crew with several close to their fifty missions. As we approached the island at 10,000 feet, we could see our invasion fleet massed just off shore. Shortly after we had dropped our bombs, the commander of the island surrendered before our invasion troops went ashore. Air power alone had forced the defenders of the island to wave the white flag, thus saving the lives of many of our foot soldiers.

Aircrew and maintenance personnel were given a few days' rest after the all-out bombing on Pantelleria. O'Hoppe headed for Setif to spend time with his French girlfriend. Passmore and I planned to go to Constantine for good food, showers, and a movie. I had to change plans after I had gone to the latrine to urinate and noticed white, flaky warts growing on my penis. I scratched one off and it started to bleed. I immediately went to see the flight surgeon, and that character said that he had to know who I had been having sexual relations with before he could treat this fungus. He had me frightened, and when I convinced him that I had not had sex since I left the States, he had a good laugh at my expense. He said that it was a common skin fungus that could be eliminated with medication. He advised me to wash my hands before I visited the latrine, since this fungus could be picked up by our hands in this environment. In three days the medication cleared up the infection and I faithfully washed my hands before a trip to the latrine.

June 18, 1943. This was to be a tragic day for me, one that I would never forget. My copilot, Lt. Flowers, was scheduled as the pilot for *Elaine*'s thirty-seventh mission. Lt. Richardson was assigned as the copilot for this mission to the tough target of Messina, Sicily. I was not scheduled to fly this mission but attended the briefing and went with my crew to the dispersal area. I saluted the *Elaine* as it taxied out for takeoff and experienced a lonesome and empty feeling, for this was my B-17. About a half hour before the group was due back, I joined the maintenance personnel on the airfield to sweat out our squadron's return. We heard them before we saw them and when they came into sight, we started counting. Our squadron, the 419th, was missing one! When they had landed and taxied to our dispersal area, the *Elaine* was missing! I ran to the squadron leader's aircraft and asked what happened to the *Elaine*. He told me that the *Elaine* had feathered an engine after coming off the target, but that she was with the group when they came to the coast and that it may have made an emergency landing at Bone. That eliminated the tense fear I had in my mind that they had been shot down.

About 9:00 P.M., an Army truck arrived in the squadron area with the crew of the *Elaine* on board. They were okay, but the *Elaine* was no more. Heavy flak over Messina had not only damaged an engine, but had also punctured the fuel tanks. Flowers miscalculated his fuel reserves and passed up landing at Bone. About thirty-five miles from St. Donat, *Elaine* ran out of fuel and Flowers crash landed in a sheep pasture. The *Elaine* was damaged beyond repair and would be used for parts. I was very disappointed in Flowers and felt that he should have landed at Bone. With the fuel leaks, the *Elaine* could have exploded, killing the entire crew. To top it off, O'Hoppe told me that Flowers even smoked a cigarette just before they had to make the crash landing.

The next day I met with Major Duval, the squadron commander, and expressed my disappointment in Flowers as a first pilot and suggested that he be returned to copilot status. Major Duval agreed to this but was concerned about my relationship with Flowers from here on. Major Duval had a long talk with me, asking me to look at the positive side—that the crew was safe, that we were at war and the loss of the *Elaine* could happen on any mission, and it could be replaced. And in my mind I knew that Major Duval was right.

June 25th. Our crew was scheduled to fly B-17 number 41 24346 and Flowers was on the aircrew list as my copilot. This mission helped ease the tension between us. The target was the Messina Straits and our aircraft was loaded with sixteen 300-pound bombs. We flew on the deck until north of Sicily, and then started our climb to our bombing altitude of 24,000 feet. During the climb, we were attacked by ME-109s and Italian RE-2001s. Our experienced gunners shot down several of the fighters before we entered the flak area. The flak was very heavy, and one of the flak shells exploded just above the nose of our aircraft. The heavy base of the shell crashed through the navigator's ceiling, tearing the heavy altitude clothing off Passmore's back and leaving a red welt the entire length of his back but drawing no blood. Another piece of flak came through the cockpit, just missing my head. Our aircraft had several holes in the wings and fuselage, but I was able to complete the bomb run. As we came off the bomb run, the fighters attacked us again and again. Laky was so busy firing at the fighters that the barrels on his fifty-caliber machine gun drooped. My gunners fired more ammo than on any of our other missions. When the fighters departed, I had the crew check in and not a one of them had been wounded. Other crews in our group were not so lucky. St. Donat never looked so good as it did this time. We had been in the air seven hours and forty minutes but it seemed a lot longer.

The next day Major Duval asked me how Lt. Flowers did on the mission to Messina with me. I replied okay, that Flowers was an excellent copilot. The major then told me that he was having operations schedule Flowers for a recheck as to his qualification to be a first pilot. This order was posted on the bulletin board the next morning and what a surprise! I was listed as the check pilot. Major Duval had put the monkey on my back. I really felt that one of the instructor pilots in operations should give this check ride. On the 27th of June, with Flowers in the left seat, we took off in a B-17 that needed time on a new engine. I gave him a thorough flight check for a first pilot, and Flowers was very cool and professional during the check ride. After we landed, I looked him straight in the eye and asked him that if he were returning from a mission to northern Italy and had a fuel leakage, would he make an emergency landing and where? He replied, "Bone." I held out my hand and said, "Leo, you are a good first pilot." We shook hands and I approved his check ride. Major Duval had taken the right action for both Flowers and me.

June 28th. This day's target was the harbor at Leghorn, Italy, on the Ligurian Sea, just a few miles south of Pisa. Our B-17 was built just a short time before our *Elaine* and was a good one. It was loaded with twelve 500-pound bombs. We flew on the deck off the west coast of Sardinia and Corsica. We turned to the north side of Corsica and started our climb to our bombing altitude of 24,000 feet. We had medium flak over the target and our bombing was very accurate. As we turned off the target, several Italian fighters appeared and flew parallel to our bomb group. O'Hoppe started firing a few bursts at them, and I called him and asked why he was firing at them when they were out of range of our guns. His answer was that he wanted them to know that he knew they were there. I could not argue with that reply and that may be the reason they never did attack us. We returned by the same route that we had flown to the target and landed at St. Donat after seven hours and forty five minutes in the air. A very successful mission.

June 30th. Our crew was assigned B-17 number 42 5082, the same aircraft we had flown on our mission to northern Italy on June 28th. It was loaded with twelve 500-pound bombs to drop on the German military compound at Palermo. Again we flew on the deck to north of Sicily, then climbed to our bombing altitude of 24,500 feet, and with very light flak, our bombs destroyed the compound. We came off the target ready to defend ourselves against the fighters, but none appeared. It was unbelievable that we had such an easy mission on one of the toughest targets in the past.

Our crew had the next three days off so Flowers and I hitched a ride to Constantine, about forty miles from our base. It was an interesting town, built on a high rocky bluff, cut in half by a deep ravine. The one half was the French part with white houses and apartment buildings, while the other half was the Arab area with mud and stone huts and the smell of centuries of open urination. The French commercial area had a public bath facility where we could clean up, which was worth the trip. A USO fed us a decent meal and accepted Army script since we were not paid in American dollars. When we returned to base, the mail from June had arrived. The next two days were spent reading and answering our Victory mail.

July 4th. We celebrated the Fourth of July by flying a mission to bomb the German airfield at Catania, located on the east coast of Sicily near Mt. Etna. We were briefed that the 2nd Bomb Group would drop their bombs first, followed by our group. Spitfire fighters from Malta would be our escort. Over Malta they joined up with us, each one flying in close formation with a B-17 to be hidden by the bomber's silhouette. As we approached the Sicilian coast, ME-109s came from behind the clouds to attack us.

When the Spitfires broke away from our formation, the ME-109s scattered in all directions. The dogfights that took place were like watching a movie. As we entered the bomb run, the flak was very heavy with several of them exploding within our squadron formation. The 2nd Bomb Group was late, so we bombed first. Our B-17 received several large and small flak holes. When the 2nd Bomb Group came off the bomb run, there were at least fifty fighters who attacked them. They had two aircraft shot down and had many aircrew members wounded. It was a miracle that we had flown through such heavy flak, with many aircraft damaged, yet not one of my crew were wounded. This was a long and rough mission of seven hours and twenty-five minutes.

July 6th. This day's target was the airfield at Gerbini, located in southeast Sicily. I was scheduled as copilot for a new replacement crew; Lt. Dodge was the pilot. It was squadron policy to use experienced pilots with new crews for their first four missions. This B-17G was the latest B-17 model and had a nose turret. It was loaded with sixteen 300-pound bombs. During our climb to bombing altitude of 23,500 feet, we flew into bad weather and poor visibility and became separated from the squadron. When we broke on top of the weather, we saw the group and slipped into a vacant spot in the nearest squadron. We had medium flak over the target and were attacked by fighters as we came off the bomb run. I really sweated out this attack because this was a new crew and the gunners were inexperienced. However, my Guardian Angel was with us and we came through unscathed. A long mission of seven hours and fifteen minutes.

July 7th. The target was an airfield on the toe of Italy. I was scheduled as pilot on a new replacement crew with their pilot as copilot. We climbed to our bombing altitude, and the target area had a solid cover of clouds and the airfield could not be seen. The entire group returned with its bombs. The group did not receive mission credit.

July 10th. I was scheduled to fly with some new crewmembers to replace the *Elaine* crewmembers that had finished their fifty missions. The target was the Gerbini airfield in southern Sicily and we were loaded with twelve 500-pound bombs. We had no problem climbing to our bombing altitude of 23,800 feet and had medium flak on the bomb run. We really destroyed this airfield and when we returned to St. Donat, we were told that the main reason we had destroyed that airfield was that the Allies had invaded Sicily that day. We had a couple of small holes from flak but none of the crew was wounded.

July 12th. The target was the railroad yards at Messina. Supplies from Italy were being unloaded here to supply the German troops fighting the Allied invasion forces in Sicily. We carried twelve 500-pound bombs and had no trouble climbing to our bombing altitude of 23,800 feet. Our bombing was accurate in spite of very heavy flak. We suffered several hits from flak with one piece hitting the navigator but not drawing blood. Two pieces came into the cockpit but missed both of us pilots. None of my aircrew was wounded. Another long mission.

July 14th. Again the target was the railroads and docks at the Messina Straits. Our

B-17 was loaded with twelve 500-pound bombs and we flew on the deck over the Mediterranean Sea to about forty miles north of the target. We started climbing to our bombing altitude of 24,300 feet without seeing any enemy fighters. Just as we started our bomb run, we received heavy flak that damaged the aircraft but did not prevent us from doing heavy damage to our target. We then prepared for attacks from enemy fighters, but to our surprise none appeared. We had a safe flight of six hours, forty-five minutes back to St. Donat.

July 15th. The target this day was the railroad yards at Naples, Italy. We flew a replacement B-17 number 42 5082, which was loaded with twelve 500-pound bombs. We flew on the deck to the northwest tip of Sicily, and then climbed to our bombing altitude of 24,000 feet. Flak over the target was very heavy and since our squadron was the last one to drop our bombs, we were attacked by two dozen Italian fighters. They were very persistent and attacked us for thirty minutes. Our squadron shot down six of them—two of them by Laky, my tail gunner, and one by my top turret gunner, Jaranson. By the time the fighters withdrew, my gunners had fired over 2,500 fifty-caliber shells. Our bombing was accurate and several of the boxcars loaded with ammunition exploded, thus blowing up other boxcars. The B-17 had some damage but not one of our aircrew was injured. This was Lt. Flowers and Sgt. Jaranson's fiftieth mission, so their combat tour was over with never an injury.

July 16th. The target was the ferry terminal across the sea from Messina at San Giovanni, Italy. We were loaded with twelve 500-pound bombs. This terminal was unloading German troop ships coming from Messina. We approached the terminal from the north at 23,000-foot altitude with no enemy fighters in sight. The flak was heavy but our bombs destroyed many of the terminals and troop ships unloading German soldiers. As we came off the bombing run, the fighters attacked us. Our gunners were kept busy for fifteen minutes and the aircraft's tail assembly was damaged but none of our crew were injured. This was a long mission of seven hours and thirty-five minutes.

July 17th. We returned to Naples to bomb the railroad yards again. The flak was heavy but no fighters were in sight. Our bombs hit the yards and left them in shambles. The fighters attacked us as we came off the bomb run, but they only made a couple of runs due to the heavy fire from our gunners. Our plane was free of any damage and none of our crew was injured. We returned to St. Donat after a long flight of seven hours and ten minutes. We had flown four long-range combat missions in four days. We were getting exhausted.

July 19, 1943. What a target intelligence briefed us on today: the railroad yards at Rome, Italy! The Germans and Italians had made it known, through Axis Sally, that if we ever bombed Rome, not a single bomber would survive. The briefing officer, Lt. Col. Brigham, stated that if any crewmember, because of his religious convictions, wished to abstain from this first raid on Rome, he was free to leave the briefing and there would be no action taken against him. Talk about patriotism and dedication to the war effort—not one crewmember got up and left the briefing. This was to be an all-out mission by the Northwest African Air Forces with four B-17 groups, two B-24 groups, two B-25 groups, and B-26s. My group, the 301st, was assigned to be the first group across the target, led by Col. Gormly, our group commander. We would be escorted by scores of P-38s and Spitfires.

Residents of Rome had been warned with leaflets dropped by the British Mosquitoes the day before that the Allies were planning to bomb a military target in Rome. We were edgy crews when the trucks dropped us off at our aircraft, especially since the planned bombing altitude was 19,000 feet. The reason for this lower altitude was to ensure bombing accuracy. We climbed to our bombing altitude over the Tyrrhenian Sea and approached Rome from the north. We had headwinds stronger than what was forecast which changed a normal two-minute bomb run to one of five minutes. It was a very tense situation, and it was ages before my bombs away light came on. The big surprise was that we didn't have one burst of flak! We turned right off the target for the open sea. We looked back to see the 97th Bomb Group, lead by General Doolittle, come over the target, and they received heavy flak. We all had our ideas as to why we didn't get flak but the most common one was that the anti-aircraft gunners did not believe we would bomb Rome and were surprised when our group dropped its bombs. Several Italian fighters appeared but they flew parallel to our group and never attacked us! It would have been a different scenario if the fighters had been ME-109s. We descended to the deck and flew between Sardinia and Sicily back to St. Donat.

Our bombing was accurate as well as the bombs from the other groups. The railroad yards, freight cars, and buildings were destroyed. We had feared that this mission to bomb Rome would be the most hazardous of any of our missions to date, and then it turned out to be almost a milk run with no aircraft lost and not one crewmember wounded. This was a long mission of seven hours and forty five minutes in the air.

July 23rd. It was back to Italy to bomb the German/Italian airfield at Livorno. We flew up the west coast of Sardinia and Corsica, starting our climb north of Corsica to our bombing altitude of 23,300 feet. No fighters appeared as we approached the Italian coast, but we had medium flak before, during, and after the bomb run. We turned west over the sea, descending to the deck between Sardinia and Sicily. When we had the African coast in sight, we checked the fuel gauges which showed not enough gas to make it to St. Donat. We landed at Bone, the British airport. It was dark before we were done refueling, so we remained overnight. We returned to home base the next morning, logging a total mission time of eight hours and fifty minutes. This was my longest combat mission and my rear end felt it.

July 27th. The target was the airdrome at Varano, Italy. The aircraft was loaded with twelve 500-pounders, and this was my first combat mission that I didn't have at least one of the original *Elaine* crewmembers on board. Thirty minutes after takeoff number one engine was losing power and I had to abort and return to St. Donat. The mission that I had aborted on the twenty-seventh resulted in the death of another close friend, J. Pearson, who was in the Aynesworth Group with me. He was flying copilot with a new crew when they got shot down. Within one year, I had lost three close comrades. I have never forgotten them. Three great Americans who gave their lives so that we could live.

July 29th. The target this day was the German/Italian airfield at Viterbo, Italy. The bomb load was sixteen 300-pounders to be dropped from 21,500 feet. We had no fighters but medium flak over the airfield. Our bombing was accurate and destroyed many aircraft on the field. Another long mission of seven and a half hours.

August 1st. The big day was here! My fiftieth mission and the target was the Capodichino Airdrome, Naples, Italy. My B-17 was loaded with sixteen 300-pound bombs to be dropped from an altitude of 23,500 feet. Shortly after takeoff I had a severe maintenance problem and had to abort. Very discouraging.

August 4th. Another try to complete my fiftieth mission. All the crewmembers with me on this mission were on their fiftieth mission! We had decided that we all were going to make it or go down together. The target was a tough one, the harbor at Naples. We flew on the deck between Sardinia and Sicily and when north of Sicily, started our climb to the bombing altitude of 23,000 feet. The first piece of luck: no fighters! We had heavy flak over the harbor and we could hear pieces of flak hitting our aircraft, and again lucky. No bad damage to our aircraft and nobody wounded. As we turned off the bomb run toward the ocean, our luck ran out. We got attacked by the fighters in force. Even though I had the most experienced gunners in the squadron, I asked God and my Guardian Angel to help us through this last battle. Even though it was thirty degrees below zero inside our fuselage, I was sweating and had to remove my oxygen mask several times to crunch the ice out of it. I flew in very tight formation so as not to be spotted as a strangler. After a long fifteen minutes, the fighters departed and although we had some damage, not one crewmember was wounded. We landed safely at St. Donat after seven hours of tense flying. As we disembarked from our B-17, one of the crewmembers suggested that we offer a silent prayer of thanks to God for having helped us through these fifty combat missions—which we did, and then we celebrated!

It was not to be a quick departure for me to the States. Our group had received orders to move to a new airfield at Oudna, Tunisia, around twenty miles south of Tunis. I was assigned a B-17 to fly to our new base with my personal items and also several aircrews and their belongings. We said goodbye to St. Donat on the 7th of August and arrived at our new base that was a big improvement over the one we had just vacated.

Flowers and I were the only *Elaine* crewmembers still with the group and with our missions completed, we had time on our hands. We decided to go to Tunis to see what damage we had done with our bombs. We were amazed at the destruction before our eyes. The warehouses in the dock area were just skeletons. The docks were nothing but piles of trash. Buildings in the area were just bare walls. It was not a good feeling to realize what terrible damage we had done but we had no choice: we were at war.

In the early afternoon we started to walk back to our new base and we noticed a huge grape vineyard and those big juicy grapes. We were as hungry as we had been ever since we arrived in Africa, which forced us into the vineyard to sit down and eat a ton of grapes. We paid for this feast that night and all next day. We had diarrhea like we never had before. Our digestive system just was not used to this good food.

The days were really hot and when Flowers and I recovered from our diarrhea, we were able to obtain transportation to the beach near Tunis. We were in for a real surprise at the immodesty of the daughters of the wealthy Italian families that owned plantations in Tunisia. They would change into bathing suits right on the beach, but they did turn their backs to us. They did not wear tops, which embarrassed us but not them. We went behind sand dunes to get into our trunks and the girls laughed at us. I was going to return to the States a lot more sophisticated than when I left there many months ago.

One week after I arrived at Oudna and was waiting for my travel orders to the States, I was assigned to the group as the assistant provost marshall. We had to increase our security because we were having trouble with thieves and saboteurs, especially in our aircraft dispersal area. I helped organize and schedule patrols utilizing aircrew personnel who had completed their fifty missions. We really had to be alert on the 16th of August because entertainer Bob Hope was scheduled to be at Oudna. The extra alert was not for his security but for our dispersal area since almost all personnel would be at Hope's show. This would be an ideal time for the enemy to infiltrate our dispersal area. Daybreak came without an alert firing from any of our patrols.

The 16th of August found Flowers and I flying locally for two hours to put flying time on a new engine. We flew down to Sousse and viewed the damage we had done there, then up to Bizerte for a buzz job over the docks to view the damage we had done there. It was awesome and would take years to clean up and rebuild.

A couple of nights later while I was on duty as the provost marshall, a military policeman (MP) on patrol drove up in his jeep (which had blackout lights) and reported that he had spotted Arabs in the B-17 dispersal area. I jumped into the jeep and we drove to the dispersal area, walked to where the MP had spotted the Arabs, and turned on our flashlights. There were three Arabs at the fuselage door of a B-17. We shouted for them to put up their hands and they started to run. We officers always carried our Colt .45s with us and I had qualified as an expert marksman. The MP and I fired in the air and when they did not stop, I fired a shot at the Arab in the middle and he fell forward. The other two Arabs stopped and raised their hands. The MP handcuffed them and I went to the Arab on the ground and saw that he was dead from a gaping hole in the chest. The senior MP on duty drove me and the two Arabs to the French military office in Tunis since Tunisia was under French Military Law. There was a French officer on duty and I explained to him in English, which he understood, what had happened. He went up to the Arabs, backhanded each one across their cheek, drawing blood with his huge signet ring, and asked each one in French if they were working with the Germans to sabotage the B-17s. Each one said yes and he shoved them over in front of a six-foot stone wall, and then turned to the MP and me and asked us to sit down for a few minutes.

About five minutes later, several sleepy looking French soldiers appeared and formed a line about twenty feet in front of the Arabs. The French officer gave a command in French, and the soldiers shot the Arabs. I was speechless from seeing what had happened. Even though I had just shot one of them, I thought that I might be in trouble. Although I had killed hundreds of the enemy from my bombs, I was at a very high altitude and did not witness their death like I had just experienced. I knew that we were at war and these Arabs were our enemy, also of the French, and their retaliation was swift. The MP and I drove back to the base, arriving at daybreak. The group commander was already up and we briefed him on the night's activity. He complimented us for having done our duty and then I asked about the Arab that was lying dead in the dispersal area. The colonel said that the Arab had already been buried.

Four days later a sergeant came to my tent and said that Colonel Gormly wanted to see me in his tent right away. I gave him a salute as I entered his tent and he introduced me to a Frenchman that spoke English. He was a top French official and asked me to tell him exactly what happened the night we caught the Arabs in our dispersal area. I gave him my experience and he said to me, "Lieutenant, Tunisia is under French Martial Law, and if you see any Arabs in your aircraft area, just shoot them and bury them. You don't have to bring them to our office in Tunis." He got up, shook hands with the colonel and me, and departed. Colonel Gormly then said to me, "Lieutenant, you have your orders!"

A few days after my copilot Flowers departed for the States, I received notice that two pilots from the 301st Bomb Group were selected to fly the Northwest African Air Forces staff B-17F to the States, and that I was named as one of the pilots. *What a morale booster!* The staff B-17F was delivered to our base at Oudna and Lt. Ellis, the other pilot selected, flew it locally on the twenty-eighth to see if it required any maintenance before we departed. The same day, we received orders from the top command, one authorizing the flight and naming the crewmembers, classified Confidential and signed by General Eisenhower. The other order from top command gave instructions as to the purpose of the flight, classified Secret and signed by General Spaatz. The next day, August 29th, we all boarded the B-17 and took off for Algiers. We remained overnight because we were going to have passengers coming aboard the next morning for the trip to the States.

The next morning, August 30th, we loaded our passengers, who were soldiers that had lost an arm or a leg, or one of each. It was a sobering experience and I would never forget these young men who had sacrificed so much for their country. After the medical personnel made our passengers comfortable, we took off for Marrakesh, landing there four hours later. At Marrakesh we were under the jurisdiction of the Air Transport Command (ATC), which had been ordered to treat us as VIPs at all stations en route to the States. Our passengers were taken by ambulance to the local military hospital, while we saw to refueling, route briefing to Prestwick, etc.

August 31, 1943. After breakfast and our medical passengers had been made comfortable, we departed for Prestwick, Scotland. We flew north over the Atlantic Ocean, entering the British Isles off the west coast of Wales, England. Prestwick was zero-zero, as were all the airfields in the British Isles. We circled on top of the fog layer above Prestwick, and when the tower reported a one to two mile visibility, we made an instrument approach. When we had descended to the minimum altitude published and could not see the runway, we had to climb back up to the top of the fog. We flew out over the Firth of Clyde and spotted a hole in the fog. We descended through the hole to just a few feet above the water and had about a mile of visibility. We canceled our instrument flight plan so that we could try for a visual approach to the Prestwick runway. We lowered the flaps and landing gear to slow our speed to be in a landing configuration. With straining eyes we spotted the city of Ayr and our navigator gave us the heading to Prestwick. We flew just above the treetops, and through the swirling mist we saw the runway directly in front of us. Full flaps, throttles back, and we greased our B-17 onto the runway. A sigh of relief issued from all of us because we had prepared the crew and passengers for a possible ditching into the water.

Medical personnel claimed our passengers and our crew was billeted in Adamton Manor, the VIP quarters. About one hour later a bus pulled up in front of Adamton Manor with Bob Hope's show troupe. We had a very enjoyable visit that evening with Bob Hope, the female singer Francis Langford, Tony Romano the guitar player, and other troupe members. Like us, they were on their way back to the States.

Early the next morning, after having the best breakfast since leaving the States, we took off for Reykjavik, Iceland. It was a smooth five-hour flight and we descended through a gray cloud layer and made a normal landing. The medics took custody of our passengers and our crew was billeted in the VIP quonset. Before long Bob Hope and a few of his troupe were billeted with us in the same quonset. Their aircraft had stopped to refuel and continue on to Goose Bay, Canada, but the weather was below minimums at Goose, an unscheduled overnight there. What a trooper that Hope was! Rather than spending a relaxing evening at the officers' club, he contacted the commanding general and volunteered to put on a show at the base theatre that evening. The general approved and it was announced over the base loudspeaker system. Our crew volunteered in helping to unload their props from the aircraft and place them on the theatre stage. Just a few minutes before 8:00 P.M., I peaked through the stage curtains and saw that the theatre was jammed. I wondered if all the soldiers got in, so I opened a side door and there were several scores of soldiers that could not get in. I informed Mr. Hope of that situation. When Hope went onto the stage and after the applause had died down, he said to tell those troops outside that there would be a second show at 9:00 P.M. for them! I have never forgotten that unselfish act on his part and of his troupe.

The weather at Goose Bay was finally forecast to have VFR conditions at our estimated arrival time, so on the 3rd of September we took off for North America. It was a long and cold flight of around 1,500 miles across Greenland to Goose Bay. We used long-range cruise control settings and after nine hours, landed at Goose Bay, Labrador. As we shut down our engines on the ramp, a new B-17G model parked beside us. I was looking it over when two women emerged from the cockpit. *Women flying B-17s? Unbelievable.* When I got out on the ramp, I asked a member of the ground crew if these women had flown that B-17. He said yes, that they were WASPs (Womens' Auxiliary Service Pilots) that were ferrying B-17s from the factory to Goose Bay, where they turned them over to male pilots to be flown to England.

The next morning was an exciting one for us. We were taking off for the USA! When we crossed the Canadian/USA border, we notified the crew and passengers that we were in the USA and our passengers, as battle scarred as they were, cheered. We landed at Presque Isle, Maine and the medics took charge of our passengers for the last time. We were billeted in the officers' quarters, took a hot shower, and headed for the snack bar. Happiness was a real American hamburger with a chocolate milk shake. I called home and my father told me that my mother was seriously ill and in the hospital. He had kept her health condition from me so that I would not worry while in combat. This put a damper on my excitement to be coming back home to the USA. I really had a wonderful mother and I loved her.

On the September 6th we received approval to deliver General Eisenhower's B-17 to the depot at Wright Patterson, Dayton, Ohio for modification and upgrading. After a five-and-half- hour flight, we landed at Patterson Army Air Base and received a letter of delivery. We reported in person to the Commander, General Estabrook, who treated us royally. When I told him of my mother's serious and terminal illness, the general ordered personnel there to give me a five-day emergency leave and a pass ticket for the next train to Pittsburgh. I arrived in Pittsburgh at midnight and my dad was there to meet me. I was safely back home after a rough combat tour. Thanks to God and my Guardian Angel.

Chapter 5
STATESIDE WAR YEARS 1943-1945

My dad briefed me on my mother's illness during the drive to our home in Vandergrift. The hospital was keeping her out of pain with drugs knowing that her son was returning from combat. The next morning I drove my dad to work so that I could have the car to visit my mother in the hospital in Tarentum. The hospital personnel were very cooperative and said they had taken her off drugs so that she would be conscious and able to talk to me. The nurse said that it would be another half hour before the drugs wore off, and she joined me for a cup of coffee. She told me that my mother was dying from nephritis, an incurable disease of the kidneys. When we returned to her room, she was awake and recognized me. I hugged her and told her I was back home safe from combat and we both had tears. She said that she had prayed for me every day and I told her that God and my Guardian Angel had heard her prayers. I got a sign from the nurse that I should leave. I knew that she needed the drugs and told her that I would be back tomorrow.

I stopped by New Kensington on my way back to Vandergrift to see Jane and her parents and my baby daughter, Patricia Elaine. Jane was not there but her parents were, and they were very glad to see me. Patti Elaine was a doll and I was glad that I had returned from overseas in time to celebrate her one-year-old birthday the next day. I stayed until Jane came home. We hugged and kissed like a married couple that had been separated almost a year should, but the spark was no longer there. I stayed for dinner but excused myself that I had to get back to Vandergrift to brief my dad on my visit with my mother that morning.

I had good publicity in the Pittsburgh, New Kensington, and Vandergrift newspapers, being a B-17 pilot back from combat. I was invited to many dinner parties by my lifelong friends in Vandergrift. Mr. Stewart, father of my buddy Steele, whom I had sold my Buick to when I left for the Aviation Cadets, loaned me an automobile with gas coupons during my leave.

Mr. Shaffer, still principal of our high school, asked if I would speak to the students at the next Chapel meeting and I agreed. It was an exciting and unusual experience to be talking to these young students about the horrors of war and answering their questions truthfully. I closed my presentation by telling them how fortunate they were to be Americans and living in the greatest country in the world. Afterwards it was a great pleasure meeting and talking to teachers that had been my high school teachers six or more years ago. As I left the high school, I thought that this was worth fighting for.

I received a call from Mr. Orr of the U.S. Steel Corporation office located at Dravosburg, across the Monongahela River from McKeesport, Pennsylvania. He invited the wife and me to a banquet to be held in my honor since I had worked there before entering the Army Air Corp. It was a very enjoyable evening and I told them about a few of my bombing missions and answered many questions. I thanked them and the many steel mill workers that were helping our country to win this war.

In between several welcoming parties, I visited my mother in the hospital but she was usually asleep. I would talk to her, thinking that maybe she could hear me and know that I was there. The doctor told me that she could depart from this life any day. I also visited my wife's parents and baby daughter Patti. Mrs. George told me that they were very upset with Jane and did not approve her dating other men. She told me that she and her husband would always love me as their son-in-law. She proved this feeling by keeping me informed about Patti's growing up after the end of the war with her mother and stepfather.

I received a call from Mr. Lyle, a representative of the U.S. Treasury Department for the third war bond drive in our state of Pennsylvania. He asked me if I would visit several industrial mills with him to encourage the workers to buy war bonds. I agreed, and along with Michael Felock, also back from combat, we visited several plants making parts for combat weapons. When Mr. Lyle introduced Michael and me as war heroes, the workers gave us tremendous applause. I spoke first: "One of the reasons that I have been able to come back from combat alive is that you patriotic Americans have been working your asses off to give us the best weapons in the world. My aunt, Rhoda McMillian, is one of you workers and is assembling B-24 bombers at Willow Run. You workers are the real reasons that we will win this war. My sincere thanks to you." Every plant that we visited met their goal for bond sales 100 percent.

The 27th of September was one of the most unhappy days of my life. My dad left for work at 7:00 A.M. and twenty minutes later, the phone rang. It was the nurse at the Tarentum hospital. She said that Mrs. Slaker was dying and asking for members of her family—that she didn't want to die alone. I was without wheels so I called the personnel office at the steel mill and told them that Mr. Slaker's wife was dying. They said that my dad would be on his way home in five minutes. Just as he came into the house, the phone rang and the nurse ask us to hurry, that Mrs. Slaker only had a few minutes to live. Dad said that he had to change clothes and went upstairs. I waited three minutes before I ran upstairs to hurry him up, and he was in the bathroom shaving! I was really mad and told him that I was taking the car and leaving for the hospital right then. He

TREASURY DEPARTMENT
WAR SAVINGS STAFF

WAR FINANCE COMMITTEE
for PENNSYLVANIA

WESTMORELAND COUNTY
FIRST NATIONAL BANK BUILDING
GREENSBURG, PENNSYLVANIA

October 7, 1943

Lieutenant Kenneth Slaker
1350 Leishman Avenue
New Kensington, Pa.

Dear Lieutenant Slaker:

In behalf of the War Finance Committee, I should like to take this opportunity to sincerely thank you for your outstanding contribution to the Third War Loan Drive. You have not only distinguished yourself on the fighting front but you have performed a service here on the home front that will do much to bring this war to an early victory.

I have taken the privilege of writing the Secretary of the Treasury, Mr. Henry Morgenthau, about your part here in behalf of the Third War Loan Drive and also enclosed the editorial from our local newspaper.

I consider it an honor and a privilege to have made your acquaintance and I want to personally thank you for the fine work you have done in our behalf.

Sincerely,

Fred J. Lyle

FIL:vrm

Thank you letter from the U. S. Treasury, 7 October 1943.

could see that I was serious, he dried his face, and we got into the car. I was already in the driver's seat and exceeded the speed limit getting to the hospital.

Twenty minutes later I drove into the hospital parking lot and ran inside to my mother's room. A doctor and a nurse were standing outside the doorway, and I knew that she had passed away. My dad arrived and we both entered my mother's room. She looked very thin and emaciated. I left the room, took the nurse by the arm, and walked down the hallway. I asked her if my mother was awake when she died. The nurse said yes, she was awake and kept asking for "the kid" when she quit breathing. That was her nickname for me. I was really angry at my dad for having taken that extra time to change clothes and shave. Otherwise, we would have arrived there before she died. I then realized that it was partly my fault because I should have waited outside and when he arrived, got into the car and told him that we were leaving right then for the hospital.

My dad signed and received the necessary death papers and requested that my mother's body be delivered to the Thompson Funeral Parlor in Vandergrift. Driving home, my dad said that he would make the funeral arrangements and have her interned in the Hawk plot with her parents. I told him that I would get in touch with my brother who was an Army pilot stationed at Marana, Arizona, to see if he could get an emergency leave to come home for the funeral service. He managed to do this and flew home in time to attend the funeral.

My mother had joined the Methodist Church during the Depression, and when I was a senior in high school, she asked me to transfer from the Lutheran church to her church. I did this as a favor for her since my dad never went to church with her and she never drove an automobile, so then I could drive her to church. Reverend Little, the Methodist minister, delivered the sermon at the funeral home. I rode with him to the cemetery, at which time I decided to tell him of a theological problem that was bothering me. I had been taught to obey the Ten Commandments, and now in combat I had to kill or be killed. I told him that I felt that I was doing the right thing since the Nazis were atheists. He replied that my killing the Nazis was not justified because of their disbelief in God, that I had sinned, and we would pray to God to forgive me. His reply did not ease my mind as I had hoped it would. I gave a lot of thought to his canned reply and decided that he was not cognizant of the serious situation our country was experiencing at this time. I wrote a letter to him containing my resignation from the Methodist Church.

The second week in October I said goodbye to Jane, my baby daughter Patti, my in-laws, and my dad. After two days of slow train rides, I arrived at Miami Beach, Florida. My military orders assigned me to the Rest and Recreation Center (R&R) located on the beach. Since I was a combat returnee, I was given a suite in a first class hotel on the beach along with the best food that I had eaten in nearly a year. I was given a flight physical examination, along with a schedule of entertainment activities. I then reported to Colonel Clagget, the commander of the R&R Center. While answering his questions about my combat experience, his daughter, Louise, stopped by and we were introduced. I saw her later that afternoon and asked her to join me for a cocktail. She agreed and we had a friendly chitchat, and she was very personable. When she got up to leave she invited me to dinner at the Clagget residence the next evening, and I accepted.

I had never been to Miami Beach and Louise, knowing this, picked me up the next day and we spent the afternoon touring the beach area. Dinner that evening was very enjoyable and relaxed. Mrs. Clagget told me that they had a daughter living in Pasadena, California who was married to the colonel who was responsible for the defense of the California coast. She wanted to visit her daughter but travel by train was very difficult and she did not have the gas coupons to drive her car that far. I told her that official orders were to be published sending me to Salt Lake City, and she could use my gas coupons if she would let me drive her car to Pasadena. She thanked me and said that she would let me know her decision.

I received my orders on October 29th and Mrs. Clagget had already agreed to accept my offer. I called her and told her that I had received my orders, and we departed for Pasadena the next morning. We stopped at Tallahassee for the first night with no problems except most gasoline stations would not sell us more than ten gallons of gasoline. As a result, we stopped more times for gasoline than we did for meals and rest stops. We experienced this gasoline restriction all the way to California. Later the next day we were ten miles east of Marshall, Texas when we heard a loud slapping noise under the hood. I pulled to the side of the road, raised the hood, and found that we had a broken fan belt. I told Mrs. Clagget that I would hitch a ride to town and get a wrecker to tow the car to a garage in town. At this very moment, a car pulled up in front of us and the driver, wearing a Coast Guard uniform, asked if we were in trouble. I told him our problem and he said that he had a tow cable and would pull us to a garage in town, which he did. Mrs. Clagget then asked him and his passenger to have dinner with us in appreciation for the help he had given us. He politely refused and we decided to spend the night in Marshall.

The next morning I had a new fan belt installed and four days later without any more problems, we arrived at her daughter's home in Pasadena. Both of us were given a warm welcome, and when they got Mrs. Clagget settled for her stay, the colonel informed me that he had a room reserved for me at a hotel in Los Angeles. The Army had several rooms blocked in this hotel for visiting officers and I would be a welcome guest with no charge. The colonel said that he would pick me up the next evening to join the family for dinner. I spent the next day resting after the long six-day drive from Miami.

The colonel picked me up that evening and the four of us—he, his wife, her mother, and I—went to Slapsie Maxie's Night Club for dinner where Phil Harris and his orchestra were playing. The husky doorman recognized the colonel and opened the door for us. I gave my military cap to the very attractive hatcheck girl who was topless. She reminded me of my swimming at the beach at Tunis the past summer with the Italian girl who was topless. We were seated three tables from the orchestra, and the waiter was there to take our orders for cocktails. I ordered white wine because I had not yet acquired a taste for whiskey or beer. When the orchestra finished their dance number, the colonel went to Phil Harris and talked to him, and Phil gave the colonel an introduction to customers and turned the microphone over to him. He then said, "It is my pleasure to have as my guest this evening a B-17 pilot who has just returned from Europe and Africa, having flown fifty bombing missions against German military targets, First Lieutenant Kenneth Slaker." He extended his arm towards our table and I stood up and received a loud applause from the customers. The dinner and service were excellent.

While eating I noticed that Alice Faye, the movie actress now married to Phil Harris, was at the table next to the orchestra. I mentioned that to the colonel and he asked me if I would like to meet her. I told him I would be thrilled. We walked over to the table and I was introduced to her. She asked me to be seated and the colonel went back to our table. We talked for a few minutes and the orchestra began to play a dance number. As a courtesy I asked if I could have this dance with her and to my surprise she agreed. About halfway through the dance number, the orchestra stopped playing and Phil Harris looked at the two of us and said into the microphone, "Lieutenant, she is my canary and she is in my cage." Then the band finished the dance number and I escorted Alice Faye Harris to her table, thanked her, and walked over to the front of the orchestra. I gave Phil a smart salute, and he returned it and the customers laughed and applauded. The four of us left the nightclub and Colonel Thorne drove me to my hotel. I thanked all of them for a wonderful evening and wished them well. I wasted no time in going to bed, for I had to be at the train station early the next morning for my ride to Salt Lake City.

While I was on the train to Salt Lake, I did a lot of thinking about my marriage situation. I finally decided that since both Jane and I had gone through a tough time in our lives, and especially since we had a young daughter, we should make a try at being married again, if she was agreeable. When I arrived at Salt Lake, I called Jane and gave her my thoughts and proposal. She was agreeable and I suggested she come alone, leaving the baby with her mother until I got assigned to my permanent station. Then her mother could bring Patti to us. The personnel officer at the 18th Replacement Wing told me that since I was an early combat returnee, I could ask for any station. I replied that I would like to be assigned to a base located near a large city.

Jane arrived at Salt Lake three days later and I got us a room at the best motel in town. I was tired of trains and taxicabs for my transportation so we spent an entire day looking for a 1941 or 1942 model car in good shape. The used car lots did not have much to look at, and I was about to give up when late in the afternoon we found a 1942 Ford sedan with low mileage. The price was higher than what it had cost new but I bought it. The next day I got a call to report to the wing personnel officer. He said there was an opening for a pilot at the air base at Lincoln, Nebraska, but he said that the pilot had to be a graduate of the Weight And Balance School at Yale University. It was a two-week course, and I was authorized commercial air but no dependents. Without any hesitation, I accepted this assignment, and my orders would be ready the next day.

I gave Jane the choice of taking the train back to New Kensington and joining me at Lincoln in two weeks, or staying at Salt Lake City until I came back from New Haven. We could not have her drive to Lincoln because we didn't have the gas coupons for that long of a trip. Jane chose to stay at Salt Lake, and the motel manager gave us a good rate for her two-week stay. I arrived in New York City one day later and took a bus to New Haven. I was assigned a room in a dormitory located on the Yale campus.

The first week was spent in the classroom studying a very important subject pertaining to the correct method of loading an aircraft. If an aircraft is loaded without respect to the center of gravity, the pilot could lose control of the aircraft on takeoff or landing. This subject was not a part of our curriculum when I went through B-17 training at Gowen Field. Its importance is now recognized with a Military Occupational Specialty (MOS). Upon graduation I would be awarded this MOS as a Weight & Balance Officer.

My second week at Yale was spent at the local airport applying what we had learned in Weight & Balance to a real multi engine aircraft located there. You had to complete a weight and balance form for the aircraft, then take it off and land it after a flight of one hour. Your weight and balance form was then checked against the actual flight results. At the end of that week we had a graduation ceremony and were awarded the MOS of a Weight & Balance Officer. I departed Yale University the next day, arriving at Salt Lake City that evening.

Jane picked me up at depot and we had a good dinner and then went to bed, for we had just Sunday to get ready to depart Monday morning for Lincoln, Nebraska. Sunday evening I signed out at the replacement wing headquarters, filled our Ford up with gasoline using my new gasoline rationing coupons, and crawled into the sack.

I awoke Monday morning feeling better than I had for weeks. At last I would be on my way to my permanent assignment at Lincoln Air Base located next to the city of Lincoln, the capital of Nebraska. The wife and I dressed and walked to a nearby restaurant for a big breakfast. On the way back I stopped at the motel office and paid the bill for the wife's stay the last two weeks. The manager expressed his appreciation for my combat duty and shook my hand. How excited I was to get behind the wheel of my Ford and head for the Midwest.

We drove to Denver and stayed at the Brown Palace that night and then went all the way to Topeka, Kansas the next day. The next morning I signed in at the Headquarters of the 21st Bomb Wing and reported to the director of operations. He was very glad to have me on board and said that I was to contact him directly if I did not receive good treatment at Lincoln. I drove to Lincoln that afternoon, signed in at headquarters, and then visited the housing office to be informed that there was no housing on base available. He did have a large house in the city that was available on a month-to-month rental and fully furnished. I accepted it, and we drove to the city and located the house in an area of first class residences. The only thing we needed to buy to feel at home was groceries.

The next morning I drove to the building that housed the Director of Operations for the 12th Heavy Bomb Processing Headquarters. Here I met my boss, Major Wallace Fields, who had already flown combat in the B-17 aircraft. I was assigned as the test pilot for every shakedown flight of every new B-17G bomber that we received from the factory. A malfunction of any of the aircraft systems was corrected by our maintenance personnel before it was assigned to a combat crew to leave for the war zone. I was also given the additional duty as the air base weight and balance officer for all aircraft.

There was an aircraft depot on the air base, and the major in charge asked me if I could help him complete his work by test flying a couple of aircraft that the depot had repaired. He could not report them for delivery until they had been test flown. I was always eager to fly a different type of aircraft and agreed to be the test pilot for the depot. The first priority selected by the depot was an RP-322. This model later became the P 38 when the right engine propeller was changed to rotate to the left so that both props were not turning to the right, causing a lot of torque of the aircraft to the right. On the 13th of December, I read the operational manual for the RP-322, climbed into the cockpit, and taxied to the end of the runway for takeoff.

I checked each engine for power—they were okay—and then asked the tower for permission to take off. I was ready with the left rudder to correct for torque to the right, was pleased with the takeoff, and climbed to an altitude of 12,000 feet.

I did some acrobatics and the aircraft's response was smooth and it really pleased me to be flying this twin-engine fighter. As the saying goes, I got a wild hair up my ass and decided to buzz the city of Lincoln. There were no telephone poles on the main street, which was the longest main street of any city in Nebraska. I flew east of town, turned west, and went into a dive at the red line speed. I entered the main street at about a ten-story level and remained at that level until I was a couple of miles from town. I pulled up and called the tower for landing instructions. I had become good friends with a fellow pilot, and he was the tower Officer of the Day. He answered the call and told me that Colonel Gainey, the base commander, had received calls from business people in town complaining that a twin-engine aircraft had buzzed O Street, breaking windows and scaring the hell out of them. "You are to park in front of the tower where the colonel will meet with you. Be sure and tell him that you have just returned from combat and did a lot of low level flying."

Sure enough, the colonel was standing in front of the tower and when I shut down the engines, he walked over to my aircraft. I lowered myself out of the cockpit and gave him a sharp salute. Like most West Point graduates, he was holding a swagger cane in his left hand. He returned my salute and asked if I had just buzzed the business area in the city. I replied in the affirmative and said that I had just test hopped the P-38 for the depot and since I had just returned from combat, I made this low level flight as the last part of my flight test. The colonel replied that this was not a combat area and if I did any more buzz flying like that, my Army career would be short. He said that my pay would be docked to pay for the broken windows that the Army would have to replace. I replied that I understood and gave him a salute, which he did not return. Thank God he was transferred to another base two months later.

A regional military hospital had been built on the Lincoln Air Base and was well staffed with qualified medical personnel. The base newspaper had an article in it about my just returning from combat, and the nurses invited my wife and me to their Christmas party. I should have gone alone because after we were done eating, Jane left me and spent most of her time flirting with the young doctors. I met the hospital commander, Colonel Fletcher, and we became good friends and fishing companions.

Jane's mother had brought our daughter Patti to Lincoln just before the holidays. I thought that maybe our child would help bring Jane and me closer together but that was not happening. The last week in January 1944, I told Jane that our marriage was finished and suggested that she return to her parents' residence. I told her that I was going to file for divorce in Pennsylvania and that if she contested it, I had the evidence to obtain it. I took her to the train station and as she boarded, I kissed daughter Patti goodbye and walked away. I would not see Patti again until she was twenty-three years old.

Shortly after I arrived at Lincoln Army Air Base, Bob Storz, a combat pilot having flown B-24s out of North Africa, was assigned to our unit. We decided to check each other out in our respective aircraft since we were receiving new B-17 and B-24 aircraft from the manufacturers. We had to test fly each one prior to them being assigned to newly trained combat aircrews.

After Jane left and I filed for divorce, I was eligible to move into the Phi Delta building at the University of Nebraska campus. Due to the war, the building was empty and had been leased by the single officers from the air base. Bob Storz and I became roommates and close friends. Our base welcomed a new commander, Colonel Sig R. Young, a combat returnee. My boss, Major Fields, and Colonel Young were both Texans so we pilots in operations had a direct line to the new commander. Major Fields submitted my name to Colonel Young for promotion to captain. He approved it and forwarded it through channels to Army Headquarters. It was approved by General Marshall effective March 23, 1944.

With the rank of captain I was now eligible to be assigned as the base operations officer. This position put me in charge of all aircraft flying in and out of Lincoln Army Air Base. I had my own office, a secretary, a staff car with driver, and four enlisted personnel trained as flight operations dispatchers. My staff car driver was a young and attractive girl. I called the motor pool officer and thanked him for giving me such a charming driver. He said, "Since you are the big hero here on base, I gave you our base beauty queen."

The major in charge of the aircraft depot called me and again wanted me to test fly a RA-25. This was a Curtis Hell Diver used by the Marines in the Pacific area. He had contacted the Marine Headquarters requesting a pilot to test fly and take delivery for the Marines. The Marine commander informed him that they did not have a pilot available. I told the major that I would test fly it if he would transfer it to my base flight.

Wanting to get it off his books and out of the building, he agreed to my request. I gave myself a cockpit check from the flight manual and took off into a clear blue sky. I liked the quick response of the flight controls, and it had a faster cruising airspeed than any of the aircraft in base flight.

The Marines did not object to the transfer of the RA-25 to the Army. Sgt. Gobat from maintenance became the crew chief, and I had him remove the armament from the rear cockpit for a passenger. There were no flight controls but there was a radio and an intercom. I flew to Boise at least once a month to see Lee, my first love. Sometimes I took Sgt. Gobat with me so that he could spend a weekend at home a few miles from Boise. The RA-25 became my own personal aircraft until the end of the war.

The latter part of March I wrote to Lee telling her that I had filed for divorce and that I would be making a flight to Boise the first part of April and wanted to see her. Colonel Fletcher, the hospital commander, had to attend a medical business meeting at Gowen Army Airfield the first week in April. I flew him there in my base flight B-25.

Lee was now a student nurse and was able to spend one evening with me. Seeing her again rekindled the feeling that I had for her when I last saw her before leaving for combat. We were able to spend some time together the next day and she expressed her love for me. With our strong feelings for one another, we agreed to see one another as often as possible.

At sunrise the next morning, we took off for Geiger Field at Spokane and I had my engineer give his seat to Colonel Fletcher. We flew down Hell's Canyon about fifty feet above the Snake River to Lewiston, Idaho. It was a very exciting and memorable flight seeing deer, bears, eagles, and other wildlife. There was also the beauty of the rugged canyon itself. When we got back to Lincoln, Colonel Fletcher thanked me for one of the best flights he had ever been on.

April was a very busy month test flying the many new B-17s and B-24s that we were receiving from the manufacturers. I was also assigned by the 2nd Air Force to pilot the "Lincoln Wings" basketball team to exhibition games against other military teams. Most of our team members had been drafted from the professional team named the Globetrotters. Our ace player was Goose Tatum, who with his long arms and height, could really put on a show. The team's coach was Captain Hall, a former athletic instructor at the University of Illinois. We always flew to the game site in base flights B-17F. Coming back to Lincoln one night after defeating the University of Colorado basketball team in Denver, we had to penetrate a huge squall line extending through the Midwest from Canada to Mexico. I had flown through several of these before in a B-17 and knew that it was a tough aircraft. I had all the passengers fasten their seat belts as we entered the black storm. It was very turbulent with many strong daggers of lightning and very loud rolls of thunder. As we came out of the storm into clear skies, Captain Hall came up to the cockpit and I asked him how the Goose was doing. He said, "Ken, Goose is the whitest black you have ever seen."

Col. Sig R. Young, Lincoln Air Base Commander, awarding me the Air Medal with three oak leaf clusters. I later received 5 more oak leaf clusters and the silver cluster to the Air Medal.

Lee and I kept in touch by mail and telephone until the third weekend in May when I flew to Boise in my A-25. I called her from Gowen Field and we agreed to meet in front of the state capitol building. I took a cab to town and went to a jewelry store. I purchased a diamond ring along with a matching wedding ring and arrived at the capitol before she did. When I saw her coming, I raced to meet her and we embraced and kissed for a long time. We sat down on a bench and briefed each other on our activity since our last meeting in April. I wanted to make sure that she would accept a proposal of marriage before I presented her with the engagement ring. I took both her hands into mine, looked into her eyes, and asked if she would marry me. Without any hesitation she said, "Yes, Ken, I love you and want to be your wife." I then slipped the diamond ring onto her finger and she looked at the ring for what seemed a long time to me, and when she raised her head she had tears in her eyes. We embraced for a long time and I knew that I had made the right choice for a mate. We spent the entire day together and were not about to leave one another that night. We spent the night at a hotel and kissed each other goodbye early in the morning because she had to be back at the hospital at 7:00 A.M. I flew back to Lincoln in my A-25, feeling better than I had all my life.

On the 12th of June we received a call from 2nd Air Force Headquarters that we were to fly the very popular Dr. IQ radio show personnel from Omaha to North Platte on the thirteenth in support of the war bond drive. Major Fields assigned me as the pilot utilizing a new B-24J already test flown. I arrived at Omaha late the next morning and my flight engineer saw to the loading of the show personnel. When I filed my flight clearance in operations I noticed that one of the names on the passenger list was Carole Landis, the movie actress.

When we reached our flight altitude, I sent my flight engineer back to where the passengers were seated and told him to have Carole Landis come up to the cockpit. She came to the cockpit entrance with an amazed look on her face, and I pointed to the copilot's seat and asked her to be seated. As I fastened her seat belt, I told her that my name was Ken and that I had seen her on the screen and it was a privilege to have her on board. I told her that I had read that she had attended the University of Washington in Seattle and that if I got through this war alive, I planned to obtain my college degree there. Then I told her that I was going to teach her how to fly this big bomber and explained the instruments and flight controls to her. Before she came up to the cockpit I had trimmed the B-24 for level flight and put it on autopilot. I answered her various questions about the aircraft and my bombing missions in Europe. I then asked her how she liked Hollywood. She said that it was a fantastic place with wonderful and talented people, but the ones that she had the highest respect for were the makeup artists. They could change your face and body into whatever the script called for. I noticed on the horizon that there was a dark looking squall line west of North Platte. I pointed out the storm to Miss Landis and told her that I would need the flight engineer back in the cockpit. I told her that I had enjoyed visiting with her and she thanked me, saying that I had made her trip to North Platte a very exciting one. As she left the cockpit she planted a kiss on my forehead.

I could see huge thunderstorms in the squall line approaching our destination from the west. I contacted the North Platte tower and asked for their weather report and forecast. They reported that there was a slow moving storm approaching the airport from the west but according to our time of arrival, we would be able to make a VFR approach to the airport. I requested permission to make a straight in approach to the runway and it was granted. I decreased power and started our letdown to approach altitude and we encountered moderate turbulence. About three miles from the runway I ordered the engineer for flaps and gear down. And that was when the hail hit us. It was the size of golf balls, and the noise inside the fuselage from the hail hitting the metal aircraft was very frightening. As I pulled back on the power and started my flare for touchdown, both windshields cracked. The landing was soft and I braked to a stop and shut down the engines. We sat there for several minutes and I could not talk to the passengers due to the terrible noise from the hail bouncing off the metal skin. When the hail stopped I was able to call the tower and request that the bus for our passengers be escorted to our aircraft on the runway, for the aircraft would have to be towed off the runway because of damage to it. While waiting for the bus, the heavy rain slacked up and we were able to get out of the aircraft and inspect the exterior for damage. In addition to the broken cockpit windows, there was damage to the flaps, tail empennage, de-icer boots, and possible damage within the engine cowlings.

I called the aircraft maintenance office at Lincoln Air Base and told the officer on duty of the damage to our B-24, and that I would not be able to return my passengers to Omaha the next day in this aircraft. He returned my call within a few minutes and said that he and selected maintenance personnel would arrive at North Platte tomorrow morning in a new B-24 that I could use to fly the show people back to Omaha. He and the maintenance crew would stay with the damaged B-24 and repair it.

All of our crewmembers were honored guests at the theatre that evening, and when Dr. IQ told the audience that the pilot, Captain Slaker, had recently returned from flying fifty bombing missions against the Axis, I received a very loud applause. It was a good show and they sold a huge amount of war bonds.

The flight back to Omaha the next day was smooth and uneventful. I had my flight engineer send Dr. IQ to the cockpit and had him sit in the copilot's seat. He said he was surprised that I did not have a rated copilot because he thought that these bombers had two pilots on the crew. I told him that I had been authorized by General Ent, Commander of the 2nd Air Force, that since I had more than 1,500 hours in four-engine aircraft, and since there was a shortage of trained pilots for combat duty, I could fly without a copilot using a qualified flight engineer as the copilot. When we landed at Omaha, all the passengers thanked our crew for a great and safe flight.

Lee called me early in June saying that she would be coming to Lincoln on June 20th to spend a week with me. I knew a desk clerk at the Cornhusker Hotel and told her that my fiancée was coming to spend a week with me. She said to be sure and register for two persons since it was against the law to have one person registered with two parties using the room. Heeding her advice, I registered Lee as my wife.

This photo was taken by a Lincoln, Nebraska photographer in 1944 for an article in the Sunday edition. I had just finished test flying this new B-24 that had arrived from the factory in Michigan.

I was waiting at the station when her train arrived and when I saw her step off the train, I really came alive, for she looked wonderful and I knew that I was truly in love with her. When she spotted me, her face broke into a smile and she came running into my arms. She was surprised that I had a late model car: the 1942 Ford that I had purchased in Salt Lake City. After we checked into our room and Lee finished unpacking, we decided to go out for an early dinner since she had very little to eat on the train. We ate at one of my favorite restaurants and then went back to our hotel room.

There is nothing greater in the entire world than getting into bed without any pajamas on and curling around the woman you love and who loves you. We made love until we both fell asleep. I had to get up early and get to the air base because I was scheduled to test fly a new B-17G at 9:00 A.M. I told Lee that I would be back in time for lunch. That afternoon I drove her around town to become familiar with this capital city. We then drove to the air base and to the hangar where my office was located. I introduced her to my secretary and to my office help. I then took her to the base headquarters and introduced her to Major Fields, my boss. After a short visit I said goodbye to my boss and he had a smile on his face and shook it in the affirmative. The next stop was the officers' club where I introduced her to many of my friends. When Lee took a trip to the ladies restroom, Captain Roberts, a good friend, asked me, "Where did you find that cutie?" We then drove to my living quarters at the Phi Delta building, next to the University of Nebraska campus, where she met some of my officer friends living there. My roommate, Bob Storz, joined us for dinner that evening, and after dinner, we went back to our room at the hotel.

I had arranged with maintenance to have all my test flights in the morning hours, giving me the afternoons off to spend with Lee. We spent the last two days at the hotel, talking about our future plans and not wanting the visit to end. The last day together we agreed that she would finish her nurse's training, and I would attend college when the war ended to get my degree. It was a quiet drive to the train station. The train was on time and we walked to the passenger car, where we embraced and kissed. She turned to step up into the passenger car entrance, and I said to her, "Lee, this has really been our honeymoon!" She nodded her head in agreement and we both had wet eyes as she disappeared.

When I became the base operations officer, there were no printed instructions on how flying was to be conducted at the Lincoln Army Air Base. I mentioned this to my boss, Major Fields, and he said that was one of the reasons he wanted me in this office. The officer that I replaced was not a pilot, which was a disadvantage to him. I asked my chief flight dispatcher, M/Sgt. Evans, to work with me in drafting a set of printed instructions for aircraft operation here at Lincoln since he had a lot of experience in this area. He was very enthused that we were finally going to have printed flying regulations.

We started working on this task the middle of April, and by the end of June we had a draft ready to submit to Major Fields in operations. He had a couple of suggestions, which we included in the draft, and we submitted it to the base commander for his approval. The draft came back with the endorsement: Great, print it. My secretary typed up the final draft and I hand carried it to a commercial printer in Lincoln. This was on the 8th of July with a printed date of July 10th. We kept twenty copies at base opera-

    Colonel F Wright
    Lincoln Air Base
    Lincoln, Nebraska

    Dear Colonel Wright:

        I wish to thank you in behalf of all members of the Dr. I Q unit which your very able crew took to North Platte yesterday and returned to Omaha this morning.

        Captain Slaker, Lt Roberts, Sgt Kerr and Sgt Dolan made each of us comfortable. They are very fine gentlemen and experts in their line.

        Frankly, I personally was delighted with the trip and I want you to know that the people of North Platte cheered to the rafters when Captain Slaker and his crew were introduced at the Paramount Theatre just before the Dr I Q show went on the air.

        I might interest you to know that this presentation in in North Platte (population, 12,451) was instrumental in selling $606,285.50 worth of war bonds. This is better than an average of $5,000 from each adult and child in North Platte.

        Thank you sincerely for Dr I Q, Allen C Anthony, Mr. Flaig of Mars, Inc, and the WOW crew of entertainers who completed the troupe.

        Sincerely,

    s/ John J. Gillin

    President
    RADIO STATION WOW, INC

A thank-you letter from Radio Station Wow, Inc., 14 June 1944.

tions and submitted thirty copies to the Base Distribution Center. I was so pleased getting printed flying regulations for the base that I called Sgt. Gobat, the flight engineer for the A-25, to get the plane ready for a flight to Boise on the tenth.

I called Lee and asked if she could spend the afternoon and evening with me. Since Boise was on Mountain Time, we gained an hour, landing at Boise at 11:00 A.M. Sgt. Gobat left to spend the night at home and I got a taxi to town. Although it was only a short two weeks since I had been with Lee, it was wonderful to be with her again. We spent the beautiful afternoon holding hands and walking the tree lined streets of Boise. She took me to meet her relatives with whom she had lived while working at the base. They were very hospitable and pleased that Lee and I were in love. With the sun setting, we went to a fine restaurant for dinner. During the meal I asked her if she remembered the photo that she had given to me when I departed for combat training in the fall of '42. She said that she did and I received a beautiful look from her when I told her that I had flown all fifty of the bombing missions with her photo in my flying suit pocket and that I still had the photo. I walked her to the hospital because she had to be in the student nurses' quarters by 10:00 P.M. We parted as lovers do and I took a taxi to the base.

The next morning I arrived at base operations and Sgt. Gobat was already there. He said that he had pre-flighted the A-25 and it was refueled and ready for the flight to Lincoln. I checked the weather and we would have a good tailwind at 11,000 feet going east. We took off at noon, climbed to 11,000 feet, and arrived at Lincoln in four hours. It was 1,200 miles from Boise, which meant that with that tailwind we had a ground speed of 300 miles per hour. This A-25 was the fastest aircraft we had in base flight and I was its only pilot.

My parent organization at Lincoln Air Base was the 12th Heavy Processing Group. We scheduled a summer picnic at Seward along the Blue River, about twenty miles west of Lincoln. My roommate, Bob Storz, insisted that I drive his new Harley Davidson motorcycle to the picnic. Since I had never driven a two-wheel cycle with power, Bob checked me out with several trips around the Phi Delta building. He drove his Cadillac full of our work mates and I followed with the new Harley.

It was a beautiful sunny and warm day, and Bob suggested that I give a cycle ride to any one of our service or civilian personnel that wanted a thrill with Big Ken. The route was the hard dirt road direct to the river, then a right turn along the river for half a mile, then west, then a right turn north to the picnic area. Betty, my secretary, was the first in line. We had a fun ride and returned to the picnic area. I now had full confidence in my driving this motorcycle. One of our enlisted clerks crawled on behind me and put his feet on the footrest rods. As I approached the right turn of the road at the river bank, I pushed my leg down to disengage the clutch and at the same time gave a quick turn up on the throttle to make loud show off turn. My passenger had his foot under the clutch pedal and it did not disengage. As a result, we shot out over the bank into the middle of the river. Fortunately, I pushed myself and rider off the motorcycle before we hit the water. If we had ended up under the Harley, we would have drowned because there was a good foot of heavy mud on the bottom. My Guardian Angel was still with me.

Bob was there first, and we took off our clothes and dove into the river which was about eight feet deep where the Harley was stuck in the mud. It took us almost an hour to free the cycle from the mud and get it onto the bank where we washed it clean, still in the nude. It was quite a show, especially for our female employees. The crankshaft was cracked and the oil had leaked out. I really felt bad but Bob was not upset and said it could be repaired. I offered to pay for the repairs but Bob refused. Bob and I were good friends and I had many good times at his home in Omaha, even attending his wedding later on.

The first week in August Colonel Fletcher called me and asked if we had anything going to Boise the next few days because he would like to do a little fishing. I suggested that he tell the base commander that he would like to get to Boise to visit the base hospital at Gowen, and I was certain that he would okay a flight there. He did just that and early on the morning of August 8th we took off in a new B-17G that I had test hopped. We arrived in Boise at 10:00 A.M. and the colonel's fishing buddy was waiting for him. They dropped me off in town and went into the mountains to fish. I had a pilot friend in town loan me his car. I picked up Lee and we drove into the mountains. We could not resist one another and our love was made stronger than ever. At dusk we went into town for dinner and then I dropped her off at the hospital. I took the car back to my friend and he drove me to the base. I got up early because I was also going fishing with the colonel. We spent the morning and most of the afternoon fly-fishing for rainbow trout. We did very well and returned to the base with twelve large rainbow that we packed in ice for the flight to Lincoln. We departed Boise at 6:00 P.M., arriving home at 11:30 P.M. Central Time.

During the spring and summer I became friends with Lt. Matias Palacio, a single officer who, before the war, was a professional golf instructor at the Marin County Country Club in California. He told me that he had enrolled to compete in the annual Broadmoor Golf Classic in Colorado Springs. I offered to fly him there and he accepted. I flew him there in my A-25, dropped him off, and returned to Lincoln. He won the tournament and when he returned to Lincoln, he invited me to have dinner with him and his fiancée. She brought a friend with her by name of Peggy, who was a WASP (Women's' Auxiliary Service Pilot) in the Army Air Corp. I told Peggy about the first WASPs that I had met who were flying B-17s to Goose Bay, and what phase of flying was she enjoying? Peggy said that she was stationed at a Basic Flight Training school in Arizona, teaching cadets how to fly the BT-13 aircraft. Lt. Palacio then told Peggy that I was the base operations officer at the air base and had flown him to Colorado Springs in an A-25. She said, "That must be fun to fly a fast and powerful plane like that." I said

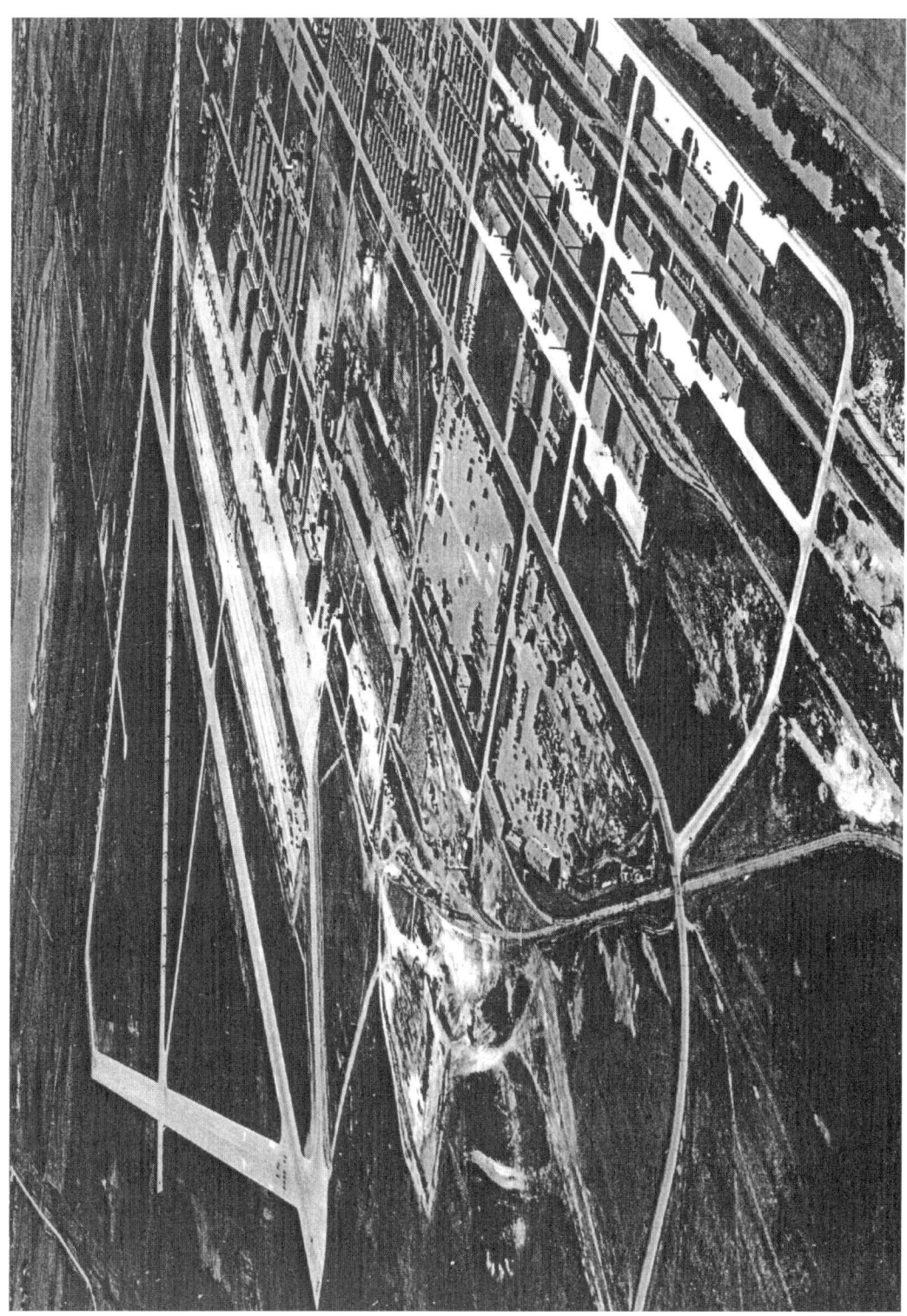

Lincoln Army Air Field, looking SE towards the city. The east-west and the northeast-southwest runways are full of new B-17Gs. Hangar ramp is full of B-17s. A new ramp next to the hangar ramp is almost completed. The other half of the base lies west of the creek seen at lower right.

that if she would like to fly the A-25, the next time she came to Lincoln, I would check her out. She said, "Lincoln is my home and I will be back in two or three weeks and will make you keep your promise."

I received a call from Peggy that she would be coming to Lincoln on the 12th of August for the weekend and would like to see me. I made a date with her for dinner Saturday night at the officers' club. She told me how to get to her home and I picked her up there Saturday evening. After dinner we joined a pilot friend of mine and his wife and enjoyed dancing in the ballroom. About 10:00 P.M. I told Peggy that I had to take her home so that she would be rested and alert Sunday morning for her check ride in the A-29. I drove her home and saw her to the front door. I gave her a hug and a kiss, not of love but of friendship.

Lt. Palacio's fiancée, Lorraine, drove Peggy out to the base Sunday morning and the weather was perfect for flying. I put her into a flying suit and fitted her to a seat pack parachute. We made a visual inspection of the A-25, and then seated her in the rear cockpit which had no flight controls but flight instruments and intercom. After clearance for takeoff from the tower, I talked to her continuously about airspeed, trim, etc. as I made two takeoffs and landings. I taxied off the runway, set the brakes, got out of the front cockpit, and told her to get into the front cockpit. Without any hesitation she climbed into the front cockpit, fastened the seat belt, and gave me an excited look. I got into the rear cockpit, contacted her on the intercom, and told her to make one takeoff and landing. She did quite well since she already had several hundred hours in the BT-13. I told her that I was getting out of the cockpit and that she was to make two landings and taxi to the parking ramp. Her approach for the first landing was a little fast and she landed about one-third down the runway. Her second landing was fine and Sgt. Gobat signaled her to a parking space and helped her out of the aircraft and her parachute. I took her up to my office, signed the checkout form that had been typed by my secretary, and congratulated her with a handshake and a hug. I walked with her and Lorraine to the parking area and Peggy kept telling Lorraine what a wonderful experience it was to have flown that A-25. As they drove off, Peggy waved goodbye and blew me a kiss.

The rest of August I was busy with test flights and administrative trips in support of our mission in supplying the European and Pacific combat groups with trained crews flying new B-17s and B-24s. With Labor Day coming up, the schedule gave us pilots a break and I decided to fly back to my hometown for a day or two. I had not seen my dad for almost a year and since he had never been in a B-17, I flew our B-17F to Pittsburgh. I landed at the Allegheny County airport and the ground crew was so pleased to have a B-17 there, they parked us where we could be seen by airport visitors.

My dad greeted me and drove to my hometown of Vandergrift. Since he had sold our house, I stayed in the only hotel in town which was owned by my ex girlfriend's father, Art Brideson. We had dinner at a local restaurant with some longtime family friends that kept me busy answering their questions about my combat missions. Early the next morning before breakfast, I walked the streets past the house I grew up in and the beautiful high school I graduated from, bringing back many memories. My classmates were not to be seen, for they had gone to war, but I did talk to some of their parents. When we finished breakfast, I told my dad that when we got back to the airport, I was going to show him the inside of the B-17.

My flight engineer was waiting at the airplane, and I introduced him and we boarded the aircraft. My dad asked me where the copilot was and was surprised when I told him that I was authorized to fly with just my engineer. I told him to get into the copilot's seat, that we were going to fly over Pittsburgh. He said no thanks and got off the plane. My father lived to be ninety-four and never flew in an airplane, even though I was the pilot! I walked with dad to the ramp and what a surprise—my ex-wife, Jane, was standing there. I asked her how our daughter Patricia Elaine was doing, and she said fine and really growing. After some small talk, I said goodbye to her and my dad and boarded the B-17. As I taxied out I waved to them both, and as I rolled down the runway, I could see them watching the takeoff. Five hours later my engineer and I landed safely at Lincoln Army Air Field.

I was at my desk on the morning of August 8th when I had a call from Lt. Palacio. He said that Peggy was in town and could I have dinner with him, Lorraine, and Peggy that evening at the Cornhusker? I met them at the hotel and we had a leisurely dinner. Peggy told me that she had been with her folks for two days and had to leave the next day for Arizona since she was scheduled to fly Sunday. Since I had nothing planned for the weekend, I asked her if she would like to fly to Arizona tomorrow in my A-25. She said, "Oh my God, that would be great, what time do we take off?" I said, "Let's plan on 10:00 A.M."

I filed a flight plan to Pueblo Army Air Base and told Peggy that I would fly the first leg to Pueblo and that she could fly the next leg to Arizona. The weather was ideal for flying and we had an easy two-hour flight to Pueblo. We refueled and had a bite to eat, and Peggy filed a flight plan to Marana Army Air Base in Arizona. Peggy had no trouble starting the engine and taxiing to the runway for takeoff. The control tower was off the far right side of the runway and she received clearance to take off. When she reached flying speed and started to climb, the torque from the engine pulled the aircraft to the right, heading for the tower. I told her by intercom, "Left rudder, Peggy, left rudder." She had not taken off at this higher altitude before, which required more rudder to overcome the torque in this thin air. Just when it looked like we were going to run into the tower, she got enough rudder to miss the control tower. The tower controller called and asked if we were in trouble and I replied that we had trouble with the trim tab but were okay now. I also apologized for frightening them but that I was just as frightened as they were.

A few minutes out of Marana, I briefed Peggy on final approach speed, flap setting, landing speed, etc. At her first attempt to land she came in too fast and I told her to go around. Her second approach was too short and she would be short of the runway. Again I told her to go around and knew she was tense, especially since the noise of the A-25 had brought out several of Peggy's fellow instructors. I told Peggy to make the same approach to land as she would in her BT-13 with the approach speed that I gave to her. This time she came over the end of the runway at the right speed and altitude and made a good landing. I waited until she got out of the cockpit so that her pilot friends could see that she was the pilot of this A-25. They swarmed all around her and then I told her not to wait on me, that I was going to get the A-25 refueled, then to the VOQ, and then to the officers' club. I did not see Peggy again until the next morning when I was having breakfast. She introduced me to a WASP that was with her and asked if I could drop her off at Sweetwater, Texas on my way back to Lincoln. That was going to be 500 miles out of my flight path to Lincoln, but Peggy's charm got an okay from me.

I filed my flight plan for Abilene with a passenger drop at Sweetwater. This was a WASP training base with no transient aircraft service on Sunday. I dropped my WASP passenger and landed at Abilene three hours after leaving Marana, Arizona. There was no refueling service after 4:00 P.M. on Sunday. I was scheduled to make a test on a new B-24 arrival the next morning at 9:00 A.M. and would not get back to Lincoln if I remained there overnight. I did some pencil computation and with no passenger weight, no weight from half of the gasoline consumed, and setting RPM and throttles at maximum cruise, I should arrive Lincoln with twenty minutes of fuel remaining.

I contacted flight service for weather en route and they reported no storms. Lincoln had scattered clouds at 2,000 feet with fifteen miles' visibility. I filed a flight plan for Lincoln, took off, and climbed to 5,500 feet. About an hour later I was halfway through western Oklahoma when the sun set. I turned on the exterior running lights and the instrument panel in the cockpit. I had been airborne about an hour and a half and had just tried to tune in a radio station from Wichita on my radio compass, but it was silent on all frequencies. All of a sudden all of the exterior lights and the cockpit and instrument panel lights went out. I found all the light switches with my fingers and turned them on and off with no luck. I had a flashlight in the right pocket of my flight suit. I reached for it and as I pulled it out, it caught onto the seat belt and fell into the bottom of the fuselage, which was out of reach.

I had a good night horizon and a clear sky and to keep on the heading I had been flying, I kept the nose of the aircraft pointed to the brightest star that was on my flight path when the lights went out. After a few minutes I became aware that I had lost visual contact with the ground below due to a solid undercast. As time passed with no clearing of the cloud cover below, I knew that I could not be too far from Lincoln and decided to continue status quo. I did have one good thing: the engine was still running. I decided that if the undercast didn't clear off in a few minutes, I would descend through it, hoping to have enough ceiling and visibility to watch for a town of any size and fly around it to see if it had a small airport. If not, I would circle the town until the engine quit and then bail out on the outskirts of the community.

At this very moment, I noticed a lighted area coming through the cloud cover and decided to descend through the lighter cloud area. I broke out of the overcast and directly ahead of me was the state capitol building! I turned toward the air base and could not contact the tower. I decided that I would buzz the tower and then they would turn on the runway lights. At that very moment they came on and the tower gave me a green light. I was happy for just two seconds when I realized that with the power failure, my landing gear may not come down. If not, should I land on the concrete runway or the grass area between the runways? I decided that since I had very little gasoline left and the A-25 was not a nose gear aircraft, that I would make a three point landing on the runway. When I had the aircraft lined up with the runway, I activated the landing gear control and oh happy me! The gear came down and locked. I taxied to the ramp and Sgt. Gobat, my flight engineer, was there to park me. I got out of the aircraft, told him that I had to go to my office to make a couple of calls, and would be back in a few minutes.

Since I was not able to contact the tower, when I got to my office I called the tower and told them of my electrical failure and asked if they had been able to see me and turn on the runway lights. They said no, that they had my flight plan with estimated time of arrival, so when it was five minutes before I was to arrive, they turned on the lights. I thanked them and went out to my A-25 and the refueling sergeant said that I didn't have more than five minutes of fuel left. As I walked to my car in the parking lot, I looked up at the cloudy sky and thought, "You are one lucky pilot," and thanked God and my Guardian Angel.

A couple of days after the exciting flight in my A-25, Colonel Fletcher called me and wanted to know the chances of flying to Boise that weekend to attend a medical meeting and if we had time, some fishing. I told him no problem because I had a request from two officers that needed to get to the air base at Ephrata, Washington, and we could leave Saturday morning, drop them off, and fly to Boise and RON (Remain Over Night). That would give us all day Sunday to fish. I called Lee and told her that I would be in Boise the evening of the fifteenth and hoped that she could spend the evening with me.

We arrived in Boise late in the afternoon and I took a taxi to my favorite hotel and got a room. Lee met me at our favorite restaurant and we had an enjoyable dinner, especially since we were together. I told Lee about Peggy, the WASP, almost flying into the control tower, and my electrical failure at night when I came very close to having to bail out of the A-25. Lee said, "Ken, you sure keep your Guardian Angel busy." We went to the hotel where a very happy couple made love. We discussed our relationship and our future and decided to get married at Gowen Air Base that Christmas with the base chaplain tying the knot. Lee said that she would tell her parents of our plans. I had never met her parents since they didn't live in Boise. Lee had to be back at the hospital not later than 10:00 P.M. It was another one of those sad times that we had to say goodbye to one another. Colonel Fletcher and I fished all morning and afternoon the next day. We departed for Lincoln at dusk and had a smooth and enjoyable flight home in our new B-17G. We could not use our administrative B-17F for this trip since it was out for maintenance.

In October I was ordered to fly the base executive officer to Forbes Army Air Corp Base at Topeka, to attend a meeting at our wing headquarters. I selected the B-25 in our base flight since it had not been flown for a couple of months and needed some hours put on it. My flight engineer made sure that my three passengers were buckled in, and I took off to the north and climbed to 500 feet. I started a 180-degree turn to the left to head south to Topeka when there was a loud explosion at the rear of the cockpit with flames and choking smoke coming from the electrical panel. I immediately called an emergency to the control tower that I was on fire inside the fuselage and that I was going to attempt a landing on the northwest taxi strip. It was the first runway or taxi strip that was clear of parked aircraft. The engineer and I opened our side windows to draw the smoke outside and give me visibility and fresh air to make the landing. The fire trucks were waiting for us and as soon as I could brake to a stop, we evacuated the B-25. The ambulance and medics were there and checked us for burns and smoke inhalation. Fortunately, none of us had to go to the hospital. The one thing that I had always feared about flying was fire. The B-25 was going to need major repairs, which left my base flight with only one multi passenger aircraft, the B-17F.

The first week in October I had a call from Lee asking me how soon could I come to Boise—that she had told her parents of our wedding plans and they wanted to meet with the two of us. I told her that I could fly to Boise on the 12th of October. On the morning of October 12th, my flight engineer and I departed for Boise in my A-25. When we landed at Boise, base operations had a message for me from Lee that I was to meet her at a hotel where her parents had a room. When I got to the hotel I thought that Lee would be in the lobby to meet me. She was not there and the desk clerk gave me the room number where she and her parents were staying. The door to the room was open, and I walked in and the parents were seated with Lee standing behind them. Lee introduced her parents to me and I could see that her eyes were red from crying. Lee didn't come from behind her parents to greet me, which I really expected. Then her mother said to me, "We cannot approve of Lee's marriage to you since she is of the Mormon faith and you are not." Then she turned to Lee and said to give me back the engagement ring. Lee came from behind her parents, and as she handed me the ring she looked at me through tears. I could see that she loved me, and I also shed tears because I was crushed and realized that I was losing her. Her parents got up, took Lee's hand, and as they walked out of the room, Lee was crying. I was stunned. The parents didn't even say they were sorry or goodbye. When I finally got my eyes dry, I left the hotel and took a cab to the base. I spent the night in my VOQ room, trying to get some sleep which never came. I didn't realize how much control Mormon parents had over their children. To me, true love had priority over any circumstance.

The flight back to Lincoln was very depressing since every mile was taking me further away from Lee. I could not believe that her own parents would cause her to cry and suffer the agony which I witnessed. I would never forget the sad look on her face and in her eyes when she handed me the engagement ring. I had the urge to pick her up and carry her out of there. To make her suffer like she did in the name of a religious faith did not present the Mormon faith to me as a very desirable one. I had a short thought that maybe for Lee's sake I should become a Mormon, but my brain tossed that aside. Up to this time I had been a member of three different Christian faiths which didn't bother me because I felt that if you truly believed in God, the prime mover of creating the universe, that there were many paths to His Domain.

I was very busy the following week flight-testing ten new B-17Gs that had just arrived from the factory. This kept my mind busy and not spending all day brooding over my loss of Lee. James Passmore, my navigator during our combat tour, called me to tell me that my bombardier, George O'Hoppe, was an instructor at the Army air base in Pueblo, Colorado. My very understanding boss, Major Fields, gave me permission to fly one of the new B-17Gs to Pueblo to see O'Hoppe and to let his students inspect the new B-17G model which they did not have there at that time. I called George and gave him the time of arrival on Saturday. I had not seen or heard from George since we had finished our bombing missions in August 1943.

George was waiting for me at the air base, and seeing him again was a great boost for my morale. When he departed from Africa, I told George to marry the girl whose picture he kept showing me—that he was then almost thirty years old and wasting his life. On the way to his residence in town he said that he had married her shortly after arriving stateside and was now a father. When we arrived at his house, his wife came running to us and put her arms around me and said that she knew all about me; that George had the highest respect for me as his combat pilot. My two days with them were enjoyable and relaxing. George asked me about my wife Jane that he had met before we went overseas, and I told him that I had divorced her and why. I then told him about my busted romance with Lee. George then suggested that I close the book, that I would be better off since I could have had a rough and unhappy life with Lee's Mormon parents as my in-laws. George drove me to the air base and walked with me to the B-17G, and turned to me and said, "Ken, you and I have had an exceptional period of our lives together and I will never forget our combat crew and our own B-17, the *Elaine*." We embraced each other and agreed that we would be brothers the rest of our lives. I flew back to Lincoln, feeling more like my old self and taking a new look at the world around me. *Thanks, George, you have already been an outstanding brother.*

A week later Peggy called and was home for the weekend. She invited me to dinner Saturday evening if I didn't have any plans. I had enough gas coupons to fill my Ford's gas tank, so I asked if she would like to drive to Omaha for dinner and dancing. She agreed and I picked her up at a girlfriend's house. I had never called for her at home and had never met her parents. We had a first class dinner and danced the evening away. We arrived back at Lincoln around midnight and it was a beautiful night. I drove out of town to a quiet country dirt road and we became intimate. It was not that we were in love but we enjoyed one another's company. We were both pilots, and it was a physical need for both of us.

The first week in November the major in command of the repair depot wanted to see me. I walked into his office and his secretary said that he was busy with another caller but it would only be a few minutes and suggested that I sit down. I had seen and greeted her before on my visits to his office, and she was always very cordial. We started to converse and I learned that she was single, lived at home, and had an older sister who was married to a marine pilot who currently was fighting the Japanese. I was only in the major's office a short time and on the way out, all of a sudden I decided to ask her for a date. Her name was Glenna, and she accepted my request and gave me her address.

I arrived at her parents' house, located in a middle class neighborhood. Glenna answered the door and ushered me into the living room where she introduced me to her mother, Mildred, and to her sister, Dolly. She told me that her father was not home because he worked for the Burlington Railroad and was gone to work half the time. We drove into the city and had a very pleasant dinner with lots of conversation, then to a movie and to her house. I walked her to the front door and she invited me in but I didn't feel that I should and declined. I asked if I could see her again and she agreed. I gave her hand a squeeze and departed.

All of our four-engine combat aircrews were processed through the 12th Heavy Processing Group at Lincoln Air Base, where they were assigned their new B-17G or B-24J. The majority of the aircrews were being assigned to the European theatre, so from Lincoln they were sent to Bangor, Maine. Here they had a days rest, their aircraft refueled, and a route briefing before taking off for Reykjavik, Iceland. We had an Army Air Corp group there to service these aircrews and get them on their way to England. While flying the route to Iceland, BW 1 was an alternate strip on the southern tip of Greenland that could be used in an emergency. A few aircrews had used this strip, but the worst emergency was the landing of a B-17 near the middle of the Greenland icecap. That B-17 would not do battle in this war. Higher command decided that these crews should be given long-range cruise instructions before leaving Lincoln Air Base.

I was alerted by Personnel that I would be on orders to attend the Long-Range Cruise Control School at the Miami airport in Florida, on the 18th of November. The weekend before leaving for Florida, I received a call from Peggy, whom I had not seen for three weeks. I made a date to take her to the officers' club for dinner and dancing.

A couple of my pilot friends and their wives joined us for dinner. The main subject was of course flying. The orchestra was an excellent one from town, and I asked Peggy for the first dance. When we finished the first dance, a young lady rushed up to us, grabbed Peggy, and they embraced, both very excited to see one another. The lady then asked Peggy, "How is your husband?" Peggy said okay and then excused herself and she and her friend went to the ladies' room. The young man that was with Peggy's lady friend introduced himself to me and asked how long had I known Peggy. I told him since early spring and that since we were both pilots, I had checked her out in the A-25.

The young man then said, "I can see she didn't tell you that she was married and that her husband is in the Army and overseas in England." I was shocked, for married women were off limits to me. When Peggy came out of the powder room I told her to get her coat and that we were leaving. Peggy knew I was upset and there was no discussion on the drive to her parents' house in Lincoln. I got out of the car, opened the door for her and she just stood there, looking at me. I said goodbye and drove away. I never saw her again.

Driving to my quarters in the Phi Delta house, I thought, *What the hell is wrong with me and women? First it was Jane, then Lee, and now Peggy. When it comes to women, I have a black cloud over my head.*

My roommate, Bob Storz, flew me to the Miami airport on November 12th to attend the Long-Range Control Course. Several days were spent on the desirable fuel air mixtures with specific RPM settings with the various weights of the aircraft, along with the best altitude and outside temperatures. Reliable wind forecasts are very important and if not accurate can cause a serious situation. I could support that statement, for I told the class of my experience in January 1943 of flying my B-17 from Dakar, Brazil with a flight plan of seven hours to Ascension Island. It turned out to be eight hours and I landed with all fuel tanks showing empty.

On the 18th of November, I was assigned along with two other pilots to fly a B-24J to Bermuda, then to a point in the Bahamas, and then to the Miami airport. We were given the weight of the aircraft, all fuel tanks full, and the takeoff time. All the other items to be considered for this flight were for we three pilots to resolve. We checked the weather reports and forecasts for the best altitude, the best fuel settings for the weight and altitude, and submitted our flight plan to operations with the estimated time en route.

From the very start of the takeoff roll until the end of the flight, we kept a detailed log of all our settings and any changes that were made during the flight. Computations were made every half hour to see if we were going to have enough fuel to complete our original flight plan. We landed at Miami without any changes to our flight course, and the B-24 was weighed and then refueled. The next day we met with the instructor who evaluated our fuel and engine settings, altitudes, etc. He said that we had done very well.

86 ★ A Military Pilot's Exciting Life and Visit from the Hereafter

The next day we were assigned to fly a B-25 with a different flight course. Although the B-25 was only a two-engine aircraft, we used the same criteria for obtaining the longest range for fuel used as we did the B-24. Here again we made no changes to the original flight plan and landed at Miami where it was weighed and refueled. Our log was turned over to the instructor, who was pleased with our success in both flights. I called my office at Lincoln Air Base and had them fly our B-17 to Miami to pick me up. I was back at my desk on the 22nd of November.

```
                      HEADQUARTERS
                AAF, AIR TRANSPORT COMMAND
               LONG RANGE CRUISE CONTROL SCHOOL
                    Miami Army Air Field

                                             Miami 30, Florida


    SUBJECT:  Long Range Cruise Control Course

    TO     :  Commanding Officer

              Lincoln Army Air Field

              Lincoln, Nebraska


          This is to certify that on the day of  21 November 1944

    Captain Kenneth W. Slaker  O 791 512      successfully completed

    the Long Range Cruise Control Course conducted by the Air Transport

    Command.

         Instruction Consisted of:

              (a) Long Range Cruise Theory.
                                         B-24 J
              (b) Flight Training in  B-25 J  aircraft.


                                 FINAL GRADE  Above Average

                                     Donald L. James Jr.
                                   DONALD L. JAMES, Jr.
                                   Captain, Air Corps
                                   Director
```

Certificate of completion of the Long Range Cruise Control Course, Miami Army Air Field, 21 November 1944.

The next day I visited the repair depot where Glenna worked to ask her for a date that coming weekend. She was very glad to see me and I asked her if she liked basketball because the Lincoln Wings (former Globetrotters) were hosting a match with a visiting team at the University of Nebraska that weekend. I told her that Captain Hall, the Wings coach, asked me to take care of the scorebook, which I did when I flew them to games away from Lincoln. She quickly agreed, for she had heard about the show the Wings put on during the first half of any game. After the game ended, which the Wings won, we had dinner with Colonel Fletcher, the hospital commander, and my fishing partner.

I drove her home after dinner and accepted her invitation to come in and meet her father, who was home that weekend. Mr. Buck and his wife, Mildred, were very hospitable and I enjoyed my visit with them. When I got up to leave, Mildred said that if I didn't have any plans for Christmas, to please join them for dinner.

The first two weeks in December didn't give me any time to attend social functions. In addition to my regular duties as the base operations officer, serving on the base Aircraft Accident Board, and flight-testing ten new B-17Gs that just arrived from the factory, I was lucky to get a good night's sleep. Flight-testing aircraft in Nebraska in December was stingy with clear weather. More than half the time I climbed to the top of the overcast to accomplish the test requirements. Then I had to make an instrument approach to the air base. These were the last B-17Gs that we were going to receive until January. We were not going to send any air combat crews overseas during the Christmas holidays. The Lincoln Wings were also off until the 14th of January when I flew them to a game in Denver, which they won.

One week before Christmas I had lunch with Colonel Fletcher at the officers' mess and he asked if it would be possible for me to fly him to the East Coast before the holidays. He had not seen his family for many months since organizing and getting the talent for this new hospital at the air base. I told him that I would if our B-17 was not scheduled. When I returned to my office, I called my base flight and they said the B-17 was mine. I called Colonel Fletcher and told him that we were leaving the morning of the nineteenth for Mitchell Field in New York City.

We departed on the morning of the nineteenth as scheduled with me, my flight engineer, Colonel Fletcher, and two hitchhikers on board. It was a smooth flight of six hours with no weather en route. The colonel's family was waiting for him in base operations. My flight engineer was going to stay on base, and Colonel Fletcher asked me what my plans were. I told him that I was going to stay at a hotel in the city. He gave me his phone number so that we could keep in touch. We shook hands as he started to leave with his family, and from his hand he passed me a signed personal check with no amount entered that I was to pay my hotel bill with.

I enjoyed myself in the city. I saw a good stage show and stayed at the Roosevelt Hotel, where Guy Lombardo and his orchestra were playing. His style of music invited you to dance, which I did with a couple of unknown friendly types. I called the colonel after a couple of days and we decided to head back home on the twenty-second, which only left two days before Christmas. The colonel arrived while I was filling out the flight plan. My flight engineer had the B-17 refueled and ready to go. Colonel Fletcher walked out with me to the aircraft and asked me if there was any way that we could have his son fly back to Lincoln with us. I told him that there was no legal way to list him on the manifest. Then before entering the aircraft, I turned to him and said, "When I get into the cockpit I don't know who gets on board," and I winked at the flight engineer, who caught on.

I had filed an instrument flight plan on controlled airways because there was bad weather most of the route to Lincoln. About a half hour after takeoff, Colonel Fletcher came up to the cockpit and asked if he could bring his son to the cockpit to meet me. I acted surprised and in a serious tone asked, "How the hell did he get on board?" Then I laughed and said to bring him here. When he appeared, I shook his hand and told him that the engineer was going to let him in the copilot's seat for a few minutes. I gave him a quick briefing of what was going on with all these instruments and he was all eyes and ears.

I had given Air Traffic Control our ETA over the Chicago beacon to the Pittsburgh center as I left their control area. We arrived at the Chicago beacon on time, and I reported in and received approval of my present altitude. There existed a pocket of good visibility in the clouds when, directly in front of me and coming head on, was an aircraft at the same altitude. I immediately turned hard right to avoid a collision. As he flew past on my left side, I was able to see the type of aircraft and the name of the airline. I contacted Air Traffic Control and reported the near miss. They thanked me and said they were trying to contact the aircraft. Colonel Fletcher never asked me about the hard turn to the right nor did I mention it to others except to my boss. We arrived safe and sound at Lincoln with two days left to get ready for Christmas. About two weeks later I received a letter from CAA asking me for a complete description of my near miss over Chicago on the 22nd of December 1944.

We arrived from New York late in the afternoon and I went to my office to check the in-basket for items needing immediate attention. There was a note from my secretary that I was to call Glenna Buck ASAP. She answered my phone call and asked me if I was planning to join the Buck family on Christmas day. I told her that I planned to be there unless there was a military emergency. I asked her what could I bring the family for Christmas and she said, "Just you."

I knew I had to give Glenna a Christmas gift of some sort, and my secretary came through with the suggestion that I purchase a gift certificate from a high-class department store in the city. That, I did. A gift for her parents was more difficult, for I had known them only a couple of months. I visited several retail outlets looking for a suitable gift when I saw a sidewalk market with a large decorated box with several compartments filled with a variety of fruit and nuts, etc. I bought that item for the family and it was well received by them. I was treated like one of the family Christmas Day, which I had not experienced for four years. My dad had sold our home and lived in a boarding house. With my dear mother in heaven, and no sisters and my only brother in the Army Air Corp, my home now was the Army Air Corp.

January 1945 was a very busy month, flight-testing new B-17G and B-24 aircraft, processing aerial combat crews for the European and Pacific battle zones, and flying the Lincoln Wings to various military bases for exhibition basketball games. I dated Glenna whenever I had free time and we developed affection for one another. The last week in January, and in a weak moment, I asked her to marry me and she accepted. I felt that once we started to live together that our feelings for one another would develop into love. She and her mother selected Valentine's Day in February for the marriage ceremony. I did not love her like I did my Mormon girlfriend. I felt that I had to let Lee know about my coming marriage to help us close the book on our love. I wrote Lee a short letter about my coming marriage but that there would always be a part of my heart that belonged to her. I signed it, *Love, Ken*.

Captain Roberts was the maintenance officer that I worked closely with on test flights and aircraft maintenance problems. One of the reasons we became friends was that we both were from Pennsylvania. He had met Lee when she was there for a week the past summer and said how lucky I was to have her the rest of my life. I told him of the separation caused by Lee's parents and he sympathized with me. He was the first person that I told about my coming marriage to Glenna, and I asked him to be my best man and he agreed.

A few days before the wedding Mildred Buck called me and asked if I could meet with her at the house an hour before Glenna would be home from work. I agreed and then wondered the reason for this meeting without Glenna being present. Mildred opened the door and escorted me to the parlor. She said she wanted to talk to me about Glenna, but first she said that the family was very proud to have me as a member of the family. She told me that Glenna was not a social person and was not friendly with her classmates, especially the boys. "Our family has seen a big change in Glenna in her personality since she started dating you. She has not had any sexual experience, and to the best of my knowledge she is still a virgin." Mildred said that I was to be patient with Glenna, and since I had been married I would know how to treat her on the honeymoon. When Glenna arrived from work, she rushed up to me, gave me a big hug and kiss, and was surprised to see me there. I told her that I had just stopped in to visit with her. I believed her to be a virgin, and for the entire time that I had dated her, I never made any sexual approaches, nor did she. At times this was difficult for me since she had a beautiful figure and the urge was there.

I had invited both my dad and my brother to the wedding because I felt that the groom should have at least one family member at the ceremony. My brother was an instructor pilot in California and could not get time off. My dad was with U.S. Steel and working full time on defense contracts. When I told him that we were going to Chicago for our honeymoon, he said he might be able to visit us there. I invited all sixteen officers living in the same building with me to the wedding.

On the evening of the 14th of February, I was to be at the church not later than 7:50. It was only a five-minute drive to the church so I planned to leave my abode no later than 7:45. Just as I reached the front door, the house phone rang. I was the only one in the building and I thought to just let it ring. Then I realized it could be for me with an emergency situation existing at the air base. I answered it and what a surprise! It was Lee's mother in Boise. Lee had shown her my letter and told her mother she still loved me and wanted to marry me even if I was not a Mormon. Her mother told me that she and her husband had agreed and they would give us permission to marry one another in a civil court! I was shocked! What should I do now? I still loved Lee but had an obligation to Glenna and her family.

I was in one hell of a situation. I was getting married but not to the one I really loved. I walked in circles in the hallway, trying to decide which way to go. I finally decided that I was not going to marry either one at this time. I got into my car, drove to the church, and entered the choir room from the outside. Captain Roberts was waiting for me and said that I was ten minutes late and the organist had kept busy with her music. The minister had just been there asking if everything was alright. I said, "Wes, I have changed my mind and am not going to get married."

Wes then said, "Ken, every man gets the jitters like you have just before the ceremony," and he opened the door to the interior of the church. There sat over 300 individuals looking at me. I now knew that I had to marry Glenna and walked in to the altar and got married.

Glenna's father had a good position with the Burlington railroad and had reserved a VIP stateroom for our honeymoon trip to Chicago. The family took us to the railroad station and her dad escorted us to our stateroom. We had our own steward and we both ordered hot chocolate. I decided that this was the time to talk sex with her. I told her that it was the custom for newlyweds to get to know one another physically on their honeymoon and that her mother had told me that she was a virgin and to be gentle with her. She surprised me! She said that she was not a virgin, that a senior she had a date with had forced himself upon her. She said that it not only hurt her physically but mentally as well. She did not tell her mother or anyone. We were both tired and decided to wait until we got to our hotel room before making love.

The day after we arrived in Chicago, my dad showed up and stayed a day with us in the Hotel Stevens. He was on good behavior and didn't have any hard liquor, but he chained smoked. Glenna didn't drink the hard stuff nor did she smoke. That, I liked, for neither did I. Dad and I talked to one another in the lobby as he was leaving, and he was quite frank. It was his opinion that Glenna was not my type and very green. He suggested that I not have any children for a couple of years to see if she could become a good wife. I had never told Dad about my first love with Lee. He knew all about my first wife Jane and her affair and had helped me to obtain a divorce in Pennsylvania.

Glenna and I tried sex at the hotel, but she didn't really respond or enjoy it. She told me that her uncle, whom she visited every summer in Colorado, was a member of a Christian spin-off church and a bible salesman who had educated her in his beliefs of how we should live our lives. One of his beliefs that he stressed to her was that you didn't have sex for the physical enjoyment, but only when you wanted a child. I thought that if my dad was to know of Glenna's relationship with her uncle, he would have advised me to send her back to Lincoln alone. As far as I was concerned, our so called honeymoon was a bust. I was a very disappointed man when we arrived at Lincoln.

The first two weeks in our apartment in the city, I learned a lot about Glenna that was very upsetting. The first week she complained about me sleeping in the nude. I told her that I had slept in the nude all my life except the year in North Africa when I never took my combat clothes off and slept in a pup tent. I also told her that you do not put clothes on to go to bed, you put them on when you get out of bed. She did not buy that, nor did I change my nude sleeping habit.

After two months of marriage I received orders to serve on a general court martial at the air base on a trial that received national publicity. A military prisoner had filed suit claiming that he was brutally beaten by a military policeman. At the end of the long, hot, first day of the trial, Bob Storz, also a court member, suggested that we go to the officers' club for a short beer. Bob's family owned the Storz Brewing Company in Omaha and kept the club supplied with beer. Although I was not a beer drinker, my friendship with Bob prohibited me from declining his invitation. We had one beer while discussing the trial, and then I drove to my apartment in the city. The wife smelled the beer on my breath and in a disgusting voice said, "You have been drinking." I explained to her about having one beer with Bob Storz after a long day in the courtroom, and now was going to take a shower. When I came out from the shower, Glenna was gone. I assumed that she had gone to the grocery store but when she failed to show up after an hour, I called her mother to see if she had heard from Glenna. She told me that Glenna had come home because of my drinking. After I told her the details she suggested that I come and pick Glenna up.

I knew that Mildred was on my side and would give Glenna some motherly advice. On my way out of the apartment I went to discard some trash and there were some empty beer cans and a wine bottle in the trash basket. I had these items in the refrigerator in case some military friends stopped by. Evidently Glenna had emptied their contents into the sink. Another one of her uncle's religious teachings.

During January and February I flight-tested thirty new B-17Gs that were the last we would receive. The Boeing Company was now building the larger B-29 bombers. In March we received notice that our 12th Heavy Processing Unit was being transferred to Forbes Air Base. Command of Lincoln Air Base was to come under Air Training Command. An ATC survey team arrived to work with our people on the transfer. I was given the task of speaking to them as to the layout of the runways, hangars, control tower and radio facilities, base flight aircraft, base operations, etc. The lieutenant colonel in charge of the team met with me after the briefing was over and said that he would like for me to remain there as the base operations officer. My boss, Major Fields, said that it was my decision to make. I discussed it with the wife and she didn't want to leave Lincoln, so I decided to remain at Lincoln Air Base.

I told Major Fields that I was going to stay at Lincoln primarily because my wife did not want to move to Topeka. As we shook hands farewell, he grinned and said that neither one of us had to make that decision. Major Fields was not married but he understood the pressure a wife has over her husband.

The first four months I also flew the Lincoln Wings basketball team to several games at other military installations, and they won them all. At the end of the season, the Wings and their support personnel were given a banquet at the base hosted by the University of Nebraska Athletic Department. Special guests were Dwight Griswold, governor of Nebraska, Lloyd Marti, Mayor of Lincoln, A.J. Lewandowski, Athletic coach from University of Nebraska, and sports writers from the cities of Omaha and Lincoln.

Colonel Fletcher and I also made two more trips to Boise to do some fly-fishing in the Boise River. We both had good luck and ate part of our catch that evening in the mountains. I did suffer some sadness, for memories returned of my seeing Lee on these trips in the past.

Rated pilots to remain on flying status must pass a flight physical every year just before or on their birthday. It is a very thorough physical, and when it came time for me to have my teeth checked, I was examined by the head of the dental clinic, Dr. Schoening. I was still wearing a partial plate for a front tooth that had been broken off when I was playing basketball in the Aviation Cadets. The doctor didn't like it and said that he was going to replace it with a gold bridge which would look and feel better and should last twenty to thirty years. He did an excellent job, and I asked him where he hailed from and he said Minneapolis. I told him that I would like to favor him with a flight home some weekend. He said that he would take me up on that offer.

The first weekend in May we flew to Minneapolis in my base flight's B-25. We took a taxi into town and the doctor dropped me off at a good hotel. I was checked in by a very attractive receptionist who was very personable. She was not busy and we got to chatting, and I told her that this was my first visit to Minneapolis and could she recommend a good dining and dancing spot for me to spend the evening? She said that her shift was over at 8:00 P.M. and that she would be glad to be my escort for the evening. I could not refuse an offer like that from a beautiful blond. We had an excellent dinner and then went dancing. To my delight she was a good dancer and I was so pleased to dance again, for Glenna did not approve of dancing. We took a cab back and dismissed it a block from the hotel. By now we were really attracted to one another, and she said that she could not walk into the hotel with me, but to go to my room and she would be up in a few minutes to tuck me in. When I entered the room I thought that maybe I had been dismissed, but in a few minutes there was a light tapping on the door and there she was. We embraced and she said, "Ken, I am not a hooker and if hotel management knew that I came to your room, I would be dismissed. But I was so attracted to you that I decided I wanted to spend the evening with you." We embraced, and our clothes came off and we were in bed. I had not told her that I had not had mutual sex since I had been married, but our night together turned out to be what we both needed. She dressed and departed early in the morning, gave me her phone number, and asked that I call her the next time I was in the city.

I met Dr. Schoening at the airport for our flight back to Lincoln, and he asked if I had enjoyed the city last night. I told him about my experience with the hotel receptionist and said I guessed that I had cheated on my wife, but it was payback time for her not being a loving wife. The doctor then said, "You know that there is a war on and men young and handsome like you are scarce in this city because they are all gone into the Army. You and your lady friend were good for one another." Being a medical doctor, he asked me if I had used a condom and I said no, I didn't carry them with me because my bombardier, George O'Hoppe, who was six years older than me and had been around, told me that you don't enjoy sex wearing a saddle, that you ride them bare back, and I did.

It was noon when I taxied out for takeoff to return to Lincoln. The flight engineer was my copilot and the doctor was seat belted in the fuselage area. Takeoff was normal and I climbed to 6,500 feet, which was my off airways altitude for a direct flight to Lincoln. My estimated time en route was one hour, forty minutes, and we had been in the air about fifteen minutes when there was a loud clanking noise from the right engine and oil sprayed all over the engine and wing, then heavy black smoke. I immediately feathered the right engine, cut off its fuel supply, increased the power on the left engine, trimmed the rudder to compensate for power from the left engine only, and called Minneapolis tower for an emergency landing with fire in number two engine and emergency vehicles. They replied that the airfield was clear for me and that the emergency vehicles were already on their way to the runway. I could not contact the doctor to inform him about our emergency landing because I had to concentrate on my airspeed and altitude, and my engineer was standing by for my orders for flaps and landing gear. I kept enough altitude in case I lost number one engine, I would be able to glide to the runway. When I saw that I had the runway made, I called for flaps and landing gear. I had never made a smoother landing in a B-25 than I did this one. Just as soon as I was able to brake to a stop, the emergency fire truck was spraying number two engine. The engineer and I quickly went to the fuselage to open the door and the doctor was already there. We opened the door, jumped out, and ran away from the aircraft in case it exploded. The doctor grabbed my hand, shook it, and said, "Captain Slaker, you are a damn good pilot." I thanked him and then shook the engineer's hand.

I talked to the maintenance chief about the repair and he said there was no fire damage. The oil pump needed replacing, and he said he could have a new one by that evening, and they were already pressure washing the wing and engine. When the repair was finished, he would give me a statement of repairs to sign and he would then submit it to the Army for payment, which it had honored for previous aircraft repairs. I told the doctor that he could enjoy another day with the family and that we would plan on taking off for Lincoln at 9:00 A.M. Monday morning and would be home before noon. He was pleased to hear that, for he said he had patients scheduled Monday afternoon. I stayed at a hotel next to the airport and was at the aircraft at seven the next morning. My flight engineer and I pre-flighted the B-25 and it was okay. We took off as scheduled and arrived at Lincoln at 10:45 A.M.

With the change of command, the B-17F and the RA-25 were transferred to Forbes Air Base at Topeka. The Technical Training Command sent us a B-25J which gave base flight two B-25 aircraft. With no more B-17s to test fly and the loss of our B-17F, I was disappointed that I no longer had a four-engine aircraft to fly. I had full faith in the B-17 and really missed it because I had been flying B-17s for three years during which it had brought me home safely after fifty bombing missions. Now I was a B-25 pilot during which I had already declared an emergency in each one of them.

Come July I was ordered to fly some staff personnel to Great Falls, Montana, and to Missoula. Since there was no hurry for me to return to Lincoln, I decided to fly to Seattle to see my two uncles, Ray and Ed Hawk, whom I had not seen since their father, my granddad, had died in 1934. As I approached Seattle, I was amazed at the scenery of the Cascade Mountains with snow-covered Mt. Rainier and Puget Sound with the Olympic Mountains in the background. Although I had flown in Idaho, Utah, and New Mexico, I had never flown over the Pacific Northwest region.

I landed in Seattle at Boeing Field and Uncle Ray and his wife Mary were there to greet me. They gave me a tour of the city and we visited the University of Washington. I was really impressed with the beauty of the campus with a good view of snow-covered Mt. Rainier touching the blue sky to the southeast. I departed early in the evening and landed at Gowen Army Air Base at Boise, Idaho. Staying overnight there brought memories back again of the loss of my first love there last fall. Now that I was a married man, memories were all that were left for me here in Boise.

My sister in law, Dolly Allen, called me on August 13th that her husband, Mark, a Marine pilot, had just returned from combat with the Japanese, and was at the Marine base in San Diego, and she would really appreciate it if I could fly to San Diego and bring him home to Lincoln. I told Dolly that she was in luck, for I already had a flight to Alamogordo, then to fly Colonel Fletcher to Boise for a business meeting. I told her to tell Mark that I would arrive at the Marine base on the fifteenth in the early afternoon.

I took off early in the morning for Alamogordo where I dropped off a passenger, then took a direct flight to Gowen Air Base at Boise. It was late afternoon, and Colonel Fletcher and I took a taxi into town. He went to his meeting and I walked for a few blocks to limber my legs after sitting in the B-25 cockpit for eight hours. As I approached city center, hundreds of people were in the streets shouting and laughing and throwing whatever they could get their hands on. I was in uniform and I became surrounded with women hugging and kissing me, and men shaking my hands. Then one of them said to me, "Congratulations, Captain. Japan has just surrendered!" I could hardly move around and I saw a sign on a corner filling station that said No gas coupons needed, and autos were already filling up. It was a very emotional scene to see hundreds of citizens expressing their happiness to one another after such a long war. A day I have never forgotten.

I had a short night of rest at the air base before taking off for San Diego. I arrived there early in the afternoon and the follow-me jeep parked me in front of operations. As I got out of the B-25, a Marine pilot with a big smile on his face walked up to me, and although I had never met Mark, I knew that this was him from photos I had seen at the Buck residence. We had a bite to eat while the ground crew serviced the B-25. When my flight engineer reported that the B-25 was ready for the flight to Lincoln, we climbed aboard and I put Mark in the copilot's seat. When we got to our assigned altitude, the first half hour was spent discussing the various flight capabilities of the B-25, which Mark was very interested in.

Then Mark asked me how I was getting along with Glenna. I told Mark about her negative attitude on making love, social cocktails, card playing, dancing, etc. He was very surprised that I had married her because her short affair with a senior in high school ended when he no longer could take her tantrums. He said that she had spent several summers in Colorado where she had a relative who was a Seventh Day Adventist who greatly influenced her lifestyle and beliefs. It was getting dark when we landed at Lincoln, and I taxied to the ramp in front of base operations where Dolly, her daughter, and mother were waiting for Mark's arrival. It made me feel very good to see the very emotional greeting between Mark and Dolly and their daughter.

The war against Germany and Japan was now over and our aircraft combat training was at a standstill. I knew that my future as an Army pilot was at stake and decided to seek advice from the base commander, Colonel Anderson, a career officer and graduate of West Point. His secretary gave me an appointment time and when I arrived, he asked me to be seated. He thanked me for the excellent work I had done as his base operations officer and asked what he could do for me. I told him that I needed his advice as to what action I should take to become a career Army pilot. He suggested that I get a discharge from active duty and study for a college degree. He said that with my excellent war record as a pilot and a good staff officer, that I certainly would be called to active duty as a regular Army officer. Also, I would need to be a college graduate to compete with the West Point graduates during my Army career.

I followed his advice and submitted my request for a discharge the latter part of August. It came back approved the first week in October and since my home of record was the state of Pennsylvania, I was ordered to the Army Separation Center at Indiantown Gap, Pennsylvania. While waiting for the discharge paperwork to be completed, I visited Pennsylvania State College to see if I wanted to study there for my degree. I was not sold on enrolling there and decided to visit other colleges before making a very important decision.

I received my discharge certificate on the 17th of October, along with an appointment as a captain in the Army Reserves as a rated pilot. We drove to my hometown of Vandergrift, about twenty-five miles from Pittsburgh, where I visited with relatives and friends. I was well acquainted with the University of Pittsburgh and Carnegie Tech so I did not visit them. The wife and I then drove to Boulder, Colorado to case the University of Colorado. The university registrar was sorry that they could not accept me because the freshman and sophomore classes were full. We could not even find a hotel or motel room for the night, so we drove to Cheyenne, Wyoming for the night.

The next morning I called my uncle Ray Hawk, a wealthy contractor in Seattle. I told him about my need to get a college degree and I had been impressed with the University of Washington, which he had shown me last spring. He told me to stay where I was and he would be calling me back. About an hour later he called me and told me to get my ass to Seattle—that he had talked to the UW Registrar and she had an enrollment space waiting for me. Glenna had gone out for a late breakfast and when she returned, I told her that I had made up my mind, that I was going to go to the University of Washington in Seattle. I wondered how this Nebraska born gal would react to my decision. She looked at me, smiled, and then said, "Let's go!" I did not expect this cooperation from her.

Chapter 6
ARMY RESERVE PILOT GOES TO COLLEGE

We stopped at Lincoln for two days on our way to Seattle to pick up our belongings. Three driving days later we arrived at my uncle Ray Hawk's residence in Seattle. He and his wife were both were very excited to have us there and told us that we were their guests until we found a place to live. We met my two cousins, Jimmy and Cherie. I had met Jimmy when he was four years old but this was my first meeting with Cherie. The next day I wanted to get to the University of Washington to enroll, and Jimmy went with me to be my navigator through the streets of Seattle. Glenna spent the day calling on houses and rentals listed in the morning *Post Intelligencer* with no luck.

I was one of the first World War II veterans to enroll at the UW and when the registrar, Mrs. Toner, saw the schooling that I had received in the Army, she asked me if I would be interested in working in her office to analyze the Army school records of the hundreds of veterans expected to enroll to determine the number of points they could receive as credits against UW courses. I replied in the affirmative and was hired on the spot. We went through the military courses that I had completed and was awarded enough points to enroll as a sophomore.

The first weekend in Seattle, Glenna and I drove around the university area to become familiar with the streets and shopping areas. About one mile northeast of the university, we came to the Naval Air Station at Sand Point, and since I had a Defense Department sticker on the windshield, I was able to drive onto the base. I drove to the officers' billeting office and asked the seaman on duty if he might have or know of available housing for the wife and me. He said that he noticed a block of small new houses being built on the edge of a suburb known as Laurelhurst. I thanked him for his information and instructions and we found the new houses without any problem. One house, already occupied, had a *For Sale* sign on it. I knocked on the door, and the owner answered and I introduced myself and asked him the price. This house was exactly what the wife and I had in mind and the price was right. I knew that I could sell our Ford, which would be enough for the down payment, so we signed the papers.

Glenna had applied for a job at the university, and she was hired the next day when they saw in her résumé that she had been a secretary at the Lincoln Air Base. I drove the

Ford to a local dealer and he gave me a good price for it. That afternoon we signed the final papers for the house and had no trouble financing it since we were both working. I gave them my uncle's name as a reference since he was well-known by the local banks.

I enrolled in Civil Engineering and enjoyed working for Mrs. Toner. The GI Bill paid for all my school expenses and with both Glenna and me working, we did not have any financial problems. We did not need a car with both of us working and me studying every night and sometimes on weekends, and there was very little time left for going places. Public transportation was reasonable and adequate. When it was not raining, I walked the mile to the university; otherwise I took the bus, which only cost a dime.

The Army Reserves did not yet have a flight unit in operation at McChord Air Base, and it was now the end of October and I had not flown since the middle of August. There was an airfield for small private aircraft east of Seattle at Bellevue. Since I was a licensed private pilot, I went there at least once a month and rented a Taylorcraft and flew it for an hour to maintain my aerial proficiency.

Just a couple of weeks after we moved into our house, the house next door came onto the market and it was purchased by an Army Reserve captain who was a pilot. His wife Eleanor was very charming and we welcomed them to the neighborhood. They were both from New York State and like us, they drove all the way across the states to go to the University of Washington. In the spring of 1946, the Army Air Corp Reserves started operating at McChord and John, since he had a sedan, insisted that we ride together to the Reserve meetings and to meet our flight schedules. John was very considerate in offering Glenna and me transportation in his car and even loaned it to me to drive over the Cascade Mountains to Ellensburg to visit my uncle Ed Hawk.

In early 1946, I received a legal document from an attorney in New Kensington, PA, bearing the notarized signature of Jane, my first wife, requesting that I pay her several thousand dollars for the support of our daughter, Patricia Elaine, now in the custody of her and her new husband. If I agreed to pay this amount and not to interfere with their raising of Patti, I would be released of all responsibility for the rearing and education of Patti. I thought this over for a couple of days, and Glenna thought that Patti would be better off with her mother and I agreed. I had some money left over from the sale of our Ford and several thousand dollars that was a bonus paid to Reserve officers when they go off active duty. I signed the legal document and sent it back by registered mail along with a certified check for the amount she requested. She never contacted me while Patti was growing up, but Jane's mother, who really liked me, always kept in touch with me and sent me photos of Patti and her schooling and activities. I don't think Jane knew that her mother was doing this for me.

One day in the summer of 1946, Glenna chanced to meet a girl at the UW who was from Nebraska, which provided them with common background for chatting. Her name was Marjorie Johnson and her husband, Keith, was also attending the university.

They were having a difficult time finding a place to live and Glenna asked which motel they were staying at. That evening Glenna told me about the Johnsons and suggested that we let them have the spare bedroom as long as they didn't mind sharing the bathroom and kitchen. I agreed to that and Glenna got in touch with them at the motel and invited them to come out and spend an evening with us. They arrived that evening and after getting acquainted, we gave them a tour of the house. I then told them our proposal to live with us and they accepted. We got along fine, and that summer Keith and I worked weekends at a service station near the university. Then Keith took us up to his folks' dairy farm near Mt. Vernon. His parents were wonderful and we had an enjoyable weekend there milking scores of cows.

My brother, also a Reserve pilot, requested a discharge in late 1945 and enrolled at Washington Jefferson College in southwest Pennsylvania. He was not too happy there, and I convinced him that the Northwest was growing, had a better climate than Pennsylvania, we had relatives here, and that I could get him enrolled at the University of Washington since I worked in the registrar's office. He arrived there in time for the beginning of the fall quarter of 1946. He had no trouble finding a place to live since the fraternity he belonged to had room for him here. There was a young single girl working in our office, and I got her and my brother together. They went steady together for several years and ended up getting married.

Chemistry was one of my best subjects with top grades. Professor Tartar recognized this by appointing me Laboratory Advisor to the Chemistry students. One of the students—I'll call her Tex since she was not from Texas— took a strong interest in me. She was not bashful about telling me her feelings about me and I responded politely, for there was a limit. I was married and I had been a very faithful husband since my one time fling in Minneapolis. I finally told her that she was wasting her time with me and she finally eased off. This had been a great temptation for I had a very frigid wife, but since I was her husband, I had an obligation to her.

While stationed at Lincoln Air Base I not only became good friends with the hospital commander, but also a doctor by name of Dr. King. At the end of the war, he came to Seattle, where he practiced at the Virginia Masons Hospital. I started having stomach cramps in the spring of 1946, so I decided to make an appointment with Dr. King. He remembered me and asked what brought me to Virginia Mason. I explained my stomach problem and thought that it might be caused by my marriage problem. He made appointments for me with a doctor of Internal Medicine, and one for Glenna with a female specialist.

My visit to the doctor concerning my stomach cramps was not enjoyable. I had to swallow a tube with a small light on the end of it to inspect the interior of my stomach—then a tube up my rear end, plus a couple of more fun tests. I went in three days later to get the results and received good news—and a surprising instruction. There was nothing wrong with my stomach and digestive system. First, he didn't want me to go to summer school, but to do physical work. Second, I should not carry a heavy subject load like I was at present, and third and a real surprise, that when I came home from a day in school, I was to sit down and relax, and have a Ballentine Scotch and water. I was not a drinking man and he said that was why he suggested Ballentine's, for it was the mildest of scotch. I went to the liquor store on base and it worked! To this day it is the only scotch that I will drink. Glenna was really upset that I was drinking liquor, and she did not keep her appointment with the female specialist.

In the spring of 1947, I received a letter from the Army Air Corp Headquarters inviting me to meet a special board of ranking officers that was selecting officers that, if qualified, would be granted a regular commission in the Army Air Corp. If I was interested in meeting the board, I was to notify the personnel officer at the air base in Spokane and would be given the date and time to be there to appear before the board. I was very interested, for flying was my number one desire in this life. There were four of us pilots that met the board the same day. We knew that our chances were slim, and before we parted we exchanged addresses and agreed to notify one another whether we were selected or not.

I was called to active duty in the summer to attend the two-week Air Corp Reserve pilot training at McChord Air Base. It was a wonderful experience to fly again and enjoy the association with the other pilots. It also helped me make a final decision that had been going through my mind that past spring. I didn't want to be a Chemical Engineer and spend my life in a laboratory. I really wanted a degree in Transportation. I checked the majority of the universities, and the best one for that degree was Northwestern University at Evanston, Illinois. At the end of the two-week tour at McChord, I wrote to the admissions office at Northwestern, giving them my senior standing at the University of Washington, and asked if they could enroll me that fall. I got an okay that I would be accepted.

When I told Glenna that I had been accepted at Northwestern, I asked if she wanted to stay in Seattle. She decided to quit her job and go back to Lincoln. She left the house for me to sell and to stop by Lincoln on my way to Chicago. A fellow pilot I met at McChord called and said that if I still wanted to buy his Buick that we had discussed at the camp, he was ready to sell. The house sold in just a few days, and so now I had money that I made on the house and a car. I said goodbye to the Freemans and my brother, and drove to Lincoln.

I arrived at Glenna's parents' house the middle of August, and since I had two weeks before I had to be in Evanston, we drove to her relatives' summer cottage on a lake just east of Kansas City. Her relatives were very hospitable and lots of fun. Glenna was more relaxed and more companionable than she had been for a long time. When we returned to Lincoln, she decided to stay at her folks' house until I got settled at school.

I arrived at Evanston the first part of September and registered for a major in Transportation. Since I was a senior, I was entitled to live in Abbot Hall on Lake Shore Drive in Chicago, especially since most of my classes were at the Chicago campus. I was billeted on the fourteenth floor (really the thirteenth but there is not a thirteenth floor there or in any of the hotels). It was not a quiet room, for when the wind blew off Lake Michigan, it howled as it blew past our building.

I had been at Northwestern University only one month when I received a telegram from the Army that I had been selected to be granted a regular commission in the Army Air Corp dependent upon my passing a physical examination within five days. I was very excited because this was the career that I wanted. I drove to Chanute Air Base the

---

DEPARTMENT OF THE ARMY
OFFICE OF THE ADJUTANT GENERAL
WASHINGTON 25, D. C.

AGSO-R 201 - 06   10 October 1947

SUBJECT: Recess Appointment in the Regular Army

TO: CAPT KENNETH W SLAKER JR 0791512
         710 NORTH LAKE SHORE DRIVE
         CHICAGO ILLINOIS

         I LT   AC   054111   26-07-45

1. The President has appointed you under recess appointment provisions this date in the Regular Army in the grade, arm or service, and with date of rank as shown above.

2. The Secretary of the Army and Chief of Staff, United States Army, have asked that I convey to you their congratulations on your selection for appointment in the Regular Army and to extend their best wishes for an interesting and professionally profitable career in the service of your country.

3. The Regular Army Officer serial number assigned to you as shown above will be used immediately upon execution of oath of office and thereafter. Complete instructions and information are contained in separate communications herewith.

BY ORDER OF THE SECRETARY OF THE ARMY:

EDWARD F. WITSELL
Major General
The Adjutant General

10 Incls
 1. SO # 17
 2. Letter of Instructions
 3. WD AGO Form 71
 4. WD AGO Form 0409 (trip)
 5. WD AGO Form-643 (dup)
 6. Cir 281, WD, 1946
 7. WD AGO Form 41
 8. 2 Return Penalty Envelopes
 9. Information Pamphlet
10. Cir 18, WD, 1947

Slaker appointed as a Regular Army Officer, 10 October 1947.

AAF REGIONAL HOSPITAL
LINCOLN ARMY AIR FIELD, LINCOLN 1, NEBRASKA
OFFICE OF THE SURGEON

FLF-hm

201 H   7 July 1945

SUBJECT: Commendation.

TO: Captain Kenneth W. Slaker, Jr.
    Lincoln Army Air Field, Lincoln 1, Nebraska.
    (THROUGH: Commanding Officer, Lincoln Army Air Field,
    Lincoln 1, Nebraska).

    1. I wish to express to you my own and the entire Medical Department's appreciation for the exceptional cooperation you have given us. Because of your efficiency, cooperation, and sustained interest and effort, you have contributed substantially to the quality of care given to patients at this and the bases which this Regional Hospital serves.

    2. I wish, therefore, to commend you and the other officers in Base Operations on behalf of the Medical Department.

    3. It is requested that a copy of this commendation be placed in your 201 File.

Frank L Fletcher
FRANK L. FLETCHER
Lt Col, Medical Corps
Surgeon

201 - Slaker, Kenneth W. Jr. (Off)   1st Ind.   HWA-mm

HEADQUARTERS LINCOLN ARMY AIR FIELD, Lincoln 1, Nebraska, 17 July 1945.

TO: Captain Kenneth W. Slaker, Jr., Lincoln Army Air Field, Lincoln 1, Nebr.

    1. It is with pleasure that the undersigned notes the above commendation from the Base Surgeon.

    2. The manner in which you have cooperated with the Regional Hospital at this station is a distinct credit to you and to the Command, and I wish to add my commendation from this Headquarters.

    3. A copy of this commendation will be placed in your 201 file, made a part of your permanent record, and will be attached to your next efficiency report.

HERBERT W. ANDERSON
Colonel, Air Corps
Commanding

- 1 -

Commendation from the Office of the Surgeon, Lincoln Army Air Field, 7 July 1945.

next day and took the physical. On the 10th of October, I received a telegram from the adjutant general of the department of the Army granting me my regular commission as soon as I took the oath of office. I notified the university registrar that I was being recalled back into the military service and was told that since I had not completed any of my courses there would not be any academic record. I took the oath of office and gave them the Lincoln address for me to receive my active duty orders.

I drove back to Lincoln and Glenna was very surprised to see me because I had not told her about my getting a regular commission. She was furious and made some very nasty remarks about me and the service. I reminded her that I was a pilot in the service when she married me, but that didn't score with her at all. She said that she was not going to spend her life on a military base and would not have our child grow up in that environment. I was ready to ask her what child when she stunned me with, "I am with child."

The atmosphere at the Buck house was tense and communication with Glenna was impossible. We had sex at the lake in August and she ended up pregnant. I could not have worn a condom, for Glenna refused to have sex with me if I used protection. I spent most of the day away from the house and visited some friends that I had made when stationed at the air base. I also spent a pleasant day in Omaha with my former roommate at the Phi Delta house, Bob Storz. I also spent time at the National Aeronautics Club, where I could converse with other pilots.

On the 17th of October I received orders to report to the 28th Bomb Wing, Ellsworth Army Air Base, Rapid City, South Dakota. I was able to talk with Glenna's mother and she agreed that my choice to have a life career as a pilot was made long before I had met Glenna, and as my wife, she should be proud that I had secured a regular commission in the Army Air Corp. I told her mother that Glenna said she would not live with me on a military base. I told her mother that I would remain as her husband until the baby was born, and then I would seek a divorce.

The day before I planned to leave for Rapid City, Glenna came to me and said that she was going with me. I knew that her mother had given her daughter a good talking to. So in late November, we arrived in Rapid City for me to begin my career as a pilot in the military.

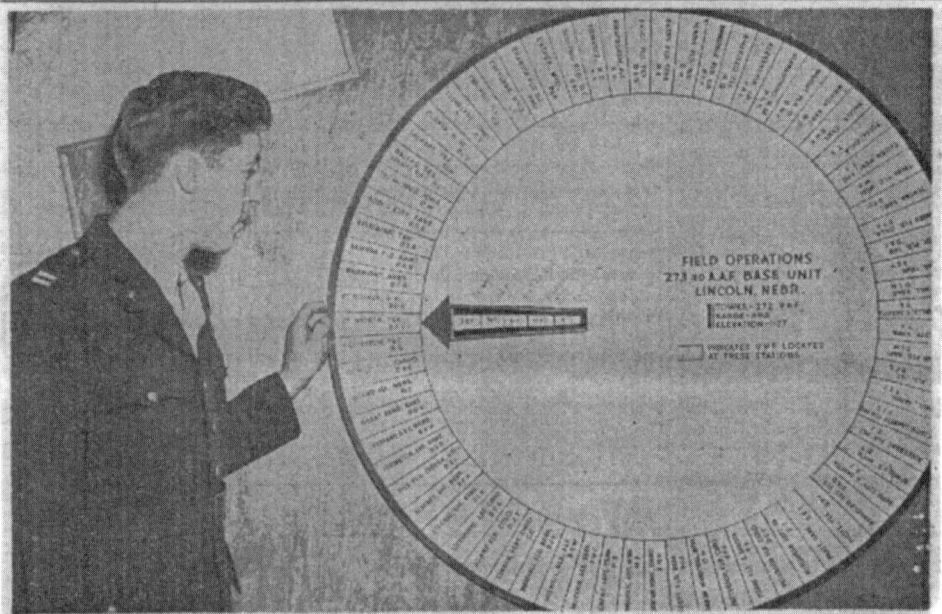

To AAFTC
LINCOLN ARMY AIR FIELD, LINCOLN, NEBR.

Captain Kenneth W. Slaker, Field Operations Officer, is shown with the flight information computer which he designed, and which saves pilots considerable time in figuring flight data to any of 72 major destinations. A turn of the outside disk and all the pertinent information which the pilot must have is immediately available. Note that the pointer happens to be directed to Forth Worth, Texas, 560 air miles from Lincoln, headquarters of the Army Air Forces Technical Command. Timely, huh?

Mileage Computer A Time Saver

560 Air Miles To Ft. Worth

No longer do pilots about to take off from Lincoln Army Air Field have to spend considerable time computing mileage and other data incident to their flights, for such information on no less than 72 frequently-used destinations can now be obtained in a second or two.

The computer, located in Operations, resembles one of those large gambling wheels used at country fairs. It is composed of two disks, the larger, outside one movable and the inner one stationary. On the inner disk is an arrow, to which any destination shown on the outside disk can be brought into line. Directly in back of this arrow is a slot in which

Continued on Page 7, Col. 4.

Article about the flight information computer Slaker designed.

HEADQUARTERS FIFTEENTH AIR FORCE
OFFICE OF THE COMMANDING GENERAL
COLORADO SPRINGS, COLORADO
10 December 1947

Captain Kenneth W. Slaker, Jr
28th Bombardment Wing
Rapid City Army Air Field
Rapid City, South Dakota

Dear Captain Slaker:

This is to congratulate you upon your recent attainment of a commission in the Regular Air Force.

You were selected for those qualities and qualifications that indicate your ability as a leader. By your acceptance you have acknowledged a trust placed in you by the government and people of the United States; you have indicated your desire to seek a career in the service of your country, and you have accepted an obligation to yourself.

Your commission is a document which, in a measure, guarantees your personal security in order that your entire life may be devoted to the welfare of our country. The Constitution of the United States guarantees the four freedoms and we in the Service have dedicated our lives to the preservation of a free and independent country in order that the four freedoms may survive.

During your war service you have seen the many problems that can arise during an emergency. There are many problems confronting us today that require everlasting energy and intelligence if they are to be met successfully. These and other issues will continue and as the years go by the burden of responsibility will grow heavier and heavier upon your shoulders. It is my firm belief that if you prepare yourself in the progress of your career, you will be equipped and ready to accept those responsibilities. Your actions may well determine whether this country survives free and independent, or whether our people become slaves of another power.

Success means various things to different people. It is my belief that success cannot be measured in terms of personal gain, but rather by a feeling in one's heart of personal pride in accomplishment. Your Air Force career may mean great satisfaction to you or it may mean disappointment and unhappiness, depending upon the energy and intelligence devoted to the job given you.

Congratulations letter, 10 December 1947.

The interests of the Air Force and the nation require that obedience and discipline be maintained. I believe the successful commander secures obedience because the orders he issues are fair, and discipline through fair and impartial decisions. Pettiness and personal grievances must be avoided. Your personal conduct should be such that it reflects credit on the Air Force, which, in turn, will obtain the support of the military establishment by the people.

I urge you to think for yourself; do not become a "yes" man. No one knows the answers to all the problems that will face you. Do not hesitate to present your views to your commander; after he has weighed the facts, his decision must have your wholehearted support.

These views are entirely my own. There are other approaches to the issue, although I do believe you will achieve great satisfaction in the knowledge that you are doing the best you know how. The idea that "my country comes first," will certainly lend toward your success.

I wish you a long career and the best of luck.

Sincerely,

LEON W. JOHNSON
Brigadier General, USAF
Commanding

Congratulations letter, 10 December 1947.

The Engineer School
Fort Belvoir, Virginia

This is to certify that

KENNETH W SLAKER   A054111

CAPTAIN, UNITED STATES AIR FORCE

has successfully completed the Post Engineer Course for the period 5 January 1948 to 26 March 1948. Subjects completed are those outlined on the reverse side of this certificate.

This certificate is issued pursuant to paragraph 16c, AR 350-110, 1 September 1942.

Lieutenant Colonel, Corps of Engineers, Secretary

Certificate for completion of the Post Engineer Course, Fort Belvoir, Virginia, 1 September 1942.

Chapter 7
Escape Through Russia's Iron Curtain

Upon arrival at Rapid City, I drove to the air base headquarters and signed in. I then talked to the base billeting officer, who informed me that there were no quarters available on base but gave me the address of a motel with small living units by a small lake west of Rapid City. We were fortunate to rent the last unit available. The neighbors, all military, welcomed us and helped us get settled. The next morning I reported to the wing commander, and then to the director of operations. When he reviewed my record and saw that I had been base operations officer at Lincoln Air Base during the war, he assigned me as the assistant base operations officer. I reported to Captain Ballentine, the base operations officer, and from the very first meeting, we got along like brothers.

I was a pilot and needed four hours' flying time to qualify for flight pay. On the 18th of December, I was scheduled on a B-29 as the copilot. It was a real thrill to be back in the cockpit of a four-engine aircraft. The pilot had been informed that I had not flown a four-engine aircraft for over two years, so he acted as an instructor pilot and we did stalls, landings, takeoffs, etc. for six hours. The pilot was impressed and told me that I had not lost my touch. An exciting day.

Flying was at a minimum during the Christmas holidays, which gave Glenna and me spare time to tour the area, driving through the Black Hills, seeing Mt. Rushmore, etc. During the last week in December the personnel officer received a request from Army Headquarters asking for the names of officers who had experience or education in Civil Engineering. Since I had three years in engineering at the University of Washington, my name and a Major Torres' name were submitted. On the 2nd of January, we received orders to report to the Engineering school at Ft. Belvoir, Virginia, to attend Post Engineering School beginning January 5th. I would be gone three months, and Glenna was four months pregnant. She could either stay there or go back to Lincoln. She decided to stay in Rapid City.

Major Torres and I were assigned to Bolling Field for flight requirements and were able to be assigned aircraft three times to fly back to Rapid City to visit our wives on weekends. We graduated the end of March and returned to Rapid City with a Military

Operational Specialty as a Post Engineer and declared critical, which meant that in the near future I would be reassigned. The latter part of April I received a telegram that the new 1948 Studebaker Land Cruiser was ready to be delivered to me by the dealer in my hometown of Vandergrift. I had ordered it in December and had a buyer for my 1942 Buick. I hitched a ride on a C-47 to Chicago and then a train to Pittsburgh, where my dad met me and drove me to the dealer. I drove it back to Rapid City, and what a wonderful driving and riding automobile.

I spent most of April and part of May making administrative flights throughout the Midwest in our C-47 and B-25 aircraft. The second week in May the personnel office notified me that I was being transferred to USAFE Headquarters in Wiesbaden, Germany. Since Glenna was in her ninth month of pregnancy, I requested a delay en route and received a twenty-day extension in the reporting date. We packed our new Studebaker with our belongings and drove to her home in Lincoln.

The evening of May 29th, Glenna started having birth pains and I drove her to the local hospital. A violent thunderstorm swept over the city just before midnight and three more women arrived having birth pains. There was only one doctor and one nurse on duty, and the nurse grabbed me and gave me instructions to assist these four women having babies, and I became a ward nurse. Glenna delivered a baby girl about 2:00 A.M. whose legs were twisted ninety degrees to the right. The doctor said this was caused by the way the baby lay in the womb and could be corrected by braces. I was helping to attend to the other women when another doctor and two nurses arrived. Glenna gave the baby her first name of Pamela, and I gave her the middle name of Ruth, my mother's name. The day after Glenna was discharged from the hospital, I departed by commercial air for Camp Kilmer, New Jersey, the port of embarkation.

My orders stated that no dependents or private auto would accompany officers to the POE. I asked the officer in charge as to when I could have my private auto shipped to Germany and he said right then, and bring it in. I immediately got on a commercial flight to Lincoln. During this flight I met a charming lady named Anne, and we visited with one another during the entire flight. Just before we landed she gave me her address and told me to be sure and call her the next time I was in New York. She was to become a very important person later on in my life. I drove my Land Cruiser to the port and two days later was on the *General Patrick* troopship on its way to Germany.

Colonel Riley, commander of the troops, named me the adjutant for this trip since I was the ranking captain on board. The first four days we had solid fog, but this didn't bother me because I was busy with paperwork and assisting the doctor with his short arm inspection of the several hundred troops on board. On the morning of the fifth day I had just got out of bed and dressed when the ship stopped. I rushed out onto the deck to see why we had stopped. What I saw took my breath away. The bright morning sun was shining on the White Cliffs of Dover, and it was beautiful. A young lady joined me and agreed that we were so lucky to see this beautiful painting by Mother Nature. She was a civil service employee also on her way to USAFE Headquarters to her new job. The ship arrived at the German port of Bremerhaven, and I was billeted at a local hotel for the night. The next day I was on the train to Wiesbaden.

I arrived at USAFE Headquarters in the middle of June, when the Russians were creating a very uncooperative relationship with our command in Berlin as to occupational policy. I reported to USAFE Personnel, and the officer that greeted me and read my orders informed me that the base I was to be assigned to as a Post Engineer had just been closed. He asked what my secondary MOS was as a pilot and I told him I was a base operations officer. He checked the officers assigned this duty at the bases in our occupied zone of Germany and found that the officer in this position at Furstenfeldbruck Air Base was rotating in August. No officer had been assigned to replace him, so the personnel officer said that orders would be published naming me as the replacement and to pick up my orders the next day. I returned to the hotel where I had been billeted and went to the dining room for dinner. Peggy, the girl that I had met on the troopship, was sitting alone so I joined her. It was a fine dinner and we departed good friends.

The next day I hitched a ride on a military aircraft going to Furstenfeldbruck Air Base, located about twenty miles west of Munich. I reported to the wing commander, Colonel Stewart, who was very cordial, which created a relaxed atmosphere. He was pleased to hear that I was an experienced base operations officer and ex combat pilot. He then informed me that the Russians had blocked all passengers and vehicles from entering Berlin, which had created a terrific tension between us and the Russians. I thought to myself, *The last time I was in Europe I fought the Germans, now I am here just in time to fight the Russians. How lucky can you get?*

After the welcome from Colonel Stewart, I went to the office of the group operations officer and introduced myself to Major Giles, who would be my boss. He was a very cheerful and understanding officer and we got along great for the rest of his tour. He escorted me to the base operations office and introduced me to Captain Marcum, the operations officer. He was really glad to see me because now he knew that he would not be extended on his tour here in Germany. He introduced me to his two assistants, Captain Castleberry and Lt. Pickett, for whom he had high praise. The next couple of days Captain Marcum briefed me on the current flying activities. We had two classified missions being accomplished by a squadron of high performance twin-engine aircraft commanded by Lt. Colonel LaPlante, and a squadron of B-17s commanded by Major Redman. I was surprised that we had B-17s there because I thought that what we had left after the war had been stored at Davis Mothan Air Base in Arizona. Since I had been a B-17 pilot during the war, Major Redman and I became close friends.

The big surprise came two weeks later when a new Post Engineer replacement arrived and it was my classmate from Engineering school, Captain Oscar Whitten. What a break for me since the one officer that I would depend upon to keep the airfield maintained in an excellent and safe flying condition was the Post Engineer. We got together for dinner and were pleased that we were here together at Furstenfeldbruck Air Base. Whitten said, "Ken, whatever you need to improve this airfield, you let me know and you will get it." And he lived up to his promise.

The news that we were getting from civilian newspapers, radio sources, and classified military correspondence became very negative about our remaining in Berlin. The last part of June the Soviets announced that the American sector of Berlin was now a part of the Soviet-controlled zone of Berlin. It was during this period that the Army Air Corp became the U.S. Air Force, equal to the Army and Navy within the military organization and command. This gave us pilots a terrific boost to our morale and prestige. President Truman announced that we Americans were staying in Berlin, which placed the responsibility for providing the Berliners with the food and supplies necessary for life upon the new Air Force.

With our air bases at Frankfurt and Wiesbaden loaded with transport aircraft flying supplies to Berlin, Furstenfeldbruck became the primary choice for being the home base for the 36th Jet Fighter Group coming to Europe from Panama that summer. Also Fursty (short for Furstenfeldbruck) would be used as an alternate for B-29s flying in and out of England and flights coming to Fursty for rest and recreation at the Garmisch R & R south of Munich. Now that I was the base operations officer, my primary task was to upgrade the single runway to handle four-engine aircraft and jet fighters. The west end of the runway had a short grass overrun of only 200 feet with heavy poles set in concrete connected together with heavy cables. If an aircraft landed long and into the overrun, it would crash into the poles and cause casualties and heavy damage to the aircraft. I called Captain Whitten to join me in eliminating this flight hazard, and he agreed that this had to be corrected immediately.

Captain Whitten called me two days later and said that the heavy poles had been removed but that the farmer who owned the land to be used to construct a 2,000-foot overrun was not too happy. I told Whitten to tell him that we won the war and had the right to utilize that land for a longer runway. Captain Whitten contacted me a few days later and said that he had obtained some money to give to the farmer who was now happy. The new runway extension was completed within two weeks—just in time, since a B-29 squadron was due in from England the coming weekend. That September I was to experience the most dangerous and critical event of my entire life.

The airlift to Berlin was in full operation come August, and since the transport groups didn't have enough pilots to meet the really tight schedule, we were to supply a pilot from our base to the 60th Troop Transport Group at Wiesbaden. My assistant, Captain Castleberry, was sent TDY for two weeks the first part of August. When he returned, my other assistant, Lt. Pickett, was sent the latter part of August and the first week in September. When he returned, I was put on orders to report to the transport group at Wiesbaden on the 9th of September for two weeks.

It was a gray, rainy day as I made my way from my room in the old Luftwaffe barracks to flight operations for the briefing of newly assigned pilots. When the operations officer completed a pitch on flight procedures in the air corridors through East Germany to Berlin, the intelligence officer added to the gloomy day with this statement: "The Russians say they will shoot down any aircraft that strays out of the Berlin air corridor, and that captured airlift pilots will be treated as spies. This is a serious threat to our pilots, and if you should find yourself down in the Soviet zone of East Germany, we cannot say that you should turn yourself in, or that you should try to escape. There is no published or firm policy on this, and it would be up to you or your crew as to what action you would want to take."

I was scheduled for my first flight to Berlin the night of September 10th. I was hoping that I would be on the daylight schedule so that I could visually orient myself with the air corridor and Templehof airfield. East Germany was really dark at night. Their cities didn't burn streetlights all night, and traffic on their roads was practically non existent. On the second night I did see the reflection of the moon on the Elbe River near Wittenberg. The third and fourth trips were made in bad weather, and we had to make GCA (ground controlled approach) at both Berlin and Wiesbaden. We never flew the same C-47, and we rarely had the same cargo as we had carried the previous run. One trip it would be flour, the next would be sacks of charcoal, etc. I had four trips under my belt when I reported to the flight line the evening of September 14th. The aircrew consisted of first Lt. Clarence Steber, an experienced C-47 pilot with the 60th Troop Carrier Group, and myself. Because of the critical weight factor, we could not afford the luxury of a flight engineer or a navigator. We reported at 1800 hours for the weather briefing. It was all bad with low visibility and ceiling at Templehof, and solid instruments en route. We received our aircraft assignment, signed for our parachutes, and sloshed along the flight line, squinting through rain-dampened eyes in search of our assigned aircraft.

When we finally spotted our C-47, I suffered a nauseous feeling in the visceral area. The faded pinkish tan on her metal skin exposed her as a relic from the North African desert campaign conducted by the British during the early part of World War II.

Since this C-47 was overdue for the graveyard, our exterior preflight inspection was very thorough. When we were satisfied that she was properly wired together, we kicked the tires and climbed aboard. When I saw the cargo that we were to carry to Berlin, I entertained the idea of going on sick call. The interior of the fuselage was jammed with fifty-give-gallon drums, and the strong pungent smell was unmistakably that of gasoline! I was not happy with our second mission the night before, since it was loaded with French wine for the French personnel in their Berlin area. And now I could not believe that we were hauling drums of gasoline! Visions of this old crate catching fire filled my head, and I immediately snaked my six-foot-three-inch frame into my parachute harness. It was the habit of many pilots to unbuckle the parachute harness and lay it on the floor near the rear exit. Steber followed this habit but did not unbuckle the harness. We crawled over the gasoline drums to the cockpit, and Steber slid into the left pilot's seat. He always flew left seat to Berlin and I flew left seat back to Wiesbaden.

We started the engines, received our clearance from the control tower, and taxied slowly over the dark, wet ramp to the runway for takeoff. This was going to be a long and tiring night because we were scheduled for two trips to Berlin. We performed a quick mag and power check, opened the side windows to siphon out the strong gasoline fumes, and eased the throttles into full open position and rolled down the runway. Immediately after becoming airborne, the runway lights were blotted out by the thick black soup. We climbed to our assigned altitude and entered the south air corridor to Berlin at the Fulda checkpoint. The thick murky night caused an eerie glow from our wing navigation lights, while the heavy rain hammered itself to pieces on the cockpit windshield. We left the side windows open because the stench of gasoline was strong, especially whenever we had rough air. We were two very tense pilots as we made our GCA approach two hours later to Templehof airdrome. We both relaxed and smiled when the runway lights sparkled onto our windshield. The German ramp crew off-loaded the gasoline drums within ten minutes, and five minutes later we rolled down the runway and lifted the nose of our pink gooney bird into the wet black night.

Our return flight to Wiesbaden was without incident, and as we cut our engines at the loading ramp, we were pleased to see a flatbed truck loaded with sacks of flour pull up to our cargo door. While the German crew loaded our fuselage with the flour, our own refueling crew serviced both our main and auxiliary tanks with enough gasoline for six hours of flying time. We were more relaxed for this second flight to Berlin with a less dangerous cargo and confidence in the capability of our pinkish tan gooney bird to fly.

We taxied out to the runway and received clearance to take off immediately, climb to 6,000 feet, and maintain an indicated airspeed of 140 mph. We were pleased to be assigned the lowest altitude in the air corridor, for we were carrying a heavier load than normal as shown on the weight and balance sheet for this load of flour. The takeoff roll was longer than usual and after becoming airborne, we had to increase the RPM in the climb to maintain the required climbing airspeed. We were in heavy rain, and it was leaking into the cockpit and onto our clothes. We leveled off at 6,000 feet and had to use increased manifold pressure and RPM to obtain the assigned airspeed for lateral separation from the aircraft behind us also at 6,000 feet. We reported over the Fulda beacon and turned to the magnetic heading of the south corridor into Berlin. We settled down for a wet and bumpy ride through the Soviet zone of East Germany. Lt. Steber was flying the first half of the route, and then I would fly the second half to Berlin. I closed my eyes and relaxed before my turn at the wheel.

About twenty minutes into East Germany and without any warning, both engines quit simultaneously! The sudden loss of the forward momentum of the aircraft caused me to lurch into the wheel, and thinking that Steber had pulled the power off the engines for some reason, I shouted, "What's wrong?"

"I don't know," he replied as he struggled to maintain control of the aircraft. I immediately checked the instrument panel. The fuel pressure for both engines was in the green, the outside temperature was twelve degrees above freezing, and all four gas tanks showed plenty of fuel. "Change to auxiliaries!" Steber shouted. We had taken off and flown this far on the main tanks. As I changed to the auxiliary tanks, I operated the wobble pump with my left hand to ensure adequate fuel pressure in the lines. With the roaring sound of the engines no longer in our ears, the staccato of the heavy rain on our metal fuselage was very loud and seemed determined to puncture the thin aluminum skin of the aircraft.

Steber was concentrating on keeping the aircraft from stalling while I turned the master switch off and then on, then the mag switches off and on with no response from the engines. "It's just some damn little thing if we could only find it," said Steber. "What is the highest terrain in this part of the corridor, Slaker?" asked Steber. Fortunately I had studied the elevation of the mountains in this corridor and told him 4,200 feet. The altimeter was showing a little less than 5,000 feet. Steber shouted, "Go back and open the cargo door and lay out my harness while I go through the emergency procedures again." I scurried over the bags of flour, my parachute harness getting caught several times on the tie down rods extending above the bags. I attempted to open the cargo door but it was jammed. I pulled the emergency release handle and the door was sucked off into the black void. I unbuckled Steber's backpack parachute and laid it on top of the flour sacks and crawled back into the cockpit. Steber had just completed emergency procedures without any response from the dead engines.

"We are going to have to bail out at 4,000 feet unless these engines start!" shouted Steber. In a final desperate effort, we switched to main tanks, turned the master switch off and then on, but the propellers continued to windmill. We were now at 4,000 feet and Steber shouted, "Let's go!" We scampered over the sacks of flour to the rear cargo door. I grabbed Steber's chute and held it for him while he slipped into the harness. He shouted, "For God's sake, Slaker, jump! We are going to crash any second!" I immediately turned and fell headfirst through the door opening. I pulled the ripcord as my feet left the floor of the fuselage, and the chute deployed at once. As I swung upwards towards the disappearing aircraft, I watched the doorway for Steber to bail, but he never appeared before I hit the ground very hard. A million lights flashed all around me and my last thought was, *This is it*. Then there was nothing.

Amnesia is a terrifying experience after you no longer suffer from it. The return of your memory is a sudden shock that can result in a variety of mental and physical reactions. Since I had no memory, lying on my back in a muddy field under a gray sky was accepted without any question. When my memory suddenly returned, I shook all over and vomited. I now realized what had happened because I had read about this very experience in medical journals. I had bailed out just before midnight and now the sky was gray and getting lighter; therefore, I had been unconscious for five hours. I tried to sit up and discovered that my back was injured and I didn't have any feeling in my legs. I discovered that I had cut my tongue with my teeth when I hit the ground because it was swollen and sore. My head ached and the back of my head was caked with dry blood. *My God! Steber!* I never saw him bail, and at that low an altitude, he must have perished in the crash. I raised my head and scanned the countryside for signs of a crashed aircraft, but there was nothing but brown potato fields and silence.

Then I heard it. A whine of an airplane that became a grinding roar as it passed over me, unseen in the gray sky. From the sound of the engines I recognized it as a C-47, undoubtedly an airlift gooney on its way to Berlin. Since I had bailed out about twenty minutes after we had crossed the border into the Soviet zone of East Germany, the American zone could not be more than fifty miles to the west. But if you could not walk, fifty miles would not be any closer than 500 miles if you could walk. The feeling in my legs was slowly returning and the words of the intelligence officer came back to me: *What action you take is up to you.* I decided that if I could walk, I would attempt to avoid capture and escape through Russia's Iron Curtain at the border. I knew that if the Russians took me into custody, I would have a very slim chance of being released, especially since I was privy to two classified missions operating out of Furstenfeldbruck Air Base. The Russians said that we pilots would be held as spies. Which means that you could end up at a work camp in Siberia never to be seen again, or to be shot. I decided that if I was going to die it would be by trying to escape and not by turning myself over to the Russians. The pain from my injuries became secondary as the will to survive became dominant within me.

At this time an ox cart occupied by an elderly couple creaked by on the dirt lane just fifty or sixty feet away. They did not see me, but I knew that as the day progressed someone would spot my white parachute strewn on the harvested potato field behind me. I could hear the far off sound of a truck and since time was now of the essence, I rolled over onto my stomach and with great effort, pulled myself up onto my knees. A sharp pain shot across my back and I became nauseated and vomited again. For a fleeting moment I thought of giving up, but after the pain stopped, I began to feel much stronger and that thought never entered my mind again.

My first task was to hide the parachute and then take cover for myself. Surely the Russians had found the crash by now and they would be searching for me, for in my mind, they had found Steber's body. Again with great determination, I was able to stand on my feet, but I could not lift the wet parachute. I then walked on the parachute for several minutes, pushing it into the mud. I could see some farm workers entering a potato field about a half-mile away and knew that I had to get moving immediately. I turned my brown leather flight jacket inside out to hide my name and pilot's wings embossed in silver on the outside of the jacket. I rubbed dirt to hide the shine on my shoes.

I walked slowly toward the dirt lane lying less than a hundred feet from me. The trees lining the lane had moss on one side, and remembering what I was taught as a boy scout when lost in the woods, now I knew that the other side of the tree was south, and that was the direction I took on the lane. The sky was still a solid gray with no sun visible.

I had not walked more than two kilometers when the lane intersected with a narrow and very worn black top road. I looked both ways and seeing no one, I turned towards the west and walked along the right side of the road next to a deep drainage ditch that was thick with weeds that could provide me with cover. My objective became to reach the woods covering the hills west of me. I planned on traveling through the woods as much as possible on my way to the border. I was about half the distance to the woods when I heard a vehicle approaching from in front of me, and I dropped quickly into the ditch. I lay flat in four inches of water until the vehicle had passed. My clothes were already soaking wet so the water in the ditch didn't make my clothes any wetter except that it was cold. It took extra effort to climb out of the ditch and get back onto my feet. I glanced back, saw that it had been a bus, and seeing no one on the road ahead, I continued walking on the road towards the woods.

My whole body loosened up as I continued to walk, and the woods were getting closer when I came to an intersection with a good secondary hard surfaced road. An old faded sign post on one of the corners had several directional sign boards, and the one on the top pointed west and spelled out: Eisenach 35K. It was here that the studying of an aeronautical map of the south air corridor a couple of days before paid off. I was elated because now I had a mental picture of exactly where I was in relation to the border. It was only eight kilometers from Eisenach to the Russian-American border. If I could successfully play this hide and seek game for another twenty-five miles, I could be at the border. The big problem would be escaping through the heavily mined and guarded Russian side of the border.

I was undecided at this point whether I should continue my walking on this secondary highway with more traffic or take to the potato fields. Since the fields had just been harvested, it would be rough walking in the soft dirt and mud. I decided to stay on this paved road and hopefully reach the woods sooner. I was about a hundred yards from the woods when I spotted a Soviet soldier on a bicycle pedaling towards me. I had no choice but to continue walking as nonchalantly as possible. I was on the right side of the road, and suddenly he veered from his right side and headed straight towards me! My heart was racing and it was obvious that he was not going to change his course to avoid hitting me. Then it dawned on me. He was going to force this German peasant off the road to remind him to show respect for the Russian military. I immediately stepped onto the dirt shoulder, and as he wheeled past, I received a cold stare. I watched him as he continued on down the highway and he never looked back. Little did he know that he had just ignored an American Air Force captain.

Within a few minutes I reached the woods and left the road for a much needed rest. My back was so painful that I was worried for fear that it might not last to the border. Although I had not slept for twenty-eight hours, I was not sleepy. Not having a knife, pistol, or any other item to defend myself with, I looked around for a club. This was no easy task because the East Germans kept the woods picked clean of fallen branches to use as firewood in their kitchens. I finally found a strong branch about three feet long that I could also use as a walking stick.

I made my way cautiously through the woods, methodically stopping and surveying the woods ahead before proceeding. As I passed by some smaller trees, I came face to face with a German walking in the opposite direction. How I missed seeing this individual in these very clean woods is not easy to explain.

I knew that I had to greet him. "Guten morgen," I said. He returned the greeting as we passed one another. My brain raced with many thoughts during the next few seconds, and I concluded that if he were suspicious of me, he would turn around and watch me. If he did so, I would have to confront him. I turned my head to see if he had continued on through the woods, and there he was, standing still and watching me. I did not know this man and could not let him report me to the Russian authorities. I gripped my club tightly and started to walk towards him. It is amazing how strong you can become when your life is threatened. The brain has sent this message to the adrenal glands, which produces and issues a complex serum during periods of danger which gives extra strength to the entire body. Here I was with all my injuries and being in danger, the glands had given me the strength I needed now. I had killed before and now I would be able to do it again to save my life.

I spoke to him in English even though I spoke conversational German. "I am an American pilot. Which way to Fulda?"

I was very tense and he stepped backwards and replied, "Fulda nein gut. Fulda Western Deutschland."

I pointed my finger at myself and replied, "For isch, Fulda gut." He looked at me very intently, and I was on the verge of letting him have a hard blow to his head when he raised both arms above his head and said in broken English, "Isch American prisoner of war," and very slowly lowered one hand to his shirt pocket and pulled out a package of official papers. He held them out to me and I took them and stepped back away from him. The top paper was a discharge from the prison of war camp at Kearney, Nebraska, with his photo on it.

"Americans good to me," he said and pulled up a trouser leg which had many scars on it and some festers. "American tank do this. I go to Deutsch hospital, doctor say must cut leg off and I say nein. Soon Americans capture us, see leg and American doctors make many operations to save leg."

I asked, "Why are you here in the woods?" He told me in broken English and German that he was looking for food for his wife and baby.

I told him that I had to get to the American Zone before the Soviets caught me, and he asked, "You Berlin Airlift pilot?"

"Ja," I replied and removed my flight jacket and pointed out the embossed silver wings. I also showed him my military ID.

"Kannath, isch help you escape but first must get potatoes for family."

"You must not help me," I said, explaining that it was very risky. He looked at me, grinned, tapped his forehead with his finger, and said, "Me not afraid, Soviet dumb." He further explained that I could not make it across the border without help, and that he knew the East Germans that would be able to get me across. Up until this time, I had faith in myself that I could do it, but looking into Rudolph's eyes, I knew that this man was being sincere and truthful. I held out my hand to him, and his face lit up with pride as he strongly shook my hand.

As we began walking, I insisted on following him. He smiled at me and asked, "Kannath no trust Rudolph?"

"Ja und nein," I replied.

Still smiling and with a shrug of his shoulders he said, "Mox Nix, kommen."

Twenty minutes later we were out of the woods and on a secondary road. Rudolph walked with a pronounced limp, but he was no weakling and as the day progressed, he had more stamina than I did. I did not inform him of my back injury but I did show him my swollen tongue so that he would understand my difficulty in talking. As we walked along this road, Rudolph pointed out Soviet cross-fire pits, well concealed from the air, even from the roadway itself. A couple of Soviet vehicles passed us, giving us no heed. About forty minutes after leaving the woods, Rudolph pointed to a typical German farmhouse and said that his comrade lived there. We would get some potatoes and then head for Eisenach.

As we approached the house, a man came out of a side door and greeted Rudolph. I was then introduced by Rudolph, who explained my circumstances. He motioned for us to come in and follow him into a large warm kitchen. An elderly woman was washing dishes, and she stopped and greeted Rudolph and stared at me. Rudolph's friend told her that I was an American airlift pilot that had bailed out of his aircraft. She became hysterical and screamed at the man that I could not stay there, for if the Soviets found that out, they both would go to prison. She shouted this several times and kept glaring at me. I knew that I could not trust this woman. The farmer ordered her to be quiet and to bring the American a cup of coffee. I was shown into the unheated parlor and asked to sit down. The old woman came in with a cup of warm coffee, glared at me, and departed. It didn't taste like coffee, but I was very thirsty and it relaxed me. I felt sleepy for the first time since I had bailed out and lay back on the couch. I dozed.

I jumped up in a panic! It was over a half hour since the old woman left, and I had not seen Rudolph or the farmer friend since. Fearing that I had been betrayed, I decided to get out of this house without going through the kitchen. I jumped up and went over to the window and started working at the latch when Rudolph and his friend came into the room. They were carrying a change of clothes for me and were not aware of why I was at the window. Rudolph explained to me that the flight jacket and flight coveralls were too conspicuous to get me safely to the border. I gave Rudolph's friend my jacket and coveralls, and he helped me put on the civilian clothes. They were worn but fit fairly well. I offered to pay him for the clothes but he politely refused. Now I no longer had any doubts about the loyalty of Rudolph. We bid his friend goodbye and took off down the road, me in my German peasant garb and Rudolph carrying a sack of potatoes.

After we had walked about two miles, Rudolph pointed to a smaller but well traveled road and said that we would take this road to the bahnhof. "Bahnhof!" I exclaimed. "Why do we want to go there?"

He replied, "To ride the eisenbahn to Eisenach."

I disagreed with this exposure of myself in public, but Rudolph brushed it aside with a grin and a pat on the shoulder. A farmer came by with a two wheeled cart pulled by oxen, and Rudolph asked if we could have a ride because I had hurt my back. Much to my surprise, he grunted approval and we bumped along several kilometers in his creaking cart. All around us were freshly ploughed potato fields being hand picked by elderly people. Their feet were wrapped in rags and strips of canvas and there were no young people there. Our driver indicated that he was turning off the road, and we thanked him as we disembarked.

We resumed our walking and I asked Rudolph about the missing young people. He told me that the Russians had taken the young men and women to work in the mines and factories in some of the other Eastern Bloc countries. I asked Rudolph that if the Russians were to see me at the bahnhof, would they not be suspicious since I was a young man? He asked me not to speak to anyone after we arrived at the bahnhof and if we were challenged, he would tell them that I was a mute. I looked at him in disbelief. I knew the Russians were looking for me and I felt that it was suicide to expose myself at the railroad passenger station. I spoke to Rudolph in a serious tone: "You are a brave man, much braver than I; therefore, I am leaving you now and will make my own way through the woods to the border."

He could see that I was very serious and beckoned me to sit beside him on the grass by the roadside. "Kannath, if we get to Eisenbach this afternoon, my friends can arrange for you to go through the border tonight. The longer it takes you to reach the border, the less chance you have of avoiding capture by the Russians." I weighed his words for a very long time and finally slapped him on the back and said, "We do it your way, Rudolph, let's go."

Rudolph knew this countryside very well, for as we walked he pointed out where Soviet technicians had installed new communication and rail lines. Some railroads had been removed, and we saw many cross fire emplacements that were very well concealed.

The only vehicular traffic was Russian military of various types. I became aware of the muffled staccato of machine gun fire and when I mentioned this to Rudolph, he shook his head and took me to a high rise along the roadway. We could see a very large training camp about a mile away, and Rudolph said it was the largest military camp in this area.

We returned to the main road just in time to witness an amusing incident. Several Russian vehicles had passed us traveling at a very high speed. Rudolph said that the Russian drivers were poorly trained and always drove with the gas pedal to the floor. We could hear a truck bellowing down upon us, and we left the road and concealed ourselves. The huge truck roared past us, and about 300 feet ahead of the truck was a ninety-degree turn to the right. The truck did not slow down. I watched in amazement as the driver started into the turn without easing up on the gas, and just as the truck started to turn over on its side, the driver straightened his front wheels and drove into the muddy potato field. As the truck ploughed to a stop, several Soviet soldiers jumped off the truck, all of them laughing and enjoying the thrill. They pushed the truck back onto the road, climbed aboard, and away it went at high speed. Rudolph looked at me, tapped his forehead, and said, "Soviet dumb."

The sun finally broke through the chilly clouds and provided the much-needed warmth as we arrived at the small railroad station. A village lay on the south side of the single track, as did the station house. We came in from the north on a dirt road that crossed the track at the station and became the main street of the village. There were about a dozen people around the station, some standing and some sitting. When I saw the three Soviet officers with sidearms standing on the west side of the road near the station, I had to fight the impulse to keep walking into the village and then run for the woods. My heart raced and Rudolph, noticing my tension, put his arm under mine and silently led me across the track to the east side of the road. As we went to sit down on the grass, everyone looked us over, including the Soviet officers. I noticed that my brown oxfords were very conspicuous, so I sat down Indian style in an effort to hide them. Rudolph got up and went into the station to purchase our inexpensive tickets. It was an eternity before he returned and handed me my ticket as he sat down beside me. Since I was supposedly a mute, we did not talk. It felt good to rest in the warm sun after eight hours of walking with my injured back.

I had not permitted myself to even glance at the Russian officers but I could feel their eyes on me. Finally I looked toward the village, then back to the bahnhof, and then nonchalantly to the Russian officers. I caught the full stare of the Russian major and my heart went into high gear. I broke eye contact with him and looked toward the village. I felt that it was only a matter of time before he would ask to see my papers and that would end my escape plan. I could feel his gaze upon me, and when I glanced his way to verify this feeling, I noticed he was not looking at my face, but at my hands lying in my lap. I looked down at my lap and realized what had his attention. There on my wrist, shining brightly in the sun, was my gold Bulova wristwatch! It was too late to remove it now; the officer had already spotted it. I dropped my left arm from view and the major said something to the other two officers. All three officers turned and looked at me. I started to get up and walk into the village when, with storybook timing, the passenger train rolled into the station. The Russian officers got up and rushed for the last two cars on the train, which were reserved for Soviet military personnel. Rudolph grabbed my arm and guided me towards the front car. We found an empty seat and I sat next to the window. Our passenger car was jammed by the time we pulled out, and I got nauseated from the stench of the body odor. I tried to open the window for fresh air but my back was too weak for the strength required to raise it. Rudolph and the passenger in front of us managed to get the window open a few inches and immediately I felt much better. With the passenger car swaying back and forth, and with no solid sleep for over thirty-two hours, I fell asleep.

Rudolph awakened me as the train entered the outskirts of Eisenach. He said that we would have to show our identification papers when we passed through the terminal gate. Since I didn't have the proper papers, he took my half of the train ticket. I was to precede him through the checkpoint, say nothing, keep walking straight through the gate and the terminal, continue out through the front door, and then turn right and keep walking. I was to play the mute game all the way and ignore any commands by the guard. I was to keep walking until Rudolph caught up with me and he warned, "Do not run, walk only." It was a very tense situation for me, and I was sure the guard would hear my heart pounding. I had no choice but to do as Rudolph said, for he had guts and knew how to handle these people.

I painfully struggled to my feet with visions of spending the rest of my life in a wheelchair if I didn't soon obtain medical treatment. We jostled our way into the bahnhof and to the gate where the guard was checking papers. I felt that it was to our advantage to be in the middle of the crowd, for certainly the guard could not abandon his post with people still pushing to get through it. As we squeezed through the narrow gate, I pointed my thumb back at Rudolph and didn't stop. The guard shouted loudly at me for the papers and then I heard Rudolph talking to the guard as I walked out of hearing range. I exited through the open door at the terminal entrance, turned right and with great restraint, continued to walk, not run. I never looked back but expected to feel a heavy Russian hand on my shoulder at any second. I had walked two long blocks when I heard Rudolph calling me. I looked back and saw him limping rapidly towards me, giving me the V for victory sign, and it was obvious he was enjoying our success.

We walked to the next corner where we waited a few minutes for a streetcar. As we seated ourselves in the streetcar, the conversation among the passengers ceased. I knew that they knew I was not one of them. They kept glancing at me, and I feared that not all of them could be trusted to not report seeing this American. Rudolph was right: the sooner I got to the border, I would less likely be captured. We got off the car early and walked several blocks to his apartment, just in case we were being followed. We entered the building, and I waited in a small hallway recess until Rudolph made sure that his apartment was clear.

His apartment was one large room: a wood stove at one end, an eating and living area in the center, and a bed at the other end. He introduced me to his wife, who was a petite, cheerful faced young woman who made me feel very welcome. They had a small baby girl not more than two years old. Rudolph told me that he was leaving to contact his friends and that I should lie down and get some much needed rest. I stretched out on their couch but I could not sleep. Every noise that I heard outside the apartment alarmed me, for surely the guard at the bahnhof had reported the mute without papers to his superior. I thought about Steber. He would not have had enough time to fasten his leg and chest straps and bail before the aircraft crashed. I did not know whether he had sent a MAYDAY signal while I was opening the back door or not. Of course they knew at Wiesbaden that we crashed since we failed to return.

The apartment door opened and Rudolph motioned for me to accompany him. We walked down a narrow street, stopped, turned around, and came part way back. We then took another narrow street and entered another apartment building. We took the stairs down into the basement and entered a dimly lit room where three men sat at a table. There were no introductions. The man in the center spoke fairly good English and asked me some questions about the airlift and German American feelings. He was silent for a minute, then threw a real surprise question to me: "When is General Eisenhower coming?"

"Coming where?" I asked.

"To Europe. He is the only American general capable of freeing East Germany from Russia." I told him that I did not know, but agreed with him that General Eisenhower was a great leader.

"We can help you in crossing the border to West Germany. Do you have any West German marks with you?" I told him that I had 500 marks. He held out his hand for them, explaining to me that he would need them to bribe the East German policeman guarding the border bridge. I opened my wallet and gave him 500 of the 700 marks that I had with me. I doubted he needed that much but I was not in a good bargaining position. Rudolph and I were instructed to cross the Werra River bridge located several kilometers west of Eisenach between 8:00 and 8:30 P.M. that evening. Due to the change of the Russian guards at that time, the only guard on the bridge would be the East German Volpo. This guard would be paid off and would not stop us from crossing on the bridge. Once across the river, we were to jump off the bridge onto the north bank and continue through the brush along the river until we came to a small clearing about 100 meters down the river. We were to wait there until midnight when two more persons would be joining us for the break across the border, which was mined and guarded. He stood up, and we all shook hands and Rudolph and I returned through two narrow streets leading to his apartment. I thought to myself that at least I didn't have to swim across the cold river.

Rudolph's wife had obtained some onions to go with the potatoes that Rudolph had received from his friend, and the smell of those two vegetables frying was tantalizing. There was neither bread nor side dishes, and realizing that this was all the food they had, I politely refused to eat. I saw the hurt look on his wife's face, and I knew they wanted to share what little they had to eat with me. I managed to eat a small helping with difficulty, due to my sore tongue. Immediately after the meal, Rudolph kissed his wife and daughter, and I shook her hand and thanked her, and we departed.

It was a beautiful evening with a strong warm sun shinning on the drab apartment buildings. We walked to a nearby corner and waited for a streetcar to take us to the outskirts of Eisenach. When we got off at the end of the line, Rudolph said that we would have to walk about five kilometers to the bridge. We took a secondary road lined with small houses, and there were many people strolling in the evening sun. I noticed the absence of young adults, although there was no shortage of children playing in the street. For the most part we were ignored and seemingly aroused no curiosity. We sighted the bridge, and seeing that we were early, we sat down along the road and relaxed. Then Rudolph surprised me when he said, "Kannath, I am going to cross the border into West Germany with you and I ask a favor." I told him that he should not do that, for he would be risking his life. He insisted and said that he wanted to get a new pair of shoes for himself and some milk for his baby. I told him that I could do that favor for him, but how was he going to get back to East Germany? He laughed and said that would be easy, for he would just show his papers and return on a commercial bus. No problem getting in, he said, but a very tough problem getting out!

At five minutes to eight, we started walking towards the bridge about 300 yards away. As we got closer, we could see the East German policeman walking guard duty on the bridge. To our dismay, we could also see standing on the far side of the bridge, a Russian sentry. We concealed ourselves at the side of the road and waited. A few minutes later we saw a squad of Russian soldiers approaching the bridge from the west. They halted, and the Russian sentry at the end of the bridge joined them. The squad then marched across the bridge, passed in front of us, and marched out of sight up a narrow road to the left and south of us. We then left our hiding place and walked towards the bridge. As we started across the bridge, the policeman spotted us and walked toward us. I got the feeling that he was going to challenge us and that I had been suckered out of 500 West German marks. If he did stop us, I would use the 200 marks that I had left in an attempt to bribe him. He walked straight towards us and was looking directly at our eyes while my heart was trying to escape from my chest. Suddenly, when he was only six feet from us, he stopped and turned his back to us. We walked right past him to the far end of the bridge.

We dropped into the thick brush along the river and struggled through the trees until we broke into a small clearing, well concealed from the bridge. We sat down, remained silent, and rested. Before very long we heard a rustling in the bushes and out came a young man accompanied by a young *fraulein*. Rudolph asked them if they were escaping across the border with us and they replied in the affirmative. The young man introduced the girl and himself and we shook hands. He had served in the German Army during the war and the girl was eighteen years old, well dressed, and very attractive. He said that the girl was from an East German family of moderate means and that they wanted her out of East Germany. He had been hired to help her get through the border.

We crawled up the bank and, looking through the bushes, could see across the fertile valley to a long hill which was the border to West Germany. Between us and the hill were cabbage fields, Russian sentry boxes to our right and left, mine fields with barbed wire fencing, and to the north at the base of the hill, the main rail connection between East and West Germany. Since it was now dusk, we could see a strong light shining at the top of the hill which was our destination—the West German Police border station. So near, yet so many dangerous obstacles between it and ourselves. Many East Germans had been killed trying to get through these obstacles to the top of that hill.

We decided that when the time came to attempt the border crossing, Rudolph would go first, then me, then the girl, and finally the young ex soldier bringing up the rear. Darkness came with a clear sky and a three-quarter moon shining brightly. This was a bad situation because we needed total darkness for cover from the sentries. The floodlights on the sentry booths came on, making it impossible to see either the booths or the guards. Lights then came on at the border rail switching station, and there was some activity although trains from West Germany were being denied entrance. After some quiet discussion, it was decided that we would crawl single file through the cabbage field and pass between the two sentry booths. Then when Rudolph gave the word, we would run through the barbed wire area and across the railroad tracks, climb the hill to the closed autobahn, and then run west on the highway to the West German Police booth. We knew that we would have to have lots of luck to avoid the mines and get through the barbed wire without the border guards seeing or hearing us and using their machine guns.

Our first lucky break came about 11:00 P.M. when the sky clouded over and obscured the bright moon. Rudolph gave the word and we quietly followed him, crawling over the bank into the cabbage field. We were flat on our stomachs and my heart was pounding so loudly that I knew it could be heard several feet away. The cabbage plants did give us cover but it was difficult not to make any noise due to the crackling of the stiff leaves. We dared not raise our heads above the cabbage heads because the sentries would see us. We had been warned at the afternoon meeting that these sentries would shoot first at the slightest noise and then investigate. It was a very slow process: crawl three feet, stop and listen, crawl three feet, stop and listen. It seemed like hours had passed. I asked myself, *What will you do if they start shooting at you? Run back to the river clearing? Make a break for the hill? What if Rudolph is blown up by a mine? Is it every man for himself?* I decided that if we were discovered, I would make a dash for the hill and it would be every man for himself. I would rather die trying to escape than suffer a slow death in a Siberian Russian work camp.

My frantic thoughts were disrupted by a sudden darkness as we crawled out of the floodlight area. I bumped into Rudolph, who had stopped in the cabbage row and was waiting for us to catch up to him. When the girl touched my foot, I tapped Rudolph and we continued on into the dark area. It was very dark but suddenly I knew that we were at the edge of the cabbage field and parallel to the rear of the guard booth. Now I could see the Russian sentry, sitting at the corner of the booth with an automatic weapon in his hands. Rudolph stopped, waited until we four were together, and whispered tensely, "Jetzt!" (Run!).

My legs were like lead from our long crawl, and it seemed like a very long time before I got them into high gear. We were running in total darkness and could not see what lay ahead of us. I ran into something, stumbled, but recovered my stride and knew that I was in the barbed wire and mined area. My momentum got me through the first wire fence but as I struggled to get through the next one, I heard shouting behind us and then the sound of automatic gunfire. Finally breaking clear of the barbed wire, I raced for the railroad tracks at the bottom of the hill with bright red tracers bouncing all around me. I ran across the tracks and bumped into Rudolph just as we started to climb the hill. The Russian guard was now raking the ridge with his machine gun and I could see the tracers bouncing off the rocks. I could not believe that I had not been hit since for every tracer there are three to five unseen metal bullets. The pain in my back was agonizing, and I had sharp pains in my legs from cuts from the barbed wire. My philosophy during this border crossing was every man for himself. What happened next was to haunt me many times the rest of my life for having made such a selfish decision. I had difficulty in climbing up the hill and Rudolph, the young man, and the girl were up ahead of me when my back gave out and I rolled back down the hill to the tracks. The girl shouted, "The captain has fallen!" All three stumbled back down the ridge, formed a chain, and pulled me up to the top of the hill, all the time with machine gun tracers bouncing all around us. It was a miracle that not one of us was injured. I felt ashamed of myself with the decision I had made during this attempt to escape. These three East Germans, at risk of great harm to themselves, had saved my life. I would have been shot or captured, and that would have been the end of Captain Slaker. I have wondered if my Guardian Angel provided these three companions with the motivation to save me.

When we got to the top of the hill, the feeling returned to my back and we stumbled through the trees, and there was the wide concrete autobahn. The four of us scrambled onto this beautiful ribbon of concrete, now closed to traffic, and we could see the light from the West German guard booth about 200 meters down the autobahn. Pain from my injuries did not hinder me from running the fastest I had ever ran in my life, and I was the first to arrive at the German booth on the west side of the border. I told the guard that I was an American pilot and showed him my military ID card. He immediately called his superior and relayed the information that I had given to him. The guard then informed me that the western border guards had been alerted of an air crash in the Soviet zone—that one pilot had been taken into custody, and that the other pilot had perished in the crash. This confirmed my thinking that Steber had perished in the crash and the Russians were confident they would capture me before I could escape through their Iron Curtain.

It was not more than five minutes when the phone rang and the guard motioned that it was for me. The caller identified himself as a colonel in the Counter-Intelligence Department located at Hersfeld. He said that he would be there to pick me up in about twenty minutes and that I was not to talk to anyone about my escape. The guard then told me that if the young man and girl were still there when the American authorities arrived, that they would be taken into custody and turned over to the Russian officials. I walked over to my three companions, informed them of this news, and gave the girl and the young man each fifty West German marks to help them get to their destination. We shook hands and they disappeared into the darkness.

Seeing that Rudolph was staying with me, the guard asked to see his identification papers. To Rudolph's and my dismay, he discovered that he had lost his papers during our dash through the Iron Curtain obstacles. If the Soviets found his papers in the cabbage patch, minefield, or the hillside, it was impossible for him to return because he would most surely go to jail. Now he was in real trouble, and I would have to do my best to keep the American officials from returning him to the Russian authorities. I had seen his papers before he lost them and I knew who he was.

The colonel arrived in thirty minutes, and after introductions, he inquired as to my injuries. I explained my bailout injuries and the cuts on my legs from the barbed wire. He placed a call to his office and left instructions to have a doctor there when we arrived. Rudolph sat up front with the staff car driver, and during our drive to Hersfeld I gave the colonel a brief résumé of what I had experienced since my bailout. About 1:30 A.M., we arrived at his office which was located on the first floor of a very large German house. The colonel said he would see that Rudolph received his new shoes and milk for his child if he still wanted to return to the Russian zone. He instructed the driver to take Rudolph to the compound. That was the last time I was to see Rudolph for almost a month.

We entered the colonel's office and an Army doctor was waiting there to examine me. It was his finding that my back was not broken but that the spinal discs were undoubtedly injured. My other cuts and bruises would heal themselves. At this time the phone rang and the colonel answered it and said, "Yes, that is correct. No, I can't give you any details." He hung up the phone and was very indignant. "That was the damn

LINCOLN STAR

LINCOLN, NEB., WEDNESDAY, SEPTEMBER 15, 1948

Telephone 2-1234 — Fire 2-2222

HOME EDITION

FIVE CENTS

U.S. Pilot Walks Through Russ Zone's Iron Curtain

...After Bailing Out Of Ailing Plane On Berlin Lift

Slaker Ignored By Russ

Formerly Stationed At Air Base Here;

This is a sample of the publicity that I was given from a canned release by the USAFE Headquarters in Germany. I was not permitted to be interviewed by either the American or international news reporters. The details of my escape through the Russian Iron Curtain were classified for forty years.

Associated Press at Frankfurt saying that they had the information that an American pilot had just escaped across the border near Hersfeld and wanted to know if it was true. How in hell did they get the word so fast? Someone paid for that tip and I'm going to find out who."

The colonel asked if I was hungry, and I said no but that I was physically exhausted and having difficulty staying awake. He told me that the maid had a hot bath and a clean bed waiting for me. The maid, an attractive white Russian, escorted me to the bathroom where I discarded my German clothes and eased myself into a tub of relaxing hot water. I dozed off and do not remember her washing or drying me or dressing the cuts on my legs. I vaguely remember being helped into bed, and then I blacked out.

The colonel awakened me at 8:30 A.M. with an apology that it was his personal desire that I not be disturbed; however, the commanding general of the Berlin Airlift, General Tunner, wanted me in Wiesbaden this morning. My body was as stiff as concrete when I tried to get out of that wonderful bed. I put on an Army flying suit that the colonel provided for me and then had absolutely the best breakfast of my life. I thanked him for his outstanding hospitality, and his staff car whisked me to the Army airstrip where an Army pilot was waiting to fly me to Wiesbaden in an L-5 type aircraft. The ceiling and visibility were almost non existent, so the pilot flew about fifty feet above the autobahn to Frankfurt, where the pilot then followed the Main River to the Constabulary airstrip just outside of Wiesbaden.

As I untangled my sore body out of the L-5, I was shocked to see a score of newsmen and cameramen rushing towards me. It was a mystery as to how they knew that I was arriving at this time at this small airstrip in the boondocks. Out of this group came an Air Force lieutenant colonel who said that I was not to say anything to the news people until it was approved by the Air Force. I thanked the Army pilot for the flight and accompanied the colonel to a waiting staff car. The reporters had gathered around the staff car and fired questions at me faster than I could answer them. As we were about to enter the staff car, one reporter asked, "Can you give us one statement please?"

"Yes, I can," and as my escort squeezed my arm I said, "We Americans don't really appreciate our freedom until we no longer have it."

The newsmen tailed us as we made our way into Wiesbaden. I asked my escorting officer if Lt. Steber had been killed in the crash of our aircraft. He informed me that the Russians had notified our Potsdam Liaison Group that one of the pilots was injured and in an East German hospital, and that the other pilot was dead! I shuddered as I realized that it was me that they had reported dead! Now I knew that Steber was still alive but in the hospital. This fact made my escape from the Soviet zone absolutely necessary, for if they had seized me after reporting me dead, I would never have been released.

"You have twenty minutes to brief General Tunner on the highlights of your experience from takeoff at Wiesbaden to your escape across the border." These were the words of his executive officer upon my arrival at airlift headquarters. General Tunner

Captain Kenneth Slaker, American Air lift pilot in Germany, had to bail out over Russian area yesterday when his supply plane developed engine trouble. He was knocked unconscious when he landed and wrenched his back. Nevertheless, he cooly walked through and out of the Soviet zone as if he owned it. He exchanged friendly geetings with Russian soldiers and went right on into the American zone where he met some M.P.'s who took him to Air Force Headquarters. And so, tonight, to Captai Slaker, of the United States Air Forces, for typical American resourcesfulness and pluck, the Kelvinator tribute...I thank you.

To Captain Kenneth Slaker, with the Compliments and admiration of Edwin G. Hill

Sept. 15, 1948.

Congratulations letter from Edwin G. Hill, 15 Septmeber 1948.

greeted me cordially, and after some forty minutes of discussion, introduced me to Colonel Red Foreman, who was to be my mouthpiece to the news people the next few days. He was not too happy about this assignment but he was a good buffer between me and the very persistent reporters. The rest of the day I spent in the military hospital for examination and treatment of my injuries. Late that afternoon I was released by the medics, and Colonel Foreman's staff car driver returned us to airlift headquarters. I was escorted to a room where standing there to meet me, was a very great surprise: Lt. Steber! Only a reporter/photographer from the *Stars and Stripes* was permitted to witness our reunion. Our photo appeared on the front page of the *Stars and Stripes* the next day with a trumped up story that I had walked out of the Soviet zone without any problem! This story was released to the Associated Press and was printed in newspapers throughout the United States. The true story was classified and not released for forty years for security reasons and to protect the East Germans who had assisted me in my escape.

Lt. Steber and I reported to USAFE Intelligence the next morning for debriefing. I related my experience as stated above. Lt. Steber said that just after I had bailed, the engines started up and he made his way back to the cockpit. He flew the aircraft about four minutes and transmitted MAYDAY on the radio emergency channel. The engines quit again and he made his way back to the cargo door and bailed out. His parachute opened just before he hit the ground and he was injured. He was taken by the Russian authorities to the local Soviet headquarters, where he was interrogated. He was then taken to an East German hospital where he was treated for his injuries. He was bedded in a solitary room on the first floor with a Soviet guard outside his door. The next morning two American members of the Potsdam Liaison Committee from Berlin arrived to visit the hospital. They had diplomatic standing and were immediately shown to Lt. Steber's room. Once inside, they asked Steber if he could make it out of the room's window. He replied that he could and they went out the window and drove off in their diplomatic vehicle.

Before they arrived in East Berlin, they put Steber in the trunk and with their diplomatic passes, drove through the guarded gate and took him to Templehof airfield. There, Steber caught a ride in an airlift C-47 to Wiesbaden, arriving there that afternoon where Steber and I were reunited in USAFE Headquarters.

After the debriefing, Lt. Steber and I were not permitted to visit with one another. This was to prevent any collusion on our part as to events leading up to the crash. This was ordered by the president of the accident board which we appeared before a couple of days later. We testified separately and a board member told me later that our testimony was identical. The accident board's finding was that the probable cause of the double engine failure was a shorting out of the master switch due to the leakage of water from the storm into the switching box.

I could see that Colonel Foreman was getting bored being with me every time I appeared in public. The newsmen were still trying to talk to me and get the real story of my escape. I went to Air Force Intelligence and told an officer there of my problem with the Press reporters. He said that the newsmen were in contact with the western border guards and promised them American cigarettes and West German marks whenever there was an incident in their area of the border. There was no doubt that the border guard I approached witnessed the gunfire from the Soviet guards and called the Associated Press reporter. I then told the officer about the call the colonel got from the Associated Press reporter just an hour after my escape, which had really upset him. So the reporters knew that our press release was a cover up.

The Intelligence officer suggested that I get permission to go to the Rest and Recreation at Garmisch under an assumed name for several days, which would get the newsmen off my back. Headquarters approved this proposal and I left Wiesbaden for Garmisch. This was good for me since it gave me some rest and let my injuries heal. From there I returned to my office at Furstenfeldbruck Air Base. I spent several days catching up, for we now had the jet fighter group on the far side of the airfield with Colonel Zemke, a World War II Ace, in command. We also had several B-29s every weekend so that their crews could enjoy R & R at Garmisch.

One of the first things that I did was to call the Army CID (Central Intelligence Division) at Hersfeld asking about Rudolph. They would not give me any information at all. This really disturbed me because I had promised to help him. I waited one week and then called the Army again. They again said they didn't have any information on Rudolph that they could give me. I knew the commander at Wiesbaden, Colonel Sig. R. Young, whom I had worked for in 1944. He knew about my escape and I told him about the Army refusing to tell me what happened to Rudolph, who had helped me to escape.

Colonel Young was also curious as to why the Army would not give me any information on Rudolph. He told me that he would see what he could do to get some information from the Army. A few days later he called me and asked me if I could be in his office tomorrow at 1:00 P.M. because the Army was ordered to deliver Rudolph to him at that time. Colonel Young said that he had to request help from Air Force Headquarters in the Pentagon. I told Colonel Young that I would be there tomorrow.

I flew up to Wiesbaden and was in Colonel Young's office at 12:45. Exactly at 1:00 P.M., two Army military police escorted Rudolph into Colonel Young's office. They gave a paper that Colonel Young had to sign and then they saluted and departed. Rudolph and I rushed together and embraced and shook hands. I stepped back and asked Rudolph what had happened with him during this time. He had tears in his eyes and he said, "Kannath, Army CID beat me with rubber hoses! They wanted me to confess that I was a communist and I am not."

I was stunned! I looked at Colonel Young, who nodded his head in the affirmative. I could not believe that American military would do that! I thought that we Americans were the good guys. How could they do that to a German citizen who had put his life on the line by helping this American pilot escape from the Russians? Colonel Young then said, "Slaker, the Air Force is going to take good care of Rudolph for what he did for one of our pilots." Colonel Young then excused himself and left the office. Rudolph and I visited and Rudolph told me in detail of the bad treatment that he had received, which I have never forgotten. Now I knew why the complete details of my escape were classified for forty years.

When the Air Force contacted the city officials of Wiesbaden and explained to them Rudolph's help in getting an airlift pilot through the Iron Curtain, they really cooperated. He was given a job with the German Postal Service and an apartment for him and his wife and baby, after which the Air Force or some agency got them out of the Soviet zone. Many of my pilot friends, including my brother who later was flying C-45s out of Frankfurt in the airlift, gave clothing, food, and even West marks in appreciation of his help to an airlift pilot. Due to Air Force assignments, I was not able to see Rudolph until 1961. We did stay in touch via letters.

Rudolph Schnabel, the East German from Eisenach, who not only helped me mentally and physically to contact the right people who advised me how to possibly escape from the Russian Zone, but to my surprise, decided to accompany me in my dangerous effort to survive the obstacles creating the Iron Curtain. I would not have been successful without the help of this brave man. He saved my life.

Chapter 8
CLASSIFIED MISSION WITH CHARLES LINDBERGH

The work that Captain Whitten and I had accomplished on removing the huge security poles at the end of the runway paid off in late September. After a busy day I retired early and was awakened by a phone call from my airdrome officer to report that a B-29, arriving from England, had landed halfway down the runway and used the entire length of the grass overrun. It had stopped a few feet short of our new security fence with no injuries to the crew or damage to the B-29. I asked him if field maintenance had been notified and he replied that they had and were now at the aircraft preparing to tow it to the parking ramp. I thanked him for doing his job and went back to sleep. By the time I had my breakfast at the club and got to my office, the B-29 crew had already left for their R & R at Garmisch.

Early in October the housing officer called me that on base housing was now available for my family. I called Glenna and asked if she wanted to join me in Germany and she agreed. Military orders were published authorizing her and the baby military air to Frankfurt. I met her at the Rhine Main airfield and drove the repaired autobahn to Furstenfeldbruck. Our quarters were assigned a maid by name of Erika with a young daughter named Crystal. Erika's husband was killed during the war with Russia, and she was having a rough time making ends meet. Since I didn't smoke I gave her my cigarette ration to sell at the black market in Munich, and then she would reimburse me for what they cost me at the base exchange.

I was happy to see that my daughter's bent legs had been straightened by the braces applied to her legs at birth. She was a very active and cute baby at six months. Erika's daughter Crystal enjoyed taking care of our daughter, and we showed our appreciation by giving Crystal American clothes and candy for Christmas. After the holidays we noticed a growth on one of Pamela's legs, and the doctor at our base hospital didn't like the looks of it and made an appointment for Pamela at the Allied hospital in Munich. The laboratory made a biopsy and said that it was cancer. She was operated on, and the growth that was removed was the size of an olive. The surgeon said that Pamela had been born with that growth. She received a thorough examination and no other growths were found. After her leg healed, only a small scar was visible and she has never had another growth.

Captain Davis, a B-17 pilot with the classified unit became a good friend when he learned that I had flown B-17s in combat. He had to make a trip to Tripoli and invited me to go along. I accepted his invitation, and about one hour out of Tripoli, he put me in the pilot's seat and I made the landing. When we departed the next day, he also had me make the takeoff. What a thrill to be flying the B-17 again after a lapse of four long years. *Thank you, Captain Davis.*

Just a couple of weeks later, I was on my way to Tripoli again by way of Istres, France. I had to pick up personnel there and take them to Tripoli. I had the wing commander's C-47 and it was an enjoyable flight of five hours. I spent all next day in the city sightseeing, dining, and shopping. I bargained with one Arab that had very attractive handmade wool rugs and bought one. A couple of my pilot passengers also purchased rugs, about four by eight feet in size. The next day on the flight back to Germany, the passengers spread their rugs on the passageway floor and laid down on them to rest. About an hour from our air base all hell broke loose in the cabin. The rugs were full of fleas, which had crawled into the clothing of those lying on the rugs. They were biting and the passengers were taking their clothes off and trying to shake the fleas out of the clothing. None of us took these rugs to our quarters; we hung them outside.

At the end of February, Glenna said she had bad news for us: she was pregnant. She also let me know that she would not have the baby in Germany, and the sooner she could leave for the States, the better for all four of us. I told her we had a good hospital in Munich that would not cost us any money and that she could not go back to Lincoln at government expense until the end of my tour in Germany. Also, she would not get the money for a commercial flight back home from me, and no way would I let her take Pamela with her. I suggested that she go talk to the base legal officer if she didn't believe me. From that time on, she would not participate in any of the base social functions.

After my return from my escape adventure, I averaged two or three flights a month to USAFE Headquarters in Wiesbaden on business. I would call Peggy, the girl whom I had met on the troopship—to see if she was available for lunch. We enjoyed one another's company, and when Glenna went into her usual rotten mood, I would stay in Wiesbaden overnight so that I could have dinner with Peggy. Like me, she liked to dance and when I told her Glenna didn't dance, we really kicked up our heels at the Press club. We became very close platonic friends.

Late one afternoon I received a telephone call from Colonel Croswaite, the wing commander, asking me to come to his office as soon as possible because he had a very important subject to discuss with me. I immediately had my staff car driver take me to headquarters. I entered the colonel's office, saluted, and he asked me to sit down. He told me that I was to report to him at 9:00 A.M. the next morning to work with another individual on a classified mission. The individual I would be working with selected me out of three officers whose résumés were given to him. I was not to tell a single person—not even my wife—where or what I would be doing or whom I was working with on this classified mission.

The next morning I was in Colonel Croswaite's office at 8:45 A.M. At exactly 9:00 A.M., the provost marshall entered the office escorting a tall, slender man, and looking at him I could not believe my eyes. It was Charles Lindbergh! The provost marshall introduced Lindbergh to the colonel and me and departed. It was such a great surprise that I had to keep repeating to myself that it was Charles Lindbergh. We three shook hands and sat down. I was so excited that I had finally met this famous aviator whom I had always held in high esteem. He then briefed the colonel and me on his mission that no one else was to know about. The colonel then asked me to take Charles Lindbergh to the VIP quarters, where both of us were to occupy during his stay here at Furstenfeldbruck.

We spent a lot of hours on his mission, mostly during the dark hours, to obtain the information and results that his assignment required. We got along fine together and agreed on most of the issues that we discussed while resting in the VIP quarters. He didn't smoke and appreciated that I was a non-smoker. Neither one of us consumed alcoholic drinks, and he told me that he had read about my walking through the Iron Curtain. Since I knew that he had a high security clearance, I gave him some of the real facts about my escape. The morning after he had completed his mission, the colonel and I walked him to the staff car and Lindbergh put his hands on my shoulders and thanked me, and we shook hands. It was a letdown to see him drive away with the provost marshall. I have never told anyone what the mission was, for it was Lindbergh's, not mine. He may have mentioned it in his personal papers. Spending this time with Charles Lindbergh was one of the highlights of my career as an Air Force pilot.

The spring and summer of 1949 was a busy one. I made two flights to London, England to take our wing commander there for business meetings at the American embassy. There were also two long and very interesting trips to Ankara, Turkey to pick up our pilots there who had delivered American aircraft to the Turkish Air Force. On one of my business flights to Wiesbaden, I called Peggy and we went to the Press club for dinner and dancing. After a good American dinner, we were dancing and our feet got entangled. We fell onto the dance floor with me on top of her. We got to laughing so hard that we could not get up. The guests got to laughing at us and clapping their hands, thinking that we had been drinking, even though we had not. A couple of the Press people helped us up, and we walked the many blocks to her women's residence. Men were not permitted in the building after 11:00 P.M., so we kissed goodnight and I took a taxi to the air base.

One week later I had to fly to Wiesbaden for business at USAFE Headquarters, and operations said that personnel had a message for me. I went to the personnel office and they said that the USAFE Chaplain wanted to see me, and they had no idea why.

He said, "Captain, I am going to ask you some personal questions about you and Peggy Smith. You may think it is none on my business but I pray you will understand my concern. I have been informed that you are dating Peggy quite frequently?"

I acknowledged that I had been dating her once or twice a month since I had met her on the boat coming here in June of last year. He then asked if I were married, and I said yes I was but it was not a happy one and was going to end up in divorce. He then asked if I were a Catholic, and I said no, that I had been raised in the Lutheran branch of Christianity.

He then said, "Peggy is a devout and good Catholic girl, and you are a distraction to the life she deserves in the Catholic faith. I am asking you not to date or keep company with her anymore. If you are really fond of this girl, you will abide by my request. If you continue to see her, then I can assure you it will jeopardize your Air Force career." I got up and, since he had a field grade officer's uniform on, I saluted and walked out.

I was really shaken by his threat to my career and went to the officers' lounge to sit and do some thinking. Since I was not a Catholic and married, I could understand his concern about Peggy; however, his negative remark about my career proved that he was more a Catholic priest than an Air Force chaplain. I had to let Peggy know why we could not see one another effective this very day. I contacted her on the phone and told her about my visit to her priest. She was very upset and said that she had told the priest about dating me at confession but thought that anything said to the priest at confession was confidential. It was a very sad time for me to have to say goodbye to a wonderful girlfriend, and I wished her a good and happy life.

Flying back to Fursty, I reviewed my experience with Christian brotherly love since I had become a pilot. There was no brotherly love shown to me by the Mormon family, no endearment from the Seventh Day Adventist that I had married, and none from a Catholic priest since I was not a Catholic. These experiences raised a question in my mind about the validity of the various Christian branches, and I decided to begin doing my own research in theology. I had always believed that the church was there for the parishioners, but we had become slaves to the church. This did not shake my strong belief in God and my Guardian Angel.

Late in August Glenna started having contractions, and I drove her to the hospital in Munich. There she gave birth to my first son, Jeffrey Scott. She was not happy with Jeffrey because she wanted another girl. The wife of our headquarters squadron commander had a baby the same day as Glenna and in the same hospital. Two weeks later she called me at the office and asked if I could have lunch with her at the officers' club because she needed to talk to me. I of course agreed and met her at noon. She was a very likeable woman and a very loyal Air Force wife. She asked that I never tell Glenna what she was going to discuss with me. She said that after Glenna had delivered the baby boy, the nurse brought Glenna back into the maternity ward and put her in the bed next to her. After the baby had been cleaned of afterbirth, the nurse brought the baby to Glenna's bedside and held it out to Glenna and said, "Here is your baby boy."

Glenna did not extend her arms and said to the nurse, "Take it away. I don't want to see it." The nurse was shocked and took the baby boy away.

The commander's wife then said to me, "Ken, I had to tell you this for as you know, Glenna has not joined any of the wives' functions, is not friendly with any one of us, and lets it be known that she does not like the Air Force. We all know that you two are not in love and several of we Air Force couples have discussed your situation and agree that you should divorce this woman. She will ruin your career and that would be a shame, for we all respect and admire you as a regular officer in the Air Force."

I was not surprised by what she told me about Glenna and told her that I was planning on filing for a divorce when I returned to the States. I thanked her for talking with me and told her that Glenna would never know about our meeting. When I picked Glenna and the baby up at the hospital, she never smiled or said a word on the way back to our quarters. Our maid ended up taking care of Jeffrey, washing him, changing diapers, etc. Since there was really no home life for me, I spent my spare time at the 4P officers' club on base or in Munich.

One evening I decided to drive into Munich to the officers' club for dinner. As I walked through the lounge I spotted Colonel Zemke, the 36th Fighter Group Commander, sitting at a table with three pilots from Fursty and a civilian. One of these pilots was Lt. Eastham, a base pilot that was one of the most reliable pilots and never turned me down when I was in need of a pilot. Colonel Zemke spotted me and asked me to join them, which I did. Zemke introduced me to the civilian, who was a news reporter from New York. The discussion was all about flying, and the news reporter asked Colonel Zemke if since we now had the F-80 fighter jets, we had a much stronger defense against the Russian Air Force. Zemke's reply was, "Hell no, we could not fight our way out of a paper bag."

The news reporter then asked, "Colonel Zemke, can I quote you?" We pilots looked at each other in surprise as Colonel Zemke said, "Hell yes."

In a few days an article appeared in the New York paper quoting Colonel Zemke. In a couple of days, as the base operations officer, I received a triple X flight plan that was arriving in Furstenfeldbruck with General Vandenberg, Chief of Staff of the Air Force, with the following message: Upon his arrival, he wanted to meet with the wing commander and Colonel Zemke in the base operations office. I immediately notified colonels Croswaite and Zemke. I also alerted our transient alert crew and asked the janitor to clean my office, and the snack bar to have coffee and rolls available.

Fortunately the weather was good when the general arrived, and I walked out on the ramp with the colonels to greet the general when he disembarked from the aircraft. Greetings were short and we escorted the general to my office. After they were seated,

I left the office and closed the door and went to my dispatcher's room to greet the general's pilot. He asked me to obtain a clearance for Tripoli within the hour. Our refueling crew was already servicing the aircraft, and within ten minutes we had his international clearance to Tripoli.

Within the half hour the three came out of the office and walked to the aircraft. Colonels Croswaite and Zemke remained standing on the ramp, rendering a salute as the aircraft started to taxi out to the runway. Colonel Croswaite went back to his office, and Colonel Zemke came back to my office and asked me and my assistant, Captain Castleberry, to meet him at the officers' club and he would brief us on the ass chewing he had just received. He briefed us in detail, but the most disturbing item was that Vandenberg told him he would have a letter placed in his personnel file that he was never to be promoted to general. I was really disappointed to hear that, for Colonel Zemke was the kind of pilot we needed if we went to war.

A few years later I had business at the Pentagon and stopped in to see Colonel Zemke, who was assigned there. I was upset to see that he was still a colonel and asked him if his current boss, a general officer, could get him promoted. He said the general had already tried that and was told that General Vandenberg's letter could never be overturned. Colonel Zemke retired as a full colonel in his home state of Montana. I still think that letter should have had just a one-time pass over for promotion, for Colonel Zemke told the truth about our F-80s, and it was not the liquor talking.

The Berlin Airlift had become history in October 1949 when I received a call from wing headquarters that Colonel Croswaite wanted to see me. I walked into his office, saluted, and he asked me to sit down. He said, "Captain Slaker, I am going to recommend that you do something which I have never done to any subordinate in my entire career." He had just received a message from the USAFE Personnel office that the Russians had submitted a request to the U.S. State Department that Captain Kenneth Waverly Slaker be returned to Russia to be tried as a spy in accordance with the Potsdam Treaty signed with Russia at the end of World War II.

"This is serious, Slaker, for the State Department is considering this request. I suggest that you contact the congressman from your home area and get his help in getting the State Department to deny their request."

Air Force had not briefed me to turn myself over to the Russian authorities but had said what I did was up to me. However, what I did was, unbeknownst to me, for my own good since the Russians had reported me killed in the crash. I immediately obtained the name of the congressman from my western Pennsylvania area and wired him as to my problem and my record in World War II and the Berlin Airlift. I received a wire from his office that he had requested the State Department to refuse this request from Russia and wanted a reply within seventy-two hours. I did not receive any more information from him or the State Department, but a little over a week later I received orders from USAFE assigning me to the Western Air Defense at Hamilton Air Force Base in California, with three months TDY at Lowery Air force en route to Hamilton Air Base.

I departed Furstenfeldbruck Air Force Base the second week in December 1949. My travel orders included wife Glenna, daughter Pamela, and son Jeffrey. I thought to myself that my twenties were busier than a lifetime for many men. Here I was, returning to the States for the second time to obtain a divorce from a woman who didn't like men, didn't like the Air Force, and didn't like me. I did thank my Guardian Angel and God for returning me safely back to the States after this exciting tour.

Chapter 9
TWO LIVES SAVED AND A LOVE LOST

We flew from Germany in a Connie aircraft and landed in New Jersey at the McGuire Air Base. We took the train to Pittsburgh and my dad picked us up and drove us to my hometown of Vandergrift. The next day I got in touch with Mr. Stewart, who had sold me my Land Cruiser, to see if he had a new one available. He only had one new Studebaker, a convertible. I bought it and we left for Lafayette, Indiana the next day. We stayed two days with Glenna's sister Dolly and husband Mark, a fun couple. We then drove to Lincoln, Nebraska, where I dropped Glenna and the kids off at her parents' home. I told her that I did not know when I would see her again, that I was filing for a divorce in Pennsylvania. I would send her support money for the kids. She was not a bit disturbed about my leaving and I spent the night in a local hotel.

The next day I drove to Denver, arriving at Lowry Air Force Base late in the evening. I obtained a room at the BOQ and had a relaxed and happy feeling not having Glenna with me. The next morning I had breakfast with a pilot I knew, and he was leaving that morning for Chicago by commercial air. I drove him to Stapleton airport and then remembered that the stewardess I had met in June of 1948 spent several overnights a week in Denver. I still had her phone number she had given to me if I ever got to Denver. I decided to call to see if she still had that schedule and was single. I called and was surprised when Anne answered the phone. She remembered me and was dating but still single. She accepted my invitation to dinner that evening. We really enjoyed one another, and she agreed to have dinner with me when she would be back in Denver in three days.

We really had the vibes for one another and we dated every time she had an overnight in Denver. After three weeks I knew that cupid's arrow had pierced my heart. At the end of our next dinner I drove to a small park and asked if she would take a short walk with me. It was chilly, but we were dressed for the cold weather. We walked for about ten minutes holding hands and making small talk when I stopped, put my hands on her shoulders, and said, "I have not been in love with a woman for five years, but I am really in love with you. I wanted you to know this because I can't just keep having dinner dates with you unless you can love me too." She put her arms around me, kissed me, and said, "Ken, I fell in love with you on our first date. Let's enjoy our lives together." I drove back to my BOQ, where we spent our first night together.

In February I was assigned to fly supplies to Fargo, North Dakota to a Hollywood team making a Howard Hughes film titled *Jet Pilot*. The Air Force was supplying the aircraft for the film, and they loaned me to them with a C 47 for one week. I spent three days as a stand in for John Wayne, the main actor in the film, who had been delayed. I sat in the cockpit while they made test film shots. When John Wayne did arrive, the director introduced me to him as his backup. We both laughed, shook hands, and had a good visit. It was a fun and rewarding experience. They paid my hotel bill and my last night was on a Saturday, when the hotel was half full of high school students having a party of some sort. I was just getting ready to retire when I heard girls laughing and running back and forth in the hallways. I opened the door and there in the hallway were several girls running up and down the hallway, laughing and shouting and completely naked. When they saw me they ran into a room at the end of the hallway. I closed and locked the door. I knew that it would not be good publicity for me to be seen visiting with them.

One day in March I picked Anne up at the airport after her arrival from New York and after a close hug and kiss, she said she had something to tell me. After a minute or two of silence, she said, "Ken, I hope that what I am going to tell you won't hurt our relationship and that you wont be upset. I have missed my period and I am pregnant." I was not surprised because we had many nights of great love, and I did not use any preventive devices. I gave her a smile, squeezed her leg, and said it would be the first of several. I thought to myself, *Thank God, I am going to have a child with a woman I love.*

I had met a woman at the officers' club that knew of my love for Anne and said she could save me up to twenty percent on a diamond if I decided to give Anne an engagement ring. I had purchased it, and at dinner that night I presented Anne with the ring. I told her this was to prove my love for her. She did not have to say anything. The tears in her eyes were enough. Then she said, "Ken, when you finish your classes here, could we go back east to my home so that you can meet my mother?" I agreed with that suggestion, and when I graduated from the Base Supply Course, we put our few belongings into my convertible and the first week in April, set out for Connecticut.

Anne was a good driver so we took turns at the wheel every two hours. We spent the first night at Marysville, Kansas. The second day was good weather and we drove until dark and stopped for the night at Peoria, Illinois. The third day we made it to Pittsburgh, where on the fourth day we took the Turnpike to New Jersey, then north to Connecticut. We were exhausted by the time we reached her home and visited with her mother until bedtime. Her mother had me in a separate bedroom and Anne slept with her mother. That was the way it was in those days. If you were not married, you did not sleep together. Anne and I broke that custom in January. The next day I got the car greased and oil changed for the coming drive to the West Coast. Anne visited with her mother, telling her that she was pregnant and our plans to marry in May when I received my divorce. Her mother's treatment of me was great, and we spent the third day enjoying each other's company. We said goodbye the next morning and drove to Vandergrift, Pennsylvania for her to meet my father and his new wife, the former Mrs. Murphy. We had dinner with them that evening and I could see that my dad was really impressed with Anne. On the way out to my car, my dad whispered to me, "You have a beautiful charmer there, Kenny, you have finally picked one you deserve." That was one of the very few compliments my dad ever paid me.

When we got seated in my car, I asked Anne how she felt. She said she was ready to go, so I suggested that we take turns every two or three hours of driving and go nonstop to Denver. She agreed and we arrived late the next evening in Aurora, where she had two co-workers that she wanted to visit. We stayed in a motel for two days and then departed the morning of the third day for the West Coast. We drove west out of Denver over the Berthoud Pass, which was covered with snow and ice. We were just over the pass, and the edge of the concrete road was not visible, when the front right wheel broke through the ice and was too deep for me to steer back onto the road. I lost control and the car veered to the right down the snow-covered mountain with many trees. The snow was pushed up and over the car, and we bumped up and down and finally slowed to a stop. We could not open the car doors due to the packed snow. I got my door window down, but the snow was too packed to crawl through. Anne and I were shook up but fortunately not injured.

There wasn't much light inside the car and for a few minutes we discussed how we were going to get out when we heard a voice calling to us, "Hey inside, are you okay?"

"Yes," I replied, "but having trouble getting out." We heard the man digging through the snow outside my door window, and finally we got my door open. He said that he saw us going down the mountain between the trees and told his wife that he was going down the mountain to help us. We looked up the path that we had made down the mountain and saw that we had barely missed hitting six huge trees. Anne and I, and the gentleman who had helped us, struggled back up the mountain just as a patrol car arrived. The patrolman called for a wrecker. We thanked the man who had rescued us and waited for the wrecker. The officer stayed with us until the wrecker arrived and controlled traffic until my car was pulled up the long path it had made in the snow to the road. The patrolman said we were very lucky that we had not hit one of the trees because we would have been injured. He helped us clean the packed snow away from the engine and when we got it started, we thanked him and he wished us safe driving! As we drove off I made the remark that my Guardian Angel had saved me again.

Anne looked at me and in a taunting mood said, "You believe in guardian angels and that one of them is yours?" I told Anne what my grandmother had said just before she died and how she had saved me from being killed fifty-five times. Anne apologized and said she didn't know about my combat missions and the actual facts about my escape through Russia's Iron Curtain. She said that my grandmother must really be my Guardian Angel.

By the time we arrived at Salt Lake City, we were two very tired people. We checked into a motel and had a good night's rest. After a good breakfast, we headed west. About fifteen miles from Reno, the engine started dying, then coming to life, then dying. I looked ahead and saw a road leading toward the railroad track about 100 feet to our left. On the right side of the road was a picnic area, which I was able to drive to before the engine went completely dead. The fuel tank showed that we had a quarter tank of gasoline, so I lifted the hood to see if the fuel line or distributor cap and wires were broken from our trip down the mountain the day before. Visually, I could not see anything wrong. About that time a car pulled into the area and the driver got out to use the toilet at the far end of the picnic tables. When he returned he could see the hood up and asked if he could be of any help. I asked if he could call a tow truck to pull my car into Reno when he got there. He said that I would have a better chance of getting one right away if either I or the lady would go with him to Reno, which was his residence. He showed me his driver's license which gave his name and address in Reno. I did not want Anne to stay here in the boondocks by herself, so I looked at her and she said she would accompany the gentleman to Reno.

One hour later Anne was back, riding with the driver in the tow truck. We were towed to a Studebaker garage in Reno and rested in the customers' lounge. In less than an hour, the mechanic came into the room and said we needed a new fuel pump, which was already installed and the car was ready to drive. Since the car was new, the only charge I had to pay was for the towing. We decided to stay in Reno overnight. We did not gamble but enjoyed the evening by going to see a good stage show. We got up the next morning feeling great and with a bright clear sky above, headed west for Hamilton Air Force Base.

We arrived at the air base in mid afternoon. I signed in at headquarters, then to billeting, where I got a BOQ room. I told Anne to take the car and drive the short five miles into San Rafael and get herself an apartment, and meet me at the officers' club at 7:00 P.M. that evening. I then reported to the commander of the air base group, my new boss, who briefed me on my assignment. I was to be the assistant base supply officer, responsible for the base supply records section. I was also to be the base petroleum officer, the clothing sales officer, and would assume the responsibilities of the base supply officer in his absence. Being an administrative pilot was a secondary duty. Fortunately, I had very experienced military and civilian personnel skills in base supply organization. There was to be an air base group staff meeting the next morning, where I would be introduced to the military and civilian personnel that I would be working with. The colonel said he was pleased to have an experienced officer like me in the organization. I thanked him, saluted, and walked with high spirits to the officers' club.

Anne arrived at the club shortly after I did and was excited. A realtor in San Rafael had referred her to a family with a beautiful home in Larkspur that had an apartment for a single person above the attached garage. She liked it, and the family and I signed a rental lease with a right to cancel with a thirty-day notice. She also checked the bus schedule to San Francisco—which was good since her leave from United Airlines was up and she was scheduled to fly out of San Francisco starting in three days. I told her to use my car because I did not need it on base. Her schedule had her gone two days, then here two days, then gone two days, etc. We would be together every other two days. Although Anne was four months pregnant, she did not show any weight gain and still had her good figure.

Hamilton Air Base was the home of the Fourth Air Force with the primary mission to provide the aerial defense of the West Coast. We were equipped with F-84 jet fighters, with two of them armed and on alert at all times. They were under control of the Combat Control Center, which was underground on base. All pilots on base were on the schedule as combat control officer, which was about once every five or six weeks. Before my name went on the schedule, I received a thorough briefing on Combat Control Center duty.

A few months after my arrival at Hamilton Air Base, and on my second time as the combat control officer, we had a call from the radar station on Mr. Diablo that they had three objects on their radar screen that were heading northwest at a speed faster than sound. I asked if they were getting photocopies from the screen and they replied in the affirmative. I said that if they were exceeding the speed of sound I was not going to launch my F-84s because they are subsonic aircraft. The radar controller agreed to that and said they were then off our screen. At the end of my tour I wrote about this experience in the logbook.

Two or three weeks later I got a call from the wing executive officer that General Rush wanted to see me in his office right away. I entered his office, gave him a salute, and he asked me to be seated. There were two male civilians also seated in the room, and the general did not introduce me to them. The general directed me to tell these two individuals exactly what happened during my last tour in the Combat Center. I told them in great detail exactly what had occurred and they never questioned me. The general thanked me and then said, "Captain, when you leave this room you are to forget what you have just told us. Do you understand?" I replied in the affirmative and was excused. I thought to myself that those were UFOs and this was a cover up.

Since we had both propeller and jet type aircraft assigned to the base, we had to have storage for both 100-octane and jet fuel available at all times. When I was assigned as the base petroleum officer I met with the civil service worker who was in charge of the aviation fuel storage area and the gasoline refueling trucks. I had only been on base a couple of weeks when he called to tell me that the jet fuel that we had just received was contaminated and could not be accepted. He gave me the test results and suggested how to approach the oil company with this problem. I called the oil company, introduced myself, and told them how important it was that we have clean fuel as soon as possible. They were very cooperative and said they would have a refueling tanker there that could fill our refueling trucks until they could get an empty refueling tanker there to remove the contaminated fuel. I notified my civilian engineer of the results of my call and thanked him for his professional assistance.

The last week in May I flew back to Pennsylvania for my divorce hearing. My attorney and I received quite a surprise when we walked into the room where the Master (judge) was to listen to my reasons for dissolving the marriage. There sat Glenna with an attorney she had brought with her all the way from Lincoln, Nebraska. She knew that if a divorce action in Pennsylvania was contested, getting the divorce approved was unlikely unless you could prove adultery. I told the Master the many negative reasons that this was not a good marriage. When I told him about her refusal to have marital relations, Glenna got up and walked across the room and slapped me very hard across my face. A clerk of the court grabbed her and escorted her back to her chair. Her attorney requested permission to speak, and the Master approved his request. Her attorney said that her action just now was a result of her concern about the children, for they needed their father at home. The Master ended the meeting and left the room. My attorney and I also left the room, and outside the courthouse he said that with Glenna's physical attack on me, my chances were very good that I would receive my divorce. I flew back to California feeling very confident that I was going to become a single man.

Upon my return from Pennsylvania I briefed Anne on the divorce hearing and she, like me, was confident that I would be awarded the divorce. I was so positive about getting the divorce, especially since that was my attorney's opinion, that I went to Novato, a small town adjacent to the air base, and purchased a new house being built in an area of new homes. Anne had fun making plans for furnishing and decorating it when we got married and moved into our new home.

The Air Force had become alarmed about the physical fitness of its members and made it a requirement to spend at least one hour a week in the base gym, jogging, or engaged in a physical sport. The boss and I started spending every Wednesday afternoon at the Sonoma Golf Club playing a round of golf. One Wednesday in the middle of June we were playing our round of golf when I had an experience that had never happened before. One of the greens could not be seen due to a ridge between it and the tee. The boss teed off and cleared the ridge. I used an eight iron to get height over the wooden marker on top of the ridge. My ball had a good height right over the marker. We hiked over the ridge to the green and the boss' ball lay just short of the green. My ball was not on the green, so I walked all around the outside of the green but could not find it. Then the boss called me and asked me to come over and look into the hole. There was my ball. I had made a hole in one! And I did not get to see it happen. Of course the boss spread the news to all the pilots that played golf, and that evening I was being hit for their drinks at the bar.

Anne was on her last trip as a stewardess since she could no longer prevent showing that she was pregnant. We met the day after she returned, and I had a very tough time telling her of the negative decision on my divorce petition by the court in Pennsylvania. She lost her composure and cried, which brought tears to my eyes. It put us both in a tough situation with her being pregnant. Then Anne told me that on one of her flights in May she was able to get a layover in Lincoln and visited Glenna. She said she told Glenna, "You don't love Ken and he doesn't love you. I love Ken and am pregnant with his child." She asked Glenna, for the sake of this unborn child, please not to contest Ken's petition for a divorce. Glenna said, "That is your problem, not mine, and now please leave."

Anne and I both agreed that our main concern was the coming birth of our child. It was now time for Anne to visit an OB doctor, for the baby was due to be born that coming fall. We spent several hours discussing our situation. We both knew that even if I filed for legal residence in California and then filed for divorce there, that Glenna would contest it. We could not expect any cooperation from her. If Anne kept the baby it would cause her trouble in our society as an unmarried mother. It also would be tough on the child to grow up without a father in the house. If we would agree to give the child up for adoption to a reputable couple, the child would have a home and parents to provide it with a normal life. I also added this statement for Anne's benefit: giving the child up for adoption would give her the freedom to be herself again and not waste any more of her time with me. Anne was quiet for several minutes and then said that with the difficulty we were having with our relationship, she agreed that we should give the baby up for adoption.

Anne made arrangements for an appointment at a hospital maternity ward in San Francisco. She informed the chief nurse that she wanted to give the baby up for adoption, and the nurse introduced her to a very understanding and cooperative doctor. He said that he had a very well-to-do couple that wanted to adopt a new baby and that he could make all the arrangements. He also said they had agreed to pay all the hospital expenses, which would be of great help to both Anne and me. She had given her notice to break her rental lease and on August 1st, we moved into the new house I had purchased in May.

We didn't purchase any furniture because we knew that this was temporary and the house had kitchen and laundry appliances. New houses were still being built on this street, so we didn't have any neighbors to contend with. In September Anne started to have labor pains and I drove her to the hospital in San Francisco. Both Anne and the baby came through the delivery okay. The doctor said that the couple adopting the baby would be pleased that it was a boy. Anne told me that she signed her real name to the birth certificate but listed the father as a military pilot.

Anne recovered quickly, and in the first week in October, I told her that she should not waste any more of her life with me. I had been trying to get rid of Glenna for eight years and I was still a married man. I asked her to please go back home and give herself the opportunity to have the life she deserved. I asked her to do this because I loved her and knew that she loved me, so to do it for the both of us. She reluctantly agreed and made reservations to fly out of Reno with a United Airlines crew that she had flown with as a stewardess. I drove her to the airport at Reno, and with tears in both of our eyes, we kissed and said goodbye. I never saw her again. Two years later I called her mother to ask how Anne was doing and she said Anne was doing fine. I told her I was happy to hear that and thanked her.

When I bailed out of the C-47 in September 1948, I severely injured my back. Every two weeks I went to the hospital in Munich for therapy, and when I was returned to the States, the treatment was continued at the base hospital. The first week in October I reported for my treatment and the surgeon had good news. The lower discs in my spine were now clear and I did not need any further treatment. He gave me a sheet of back exercises and said that when I reached my sixties that I might be bothered with arthritis.

More good news in October. I had sold my convertible in July because I was offered several hundred dollars more than I had paid for it. I called Mr. Stewart, the Cadillac salesman in Vandergrift, and ordered a new Cadillac. He said it would be three or four months, since their 1950 quota was filled and I would have to wait until they received a shipment against their 1951 quota. My brother had bought a new Chevrolet in July and a few days later received orders to report to the USAFE Air Weather Service in Guam and had no need for a car there. I bought his car to use while waiting for my new car. His Chevrolet was a lemon. The rear window leaked, the engine kept dying, and there were other mechanical defects. I would sell it as soon as my new car was available.

Although my primary assignment was a desk job, I was still a rated pilot and flew several administrative flights every month. A few times I flew a high-ranking officer, who was a member of the Air Force Blue Book Project, to investigate a UFO sighting in the western division. I would fly him to an airport nearest to the reported sighting. One evening at the officers' club, I walked into the lounge as he was having an after dinner drink and he asked me to join him. I ordered coffee and he talked about his possible transfer and hated to leave Hamilton Air Base. I asked him if since I had flown him to a couple of reported UFO sightings, could he tell me the result of his investigations. He said he could not because when he became a member of the Blue Book Project; he took an oath not to relate any of his findings to a non Blue Book member. We got up to leave and as we shook hands, he looked straight into my eyes and said, "Slaker, I can tell you one thing. Don't take these sightings lightly." With that remark, he told me plenty.

September and October had been busy months, and I decided to take a break and visit my three uncles and their families in Seattle if I could hitch a ride in an aircraft flying to the Seattle area. I called the base operations officer and he said that there was a

C-46 here from Portland flown by inactive weekend pilots leaving this evening and that there was space available. I arrived at base operations around 4:00 P.M. and put my name on the C-46 passenger list. Since I had a green instrument card, I was authorized to enter the weather station to check the sequences of the weather forecast at our estimated time of arrival at Portland. The weather forecast for our ETA at Portland was marginal with low ceiling and poor visibility. The pilot was a lieutenant colonel in the Reserves and I introduced myself and told him that I was hitching a ride to Portland in his aircraft, and he nodded his head in the affirmative.

I joined the colonel on the way walking to the C-46, and as one pilot to another, said, "The weather doesn't look too good for our ETA at Portland, and if we can't land there, what is your alternative?" I was hoping that if we had to use the alternate, it was McChord Air Force Base, only thirty minutes from Seattle. In a very sarcastic tone he said, "Captain, if you are worried about the weather, you best not make this flight."

Without any thought, two words came out of my mouth: "You're right." I turned around and walked back to operations, crossed out my name on the passenger list, and while walking back to my room, thought to myself, *Now why in the hell did you do that? You wanted to get to Seattle.* I changed clothes and had dinner at the officers' club and danced until midnight with nurses and WAF officers.

Saturday morning I was up at 7:30, took a quick shower, and the phone rang. I answered it and the voice asked, "Slaker?"

I said, "Yes, who are you?"

"This is Vesowaite, your base operations officer. I thought that you were going on that C-46 to Portland last night?"

I said, "Yes, but I didn't like the smart-ass attitude of the pilot and didn't go."

"Slaker, you had God with you last night. That C-46 was making an instrument approach to the airport, crashed into a hill, and killed everyone on board." I dropped the phone and stood in my room in shock.

I walked back and forth in my room trying to believe this had really happened. I asked myself, *Why did I so abruptly agree with the colonel not to go on that flight?* Then it dawned on me. My quick response and action to leave the colonel standing there was from my Guardian Angel. I was like a robot, for she was in charge and it was not my brain that had me react like I did. My mother was right. Her mother is my Guardian Angel. I lived through the flu epidemic when I was a baby; I recovered from injuries received when I was run over by an automobile when I was seven; I was lucky to survive when I was in a head on collision; I made it through fifty combat bombing missions when I was twenty-three; I escaped death when I bailed out of the aircraft just before it crashed; and now I had avoided taking this flight of death. As I walked from the officers' club that night to my room, I looked up at the dark sky and thanked God and my Guardian Angel for helping me to survive through these life threatening events during the first thirty years of my life.

The Air Force had come up with new blue uniforms for its members and I had ordered several hundred of various sizes to be ready to issue them in November. I selected S/Sgt. Griffin to be the non-commissioned airman in charge and we obtained a building suitable for fitting tables and bins. He and his selected airmen and civilians did an outstanding job of fitting several hundred airmen with their new Blues. We received a very rewarding letter from the commander of the Letterman Army Hospital for the efficient manner in which we clothed their personnel.

The middle of November I received a call from Mr. Stewart, the salesman I had ordered my new Cadillac from, that my car was now available for delivery. I informed him that my flying and working schedule was loaded and that it would be the middle of December before I could pick it up, but to use it as a display in the showroom till I got there. A week before Christmas, I got a ride on an aircraft going to Wright Patterson Air Base at Dayton, Ohio. From there I took a train and bus to my hometown of Vandergrift. The next day I took delivery of my four-door, metallic green Cadillac. I spent the day with my father and departed the next day for California.

On my way west, I decided to stop in Lincoln, Nebraska, not to see Glenna, but to see my two children, Pamela and Jeffrey. The last I had heard, she and the children were living with her parents, so when I arrived in Lincoln, I drove directly to her parents' house. Her mother, whom I had always gotten along with, was there and informed me that her husband could not stand the cruel mental and physical way Glenna was treating Jeffrey, so he forced her to move to an apartment in the city. Her mother gave me the address and without calling, I found the apartment and knocked on the door. Glenna was really surprised to see me, and Pamela and Jeffrey were overjoyed to see their dad. And I them.

I had not eaten all day and they had not eaten dinner, so I took them to dinner at a good restaurant. The kids were really enjoying themselves and Pam could not quit talking to me. Jeffrey, not even two, was a good looking boy and never took his eyes off me. When we returned to the apartment, Glenna asked the children to go into another room because she wanted to talk to their dad. Her first question, which surprised me, was, "What about the baby?" I told her it had been adopted and Anne and I had separated for the good of both of us. Glenna then said that she had done a lot of thinking since the divorce hearing and she apologized for slapping me. She said she realized that her treatment of me and my career was wrong, and hoped I would consider a reconciliation. Then she really surprised me. She got up out of her chair and came over to where I was sitting. With tears in her eyes, she asked me to take her back!

Ever since my arrival at the apartment late that afternoon, I was having difficulty with my own emotions. I loved the children and it was going to be difficult to leave them. I looked at Glenna, not knowing what to say or do when just then, Pam and Jeff came running into the room both begging me to take them with me to California. That did it. I told Glenna to pack their belongings and that I would be back in the morning, that all of us were going to California. Three days later we arrived at Hamilton Air Base and I found a house fully furnished for rent near San Rafael. Glenna was really in better spirits than I had ever seen her. We had arrived there the day before Christmas, just in time to enjoy the Christmas day party at the officers' club.

The house next to us was a rental occupied by a lieutenant and his wife and young child. This was good because Glenna and the wife became friends and did women things together. I had very good people as my assistants for my non-rated functions, which gave me the freedom to make two or three administrative flights a week. A colonel I had done some favors for in Germany was now in USAFE Headquarters Personnel. I still wanted to get my college degree, and since they had called me to active duty when I was a senior at the university, I decided to ask my colonel friend if he could get me assigned to an ROTC detachment so I could attend classes in my spare time for my degree. In May I was notified that I was being transferred to the ROTC detachment at Washburn University, Topeka, Kansas. Prior to reporting to my new station, I had to attend Air University at Montgomery, Alabama, where I was to be schooled in the course that I was to teach, Geopolitics. My civilian and military personnel that worked for me gave me a great farewell coffee, and I was going to miss these hard working and loyal personnel. I could not have had better people. I gave Glenna the choice of staying in California six more weeks or going to Topeka then to find a place to live. She selected Topeka, so we packed the Cadillac with our belongings and said goodbye to Hamilton Field.

HEADQUARTERS
1080th Hospital Squadron
Letterman Army Hospital
San Francisco, California

MEDES-AF   24 November 1950

SUBJECT: Letter of Commendation and Appreciation

TO: Commanding Officer
         78th Fighter-Interceptor Wing
         Hamilton AFB
         Hamilton, California

1. On the 9th and 10th of November 1950 all of the airmen personnel assigned to this organization were issued their blue uniforms at the Clothing Sales Store, Hamilton AFB, Hamilton, California.

2. Captain Kenneth W. Slaker, Officer in charge of the Clothing Sales Store, was most Cooperative in arranging a schedule for our personnel. Arrangements were made to have approximately 40 of our airmen issued their uniforms each morning and afternoon Thursday and Friday the 9th and 10th of November 1950.

3. Each individual man on the "fitting line" went out of his way to give our men a proper fit. Each item of clothing was tried on for size and special measurements were taken to insure each man a correct fit. There was no limit to the amount of clothes each man tried, and there seemed to be no limit to the amount of patience of each man on the line. All of the personnel on the "fitting line" were very courteous and understanding as to the different types of problems each man had. Because of the fact that our airmen personnel had a considerable distance to travel and a limited amount of time, the personnel of the Clothing Sales Store gave our unit consideration by processing our personnel ahead of personnel from other units when we were late in arriving for our processing.

4. The entire operation of issuing clothing to the personnel of the 1080th Hospital Squadron was carried on in a very efficient and expeditious manner. All of the personnel involved in carrying out the operation so efficiently are to be commended.

Letter of Commendation and Appreciation from Lt. Col. John R. Whitson, 24 November 1950.

MEDES-AF
Subject: Letter of Comendation and Appreciation

    5. The following named personnel were responsible for the efficiency with which this clothing was issued:

                Capt. Kenneth W. Slaker (Officer in charge)
                S/Sgt. LaMar. H. Griffin (NCO in charge)
                S/Sgt. Ralph Lehman
                Sgt. James D. Thomas
                Sgt. C. Chim
                Pfc. William McViekerf
                Pfc. L. P. Hefke
                Pvt. Lonnie Reeves
                Harry Mendelson (Civilian)
                Gladys Rodoni (Civilian)

FOR THE COMMANDING OFFICER:

                DAVID L. MOORE
                Captain, USAF (MSC)
                Adjutant

MEDES-AF   24 November 1950
Subject: Letter of Commendation and Appreciation

GM 330.13   2d Ind

HEADQUARTERS, 78th Maintenance and Supply Group, Hamilton Air Force Base, Hamilton, California, 4 December 1950

TO: Commanding Officer, 78th Supply Squadron, Hamilton Air Force Base, Hamilton, California

    1. It is a pleasure to receive letters of this nature and I wish to extend my congratulations.

    2. Copies will be made for all personnel concerned and placed in individual 201 files.

                                    JOHN R. WHITSON
                                    LT COL, USAF
                                    Commanding

Letter of Commendation and Appreciation from Lt. Col. John R. Whitson, 24 November 1950.

Slaker's 30th Birthday, 14 April 1950. His fiancee at the time, Ann Richards of West Hartford, Connecticut, and him celebrated it with a party in Reno, Nevada, where this photo was taken. Yes, they gambled and lost.

Chapter 10
WASHBURN UNIVERSITY AFROTC

We made Reno our first potty and lunch stop. After we left Reno and the kids were asleep in the back seat, Glenna said to me in a very casual tone, "Ken, I have missed two periods and I am pregnant." The first five months of that year Glenna had given me the best treatment and cooperation I had ever received from her. Her remark concerned me because I thought that maybe the two of us were not ready to have another child. I remarked that my transfer to Topeka was good timing because we would be just four hours' drive from her parents and they could be of help with Pam and Jeff. Without any hesitation she said that she didn't want her parents to know she was pregnant.

We arrived in Topeka on the afternoon of the third day and found a comfortable motel with a restaurant for the four of us. I got the evening newspaper and scanned the listing of houses for sale and one caught my eye. It was a brick rambler with an unfinished interior for sale by owner. I called him and identified myself that I was going to be an instructor at the university. He was very cordial and could meet with me that evening. The house was on a good sized lot owned by his father, who lived next door. I liked the house and knew that I could finish it myself. He saw that I was interested and said I could have it for exactly the money he had in it plus the value of the lot. We agreed to meet the next afternoon in the office of the mortgage company that was going to carry his mortgage and he was sure would carry mine. The price was right, but I was three thousand dollars short of my cash on hand. However, I had a good idea as to where I could borrow it.

I left early the next morning to sign in at the office but stopped at a public phone on the way. I called Glenna's mother and explained the house situation to her and asked if I could borrow 3,000 dollars from her. I would sign a promissory note plus interest and monthly payment amount to her. She said, "None of that. It is a personal loan between us." I thanked her and told her that I was not to tell her, but Glenna was three months pregnant. She thanked me for the information and told me to let her know when I had the house finished because she and her husband wanted to see the house and visit the children.

I signed in at the AFROTC office and met my new boss, Lt. Colonel Carter. He was a true Southern gentleman and made me feel very welcome. I told him about the house I had just bought, and he said that was a good area and only a few blocks from the university, and showing that he had a sense of humor, that I could walk to the office for my daily exercise. He introduced me to two other pilots on the staff, captains Lasseter and McBride, and two airmen doing the office paperwork, M/Sgt. LaDuke and S/Sgt. Sullivan. I told them I was looking forward to working with them and that I would be back at the end of July when I finished the Academic Instructor Course at the Air University.

I drove back to the motel, picked up the wife and kids, and drove to the center of town where we had an early lunch. Then we visited a large furniture store, and they were pleased to open a charge account in my name. In two hours we had purchased the basic furniture needed so that we could move into the house before I left for Montgomery, Alabama. I took the family back to the motel and drove to the office of the mortgage company. They were delighted to carry the mortgage on the house and the deal was closed.

My orders assigned me to Forbes Air Base located a few miles south of Topeka, where I would accomplish the flight requirements as a rated pilot. A couple of days before I had to leave for Montgomery, Alabama, I drove to the base and reported to base operations. The officer in charge was Major Ottman, a very experienced pilot and one that I knew I was going to like working with. He was pleased when I told him I was current in the C-47 with several hundred hours of logged time. He said that the base had a C-47 that was General Caldara's administrative aircraft and that there were very few of the B-29 pilots here current in the C-47. He said, "Slaker, you are going to be the general's number one pilot on call to fly his aircraft." I told Ottman that was fine with me and that I would be available after I returned from the Air University the end of July.

Since Glenna didn't drive, I drove the Cadillac to the Air University located at Maxwell Field, Montgomery, Alabama. Classes were held every weekday and the instructors were tops. Weekends were free and the first weekend I flew a C-45 on an administrative flight to Dayton, Ohio, stayed overnight, and returned Sunday with a stop at Toledo, Ohio for a passenger pickup. This got my flight time in for my July flight pay. The second weekend I drove to Columbus, Georgia to the home of my World War II navigator, James Passmore, and his lovely wife, Marian. We had kept in touch ever since our aircrew finished its combat tour in September 1943. Marian and I were like sister and brother to one another, and Jim was always the quiet, Southern gentleman. I stayed overnight and enjoyed conversing with their young children. The third weekend I flew another flight to help a couple of pilots get their flight time in for July pay. The fourth weekend we had a graduation party at the officers' club, and I enjoyed the evening dancing with some very beautiful ladies from Alabama. I left Sunday morning for Topeka, now a professional instructor in Geopolitics.

Fall classes didn't start until September, which gave me time to meet the faculty and acquaint myself with the campus and the city of Topeka, the Kansas State capital. I had lesson plans to prepare for AFROTC classes, and I had to make arrangements for my own class schedule. My 150 semester hours from the University of Washington were acceptable at Washburn, except the last twenty-eight hours had to be at the Washburn University campus. Taking priority over all of these programs and duties was my primary occupation of an aircraft pilot. I felt that I must maintain my skill in this most important part of my life.

In August the new faculty members were introduced to the current members, and we received a very friendly welcome. A faculty member that I really enjoyed talking to was Arthur Sellen, the Dean of College. He had heard of my World War II experience and my Berlin Airlift disaster from Colonel Carter, my new boss, and personally welcomed me to the university. I mentioned to him that one of the reasons I was at Washburn University was to get a degree in Liberal Arts since I only needed twenty-eight semester hours on campus. I told him that I would not be wearing my uniform at any class that I attended as a student. He said that anytime I wanted to talk to him, his door was always open.

On August 22nd Major Ottman from Forbes Operations called me and said that he had me scheduled to fly the C-47 on an administrative flight to Maxwell Field on the twenty-third, returning to Forbes the next day. I was very pleased, and this was my first flight out of Forbes Air Base since 1945. It was a wonderful feeling to be back in the cockpit again.

One of the subjects that I registered for that fall was Biology with Robert Kingman as the instructor. I have never forgotten his opening remark at our first class meeting. We students were in our seats waiting for the starting bell to ring, and the chalkboard was covered with a six-foot-wide blind, top to bottom. The bell rang and he walked in and looked at each one of us for a couple of seconds, then turned around and retracted the blind up into its container, and there on the board was the diagram of a huge fish. Then he said in a very serious tone, "We are all fish!" No doubt about it, he had our attention.

The last weekend in August Major Ottman called me and said he had put me on base operations orders as an instructor pilot in the C-47. Not only could I give check rides in the aircraft, but three pilots could also log flight time, thus getting more recorded flight time out of the aircraft. I flew locally the last two days in August for a total of four hours' aircraft time, but with three pilots on board, we logged twelve hours' flight time.

The week after Labor Day the campus came alive with hundreds of students and I conducted my first ROTC class. I had twenty-five freshmen that had signed and become members of the AFROTC college program. I welcomed them to the program and gave a short review of my past experience as a pilot. I gave them the basic instructions as to how our class was to be conducted and then had each cadet rise, introduce himself, his primary activities, and his goal in life. I was already proud to be the instructor of these eager young American men.

My second class with my ROTC students was an eye opener for me. The study of Geopolitics and how it determines the existence and behavior of a particular country requires a knowledge of world geography. Some of the students had never had a course in any Geography. About half the class had United States Geography, and none of the students had studied World Geography. I asked them how many knew the capitals of all forty-eight states, and no hands went up. I asked how many knew the capital of Oregon State; two hands went up and both said Medford. Wrong. I told the class that for the next four weeks we were going to study World Geography. I gave them their assignment for the next class, which was to find out how many continents there were and their location on the earth. I suggested that they learn to use their campus library.

In the meantime I spent what little spare time I had finishing the house that I had bought. The house only had two bedrooms and a double garage. We only had one car and Glenna didn't drive, so I remodeled the garage to hold one automobile and converted the space for the second car to a third bedroom. I had a mason extend the brick wall of the house to the space for the single garage, and I framed and sheet rocked the third bedroom. This actually improved the exterior looks of the house, making it look like a larger rambler. I also sheet rocked and painted the other two bedrooms, the living room, and the dining room.

The first week in October Major Ottman called me to see if I could leave my office for a three-day flight in the general's C-47. Two of his staff officers were to attend classified meetings in the afternoon of October 6th at Great Falls Air Base in Montana, and at Fairchild Air Base on October 7th at Spokane, Washington. I agreed to take the flight and on the 8th of October, we departed at 7:00 A.M. for Great Falls. I filed a flight plan for six hours, which should put us at Great Falls at noon Mountain Time, which we did. The two staff officers said they could finish their business there that afternoon and evening and would be ready to leave for Spokane the next morning. The copilot and I spent the evening in town and found the townspeople very friendly.

We departed Great Falls the next morning at 9:00 A.M. Mountain Time for Fairchild Air Base, arriving there a little after 10:00 A.M. Pacific Time. I had flown into Fairchild before when I was an inactive Reserve pilot flying out of McChord Air Base at Tacoma, Washington. The two officers said they could leave any time the next day and it would be great if they could be home in time for dinner. I told them it would take about eight hours and with Topeka on Central Time, we should leave there at 8:00 A.M. They agreed. I spent the day with a pilot friend that I knew from flying combat from the same bomb group in World War II. We departed Spokane at 8:00 A.M. the next day and it was a smooth flight and no help with the winds, arriving at Forbes at 5:45 P.M.

I declined taking any cross-country flights during November because Glenna was entering her ninth month of pregnancy. The doctor said that the baby should arrive the first week in December but could arrive any time before that. Her doctor was a captain in the Air Force, and she would deliver her baby in the Forbes station hospital since I was assigned there for flying. This would be her second child born in a military hospital, much to her distaste for the military.

My ROTC students had made satisfactory progress in their research and class work in World Geography. I informed them that now we were going to study the politics of various countries. The first one was our ally during World War II, and now was our enemy in a cold war: Russia. I told them that from then on they could expect pop quizzes on their class assignments. I could now use my original lesson plans that I had for this class; before, I had to put them aside until we were done studying geography.

Early in the morning on the 23rd of November, Glenna started having contractions. I got the kids out of bed, grabbed their clothing, put them in the back seat of the car, and told them to dress themselves. I made a quick call to the base hospital that I was bringing in my wife, who was having contractions, and would be there in about twenty minutes. I drove directly to the emergency entrance to the hospital and the medics were waiting for her. She delivered a baby boy about an hour later. I named him Timothy and left the middle name up to her. She never did give him a middle name and was not happy because she didn't want another boy.

December was a very busy month for me, conducting my ROTC classes, attending my own class at the university, and a couple of cross-country weekend flights. Glenna had been in a depressed mood ever since Tim was born and was unkind in her treatment of Pam and Jeff. When I was at home, Pam, Jeff, and I were a threesome that went shopping, walking, and playing games. Glenna's mother called and invited us to Lincoln for Christmas but Glenna declined. Without Glenna knowing, I called her mother and asked her and her husband to visit us on Christmas day, for they had a new grandson and our new house which they had not seen. She agreed and I asked her not to tell Glenna and to make it look like a surprise visit.

I returned home from a two-day flight on the 22nd of December. Pam and Jeff and I spent the twenty-third and twenty-fourth buying and trimming the Christmas tree and outlining the outside of the house with colored lights. Christmas morning was a fun time opening packages and at noon, in walked the kids' grandparents from Lincoln. Pam and Jeff had a fun afternoon with them, and I had already made dinner reservations at one of the few restaurants open. We all went to dinner at 6:00 P.M., which was the first time in two years that we all had been together. After an enjoyable meal the grandparents hugged and kissed all of us and departed for Lincoln.

In the early part of winter 1952, I was scheduled to fly after classes on a Friday afternoon to Norton Air Base in California. I took off with Captain John Smith as my copilot, and we landed at Davis Monthan Air Base in Arizona for fuel. It was dark when we took off and gave our position report when over Blythe, California, cruising at 10,500 feet. All of a sudden, a large, bright, saucer-shaped object came out of the south of us and crossed about 500 feet in front of us at a terrific speed. Captain John said, "Slaker, did you see that?"

I replied, "See what?"

"Slaker, you had to see its lights and terrific speed."

I turned my head, looking at John and said, "Captain, we didn't see anything." He got the message and said that I was right, that we did not see anything.

We both knew what had happened to other pilots when they observed a UFO and filed the sighting on the forms carried in the Blue Book. They were questioned at length and asked if they had been drinking, if they were tired and sleepy, that it was probably a searchlight from the ground reflecting off the clouds, etc. The investigators tried to convince you that you had not really seen anything that could travel at that speed. I remembered what the colonel at Hamilton Field who had investigated reported sightings said to me: "Don't take these sightings lightly." *Yes, Johnny, there are UFOs.*

The university athletic director had made a contract with the Globetrotters, a famous colored basketball team, to play an exhibition game here in the early spring. I went to see the game since I had been the Globetrotters' pilot when they were in the Army and known as the Lincoln Wings in 1944-45. I was anxious to see how many of the players that I knew were still with the team, especially Goose Tatum. When each player was introduced onto the floor before the game, the Goose was still with the team. When the game ended, I went to the Trotters' locker room and the Goose was getting dressed. I walked up to him and said, "Goose, do you remember me? I am Captain Slaker, I was your pilot flying you to exhibition games all over the country when you were with the Lincoln Wings in 1944."

Goose looked at me and jumped up and said, "My God, hey fellows, this man here was my pilot when I played with the Lincoln Wings during the war." We shook hands and talked several minutes about our current careers, and not only shook hands but also made a quick brace of each other's shoulders. I left the locker room feeling very proud that one of the greatest basketball players had remembered me.

Glenna had not been in a good mood since the birth of Tim. She was not a good bed partner, and when I would suggest that we make love, she refused because she believed that you only have sex to have a child, and she didn't want any more boys. I was having a tough time staying true to her because there were temptations, especially at the university. When spring arrived she cheered up a bit and let me satisfy my sexual needs. June arrived, and she went into one of her depressed moods and told me that she had missed her period and was pregnant. Neither one of us was happy with this situation. I mentioned an abortion and she was furious that I would suggest such an action. That was when I made up my mind never to have sexual relations with her again.

On the 1st of August, Major Ottman notified me that I was scheduled to fly General Caldara to Puerto Rico via Cumberland, Maryland, the general's hometown. On the 3rd of August, General Caldara, myself, my copilot, the flight engineer, and the

WAF from base operations office, as a reward for her excellent work in operations, took off for Cumberland, Maryland. This was an overnight stop and the general invited the WAF to stay with his family, and we two pilots and engineer stayed at a motel.

We took off late the next morning for MacDill Air Base, located in Florida. Here we topped off the fuel tanks so we would not have to refuel in Puerto Rico, obtained customs clearance to depart the United States, and retired early in our respective billets. We departed MacDill at 9:00 A.M. for a two and a half hour flight to Ramey Air Base in Puerto Rico. It was a smooth flight with clear weather, and after we had landed and taxied to the ramp, a staff car with a general's flag on it arrived. General Caldara invited me and the WAF to get into the staff car and told the driver he wanted to make a stop at base operations. This was my first stop also to turn in the flight clearance, etc. The general told the WAF to wait in the car, and on the way into operations he told me that he was going to have the WAF billeted in the nurses' quarters, and that we would be taking off the next morning for San Juan. If for any reason I needed to contact him, I was to leave the message with the Base Officer of the Day. I went back to our aircraft and told the engineer that we would be leaving about 10:00 A.M. the next day for San Juan, about a twenty-minute flight. The copilot and I then signed in at the transient billets. At dinner the copilot asked me if the WAF was spending the night with the general, and I said I didn't know but I personally didn't think so.

The next morning, after a short twenty-minute flight, we arrived at San Juan. All of us had lunch together and before the general left in a Navy staff car, he told us that we would be departing the next day at 11:00 A.M. for MacDill Air Base. The rest of us checked into a seaside hotel. The WAF and I spent the late afternoon at the poolside enjoying one another's company. We had dinner together and even enjoyed dancing in the lounge. When it came time to retire, she had her own room, but we both knew that she was not going to use it. At breakfast the next morning my copilot joined me and told me that he spent the afternoon helping the engineer take up the flooring in the C-47 for many cases of whiskey that the Navy delivered to the aircraft. Since I was the pilot I thought that the general could have told me why we were going to San Juan. The copilot then asked if I knew where the WAF spent the night. I said, "Yes, I know whose bed she was in last night." He looked at me and I said, "Mine."

We departed San Juan late the next morning for MacDill Air Base after customs checked the aircraft and cleared us to leave. I told the engineer that the customs individual didn't even board the aircraft but just looked in through the door. The Engineer said that the Navy individual he worked with said not to worry, that the Navy took care of customs for us. We arrived at MacDill Air Base two and a half hours later and went through customs and refueled. I checked the weather at Forbes Air Base, and the forecast for our planned arrival time would be at minimums or below for landing at Forbes. I briefed the general on the weather situation and he agreed that we should RON here and leave tomorrow afternoon for home. He told me that we didn't want to arrive at Forbes until after dark. I replied that our flight time to Forbes would be four and a half to five hours depending on the winds. The general then said, "Let's leave here tomorrow at 5:00 P.M."

The next morning I checked the weather forecast for that evening at Topeka, and it would not prevent us from landing at Forbes Air Base. We were airborne a few minutes after 5:00 P.M. and had two hours of instrument flight time en route, but it became clear skies when we reached Kansas. I reported our arrival to the tower and was instructed to park on the south taxi strip where the aircraft would be unloaded. It was exactly 10:00 P.M. when I shut down the engines, and it was a very dark night. A large truck pulled up to the fuselage and the engineer and the truck driver started to remove the flooring from the fuselage. I heard the general tell the truck driver that half of these crates were to go to the officers' club and half to the NCO club. The clubs could not purchase this whiskey here because Kansas was a very dry state. We were gone six days, and I really enjoyed flying this trip to San Juan—especially the night I spent there.

Glenna had news for me when I returned from this flight to San Juan. Her brother Kenny had called and wanted to marry his girl in our house. His parents did not want him to get married until he had finished college. He would not tell his parents and then surprise them when they returned to Lincoln. Glenna agreed to have the ceremony in our house. I told Glenna that it was my house too and I didn't like it because these were her parents too and it was sneaky. Ken and his girl were coming to our house the day before the ceremony, and I suggested that just before they arrive there, she should call her parents and suggest they drive down there for the wedding and as a surprise. To my surprise, Glenna agreed and the folks thanked her and said they would be there for the ceremony. Glenna gave them the time of the ceremony and they arrived about an hour before the minister arrived. Glenna had a florist decorate the living room with flowers and had a wedding cake delivered just after the ceremony. We liked his girl and knew that she would make Kenny a good wife. They had one habit that bothered me. They both smoked, and this bothered me because I didn't smoke and neither did Glenna.

Fall of 1952 was a busy one. In addition to teaching my morning ROTC class about the rise and fall of Germany under Hitler, I was taking two college courses—one in the afternoon and one in the evening. At the same time, I made seven administrative flights with General Caldara on three of them. These flights took me away from home for a total of eighteen days. I didn't miss gloomy Glenna, but the kids and I missed each other.

The last Saturday in November I was not scheduled to fly and went to the office to catch up on paperwork, and one of our sergeants who lived in Kansas City was also there completing office records. About lunchtime his wife came in and had a lady friend with her. We were introduced and she was very attractive and congenial. We were able to converse with one another for about fifteen minutes before she had to leave with the sergeant and his wife. I asked her to call me the next time she was in the area and that

I would show her the campus and take her to lunch. She thanked me and said she would take me up on that invitation. That was to be the beginning of a close relationship.

Her name was Helen, and she didn't waste any time getting back to Topeka. She called me the following Friday at the office to see if I could meet with her Saturday evening. I told her that I was scheduled to fly to Minneapolis Saturday but would be back by 4:00 P.M. and could spend the evening with her. On Friday I told Glenna that I had a flight to Minneapolis Saturday and would be back Sunday. She couldn't have cared less and was complaining that she would be eight months pregnant during the Christmas holidays. I reminded her that she would not have any work to do because we were invited to her folks' home for Christmas. She said that she didn't care to go and that I could take the kids to spend the holidays with their grandparents.

I returned to Forbes Air Base about 4:00 P.M. Saturday, changed clothes, and drove to my office on campus. Helen was waiting there in her car, and I suggested that she follow me to Lawrence where she could leave her car and we would drive on in my car to Kansas City. She knew of a good dining restaurant where they had a live orchestra for dancing. That was where we really got acquainted, for I was starving for female companionship. When we got into my Cadillac to drive to her car, we got to embracing and kissing one another and ended up making love. When we arrived at her car, we agreed to see one another again and soon. I drove to Topeka and spent the night at the air base.

A week before Christmas our sergeant that lived in Kansas City invited the ROTC staff to his house for a Christmas party. I informed Glenna of this invitation and she didn't care to go but knew that I was obligated to be there. I called Helen and made arrangements to meet at her home when our early dinner was over.

I excused myself immediately after dinner and confided with the sergeant, who knew that I had dated Helen, that I was on my way to see her. She answered the door and asked me in to meet her aunt. From there we went to the Continental Hotel restaurant for Helen to have her evening meal. I obtained a room at the hotel and we bedded together until 2:00 A.M. She took a cab home and I drove home and was in bed by 4:00 A.M. without waking Glenna.

On the 21st of December I flew General Caldara's C-47 on an administrative flight to Maxwell Air Base. The flight schedule called for me to remain overnight there, and then leave the next day for Tinker Air Base in Oklahoma. I had to remain overnight and departed the next day, the 23rd of December, for Forbes Air Base. I got home that evening, loaded the car with Christmas presents and food, and the kids and I took off the morning of the twenty-fourth to their grandparents' home in Lincoln. The next couple of days the kids got to know their aunt Dolly, their mother's older sister, and her husband Mark. Dolly's personality was just the opposite of Glenna's, and both she and her husband Mark Allen were fun to be with, as were their children.

The kids and I left Lincoln for Topeka after three days of Christmas fun with the grandparents and the Allen family. I was busy at the office until New Year's day. Glenna had hired a lady to take care of the kids and house on a daily basis since I was all day and evening at the university or flying. We were invited to the AFROTC New Year's party but Glenna was very uncomfortable with her pregnancy, and we spent the evening at home. I was scheduled to make a long administrative flight to March Air Base in California the day after New Year's and returned the next day. The 4th of January I was back to the daily routine of classes in the morning, afternoon, and evening.

I had not seen Helen since before Christmas but had called her from Lincoln to wish her happy holidays. We were able to spend the evening together the Friday after my return flight from California. Her aunt was gone for the evening and would not be back until midnight, so we were able to make up for lost time. Sunday I went to the office to complete some paperwork and the sergeant whose wife had introduced me to Helen was also there catching up on office paperwork. He said that he needed to talk to me when I finished my work.

We got together about an hour later and he said he had something to tell me about Helen since he didn't realize that she and I would become such close friends. He asked if I had ever heard of the Pendergast Political Machine in Kansas City. I said yes, that I remembered that it played an important part in Harry Truman's political career. The sergeant said, "Yes, and Helen is the girlfriend of the Head Man. I wanted you to know just what you were getting into by dating Helen." I thanked him for telling me.

I didn't waste any time in calling Helen and asked how soon could we get together. She said that she could see me Friday evening and we agreed to meet in Lawrence, Kansas. We had a warm welcome, and then she asked what was bothering me. I repeated what the sergeant had told me and that I wanted to hear it from her. She said yes, that the top man was a dear and very close friend and that she had already told him about me having a loveless marriage, that I was a pilot that had fought against the Germans in World War II and was now an associate professor at Washburn University. She also told him that I was a wonderful companion to her. I told her that I didn't want to interfere with their relationship, and she said that their love for one another was platonic and that he was pleased that I was a good companion for her because he wanted her to be happy and he wanted to meet me. I found that hard to believe, and in my mind I thought that I should not see Helen again. She strongly insisted that there would be no trouble with me meeting him and asked me to please let her arrange a date and time for the two of us to meet with him. I knew that she was sincere and told her I would have to have the address for me to leave with my boss in case of an emergency. Helen agreed.

Why do pregnant women usually seem to start their labor pains during the dark hours of the day? In the early dark hours of the morning of January 15th, Glenna started having labor pains and I rushed her to the Forbes Air Base hospital. I then returned to the house until the house sitter arrived at 8:00 A.M. I returned to the hospital and Glenna delivered a baby boy just before noon. I knew that she would be unhappy because she wanted a girl and so did I. We had not discussed any name for either a girl or boy but I told Glenna that I would like the boy to be named Stephen. Without my knowledge, she filled out the birth certificate and named the boy Kenneth Stephen. I really didn't like that because I had been named after my dad and resented it, so I didn't want any son of mine named after me, and Glenna knew this. Glenna didn't have any complications but it was hospital policy to stay three nights. The woman that Glenna had hired to watch the house and children was very good and stayed overnight for several days even after Glenna had returned from the hospital. A week before the baby came, I was scheduled to fly to March Air Base in California on the sixteenth, which I completed and returned on the seventeenth. Glenna was discharged with the baby on the eighteenth, and I drove her and the new baby home. The kids made a big fuss of joy having a new brother, but Glenna was very sullen. She had been in a bad mood for several weeks after Tim was born and it looked like this mood was being repeated.

I had never bored Helen with my married life except to tell her that I was married with three children and was planning to file for divorce after I completed my assignment at the university. A few days after I returned from California, Helen called me at the office and said that we had an appointment to meet her political friend. On the date of the meeting, I met Helen in Kansas City and we drove in her car to her friend's estate; the guard at the gate knew Helen and the car. The estate was located a few miles outside of Kansas City and as we turned into the entrance, the guard greeted Helen by name. She told the guard that I was her close friend, Ken, who had been invited to come with her today. The guard opened the iron gate and Helen drove up to a large and impressive house. We were greeted by another guard who greeted her and took care of the car. As we approached the front door, it opened just as we got there and the butler greeted Helen, who introduced me to him. The guard at the gate had no doubt notified the butler of our arrival.

The butler escorted us through the hallway to a large living room where a gentleman was relaxing in a lounge chair. He got up and Helen walked over to him, where they embraced and kissed. She introduced me, and we shook hands and he asked us to sit down. He looked at me and said, "Helen tells me that you are a pilot and helped us win the war against the Germans."

"Yes sir," I replied.

"I certainly thank you for that, and Helen tells me that you voted for Harry Truman to be President?"

"Yes sir, it was the first time I had ever voted, and Truman had proven himself a good President after Roosevelt died."

He then asked me what I did at the university, and I told him besides flying General Caldara to various meetings, I was teaching ROTC cadets about Geopolitics in the world today, "and from what Helen tells me, you are well versed in that subject." He laughed and then Helen and he had a few items to discuss. I felt that the time was appropriate for me to leave. I got up and shook his hand and told him that it had been a pleasure to meet him. He said that he was also pleased to meet me and appreciated that I was being a good companion for Helen. I told Helen that I would be out in the hall and left the two of them alone. About five minutes later Helen came out into the hallway and Helen bid the butler goodbye as he opened the door. A guard had the car out front and Helen bid him goodbye as we got into her car. As we drove through the open gate, the guard saluted us. Helen then asked me what I thought of the boss. I said that I really liked him and felt very comfortable with him. She said, "Well he liked you too, and said I was to feel free to bring you with me anytime that I came to visit with him."

The middle of February I had to make another flight to March Air Base and had to stay overnight. The next day I had to stop at Colorado Springs and didn't arrive at Forbes until 11:00 P.M. I got home about midnight and was able to get to bed without waking the kids or Glenna. About 3:00 A.M. I awoke because the bedroom light was on. Glenna was sitting on her side of the bed with a kitchen knife in her hand. I asked her what in the hell was she doing with the light on and a knife in her hand. She said, "I was going to kill you!" I thought this woman was insane! I jumped out of bed and told her that this was it, she would never see me in her bed again. I grabbed some clothes, drove to the base, and checked into the BOQ, which became my home.

I never slept in that house again, nor with her. I would see Helen once or twice a month and had to tell her why I was living on base in the officers' quarters. She said I was a very lucky man to wake up when I did. I then told her about my Guardian Angel who had saved my life over fifty times and that there was no doubt that she woke me up before Glenna could use the knife. I did stop by to see the children when the babysitter was there and Glenna was absent. Pam and Jeff asked me why I didn't come home anymore and I was honest with them. I told them that their mother no longer loved me and I no longer loved her, so we would never live together again.

The 1st of April I received good news. My good friend at the Pentagon, Colonel Bennet, said that I was on the promotion list to major. I had been a second lieutenant six months, a first lieutenant one year, and a captain ten years. I had been on the promotion list twice before, but the board believed the untruthful letters that Glenna had written to the Air Force and not my truthful denials. She would be surprised when she heard that I had been promoted.

The school year would be ending in June and I would have my college degree. At that time I would be reassigned to another air base, so I arranged a meeting with Glenna the last week in May to discuss a property settlement. I told her that our marriage was over and that I would be leaving Topeka in June. I told her that she could have the house and the furnishings and that from this house it was only a four-hour drive to her hometown of Lincoln and her parents. She told me that she did not want to stay in this area and wanted to live her life in Bellevue, Washington. I was surprised because we had never spent any time in that city nor had we any friends or relatives there. I knew better than to argue with her so I agreed to drive her and the children there and purchase a house for her and the children to live in.

In the middle of June I sold the house just two days after I placed the *For Sale* sign in the front yard. The house had increased in value enough to pay back the money I had borrowed from my mother-in-law, and enough to purchase a house in Bellevue. I received my new assignment a couple of days after graduation and I was not happy with them. I was given thirty days' leave, then to report to Parks Processing Facility, California, and then report to the Weather Recon Squadron at Eielson Air Force Base, Fairbanks, Alaska for duty. I was not happy with this assignment, so I drove to the Pentagon at Washington D.C. and had a meeting with Colonel Bennet. I told him that I was going to be a single man, and this was not a very good place to be for two years. He asked if I had ever been to Alaska and I said that I had not. He then told me to take the assignment and if, at the end of six months, I felt that I was not being utilized in a position relative to my rank and experience, to write him a personal letter and he would get me reassigned. I thanked him and drove back to Topeka feeling much better.

When I got back to Forbes Air Base, I called Helen and told her of my transfer to Alaska and she agreed that I could see her the next day. She was alone at home and we sat down on the couch and looked at each other, knowing that was a sad time. I thanked her for being a great morale booster for me during my assignment at the university. We both agreed that we had enjoyed our companionship and that we had needed our sexual relationship. I told her to give my regards to the boss and that the two of them were always welcome to come to Alaska and visit me in my igloo. I stood up to leave, and she got up and we embraced and kissed and I hurried out of the house and drove away. I had a great affection for her, but not the true love that I had felt for Lee, my Mormon sweetheart. I never saw Helen again.

I made my last flight out of Forbes Air Base on the 9th of July. General Caldara had already been transferred to another air base, so I would miss being his pilot. I thanked the base operations personnel for the great cooperation they had given to me in retaining my skill as a pilot.

According to the sales agreement on our house, the buyer was to have possession on the 15th of July. Our furniture was picked up on the twelfth and we departed the same day for Lincoln, Nebraska so that the children could say goodbye to their grandparents. After we got settled in the Buck house, I got Mildred, my mother in law, cornered in the kitchen. While paying her back the money I had borrowed from her, Glenna walked in on us and wanted to know why I was giving her mother all that money. I told her, and she was upset that I had borrowed money from her mother. I told her that thanks to her mother, we had lived in a good house in Topeka. We stayed one whole day and then left early the next morning for Washington State.

We spent the first night at Scottsbluff, Nebraska. Jeff and I shared one room and

Glenna had the three other children with her. The next day we stayed at Yellowstone National Park so that the children could see the beautiful falls and Old Faithful blowing its steam. We stopped at Missoula, Montana the next day because Pamela was taken ill, and Glenna took her to a local doctor. He examined her and said it was not serious and gave Glenna a prescription, which she filled at a local drug store. Glenna had Pam with her for the night, and I ended up with three sons in my room. Pam was feeling fine the next morning, and I drove all day to reach Seattle that night. I put the family in a two-bedroom suite in a Seattle hotel and went to my uncle Ray Hawk's house, where I spent the night.

The next day I drove across Lake Washington on the floating bridge to Bellevue, where I spent an hour driving the city streets to become familiar with the city layout. I found a new group of houses about fifteen blocks north of the city center. I looked at a rambler that had just been finished and purchased it from the contractor who was finishing the house next door. I called the warehouse in Seattle that had our furniture in storage, and they promised to deliver it to the new rambler the next day. I called Glenna and told her that I had bought a new rambler and that I would pick them up the next morning. I drove back to my uncle's house in Seattle and enjoyed the evening with my uncle, aunt Mary, and two cousins, Jim and Cherie.

When I arrived at the hotel the next morning, the family had already checked out and were waiting for me. The kids were excited about going to a new home and even Glenna showed some interest. The furniture arrived just a few minutes after we did. The house had three bedrooms and two baths, with the usual dining room, living room, and kitchen. Glenna enjoyed telling the movers where to put everything, and I went next door to talk to the contractor. I asked him to pour a fifteen by twenty foot patio adjoining the back door, and install a wooden fence around the back yard. I paid him his estimated cost of this improvement on the spot. Jeff and I then went to the nearest grocery store and bought enough food for an army. I stayed two more days before I had to leave, helping them getting settled. Jeff and I stayed in one bedroom, Tim and Steve in the middle bedroom, and Pam and her mother in the master bedroom with its own bath.

It was now time for me to leave for the Overseas Processing Unit at Parks, California. I got Glenna aside and told her that I would give her 100 dollars per child per month, and make the mortgage payment on the house and valid doctor bills. If she needed more money than that, I suggested that she go to work or file for a divorce. The kids didn't want me to leave, especially Pam and Jeff, but I explained to them that flying with the Air Force was my career. I gave them a hug and a kiss, but only gave Glenna a verbal goodbye.

I was at Parks for a week getting a physical examination and shots that were due, and making sure that my military records were up-to-date. I drove the Cadillac back to Bellevue because I would not need it in the tundra of northern Alaska. I would go by military air out of McChord Air Base to get to Alaska. Glenna was surprised when I handed her the keys to the car, and I suggested that she learn to drive. The first week in August I was in a MATS aircraft out of McChord Air Base on my way to Elmendorf Air Base at Anchorage, Alaska.

Washburn University of Topeka

To the Friends of Learning Everywhere, Greetings:

is this day, by action of the Faculty and of the Board of Regents, declared a

Kenneth Waverly Slaker, Jr.

of Washburn University of Topeka and is admitted to all the rights and privileges belonging to this degree.

Bachelor of Arts

In testimony whereof, this diploma is issued with the signatures of the proper officers and the seal of the University, affixed at Topeka, Kansas, on this, the first day of September, in the year of our Lord, nineteen hundred and fifty-three.

For the Regents
Chairman
Secretary

For the Faculty
President
Dean

Diploma from Washburn University of Topeka.

Chapter 11
CHASING WEATHER TO THE NORTH POLE

I was surprised when I arrived at Elmendorf Air Force Base. The buildings were large, modern, and clean. I checked into a very modern BOQ and walked to the officers' club. The club atmosphere penetrated my mind and it felt great to be back on an air base where I belonged. I looked through the base telephone directory for pilots that I might know stationed there. I found Colonel Quentin T. Quick, a second cousin of mine from Bellingham, Washington who I had not seen since 1943 in North Africa. There were also two pilots that were with me in Germany in 1949.

The next morning I signed in at the Headquarters of the 7th Weather Group, the parent headquarters for the 58th Weather Recon Squadron at Eielson AFB, to which I was to be assigned. The commander was pleased to see me and said that I would receive a briefing of the missions in a couple of days. In the meantime, I was to become familiar with the base and Anchorage. I called Colonel Quick at Alaskan Air Command Headquarters, and we had a long lunch talking about our World War II days flying B-17s in combat out of North Africa. I spent a day in Anchorage, a small city of about 25,000, all of whom I found very friendly.

I spent two days at the 7th Weather Group Headquarters being briefed on the two missions being accomplished by the WB-50 aircrews. The first mission was the gathering of weather data from two routes, one from Eielson to the North Pole and back, and the other route west to the end of the Aleutian Islands, then north on the dateline to St. Lawrence Island, then east to Eielson Air Base. The second mission was classified because on each flight air samples were taken at a high altitude and given to civilian technical personnel at Fairbanks. These people then could analyze the samples for residue from atomic blasts by the Russians and know their progress in the development of the atomic bomb.

The first week in September the 7th Weather Group got me passage on a C-47 to Ladd Field at Fairbanks. I was greeted by a Lt. Don Mendiola who was assigned to drive me the twenty-six miles to Eielson. On the way the lieutenant told me that I had been assigned to a singles suite in the field grade building. Also since I was shown as a married man but separated from his wife, I was to have dinner that evening with the sister of a pilot and his wife at 8:00 P.M.

During the flight to Fairbanks, I had taken a look at myself. Here I was thirty-three years old, had two bad marriages, lost two women that I had loved, and I was on my way to an isolated base in Alaska. I decided that I had enough of love and marriage and from then on I was just going to screw them and leave them. And now this lieutenant tells me that I have a date the first night here in Fairbanks, Alaska.

I met Lt. Mendiola at the officers' club that evening at 7:30 and he briefed me in detail about the WB-50 flights. The one to the North Pole was a fifteen to sixteen hour flight, depending on the winds. A surprise was that the crew contained three navigators because there were no landmarks, just solid icecap below, and no radio guidance systems. The magnetic compass was not reliable because when you are over the pole, the only direction is south, so we had electronic compasses and the navigators could use celestial to keep us on course. A few minutes before eight, two ladies walked in, and they were chubby. I looked at Lt. Mendiola and he just shook his head no and smiled. At exactly five after eight, a threesome walked into the lounge. The officer was tall and slender like me. On his right arm was a short, dark haired young lady, and to her right was a young girl about 5' 7" with blond hair, a slim figure, and very attractive. I turned to the lieutenant and said, "That blond is a beauty that I could go for," and he said, "She is your date, let's go meet her."

We got up to meet them and the lieutenant introduced me to Captain Glenn Stanislaus, who then introduced me to Dorothy, his wife, and then to his sister, Lee Ann Stanislaus. We had an enjoyable dinner during which Lee Ann told me that she had only been there one month. Her brother had asked her to accompany his new bride to Alaska because she had never flown in an airplane nor been very far out of Mississippi. The base was very short of civilian help and the base supply officer had talked her into staying and working for him. After dinner Lee Ann told me that we were invited to a private party in the nurses' quarters and hoped that I could go with her. I quickly agreed, thanked Glenn and his wife for the dinner, and told them that it was a pleasure to have met them. The party was good for me since I was new on the base and was able to meet so many of the permanent party the first day here. About 11:00 P.M. Lee Ann said she had to leave because she had to be at work early the next morning. I walked her to the women's quarters, we shook hands, and I thanked her for the invite to the party. I started to walk to my quarters and realized that I didn't know the base layout, so I stood at one of the corners trying to figure out where my quarters were, when the Officer of the Day drove up and asked if he could be of help. I explained my problem; he laughed and drove me to my quarters. So ended my first and long day at Eielson Air Force Base in Alaska.

I reported for duty the next morning to Lt. Colonel Lipe, the squadron commander. He asked me to be seated and started to brief me on the squadron mission, and I informed him that I had been thoroughly briefed at the 7th Weather Group Headquarters at Elmendorf. I then asked him just where I would fit in to the squadron operation. He told me what I had to accomplish before I could become a WB-50 aircraft commander. First, I would have to attend the Arctic Survival School at Fairbanks before even flying on a mission. Also, even though I had over two thousand hours as pilot of four-engine aircraft, I had to fly as a copilot with a pilot that already had flown several of the arctic missions. The remainder of September I spent attending mission briefings and attending ground school studying the various systems on the WB-50.

The first week in October I was assigned a room in the transient quarters for the week to attend the Arctic Indoctrination School at Ladd Air Base at Fairbanks. The instructor was a middle-aged sourdough born in Alaska and was very experienced in living and surviving in the Alaskan and arctic region. On the last day of ground school, we were briefed that there was one more phase to complete before we would be given graduate status. We could now fly our squadron missions but on one of the three or four missions when we returned to home base, there would be a bus waiting for us. We would go directly from the aircraft and enter the bus. The instructor said, "You have just bailed out of the aircraft in the arctic region where the bus is going to drop you, and you will be there for four days to survive with what you are wearing along with one of the survival packs that has been released from the aircraft." There were some questions, and the instructor hoped that we would never have to experience what we had just learned and to remember that Alaska was two times the size of Texas. A pilot from California sitting beside me said in a loud voice, "Two times nothing is still nothing!" There was very little laughter and the instructor just smiled and dismissed us.

Before I had gone to Arctic School, I had started eating some of my breakfasts at the civilian mess and when Lee Ann came in, she would join me. She had a terrific personality and I got her to talk about herself and her family. She was born in Vinita, Oklahoma, and her mother was second generation from an English immigrant family. Her father was third generation from a Polish family by name of Stanislaus. Her father and his brother were in the farm implement business in eastern Oklahoma and doing very well. She had two brothers, the one I had met here who was an Air Force pilot, and her other brother worked for the public school system in Wichita. I have never asked people their age, nor did I with Lee Ann, but I assumed she was in her early twenties.

When I returned from Arctic school, I went to base supply and asked Lee Ann if she would let me take her to the officers' club that weekend to a bingo game night. She was very pleased and pleased me by saying she would love to. We had a fun evening and she even won a game. Then after the game there was a local GI band that played dancing music. I loved to dance and asked Lee Ann to dance. Wow! She was an outstanding dancer, and what a fun time we had. She told me that she had played saxophone in the high school band and the church organ on Sundays. From that night on we dated once or twice a week. The third week in October, I was scheduled for my first arctic mission as a copilot with a major that was one of the exceptional officers in the squadron.

My first mission to the North Pole exposed me to new and important information that I needed to know as a pilot. After takeoff and across the Brooks Mountain Range, all systems and instruments were checked and when no trouble was found, we started our climb to 18,500 feet pressure altitude, not sea level altitude. Since there was no land surface in the arctic and it was completely covered with ice, the temperature was fairly stable and you don't have the tall cumulus buildups like you get further south. At our altitude the clouds were below us but we did have a problem. It was very difficult to tell from what direction and what speed the winds were at our altitude.

After a few hours on course, there was a mark on the course called "The Point of No Return." Here, the crew checked all systems and instruments for normal operation. If there was any indication that an engine was showing a possible problem, then the mission should be aborted. If the pilot decided to continue and the engine was lost plus other related problems requiring a bailout, Air Rescue Service in Alaska would not have the capability to perform a rescue beyond the point of no return. The icecap was covered with ridges of broken ice which would be very hazardous to attempt a wheels landing. There were some areas called leads but the ice on them might not be thick enough to support a WB-50.

When over the North Pole, we did not return on the same route that we came to the Pole, but the navigators gave us the direction to Wrangle Island. This island on the eastern coast of Siberia belonged to Russia, and when we were within five miles of the Wrangle coast, we flew south five miles from the island, taking samples of the air that had originated in western Siberia. This completed the classified part of our mission and we headed for Point Barrow, Alaska and on to Eielson Air Base. This was my first arctic mission, which was fifteen and a half hours long. This was the first time I had ever flown over eight hours, fifteen minutes—which was a B-17 bombing mission to northern Italy in 1943. The crew gets the next day off after flying an arctic mission. The day after that, you check the records of the flight made the previous day for errors, etc.

I was scheduled to fly every fourth day and in the third week of October, I was on my third arctic mission when we got a surprise welcome when we got back to Eielson. There was the bus waiting for us newcomers to finish the last phase of our arctic survival course. We were not permitted to carry anything because we were treated as if we had just bailed out of the aircraft. The driver took us about thirty miles into the tundra with its small trees and dumped us. He said that he would be back to pick up our bodies the morning of the fifth day and drove off. Then we remembered that the first thing we had to do was start a fire, which would not be easy because the temperature was forty-two degrees below zero and everything was frozen. We found enough dry things on us, such as handkerchiefs and cigarettes, to cover with thin wood shavings.

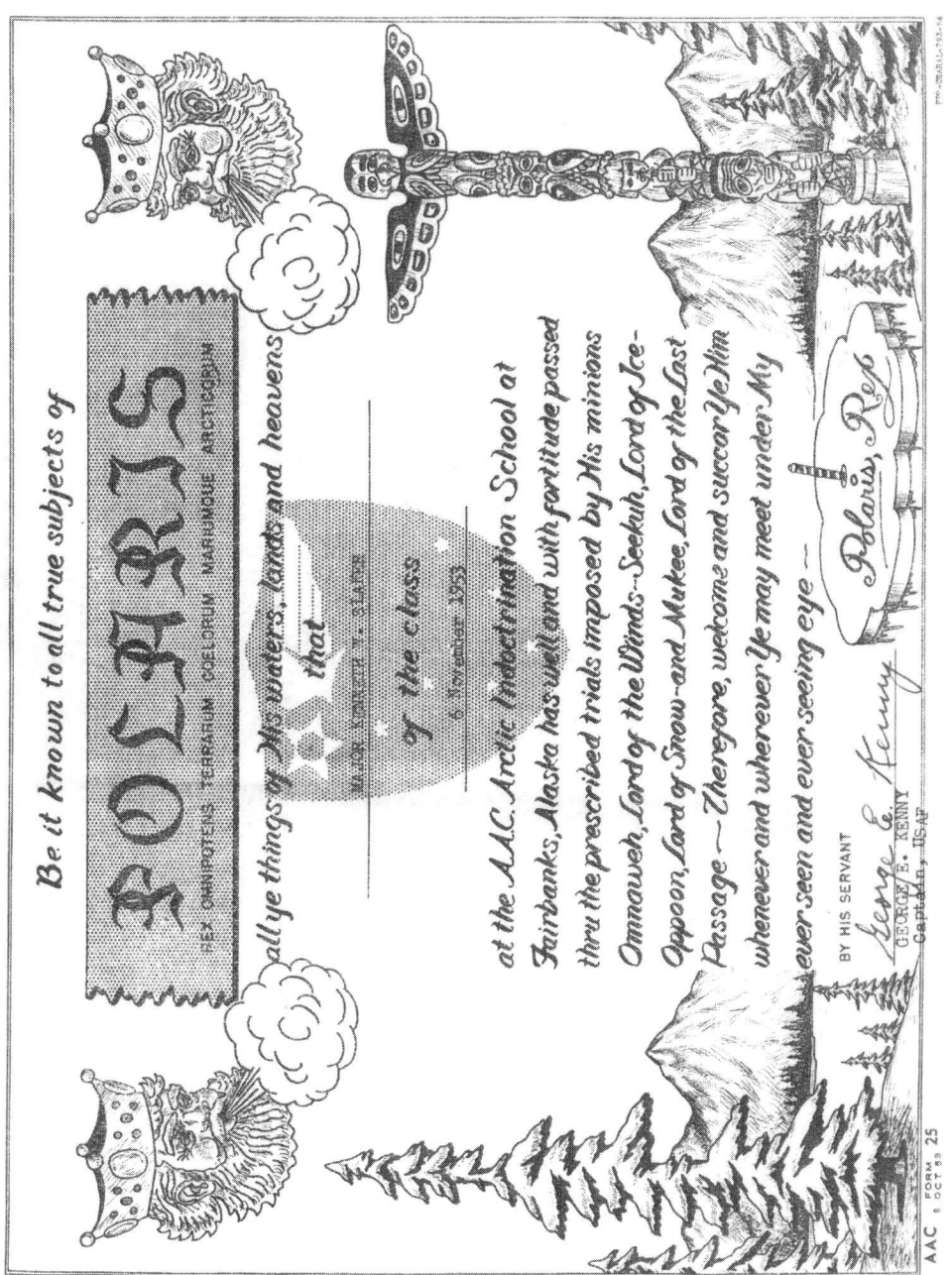

Diploma from Arctic Indoctrination School in Alaska, 6 November 1953.

We put thin frozen shavings next to the fire to thaw. It was a slow process but after a couple of hours we had a good warm fire.

At school we were taught that rabbits were plentiful and that all we needed was a couple of lengths of thin copper wire. I had this in the lining of my heavy flight jacket and found a couple of bushes with rabbit tracks. I made two loops for their heads to enter, which would choke them to death since the end of the wire was wound around a branch of the bush and rabbits never back up; they always try to run forward and that kills them. We laid tarps around the fire and tried to sleep. We really didn't sleep but dozed off and on. I finally got up at 7:00 A.M. and it would not be daylight for another three or four hours. I decided to take a look at my rabbit traps, and I was really surprised to see two frozen rabbits. We also had been instructed that before any one of us had time to take a leak, to select a spot at least a hundred feet away and mark it with a couple of rocks where you would empty your bladder. Here it would freeze and not thaw until summer. It was named Mt. Urine. The same action was to be taken for bowel movements, but further away from the fire and behind some bushes or trees.

I had purchased several Hershey chocolate bars and stuffed them into the lining of my flight jacket. These were a lifesaver for me. I had four bars and ate one each day. When the bus arrived the morning of the fifth day, we were on the bus before it even stopped. When we arrived at Ladd Air Base, I went to the transient quarters, rented a room, took a long hot shower, and went to bed. I awoke about 5:00 P.M., dressed, and was able to get a staff car to take me the twenty-six miles to Eielson where I enjoyed a steak dinner at the officers' club. On the morning of November 1st, the squadron adjutant handed me a large envelope and inside it was the graduation certificate from the Arctic Indoctrination School. This was one to keep, for not many pilots in the Air Force had this certificate.

I only flew one mission in November plus a couple of local flights in a C-47. This gave me more time to date Lee Ann a few times a week. She told me that she was working as a model on Saturdays at the biggest department store in Fairbanks. Since I didn't have a car, I asked Lt. Mendiola if he could drive me to Fairbanks the last Saturday in November. He agreed, and as we drove into Fairbanks that Saturday, I told him that we were going to see Lee Ann model some clothes. He was surprised and asked what I had in mind, and I told him to wait and see. We went to the women's clothing area and I told the hostess that I would like to see some formal gowns. She was very pleased and disappeared into a back room. She came back with Lee Ann in a formal gown, and when Lee Ann saw Mendiola and me, she was at a loss for words. She moved around to display the gown and I told the hostess that it was too formal and would like a younger looking formal. This time Lee Ann came out alone, and I told her that if she would go with me to the formal dance at the University of Alaska that evening, I would purchase that dress for her. She smiled and said, "Its a deal." I bought the dress and we went to the formal and danced . . . danced . . . and danced.

Come December, Lee Ann and I were spending the evenings together except when I was flying. We ate dinner usually at the officers' club, and if there was no activity at the club, we walked to her quarters where we talked about our family backgrounds, characters at Eielson, her job, my career, etc. I would say goodnight about 10:30 because there was an eleven o'clock curfew when all visitors had to be out of the women's quar-

Lee Ann Stanislaus Slaker, Lackland AFB, San Antonio, Texas, 1960.

ters. One evening we planned to eat at the club and I arrived early to get a table for four since my roommate, Major Levine, and his girlfriend were going to join us. The wife of a major in our squadron walked in and headed towards my table. I assumed that she was going to take the empty table beside mine, but without any greeting she sat down beside me. I greeted her and she said, "Major Slaker, I really have something to say to you and I will make it short. You are a regular officer and married with four children. You are here without them and keeping company with a nineteen-year-old girl that you are misleading. My husband and I and several other couples in the squadron dislike what you are doing." She got up and walked away. I never said a word and didn't even give her the courtesy of standing up when she departed. I had to be amused because just four years ago a major's wife had talked to me suggesting that I get rid of Glenna. Now here was a major's wife asking me to get back with Glenna. Privacy is rare when you are in the military service.

We had an enjoyable dinner with Major Levine and his girlfriend, excused ourselves, and walked to Lee Ann's quarters. I told her about the scolding I had received from the major's wife. I then asked Lee Ann if she was nineteen as the major's wife said. Lee Ann then asked me, what age did I want her to be? I told her I had assumed that she was in her early twenties and if she was nineteen, then she was the most mature nineteen-year-old I had ever met. She then said, "Ken, I am nineteen and I hope that my age will not change our relationship." I told her that her age would not change the relationship, that it was my being fourteen years older that might cause her to have second thoughts.

I felt it was time that I tell Lee Ann the full history of my marriage to Glenna. She was surprised that I had taken her back after my divorce application was denied in Pennsylvania. I told her that Lt. Mendolia's parents had given me the name of a good attorney in Reno who I was in contact with for filing for a divorce there. I was saving my leave time to get forty-two days to spend in Reno to establish my residence there. I had also promised the kids that I would see them at Christmas time. Lee Ann expressed her disappointment that I wasn't going to be there for Christmas. We walked to the door of her quarters, and we put our arms around each other and I gave her a kiss, saying nothing, and she said, "Ken, you know that I am very much in love with you." She gave me a kiss and went back into her quarters.

I had made reservations to fly commercial air to Seattle on the twenty-third. Lee Ann was very busy modeling at the store in Fairbanks in the evenings for the holiday season, but she was able to have dinner with me the night before I was leave for Seattle.

We had dinner by ourselves and were both tense and didn't do much talking. We walked to her quarters, and Lee Ann asked me to sit down because she had something to tell me before I left for Seattle. She said that just after she had graduated from high school, she married the son of a very wealthy family. She liked him, but her mother had really pushed her into getting married to him. They had lived together just a short time when he came down with a disease of his genitals. He confessed that he had contracted the disease from a streetwalker he had picked up. Lee Ann said that she called her father, who was very upset since he had been against her marriage to this spoiled classmate. Her dad told her to pack her clothes, that he was coming to pick her up. She told her dad that she had not had sex with him the several days before her husband caught the disease, but her dad insisted that she be examined by the family doctor. Her dad, who was a very well-known and liked businessman, had no problem in getting Lee Ann a divorce. The doctor had notified her dad that from his examination and tests made on her, Lee Ann was a very clean and healthy girl. Lee Ann then told me that this was one reason she welcomed the opportunity to come to Alaska—to put this mistake behind her and be herself.

I was really shaken to hear this confession by her and then think that this beautiful young girl had been married and divorced before she was nineteen. I thought, here I go again, becoming interested in a woman that was on the rebound from a bad martial experience. I got up and thanked her for being honest with me and wished her a happy Christmas with her brother and his wife. Lee Ann came up to me, put her hands on my shoulders, looked me in the eyes and was very serious when she said, "Ken, in spite of the circumstances we have lived with, I love you very much." I put my arms around her and we really hugged and kissed. I didn't say anything and turned and walked back to my quarters in a daze.

The base transportation officer said that he would have a staff car pick me up in front of my quarters at 8:30 A.M. to take me to the airport at Fairbanks. I came out of the building shortly before 8:30, and standing by the car was Lee Ann. That was a pleasant surprise and a morale booster. We put our arms around one another and she whispered, "I love you." We kissed and I got into the car. As we drove off, I knew that was not a goodbye kiss—it was a kiss of love.

Chapter 12
LOVE'S THIRD CHARM IN ALASKA

It was a cold and rainy day when I arrived at the Sea Tac airport in Seattle. I took a taxi to Bellevue, and there in the carport was my green Cadillac. I wished then that I had taken it to Alaska. I rang the doorbell and Jeff opened the door and shouted, "Dad's here!" Pam and Tim came running and hugging me, and what a joy it was to see my kids happy to see me. Glenna came into the room and we greeted each other with a hello. Most of my time that day was with Pam and Jeff because Tim was only two and Steve was still not quite one year old. Pam was a cute young girl and very affectionate. Jeff had many questions about my flying over the North Pole and I was able to answer most of them. I told Glenna that I would need the keys to the car the next day to go to Seattle to do my Christmas shopping. I asked her if she had learned to drive and she said no, that she had a neighbor who drove the Cadillac for her when she had some shopping to do.

I spent the night with Jeff in his bedroom, where I would also get some sleep Christmas Eve. I took Jeff with me the next day to Seattle to purchase Christmas gifts for the children. I did all my shopping at Frederick & Nelsons department store because they had a huge selection of gifts to choose from. Jeff and I had lunch there and had a good visit with one another. As we got ready to leave, Jeff asked me if I would ever come back home to live. I was honest with Jeff and told him that I never could do that because his mother and I did not love one another. He was silent for a couple of minutes, then he made a statement that really bothered me: "Dad, my mother doesn't like me." I could not make a decent reply to him, but I said one to myself: *Your mother is a bitch!* I could not let the love for my children pull me back into that trap with Glenna again.

Christmas morning was the usual screams of *ohs* and *ahs* when the children opened their gifts. There was a gift for me, a pen and pencil set from the four children. I had bought a Christmas card and put a fifty-dollar bill in it for Glenna. She prepared a good farewell luncheon for me and the kids, and I really enjoyed all the food. When it came time for me to say goodbye, it was not easy. Pam cried and Jeff just stood and looked at me. Tim gave me a hug and I told Glenna to take good care of them. As I turned to walk out, I shook hands with Jeff and gave him a wink with my wet eye.

My mother was one of eight children, and I spent the night with her older brother, Ray Hawk. When he was in the Navy, his ship docked at Seattle and while there, he met a very attractive daughter of Italian immigrants, married her, and lived his life in Seattle. The next two nights I was with Mother's young sister, Rhoda, married to Herman McMillian, who was a contractor in Federal Way. He took me to the airport on the morning of the twenty-eighth, where I boarded Pacific Northern for Alaska.

During the flight to Fairbanks, my thoughts came back to my first flight to Fairbanks after I had gone to the Pentagon, begging not to be sent to Alaska. Colonel Bennet would not change my assignment. My decision during that first flight to Fairbanks was to hell with women. I was not going to get serious with any woman and just play the field. Within one hour after arrival at Fairbanks, Lt. Mendiola tells me I have a date that night! Now my brain cells got together and reminded me that I have a Guardian Angel. She knew of my difficulty with love and marriage, and it was her guidance that brought me to Alaska to meet this beautiful, young, and intelligent girl who ended up telling me that she loved me. The more I thought about it, the more convinced I became that meeting Lee Ann was not an accident, but was planned to happen. I knew that I was in love with her but was hesitant to commit myself to love another woman.

I was not excited about returning to the weather squadron because there existed a clique which I was not a part of. Actually, my time was being wasted so far as my career was concerned. I decided that if I was not given a better assignment in the 7th Weather Group that January or February, I would write that letter to Colonel Bennet who had promised to transfer me.

I had asked Lt. Mendiola to pick me up when I came back from Seattle, and when I got out of the aircraft, I spotted him at the gate. Standing beside him was Lee Ann, which boosted my morale and confidence. I realized that if she had not been there, I would have been very disappointed. I walked right up to her and said, "I have not come back here to fly to the North Pole, I have come back to be with you." We put our arms around one another and had a long kiss. Lt. Mendiola said, "Come on, you two lovebirds, let's get back to Eielson."

Lee Ann and I sat in the back seat, holding hands and talking. She said that she worried I might not return because she knew that I did not like my assignment there and might get a transfer while I was in Seattle. I told her that was still a possibility, and would she come with me? She said that she would go anywhere on this earth with me. Lt. Mendiola dropped us off at Lee Ann's quarters, and I asked him to join us at the club for dinner. We entered her quarters and were instantly into each other's arms. I finally told her that I loved her more than any woman I had ever known and wanted to marry her as soon as I became a free man. We met Lt. Mendiola at the club and my roommate, Major Levine, and Loraine, his girlfriend, joined us. By the time we finished dinner and chatted, it was 10:00 P.M. and we excused ourselves and walked to Lee Ann's quarters. I was not going to have much time with Lee Ann due to the 11:00 P.M. curfew. I told Lee Ann that I was not leaving and that I would sneak out early in the morning. She didn't say anything so I started to take off my clothes. I turned to see her and she was already in bed.

The greatest thrill a man can have is to slip in between the sheets with the woman he deeply loves and to know she has the same love for you. It was a night of ecstasy for me. When Lee Ann finally went to sleep, I got dressed and quietly left her quarters. Walking back to my unit, I looked up at the cold black sky and thanked my Guardian Angel for bringing Lee Ann into my life.

By the time New Year's Eve arrived, our table had grown from four persons to eight. It included Lee Ann's brother Glenn and his wife, and Captain Jackson and his wife, a couple that I had become friends with since my arrival. The food and drinks were great, and Lee Ann and I enjoyed dancing to the live orchestra. When the clock struck twelve, Lee Ann and I kissed and I told her that 1954 was our year to enjoy. She said, "Ken, this is the best New Year's that I have ever experienced, since I am with you."

I was scheduled to fly the Polar mission only once in January. I had no other duty in the squadron so I had plenty of time on my hands. The second week in January I had a call from Lee Ann's brother Glenn, asking me if I could meet him at the club lounge at 4:00 P.M. I agreed and he was already there when I arrived, and he apologized for taking my time. He said that with his sister dating me steady and telling him that she loved me, his wife Dorothy was worried that I was just using Lee Ann and that Glenn should talk to me about my relationship with his sister. I told Glenn that I could understand his concern about Lee Ann and that I would be honest with him. I said that I was truly in love with his sister, that I wanted to marry her and that I had an attorney in Reno that would get me my divorce as soon as I had enough leave time to live in Reno for six weeks to establish residence in Nevada. "I am not playing games, Stan. I want to spend my life with her." Glenn held out his hand, we shook hands, and he said: "Major Slaker, welcome to the family." I told Glenn that from then on it was *Ken*, not *Major Slaker*. That weekend I was invited to dinner with Lee Ann at her brother's quarters.

I was not scheduled to fly either the Polar or dateline mission in February. I had to fly local for four hours in a C-47 so that I would get my flight pay. I also found out that there would not be a first pilot's space available for me until August. That did it.

The first week in March, I wrote a personal letter to Colonel Bennet explaining my situation there as a pilot. I told him that this was the worst outfit I had been in during thirteen years in the Air Force, and if he didn't have a position available for a pilot with my experience and rank, I would resign and go with the airlines. A week later he called me and asked if I would accept a position worthy of my pilot experience and rank there in Alaska. I told him that would be acceptable.

March was only a couple of days old when Lee Ann told me that her brother had received a letter from her mother that she was coming to Alaska the second week in March. I asked Lee Ann what would bring her mother there this time of the year. Lee

Ann then told me that she had written to her mother the middle of February that she had fallen in love with the man that she wanted to spend the rest of her life with. She also told her that I was separated from my wife but was getting a divorce and had four children. I asked why she told her of my situation, and Lee Ann said she had promised her parents that when she found the man she wanted to marry, she would let them know. Lee Ann was surprised that her mother was flying to Fairbanks, especially since she had never flown before. I told Lee Ann that I knew why she was coming this time of the year—it was to save her nineteen-year-old daughter from this man who was fourteen years older than her and had four children.

Lee Ann had told me about her mother during her lunch break, and after she went back to work, I had many thoughts about Lee Ann and me and her mother. It came to me that it was women who prevented me from marrying my first two loves. I decided that Lee Ann and I were going to prove to her mother that we loved one another and were planning a life together. I called the Mt. McKinley Hotel and reserved a room for three nights that coming weekend, the only weekend we had before her mother arrived. I knew that Lee Ann could get Friday off because my roommate was her boss. When Lee Ann met me at the club for dinner, I told her that we were going to the Mt. McKinley Hotel for our early honeymoon. She was all for it, and Friday morning we got on the train at Fairbanks that goes to Anchorage with a stop at the Mt. McKinley National Park. We really enjoyed ourselves, hiking, eating, dancing, and making love.

We returned Monday morning and Glenn told us that their mother was arriving by air late Wednesday night. He had borrowed a big sedan that would hold the five of us. Glenn could see that I was silently trying to name the five when he said, "Ken, you are going with us to meet Mother because you are a member of this family." I was ready to decline when I looked at Lee Ann, and she was nodding her head yes at me.

Their mother, Gladys Stanislaus, arrived at Fairbanks about 11:00 P.M. The temperature was twenty below zero. After the hugs and kisses and my introduction to her were over, I asked Mrs. Stanislaus if, after this long journey from Oklahoma, she would like a cocktail. Lee Ann had told me that her mother liked bourbon and 7-Up. She said, "That is a great idea, but where do we get a cocktail at this hour?" I told her that in Fairbanks the bars never close and she said, "Let's go!" The next couple of weeks I had dinner with the family at the club and at their quarters. Mrs. Stanislaus and I got along fine and got to know one another. She could see the love that existed between Lee Ann and me. Lee Ann told me that she and her mother had several down to earth talks and that she had convinced her mother that she and I were meant for each other.

Every month we had Commander's Call at the officers' club at no cost to club members, because our club was making money. The commanding general for April's call invited the Stanislaus family and me to be seated at his table. This was quite an honor, and my evening had a good start when I saw the major's wife who had given me a hard time about dating Lee Ann look at us at the general's table in envy. When dinner was over,

Lee Ann and I enjoyed dancing to a good GI band. After a couple of dances, Lee Ann asked me to dance with her mother when a slow number was played. When a slow number came up, I asked Mrs. Stanislaus to dance and we did very well. We were in the middle of the dance floor when the music stopped for intermission and I said, "Mrs. Stanislaus, we did quite well for the first time we have ever danced together."

She looked at me and said, "Call me Mom!" and gave me a hug. When I got back to the table and told Lee Ann what her mother had said to me, she got tears in her eyes.

My roommate (actually, we had a suite) Major Levine told me he had asked Loraine to marry him and she had agreed. He was taking leave to go back to Boston to tell the family and get their permission. I drove him to Fairbanks in his car, and he said he would call me as to when I could pick him up. Lee Ann and I were pleased because we had joined with them for many functions and activities. Four days later Bueny (his nickname) called me as to date, time, and flight number when he would arrive in Fairbanks. His plane came in on time, and we greeted each other and he asked me to drive. I didn't ask any questions and waited for him to tell me about his visit to Boston.

We were about five minutes from Eielson when I noticed his eyes were wet. I pulled to the side of the road and stopped. I asked, "Bueny, what's wrong?"

He said, "Ken, the family has refused me permission to marry a gentile and will disown me if I do. I don't know how I am going to tell Loraine this terrible news." I was at a loss for words. I thought, *Where is this brotherly love that is supposed to exist between us? I could not marry a Mormon because I was not a Mormon, my brother could not marry his Catholic sweetheart because he was not a Catholic, and now a fine Jewish officer and gentleman cannot marry a gentile because she is not a Jew. We are all God's children; isn't that good enough?* I asked Bueny if he wanted either me or Lee Ann to be with him when he told Loraine the bad news. He said no, that it was his duty. I dropped him off at the club so he could collect his thoughts before meeting Loraine.

The last week in April I received a note from Colonel Bennet that I would be receiving orders in a few days assigning me to the 10th Air Rescue Group as the group operations staff officer at Elmendorf Air Base at Anchorage. If I still wore the Colt .45, I would be outside firing away to celebrate my new assignment. I could not wait for Lee Ann to get off work; I went to her desk at base supply and told her the good news. I asked her if she wanted to stay and work there or come to Elmendorf. She said that she was ready to return to civilization.

I made my last flight to the North Pole on the 9th of May. The pilot was a captain, and when he heard that it was my last flight, when we were over the Pole, he exchanged seats with me and I finally got to fly the WB-50 back to Eielson and make the landing. I thanked him for being a fellow pilot. I was to report to the 10th Air Rescue Group the last week in May, so I spent most of my time packing my personal belongings and clearing the base.

Lee Ann gave her termination notice effective the 30th of May to the civilian personnel office. Being a woman, she had more clothes and personal items to pack than I did. Her brother had a farewell party for us in the Stanislaus quarters a couple of days before I left for Anchorage. The day before I left, Major Levine, Captain Jackson and wife, and Lt. Mendiola gave Lee Ann and me a farewell party at the officers' club. We would miss these good friends. I thanked Lt. Mendiola for getting me a first date with Lee Ann and assisting us in having an exceptional romance. The Air Rescue Squadron at Ladd Air Force Base had their C-54 pick me up at Eielson and fly me to Elmendorf Air Base. Lee Ann arrived a week later on the train.

My assignment at Eielson Air Base gave me the greatest gift of my life: a beautiful and talented lady who fell in love with me, Lee Ann Stanislaus.

Chapter 13
SAVING LIVES IN ALASKA

What a welcome change in the working atmosphere and the attitudes of the personnel in the 10th Air Rescue Group. This was to be one of the most interesting and rewarding experiences of my flying career. Our primary mission was a humanitarian one of saving lives of both military and civilian personnel.

Colonel Brecht, the group commander, introduced me to the headquarters staff at the first staff meeting in June. I also met Major Hackett, the 71st Squadron Commander there at Elmendorf, and Lt. Colonel Reichert, commander of the 74th Squadron at Ladd Air Base at Fairbanks. Major Blackwell, my immediate superior, informed me that I was to leave immediately for Ladd Air Base where I was to be checked out in the SA-16 aircraft. I always enjoyed flying another type of aircraft, and especially this one, for it was a triphibian that could fly on and off land, water, and snow. I had an excellent instructor, Captain Dallas, and I never forgot his comment at the end of my check ride: "Remember, the SA-16 is the only aircraft in the Air Force that takes off, climbs, and stalls at the same airspeed!"

Lee Ann found employment at the AACS office at Elmendorf Air Base and leased an apartment in the high rise McKinley building in Anchorage. The manager, Stan Bushka, who was of Polish descent, saw Lee Ann's Polish last name and asked me about her background. When I told him that her lineage went back to her sixth great-grandfather, who was the King of Poland, he was overjoyed. He was very attentive to the both of us and introduced us to many business people in Anchorage. We enjoyed an interesting social life in Anchorage and at the air base. The officers and wives in our 10th Rescue Group accepted Lee Ann and me as if we were already married.

The squadron always had two SA-16 crews on alert: one as the primary alert crew ready for an immediate dispatch on a rescue mission, and a backup crew to replace the primary SA-16 crew whenever it was dispatched. I told Major Hackett that I wanted to be scheduled as a pilot on either crew, any time day or night, even though I was a group staff officer. He knew that I was more interested in being a pilot than a desk jockey. Summer is a very busy time for air rescue personnel in Alaska since each day has twenty hours of daylight and good flying weather for both military and civilian aircraft.

I was scheduled as a copilot on the primary alert crew for my first rescue mission in June. Squadron operations received a call from a lady in Anchorage that she was worried about her husband, a pilot who had taken a friend on a fishing trip to a lake north of Anchorage. He was two days overdue on the day that he planned to return, and she was worried. She didn't know which lake, but she had the name of a couple that he usually flew to for fishing. We took off and searched the two lakes that she had named with negative results. We then began searching other lakes in the area and at the second one, we saw a float plane anchored at the edge of the lake which was the model and number given to us by the pilot's wife. We flew low and slow over the beach site where a campfire was burning, and the men recognized us as a rescue plane and gave us the okay signal. We returned to Elmendorf and had operations inform the lady that her husband and friend were alright. What the crew and I didn't tell operations was that there were also two females on the beach with them.

Early summer was a sad one for Lee Ann and me. She had received a telegram from her cousin, Joan Stanislaus, in Vinita, Oklahoma, that Lee Ann's father was dying from cancer and was asking for her. She and her father were very close, and I knew without asking that she had to return to Vinita as soon as possible. We were able to get her on a commercial flight leaving Anchorage that afternoon. We pooled our money for her ticket and travel expenses, and I drove her to the airport in my new Chevrolet which I had just received from the agency in San Francisco. Just before she boarded the airplane, I took her by the hand and looked into her eyes. I told her that this was her first visit home since we had met in Fairbanks last fall. After she had visited with her dad, relatives, and classmates, maybe she would realize her love for me was a result of being alone in Alaska. She was to let me know if she began to have doubts about her love for me. I told her that I would understand, but that my love for her would never die. We both had tears as we hugged goodbye and as she boarded the aircraft, she turned and blew me a kiss.

With Lee Ann in Oklahoma, and although my primary duty was the director of operations in group headquarters, I made myself available to squadron operations for rescue mission duty any time day or night. A few days later, operations scheduled me on a standby crew as the copilot. The evening was a quiet one and no missions were flown. About a week later I was scheduled as the primary alert crew pilot. I was on duty only a few minutes when we received a call from radar control that they had been directing one of our jet fighters to Elmendorf when it disappeared from the radarscope while it was over Mt. Spur. This is a snow-covered volcano about 100 miles west of Anchorage.

I was dispatched immediately to Mt. Spur and arrived at the top of the volcano to begin our search pattern. There was no smoke or crash in sight, so I started to circle the volcano, dropping 200 feet in altitude at the completion of each circle. This was a time consuming search.

We reached the base of the volcano without sighting any sign of a crash. I gave a negative report to operations and was ordered to return to Elmendorf. When I prepared to land, the landing gear would not come down. The engineer went through the checklist for the emergency lowering of the landing gear but had no success. The squadron maintenance officer got on the comnet with the engineer, but his suggestions were of no help. Major Hackett then ordered me to fly north to Big Lake and make a water landing. I had not been checked out on water landings with the SA-16, so Major Hackett gave me the basic instructions for making a water landing. The wind was calm, the water was smooth, and my landing was perfect! The aircrew, knowing this was my first water landing, applauded! They made my day.

There was a large resort hotel on the lake, and I taxied to their dock where we anchored. I called operations and was told that a maintenance crew would arrive the next morning and that me and my crew were to stay overnight and return to Elmendorf the next day when repairs would be made. The next morning Captain Gilmer, a qualified pilot for water operation in the SA-16, arrived from the squadron to be first pilot with me as copilot for the return to Elmendorf. There was wind and the lake surface was choppy, so Captain Gilmer decided that we would fire the jato bottles to assist in the takeoff. When we reached minimum speed for using jato, Gilmer gave me the order to fire, I pushed the buttons, and wham, we were airborne. We landed at Elmendorf without any gear problems. I really enjoyed this mission because I had made my first water landing and had my first experience in the use of jato for takeoff.

A few days later I was on a mission to Kenai to pick up an accident victim when I got a call on our comnet that they had just received a message from AACS for Major Slaker in the 10th Air Rescue Group. The operator asked if I wanted him to read it to me, or hold it for me to be picked up later at group headquarters. I asked the operator to read it to me, which he did: *Dear Ken, I have settled dad's business affairs and the estate and will arrive in Anchorage this coming Monday afternoon on Pacific Northern Airlines. Ego Amo Te. Lee Ann.* It was the most important message I have ever received. Lee Ann was coming back to Anchorage to live her life with me! I thanked God and my Guardian Angel for this great happening to me.

Monday found me at the Anchorage airport anxiously awaiting the arrival of Lee Ann's flight from Seattle. It was to arrive at 3:00 P.M., about thirty minutes after a Pacific Northern flight coming in from Juneau. It being a sunny day, I walked out onto the ramp just as the flight from Juneau arrived. All the passengers that disembarked were fishermen except for one very well dressed and attractive lady that I assumed was on her way to a local nightclub as a performer with an engagement here. She and the fishermen walked through the ramp gate, which was about thirty feet from where I was standing, and as they entered the terminal, the lady turned her head and looked at me. I then went into the terminal building to verify Lee Ann's arrival time, and as I came through the doorway, the attractive lady came up to me and said, "Ken, don't you remember me?" My God, it was Lee Ann! I had never seen her dressed in such attractive clothes and with great makeup and hairdo. We embraced for a long time and our eyes were moist with joyful tears. I asked how she got on that plane, and she said that when she was in the terminal at Seattle she saw that this flight would get into Anchorage before her ticketed flight, even though it was making a stop at Juneau. There was a seat available and she took it. We drove to her apartment in the McKinley building, which I had held for her if she returned to Anchorage, and we wasted no time in going to bed.

The first trip in our new Chevrolet was to Eielson Air Force Base twenty-six miles from Fairbanks, to visit Lee Ann's mother Gladys and her brother Glenn. They had not attended funeral services in Oklahoma for her father, and she needed to brief them on the burial services and the settlement of the estate. Glenn thanked her and complimented her for the efficient manner in which she settled the business matters of the estate. Lee Ann's mother, however, was not too happy because she expected Lee Ann to have some money for her from the estate. Lee Ann explained to her that after paying all the bills and notes due, and the very high medical charges for the treatment of her dad's terminal cancer, she actually had to borrow money from Uncle Oval Stanislaus to pay for her air ticket back to Anchorage.

When you are dispatched on a rescue mission you can have several situations that arise: you will find the party in trouble and give them whatever assistance they need; you will locate the missing party and find fatalities; or you will be unable to find the missing party. You never know whether you are going to return from the mission feeling great that you have saved human lives or being very disappointed that your mission was in vain.

Squadron operations had me as pilot of a primary alert crew one morning when flight control notified us that a F-94 pilot was missing. He was the wingman on a normal alert flight of two that had been dispatched from Elmendorf. The lead pilot reported that during their climb they had entered a fog bank over Portage Glacier, and when he broke out on top, his wingman was missing. He tried to contact him on the radio, but got no reply. I was given the Portage area to search and by the time I arrived, the fog had lifted. There was no sign of an aircraft either on the glacier or the lake. I expanded our search over the adjacent mountains until my fuel was low and I had to return to Elmendorf. The standby SA-16 crew continued the search along with an H-5 helicopter. They returned with no sighting of the missing F-94. Operations decided to suspend the search, and it was the opinion of most of us in operations that the pilot had suffered vertigo from the brilliant whiteout in the fog bank, crashed into the glacier, and fell into a deep crevasse.

Not too long after this F-94 accident, our headquarters received a directive, as did the fighter squadron to which the missing pilot was assigned, that his parents had received permission to come to Anchorage and were to be given VIP treatment. We were directed to give them a full briefing of the accident criteria, and we were authorized to fly his parents in a rescue transport aircraft to view the area believed to be the site of the accident. The briefing was very thorough, and their questions were answered truthfully and with all the accident information currently on record.

When the briefing was over, the parents were hosted at a luncheon at the officers' club. The weather was favorable for a flight over the glacier and surrounding mountains. The rescue transport was airborne with the parents shortly after they had finished lunch. When they viewed the rugged area and glacier over which their son had disappeared, they realized the difficulty in searching for his aircraft. When we landed at Elmendorf, they thanked all of us for our effort to locate their son's aircraft and our hospitality. They said it had been of great help to both of them to see and know the area of their son's final resting place.

Our two rescue squadrons had H-5 helicopters which were not adequate for rescue work in Alaska. Air Force was aware of this, and in the first week in November 1954, we received word that four H-19 helicopters, modified for arctic operation, were available for our group. However, unlike the H-5s that arrived in Alaska in crates, these H-19s were to be flown to Alaska during daylight hours and under VFR flight conditions only. These restrictions were in the interest of safety; however, it could take us weeks to fly to Alaska since in November we only had five hours of daylight and very few VFR flight conditions.

I was informed that Colonel Parker, our group commander, wanted to see me. I entered his office, saluted, and he asked me to sit down. We discussed our good fortune in getting the H-19 helicopters and the problems in flying them to Alaska this time of the year. He then said that I was the project officer and to organize my team and depart as soon as possible. He also said that he didn't care how long it took to pick up these four helicopters and fly them to our squadrons, "but when you arrive here, you better have four H-19 helicopters or I will have your ass."

Major Hackett, the commander of the 71st Air Rescue Squadron, provided me with four helicopter pilots and two maintenance personnel. I called Colonel Reichert, commander of the 74th Rescue Squadron at Ladd AFB at Fairbanks, and requested his SC-54 with two pilots, three helicopter pilots, and two maintenance personnel. I asked for one of the pilots by name, a Captain Frank Guelich, who was a very knowledgeable and experienced helicopter pilot, and since I had no H-19 time, would designate him as my H-19 flight captain. Colonel Riechert was very cooperative and gave me everything that I requested. One of the smartest actions that I took was to ask Mr. Harry Black, the Sikorsky Technical Representative to the 10th Air Rescue Group, to obtain approval from his boss at Sikorsky to be a member of my H-19 team. Approval was received and Blackie would prove to be a very valuable member of my H-19 team.

My H-19 team assembled at Ladd AFB, and we departed in our SC-54 the morning of November 14, 1954. Our first stop was an overnight stay at Great Falls, Montana, then on the fifteenth to Hill AFB, Ogden, Utah. This was the first location of our H-19 pickup. I introduced myself to the Director of Material and showed him the Air

Force directive authorizing me to receive a designated numbered H-19 under his command. He said he had orders not to transfer this H-19 since it did not have winterized serves; therefore it could not be ready for transfer until July 1955. When I informed Mr. Black of my meeting with the DM, he contacted the Sikorsky plant at Bridgeport, Connecticut and received serial numbers of all H-19s that had winterized serves. Our designated H-19 was on the winterized list. I introduced Mr. Black to the DM, and after Mr. Black informed him that our designated H-19 had been winterized, the DM became very cooperative. I assigned an H-19 crew to flight check the H-19, and they found seventeen discrepancies, one of which was a badly damaged Morse coupling. Because a new coupling would have to be ordered, the H-19 went AOCP (aircraft out of commission for parts). I knew that it would take at least a week to return the H-19 to flying status. I left the assigned flight crew and one maintenance airman there to bird-dog the repairs and the pilot to be my communications chief. I would contact him daily, as would each flight crew after they had received their H-19.

Our second H-19 for pickup was at Foster AFB, Victoria, Texas, where we arrived early in the morning on November 18th. I contacted the Director of Material and he gave us permission to test hop our designated H-19. Captain Guelich did the test hop and put on a terrific aerial show, including a loop! I told him no more aerial shows until we got back to Alaska. He and the aerial engineer found twenty seven discrepancies. Again I refused to accept this H-19 until all these negative write-ups were cleared. I assigned an H-19 crew there and then we flew to Robbins AFB, Georgia, the base with our third H-19.

We arrived at Robbins AFB on the 22nd of November and I made our presence known to the DM. Inspection and test hop of our assigned H-19 revealed nine discrepancies. I assigned a flight crew to the H-19, and my SC-54 pilots flew me and the remaining H-19 flight crew to Forbes AFB at Topeka, Kansas, where the H-19s from Foster AFB and Robbins AFB were to rendezvous with the team. Both of these H-19s were at Forbes AFB by November 27th, clean of all write ups. I gave them permission to continue to our final assembly base at Great Falls. The remaining flight crew and I departed in our SC-54 to George AFB at Victorville, California to pick up our fourth H-19. What a surprise! Our inspection and test hop revealed no discrepancies. It did lack an APU (Auxiliary power unit), and the proper one for arctic operation was found available at Norton AFB. I accepted the H-19 and the flight crew took it to Norton, where the APU was installed.

The only members of my team remaining were the SC-54 crew. Captain Price informed me that the SC-54 was due for a fifty-hour inspection, and that could be done at Hill AFB, Utah. We arrived there on November 30th and turned the SC-54 into the depot for its inspection. A couple of days later the depot said that our SC-54 would not be ready to fly before the 10th of December, so I went ahead to Great Falls, arriving there on December 5th. This was the assembly base for all four H-19s before starting the flight to Alaska. All four H-19s were at Malstrom AFB by the 6th of December. With VFR weather forecast for the flight to Edmonton, Canada on the 7th and 8th of December, I authorized three of the H-19s to depart for Edmonton. The remaining H-19 went AOCP for a power unit. The Malstrom DM located one at the depot at McClellan AFB, Sacramento, so I dispatched the SC-54 from the depot in Utah to Sacramento for the APU. The fourth H-19 and the support SC-54 departed Great Falls on December 11, 1954.

On the morning of December 13th at Edmonton, Canada, all team members were at the route briefing given by the Air Force Traffic Control Representative. The four H-19s were to remain together as a flight, maintain constant communication with the nearest flight center, follow the Alcan highway, and carry backup aviation fuel in fifty-five-gallon drums in each H-19. I appointed Captain Guelich as the flight leader. The weather was good and before long the four H-19s and the SC-54 were airborne on the way to Whitecourt. We refueled and departed for Grand Prairie where we refueled and remained overnight. The weather was VFR the next day and the H-19 flight took off for Fort St. John. The SC-54 could now give better support to the H-19 flight by flying out of Ladd AFB. The SC-54 crew and I departed for Ladd AFB.

The H-19 flight refueled at St. John and took off and followed the Alcan Highway until dusk. They landed by a tourist camp, refueled, and spent the night here.

The H-19 flight took three more days to arrive at Whitehorse due to bad weather and short daylight hours. Our SC-54 flew from Ladd AFB to Whitehorse with supplies that the flight leader had requested. Due to severe weather, the flight didn't arrive at Tok Junction, Alaska until December 20th. Here two of the H-19s departed for Ladd AFB, arriving there on the 21st of December. The two H-19s for the squadron at Elmendorf arrived on the December 22nd during a snowstorm. A photographer from *Life* magazine took photos of our arrival. These appeared in a later issue of *Life* magazine.

The success of this critical project was due to the great team that worked with me. Thanks to them and to my ever-present Guardian Angel, we delivered the first helicopters to fly to Alaska from the ZI (zone of interior) without an accident or an injury to any member of the H-19 team. We had been away from families and friends for six weeks, and what excellent timing to be back for the Christmas holidays.

I had flown from Ladd AFB to Elmendorf AFB that morning to be there when the H-19s arrived. Colonel Parker and I both witnessed their arrival, and he turned to me and not only shook my hand, but also gave me a bear hug. Lee Ann arrived from work shortly afterwards, and seeing her again, I was bursting with joy. I had done a lot of thinking about Lee Ann on this trip. Lt. Mendiola, who had arranged my first date with Lee Ann, knew of my plan to obtain a divorce and had given me the name of an attorney in Reno, Mendiola's hometown. When I had arrived at Hill AFB on the 30th of November and was told that our SC-54 would be in the depot for ten days, I called Mr. Rutherford's office in Reno made an appointment to meet with him the next day.

He was very cordial and positive in his discussion with me that I would not have any difficulty in obtaining a divorce after I had resided there six weeks to become a legal resident.

Captain Gilmer, one of our SA-16 pilots, and his wife were planning a New Year's party and Lee Ann and I were invited. I thought this party would be an ideal time to give Lee Ann an engagement ring. I discussed my idea with the Gilmers and they agreed that it would be the highlight of the party. I purchased a one-carat diamond, and since I did not know her ring size, the jeweler put the diamond in adjustable ring. Lee Ann could then come back and have the diamond placed in a setting of her own choosing. The guests at the party were enjoying the food and holiday drinks when Captain Gilmer got their attention and said that I had an announcement to make. I told them that I was giving Lee Ann this engagement ring, confirming my marriage to her that coming spring. During the loud applause, I slipped the ring onto her finger and she had happy tears in her eyes as I kissed her. All the pilots gave her a hug and a kiss and the wives did the same to me. Welcome to the camaraderie of the 10th Air Rescue Group.

I flew several rescue missions in Alaska before I returned to the States in March 1955. Alaska was not yet a state then. One mission was so rewarding to me that I must tell it here. On the 8th of February I was scheduled as the pilot on the primary alert aircrew for the evening shift. About 9:00 P.M., operations received an emergency call from the small fishing village of Cordova, located on the coast southeast of Anchorage, that there was a woman in childbirth labor with a serious medical problem. The midwife could not get the baby turned so that it could be born headfirst. She would have to have a Caesarean delivery, which required medical experience and equipment lacking at Cordova. We were airborne immediately, and I had flown over Cordova but had never landed at its short dirt airstrip. It was dusk and would be dark by the time I arrived there, so the operations officer directed them to have cars at each end of the runway with their lights shining on the approach area. They did not have runway lights and when I arrived, they had done a good job of lighting the dirt runway with many car lights. I made a slow approach with full flaps and our powerful landing lights on. We touched down at the very start of the runway and had no trouble slowing down before reaching the end of the strip. The ambulance was there with its lights flickering. Our medics rushed to the ambulance and helped carry the woman on a stretcher into our aircraft. I turned the aircraft around, gave it full throttle, and when we reached the near end of the strip, fired the jato bottles and shot into the air. There was an ambulance from the native hospital in front of operations at Elmendorf, and the medics had the lady in the ambulance and it was gone in a matter of seconds.

The next afternoon I drove to the native hospital to inquire as to the woman's medical condition. I explained to the receptionist who I was, and she asked me to be seated and disappeared. She returned in a few minutes, told me that the woman had given birth to the baby by Caesarean and both were doing fine and to follow her. She took

                    74TH AIR RESCUE SQUADRON
                  10TH AIR RESCUE GROUP, ARS-MATS
                   Ladd AFB, APO 731, U.S. Air Force

ARSCO   JAN 10 1955

SUBJECT: Letter of Appreciation

TO: Commander
        10th Air Rescue Group, ARS-MATS
        Elmendorf Air Force Base
        APO 942, U. S. Air Force

   1. I wish to take this opportunity to express my sincere thanks and appreciation for the excellent manner in which Major Kenneth Slaker, 11771A, carried out his assignment as Project Officer for H-19 Operation Pick-up.

   2. Major Slaker's enthusiastic approach to problems involved, persistance and cooperative efforts contributed greatly to the delivery of these aircraft without incident.

   3. It is a very comforting feeling to have realized Major Slaker's wholehearted support in the successful completion of this project.

                                        EARL T. REICHERT
                                        Lt. Col. USAF
                                        Commander

Letter of Appreciation from Lt. Col. Earl T. Reichert, Commander, 10 January 1955.

me into the maternity ward and introduced me to the native woman that I had flown to the hospital the night before. She was so happy to see me and held out her arms to give me a hug. We talked for a couple of minutes, then I wished her well, bent over, and gave her a kiss on the forehead and departed. I was really proud to have had this experience, and it's the reward for being a pilot in the Air Rescue Service.

One day during the latter part of February, I was at work in my office when Colonel Parker came in and introduced a Colonel Steely to me. I was told that he was the director of operations for the Continental Division of MATS (Military Air Transport Service) and would like to spend a few minutes with me. Colonel Steely had seen the article in *Life* magazine about our flying the H-19 Helicopters to Alaska, and congratulated me for the success of that challenging assignment. Then he said he had just had a very rewarding discussion with Colonel Parker about me and my flying experience during World War II and the Berlin Airlift. He said that he had Colonel Parker's approval to offer me a new position.

Chapter 14
CHIEF TRANSPORT CONTROL, CONTINENTAL DIVISION MATS

Colonel Steely paused and then said that I was under no obligation to accept the offer he was about to make to me, but to give it some thought and give him an answer prior to his leaving Elmendorf. He asked if I was familiar with the organization and mission of Continental Division MATS. I apologized that I was not familiar with the Continental Division. He said he would like to give me a short briefing so that I would know what I was being asked to accept.

"The Continental Division has its headquarters at East Kelly Field in San Antonio, Texas and reports to MATS Headquarters in Washington, D.C. Units within our division are the 1708 Ferrying Group, the 1700 Air Transport Group, and the Medical Air Evacuation Group. The communication and Control Center for these groups is located in our headquarters. At any given time the center has communication with any one of our aircraft in the air and control of its flight and destination. The center has the utmost responsibility for its operation and reports directly to the director of operations. Each morning the chief of the control center gives a standup briefing to the commanding general as to the current status of each of the three groups."

Colonel Steely then said, "Major Slaker, I am offering you this position as Chief of Transport Control Center, for I know that with your experience you will do an excellent job. Can you give me an answer now or do you wish to think about it for a couple of minutes?" And he laughed.

I knew this position would give me a new experience that would add to my career. Also, to have a colonel make a special visit to offer me this position was exceptional. I replied that I would be thrilled to accept his offer. I then explained that I was planning on taking six weeks' leave to get a divorce so that I could marry the love of my life. I told him she would make a great Air Force wife and that her brother was a pilot in the Air Force. Colonel Steely said that would not be a problem, for Colonel Parker was very complimentary of Lee Ann. Colonel Steely got up to leave and we shook hands and he said, "See you in Texas."

On the 6th of March I received orders transferring me to the Continental Division MATS. I told Lee Ann of my new assignment after six weeks in Reno to get my divorce. We both agreed that she should continue working in Elmendorf while I was in Reno and move into the women's quarters on base. I traded the Chevrolet in for a new Buick to be delivered in Michigan. The commander had a cocktail party for me on the eighth and I departed on the ninth of March. It was an unhappy farewell kissing Lee Ann goodbye and leaving these good people in the 10th Air Rescue Group.

When I arrived at McChord Air Base, I called my Aunt Rhoda, who picked me up, and I stayed overnight at their residence in Federal Way. My uncle McMillian was pleased to hear that I was going to Reno to divorce Glenna. He had never cared for her; in fact, none of my mother's family accepted her. My uncle took me to Sea-Tac airport the next morning, where I caught a commercial flight to Reno.

Here again Lt. Mendiola was of great help to me. His parents were close with Joe G., a World War II veteran who had been awarded the Medal of Honor. He now owned a motel in the center of Reno. Lt. Mendiola called Joe and told him that I was coming to Reno and would need to rent a motel or hotel room for six weeks to establish residence to file for a divorce. Lt. Mendiola called me at Anchorage just before I left and told me about Joe and that he had a motel room reserved for me. When I arrived at Reno I took a cab to the motel, and when I was checking in, the girl at the counter contacted Joe and he came out of his office to welcome me.

Both Joe and I, being combat veterans, became friends from our first meeting and spent many evenings discussing how World War II should have been fought. He knew my attorney, Mr. Rutherford, and said that when I had my meeting with him the next day, to tell him that Joe would be my sponsor who would testify in court that he had seen me every day in Nevada for six weeks. When Joe was not busy in the office, he would call me to see if I had any plans, and we would have lunch or dinner and discuss business. He was especially interested in my flying experience in Alaska. One evening he and his gracious wife invited me to their house for dinner.

I would usually have dinner at the Mapes Hotel and sometimes play the tables at the casino on the top floor. At the beginning of the fifth week in Reno, I called the Buick Company in Michigan and asked if the car I ordered was ready for me to pick up. They told me that it was ready for me to take delivery at the Buick dealers in Detroit. I wanted the car then, but Joe had to see me every day. I checked flight schedules and told Joe my plan. I would have a taxi pick me up at 12:30 A.M. and take me to the airport to catch the red eye to Chicago at 1:15 A.M. Now Joe has seen me this day. I would arrive in Chicago early and take the shuttle to Detroit, then the taxi to the Buick dealers. At 11:00 A.M. I would be on my way non stop to Reno. I would arrive in Reno the next day by 10:00 P.M. Joe said to go, but not to drive when I got sleepy, to take a nap. I arrived in Reno at 9:30 P.M. Joe came out to see my new Buick, and he had seen me both days!

My six weeks was completed on April 22nd and I filed as a resident of Washoe County, Nevada on the 25th of April. I had asked Lee Ann to fly to San Francisco the

25th of April, and I would pick her up there. My attorney would file the divorce petition and I was free to go. I picked up Lee Ann at the airport and she looked great! We started our long drive to San Antonio.

We arrived in San Antonio on the 28th of April, two days before I was to report for duty at Continental Division. We spent the next day casing the area and looking for an apartment that would be suitable for us after we got married. We had dinner that evening at the officers' club and struck up a conversation with a pilot from the 1700 Transport Group. When I told him that I was just assigned to the Continental Division and we were looking for an apartment close to Kelly Field, he said that the commander of his group had just rented an apartment in a new building with a short drive to Kelly. He gave me the address, and the next day Lee Ann and I went to the apartment complex located on Cincinnati, just a few blocks from St. Mary's University. There was a one-bedroom apartment left on the second floor, unfurnished, with a minimum lease of one year. We signed the lease and paid the first month's rent plus the damage deposit. The landlady told us that the best store to purchase our furniture was Joskes, located in the city center. We wasted no time in driving to Joskes and sure enough, they had a variety of home furnishings. I asked the sales woman if we could open a charge account because we needed to furnish an empty apartment. When I told her that I was a major in the Air Force just assigned to Kelly Field, she said there was no limit on what we needed for the apartment and that they could deliver tomorrow whatever we selected today.

Early morning on May 1st we checked out of the motel and I dropped Lee Ann off at the apartment to be there when our furnishings were delivered. I drove to East Kelly and signed in at the adjutant's office and reported to Colonel Steely. He came out from behind his desk and shook my hand, glad to see me here safe and sound. I told him that I was now a resident of Nevada and that my attorney had filed my petition for divorce. He then said, "Let's go to your new hangout and meet your people." He introduced me to the two officers on duty, a Captain Rutherford and a Captain Aldrich, both pilots. Colonel Steely then excused himself, and I turned to Captain Rutherford and asked him to be my instructor the rest of his duty day.

The Control Center had various types of communication equipment spaced along two walls, and on the biggest wall was a huge board with small plaques spread all over it. Captain Rutherford told me that each aircraft from any one of the three groups on a mission was plotted on this huge board as to aircraft type, last reported location, its destination, etc. At any time of the day or night, our Control Center could give the commander the current state of our air transport capability. He said, "Every morning we give the Chief of the Control Center, which is now you, the current status of our fleet for your briefing of the general at 9:00 A.M. There are six experienced pilots assigned to the Control Center, and we have our own secretary." He then closed his briefing by asking if I had any questions, and I said no. Captain Rutherford then said, "Major Slaker,

Colonel Steely briefed all of us about your past experience and we are pleased to welcome you to the Control Center."

Since I was not married to Lee Ann, she lived in the apartment and I had a room in the BOQ. One week after I was in my new job, flight operations of the 1700 Transport Group scheduled me for a check ride in the C-54 (commercial designation was DC-4). I had never flown a C-54, but with my couple of thousand hours in the B-17 and B-24, I didn't have any difficulty with this four-engine aircraft. I enjoyed the stability of this C-54 and was looking forward to piloting it. I also received disappointing news from Personnel. I had applied for the new Space Program and could not be accepted since I was three inches too tall. This was the second time being 6'3" was the reason I was disqualified for an appointment to the Annapolis Naval Academy.

Lee Ann submitted an application for a civil service position at both Kelly and Lackland Air Force Base since she had worked in civil service in Alaska. She was sent to the Air Force Security Headquarters at Lackland Air Base for an Interview. She had already obtained a Secret clearance in Alaska, and with a brother that was an Air Force captain, and being engaged to a career Air Force Major, they grabbed her at her first interview. She found transportation with a carpool from the apartment area, so we did not have to purchase another auto.

I flew a C-54 on a round trip to Brookly Air Base on the seventeenth, and when I got back to the office, there was a message to call my attorney in Reno. He said that my petition for divorce was on the court calendar for the next morning, the 18th of May. He said that he would call me tomorrow after the hearing.

I received a call from my attorney in the afternoon on the 18th of May to tell me that I was now a single man. I thanked him and told him that I would never forget what a fine thing he had done for me. I called Lee Ann at her office and told her that I felt like I had just been released after ten years in prison. She replied, "Ken, you are so deserving of this divorce, and it is also one of the happiest moments in my life now that we can live our lives together." I knew that Lee Ann had wet eyes, and I told her that she did not need to put a hundred yellow ribbons on that tree by our apartment, that one would be enough. By the time I had finished my workday and driven to the apartment, she was already there, standing outside waiting for me. We walked up to each other, held hands, and looked into each other's eyes. I had an emotional feeling that I had never experienced before and knew that God had given me this woman to spend my life with. I was really a very lucky man.

I drove back to my room at Kelly Field after a wonderful dinner with Lee Ann to prevent idle talk that we were living together and not married. Spending the weekend in my room at the air base was unbearable, so Monday evening I told Lee Ann that we were getting married the coming weekend. I told her that the location was her choice. Wednesday evening she said she had talked to relatives in her hometown of Vinita and they wanted the ceremony there, but when she talked to her brother in Wichita, he insisted that she get married there, for this was family. I told her that I agreed with her brother and that we could leave after work Friday evening, take turns driving, and arrive at her brother's before noon Saturday.

Lee Ann called her brother and told him of our decision to get married in Wichita that Saturday. He had bad news. There was a three-day waiting period after you applied for the license before you could pick it up, and the county offices were not open on Saturday. I remembered that one of my students at Washburn University had become a lawyer. I called the school, got his address in Wichita, and called him. He remembered me, and I told him my problem and asked if he could be of help. He said that since I was in the service, he could get a waiver on the three-day waiting period and that Neal, Lee Ann's brother, could pick the license up Friday. Neal went to the office Friday and the license was waiting for him.

I picked Lee Ann up at the apartment Friday evening after work, and we were on our way to Wichita to finally become husband and wife. We told Mrs. Smutts, the landlady, of our plans and that we would be back Sunday evening. We took turns driving during the night and were making good time until we neared Caldwell on the Oklahoma Kansas border. The highway was closed due to damage from a tornado that had hit the area the day before. I asked the officer on guard what was the best route to get back onto our road to Wichita, and he could not suggest an alternate route because other areas had suffered damage. So we played a game, driving east on a farm road for about twenty miles, then north on a back road until we knew that we were in Kansas, then west until we found our original route. We arrived in Wichita about 10:00 A.M. and went directly to an air conditioned motel to freshen up and to be sure that we had a place to sleep that night, for no way were we going to stay overnight at her brother's house.

We were scheduled to be married Saturday afternoon at the Church of the Nazarene, her brother's church, at 3:00 P.M. Neal and his wife Pauline were the two witnesses required to make it legal. After the wedding we had a small party at the house. I had purchased a bottle of champagne when we were in Oklahoma—the wettest dry state in the country—for our toast after the wedding. Neal had never tasted champagne, and Lee Ann talked him into having a wine glass full. About a half hour later Neal got sick and threw up that good champagne. Most of us laughed at his distress, and he would not forget this wedding party.

At 8:00 P.M. we said our goodbyes to one and all and left for our motel. We decided to take a shower, for it had been a hot and humid day. When Lee Ann opened her suitcase to get her new nightie, there was nothing in it except rolls and rolls of toilet paper and an unsigned congratulations card. So the first night of our marriage, we both slept in the nude.

We were on the road back to San Antonio at 6:00 A.M. Our new Buick had air conditioning, which was a blessing because it was a hot and humid day. In southern Oklahoma we stopped at a fruit stand to get a cold drink, and it was loaded with watermelons for sale. There was a very huge one that had a sign on it that it had won the state record. We decided to buy it and have a lawn party for the apartment building residents the next weekend. The trunk of the Buick was just big enough to hold the watermelon. The owner of the fruit stand just smiled and shook his head as we drove away.

We arrived at our apartment in San Antonio at 7:00 P.M. and put our bags in the one bedroom. That was an enjoyable moment for me since I didn't have to get back into the Buick and drive to my room at Kelly Field. We had not eaten a full meal since the prior evening, so we decided to eat at the drive-in behind our building. As we were getting ready to leave the apartment, we heard many bells ringing, drums pounding, and people shouting in front of our apartment for the newlyweds to come on outside. Friends from my and Lee Ann's offices and residents from our building were giving us a reception. We joined them, and it was a loud and fun evening. Nell Mauldin, a girl from Lee Ann's office, asked Lee Ann if she had any trouble finding her clothes on her wedding night. With a surprised look on her face, Lee Ann asked Nell just how had she managed to get to her suitcase and fill it with toilet paper? Nell said that she talked the landlady into letting her into the apartment that afternoon while Lee Ann was at work, and Mrs. Smutts became a part of the suitcase surprise. Lee Ann and Nell laughed and embraced one another, and Nell became a close friend of ours during my assignment in San Antonio.

Monday evening I removed all the shelves from the refrigerator, for the watermelon was too long to lie flat on a shelf. Before I placed it on end in the refrigerator, I made and removed a two-inch plug from the end of the melon and filled the hole with tasteless 100-proof Mexican vodka. I filled this hole every evening until Saturday when the melon had absorbed almost the entire liter of vodka. We also bought a keg of Lone Star beer and the guests brought snacks of all kinds. Saturday was a beautiful clear day with temperatures in the eighties. Before the guests arrived, I cut off the end of the melon that contained the hole. That huge watermelon lasted two hours and the guests were happy, telling jokes and laughing, and none suspected that the watermelon was the instigator of their enjoyable time. Many of the guests made the comment that Oklahoma sure grew damn good watermelons. It was almost midnight before the last guests left. The guests thanked us for a great lawn party and offered to help us clean up the front lawn. There was not much cleanup for Lee Ann and I to do. The watermelon was gone, the beer was gone, and the snacks were long gone. Lee Ann and I never told a soul about the doctored watermelon.

The stand up briefing held in General Allen's office every workday morning at 9:00 A.M. consisted of flight group commanders, the Directors of Operation and Maintenance, and myself. My briefing was to give the status of all of our aircraft airborne away from their home base as to accidents, maintenance problems, weather delays, flight crew sickness, etc. The average length of these meetings was twelve minutes. I got to know the unit commanders very well because after the meetings we would discuss the problems that I had presented at the meeting in greater depth. When the problem with one of our airborne aircraft was very serious, I would contact the unit commander before the briefing.

Lee Ann and I were kept busy with our new jobs, attending military social functions, and making and associating with new friends. In addition, I was kept busy proving to the Air Force Headquarters that the letters of complaints from my ex wife were lies. The letters from her became so numerous that I got a call from the Judge Advocates Office that I should contact my attorney and take legal action against her for the damage she was causing to my career. I did just that, and my attorney contacted her and informed her that I was going to sue her for the property and the children because she was incapable of being a good mother and was damaging their father's career. The letters to the Air Force ceased.

I sent a letter to my ex wife in the spring of 1956, asking her to consider turning the children over to me since there were three boys and only one girl, and they should be with their father. She replied that she and the children would be at her parents' house in Lincoln and that I could pick them up there. She gave me a specific date for the pickup, and Lee Ann and I were really excited to know that we were going to have the children. Lee Ann had just been examined by a top obstetrician in San Antonio and was told that she would never have children since her uterus had never developed. I went searching for a house with at least four bedrooms and two baths. A rental agency found one for me, and I signed a lease and paid the first month's rent and the damage deposit.

I made plans to drive to Lincoln to pick up the children, and two days before I was to leave, the ex wife called and said that she had changed her mind and was leaving the next day for Bellevue, Washington, and taking the children with her. I tried to reason with her, telling her I had rented a large house and that this was a blow to both Lee Ann and me since Lee Ann would never be able to have a child. With a smart tone in her voice, she said that if we wanted children so bad, to go and adopt one or two. I told her that she best take good care of the children or that I would file suit for one or all of them.

Our Continental Division had subordinate TCC's (Transport Control Center) at Travis Air Base in California and Pope Air Base in North Carolina. We had direct communication with Air Traffic Control Centers at Goose Bay, Canada; Reykjavik, Iceland; Prestwick, Scotland; Wiesbaden, Germany; Naples, Italy; Athens, Greece; Izmir, Turkey; and Lisbon, Portugal. These were on what we called the High Flight Route to NATO countries. Our 1708 Ferry Group there at Kelly had ferried aircraft to various NATO countries including Turkey.

In April 1957, General Allen decided that we should fly this route and visit the Control Centers, for we always had aircraft at several of these sites every day. He selected three staff officers—colonels Beaudrey, Schriever, and Sudbury—and myself to accompany him in his personal C-54 aircraft. We were scheduled to depart Kelly Air Base the morning of April 8th and all our wives were there to say goodbye. Just after I kissed Lee Ann and turned to board the aircraft, she gave me a small package and told me not to open it until we were out of the States.

We spent our first night at Goose Bay, Canada, and all of us had flown aircraft through there before. The next day we filed for the long flight to Reykjavik, Iceland. Four of us decided to play bridge. After a couple of hours we took a break and I decided to open the small package Lee Ann had given to me. My bridge partners watched me open the small box, for they were as curious as I. What a surprise! It contained a Trojan condom and a small card signed: *Love, Lee Ann*. The officers flipped and one of them said, "Ken, let me have this, I got to show this to General Allen." He took it to the general's compartment, and I heard the general laugh.

They both came back to our bridge table and General Allen said, "Slaker, where did you find this woman?"

"I found her in the boondocks of Alaska."

"Well, you sure got a winner in Lee Ann." One of the officers suggested that I save it and on the flight into Kelly, squeeze some toothpaste into the rubber, and when the wives greeted us at Kelly, tell Lee Ann that I brought her a gift and put it in her hand. I decided to do that.

We landed at Reykjavik, Iceland and were given a great welcome and tour of their communications and aircraft facilities. We had an elaborate dining setting, and of course the main dish was fish. The next morning we flew to Prestwick, Scotland, which brought back memories of when I last visited there in 1943 when I had dinner with Bob Hope and Frances Langford. Here again we were well received and given a tour of the base communication and maintenance facilities. We departed that evening for the American air base at Wiesbaden, Germany. We were served a special dinner at the officers' club and then went to bed to rest after a long day.

We departed Wiesbaden on the 12th of April for Copenhagen, Denmark, where General Allen had business to attend to. When we landed, the crew chief said we had a maintenance problem with one of the engines that was not serious and he could repair within a couple of days. We stayed at the di Angleterre Hotel, which was first class. Captain Frank from the flight crew and I shared a large suite with two beds, which cost less than each one of us paying the high price for a single bedroom.

Most of us had dinner that evening at the hotel and after eating, Captain Frank and I went into the well furnished lounge for an after dinner drink. We were seated at a table next to a table where two attractive young ladies were having a cocktail. We exchanged smiles, and after our waiter departed, one asked if we were Americans. We answered in the affirmative and they welcomed us to Copenhagen. We got to talking and told them that we were pilots and had flown our commanding general there for a meeting and that it was our first visit to Denmark. About this time an orchestra started playing dancing music and we asked the girls to dance. They spoke perfect English and the girl that I teamed up with was an excellent dancer. After a couple of hours of drinking, talking, and dancing, I was getting tired and unsteady on my feet, so I stood up, told the three of them that I was going to bed, and excused myself. I went to our suite, took off my clothes and threw them onto the chair, flopped into bed, and I don't even remember going to sleep.

```
                    HEADQUARTERS
                 CONTINENTAL DIVISION
           MILITARY AIR TRANSPORT SERVICE
                UNITED STATES AIR FORCE
                KELLY AIR FORCE BASE, TEXAS

CDCAD                                    4 April 1957

SUBJECT:  Letter Order 224


TO:       Personnel Concerned


     1.  The FOL-named GEN OFF, FNOA, USAF, organizations in-
dicated, this STA, PROBOUT 7 APR 57 from this STA to Mitchel
AFB, NY; Goose AB, Labrador; Narsarssuak AB, Greenland;
Keflavik, Iceland; Prestwick, Scotland; Burtonwood, England;
Wiesbaden AB, GE; Copenhagen, Denmark; Naples, Italy; Izmir,
Turkey; Ankara, Turkey; Wheelus AB, Tripoli, Libya; Nouasseur
AB, French Morocco; Lajes FLD, Azores, and Harmon AFB, NF
(CIPAP), on TDY for APRX fifteen (15) days to survey activities
along high-flight route; UCWR this STA.  PERS cleared for
access to CLAS MAT up to and INCL **SECRET *TOPSEC for PD
of this TDY.  SR OFF will comply with AFM 35-11.  IMM IAW
AFR 160-102 W/B ACCOMP IMMED.  #Denotes OFF AUTH IAW MATS
Manual 55-1 to act as ADD CR/M (over and above MAX crew
complement) (unqualified) on MATS TRANS type ACFT.  Utili-
zation of AVAL GOVT messing and QTR facilities is considered
to be impracticable in that such utilization will adversely
affect the performance of the ASG MSN:

      *MAJGEN BROOKE E ALLEN, 1287A, HQ CNTLD, MATS
     #*COL GERHARD J SCHRIEVER, 2043A, DO
     #*COL EMIL G BEAUDRY, 4201A, DO
     #*LTCOL DAVID V SUDBURY, 6201A, DO
     #*MAJ KENNETH W SLAKER, 11771A, DO
      *CAPT JAMES C LAFFERTY, A0840947, DO
      *CAPT RAYMOND S CLARK, A0834385, DO
      *CAPT EARL B ROEHM, 28453A, DO
      *MSGT ALBERT M DAISEY, AF33072302, DO
     **MSGT RALPH W CLANAHAN, AF34198980, DO
     **SSGT ARCADIO HERRERA, AF18253949, DO
     **SSGT WILLIAM H JEWELL, AF18299150, 1700th Air
       TRANS GP, MED
```

Letter Order 224, Kelly Air Force Base, Texas, 4 April 1957.

I slept solid all night, heard nothing, and awoke about 6:30. I thought I heard someone breathing, so I raised up and MY GOD! There was a woman in bed with me! I looked across the room at Captain Frank's bed, and there was a woman in bed with him. I knew that it had to be the two girls we had spent the evening with, and Captain Frank had brought them up to our suite. Then I asked myself: *Did I have sex with the girl in my bed?* The answer was obvious, for I would have remembered that. I slipped out of the bed without moving any of the covers, picked up my clothes from the chair, quietly opened the door, and went down the hall to a service room where I got dressed. It was 7:00 A.M. and I went downstairs to the restaurant to have coffee and breakfast. Then I got smart. We didn't pick these girls up. They were professionals and had picked us up. Before long, Colonel Sudbury joined me followed by Colonel Beaudry. I never mentioned a word about the two girls in our suite. They talked about planning on sightseeing that morning, then having lunch at a highly recognized restaurant. I joined them and fortunately we left the hotel before Captain Frank and the girls appeared. I never saw the two girls again.

The next day we departed for Naples, Italy. This area was very familiar to me, for I had made several bombing raids on the docks in 1943. Also in 1950, I had spent several days there on duty. We were very well received by the Italians and had an excellent briefing and a very tasty dinner. The next morning we departed for Izmir, Turkey, where the NATO office was located. I had flown into Turkey before and our reception there was cooler than any of our stops. One of the Americans assigned there suggested that for dinner we go to a Turkish nightclub located on the waterfront. We had to wear civilian clothes at all times in Turkey. Four of us agreed with his proposal and he drove us to the nightclub.

There was a monitor at the entrance, and we showed him our military identification card and he signaled for a waiter to seat us. In the center of the room was a medium sized dance floor separated from the dining tables with an iron railing. I noticed there were no women at the tables and our host told us that the Turkish men did not bring their wives to this club. There were scantily dressed female waitresses, and ours asked us in English what we would like to drink. There was no menu and she gave us one of two choices. We had nearly finished eating when an orchestra appeared and started playing music. Out onto the dance floor came four girls attractively dressed with their breasts exposed. We knew by now that the word had spread through the club that there were American officers at a certain table by the iron railing, and the dancing girls knew it. They kept looking our way as they danced, and then one of them danced away from the other three and arrived at our table. She kept dancing in front of me with her breasts not more than two inches from my face. I made no move to touch them and she suddenly stamped her feet and shook her head in disgust and danced back to her group. The Turks started clapping their hands and laughing because I had not responded to her teasing me with her breasts. Our hostess asked me if I would like to invite the girl to our table, and I thanked her but told her we had to leave.

We completed our visit to Turkey and General Allen said we should go home. We departed Turkey on the 18th of April and made a long flight to Lisbon, Portugal. This was my first visit to Lisbon and it was a pleasing one. The next day the aircrew had planned to fly to the States via the Azores, but the weather there was marginal, so we made a long nine-hour flight to Harmon, Newfoundland. The next morning we flew to Andrews Air Base where the general was to visit the commanding general of MATS. That afternoon we left for Kelly and an hour before we arrived, I called my Transport Control Center and asked Captain Rutherford, my assistant, to call our wives and give them our arrival time. I took the condom Lee Ann had given me and squeezed toothpaste into it. The wives were waiting for us and General Allen was the first to disembark, followed by the colonels and then me. We hugged and kissed our wives, and then I said to my wife, "Lee Ann, I have a gift for you." They all watched as I placed the gooey condom in her hand. She was surprised, and an okay smile appeared on her face and all the guys laughed. She looked at them and said, "You guys are all bad." They then explained to their wives what all the laughter was about. The next night we were all guests of General Allen for dinner at the officers' club.

One week after the long inspection trip to Europe, the personnel officer walked into my office and greeted me with, "Major, you are on the way up the ladder. Here is a wire we just received from the Air Force Institute of Technology." I read the wire and it said that with my high grades in college and outstanding rating as an associate professor at Washburn University, I had been selected to attend the University of Southern California to study for a master's degree in Industrial Management. I was really surprised, for I had never applied for graduate school and especially at Air Force expense. I could not wait until Lee Ann came home from work, so I called her at the office and told her we were moving to the Los Angeles area for at least a year. She was really surprised and thrilled that I was going to graduate school.

When we signed the lease for our apartment, we were permitted to cancel the lease with a thirty-day notice since I was in the Service. We had lived in the apartment for two years, and our landlady had taken a liking to us and was upset that we were leaving. We also had to leave some close friends that we had made, especially Major Wudeck and his wife Peggy. We had played bridge many evenings, attended social functions together, etc. We stayed in touch with them for many years.

The last week in April, I had a flight to the West Coast and was able to spend a day at the Chino airfield. I rented a car and drove to Pasadena to look for an apartment. I had always liked that city after visiting there in 1943, and there was a freeway from there to USC. I found a one-bedroom apartment in a good area and leased it for one year. I got back to San Antonio on May 1st, and we started packing and making shipping arrangements for our furniture. I had to attend summer school to take two undergraduate courses required to enter graduate school. They were Accounting and Marketing. Before I could leave my position as Chief of the Transport Control Center, I had to complete the efficiency report on each one of my officers. I gave them all above average, except I gave Captain Rutherford the outstanding rating, which he deserved. In the comment section I stated that he should be granted a regular commission in the Air Force. He notified me some months later that he had received a regular commission. That really pleased me and made me believe in the Air Force.

Lee Ann gave her two-week notice of resignation to the Air Force Security Service, which made our date of departure the middle of May. A couple of months before this change in our plans, I had traded our '55 Buick for a new 1957 Buick hardtop that we really enjoyed driving to the West Coast. Our furniture was scheduled to arrive three days after we did, so we stayed at a motel near the USC campus. I registered at the university and familiarized myself with the USC campus and the freeway system. We drove to Norton Air Force Base, where I was assigned for flying duty while at USC.

Chapter 15
AN AIR FORCE PILOT STUDIES FOR HIS MBA

We drove to our empty apartment the day our furniture arrived, and the tenants in the apartment below us on the first floor came up and welcomed us to Pasadena. Their names were Penny and Max Van Praag, and we became good friends with them. Max informed me that our apartment had a single car space in the building behind ours.

My summer school classes were in the morning, but come fall, all the graduate classes were in the evening. Lee Ann was not one to sit around in the apartment while I was in school most of the day. She registered with a private employment company, and they found a position for her with the Forest Lawn Memorial Association as a flower consultant for funeral and wedding functions. It was located in Glendale, just a few miles from our apartment. From that day on, our apartment never lacked for fresh flowers.

The University of Southern California is a private school and does not have to comply with many of the operational requirements that state schools do. Our graduate classes were restricted to fifteen students, and some class sessions were two hours long with a five-minute break after one hour. Some subjects were taught three times a week, some were five times. What really impressed me was that the particular subject being taught was done by professionals and not by career teachers. My Principles of Marketing class was conducted by Mr. Barker, President of Barker Furniture Corporation. Mr. Mautner, who was an executive officer in a large personnel management company, taught us the requirements for personnel at the various management levels. Business Law was taught by an attorney who had contracts with several local corporations. They had our attention and respect, for we were getting business as it really was and not from a textbook.

I usually got home about 10:00 P.M., and Lee Ann waited up for me to discuss any exceptions to the daily routine. One evening the first week in October, she was so excited to tell me about a new lady employee that was meant to work with her. She lived in Burbank and her name was Rosalie. Her husband was a doctor who had just recently been killed in an automobile accident. As a result of his death, a narcotics investigator by the name of Robert King called on Rosalie. He explained to her that for several weeks before her husband's death, he had been assigned to watch her husband to make sure that he was not one of the doctors supplying drugs to the Hollywood users. He said that he had found nothing and that her husband was clean. Their meeting was very amiable, and a few days later he called her and invited her to dinner. She accepted and they started dating, and she had invited Lee Ann and me to her house the next Saturday to have cocktails and meet Mr. King. That, we did.

After an hour of drinks and getting to know one another, Bob suggested that we go to dinner at a nightclub of his choice. Bob knew his way around Los Angeles because of his profession, and we had a fine dinner and entertainment at a nightclub that the other three of us had never attended. We enjoyed each other's company so much that our weekend dinners became a habit. Bob and I became close friends since I was a federal officer with a classified clearance and he was a state narcotics inspector. It was not unusual for Bob to receive a call while we were having dinner to leave to take part in a drug bust. Bob even confided in me the names of some of the successful people in Hollywood that were on drugs. It was difficult for me to understand why such successful people would end up with a drug habit.

I spent from noon to 10:00 P.M., five days a week at school, and one and sometimes two weekends a month flying cross-country trips out of Norton Air Base. During the weekends that Lee Ann and I could be together, we lived it up, mostly with Bob and Rosalie. We were able to be together the first weekend in November, and the four of us had an excellent dinner in Chinatown. When we got home, Lee Ann got sick and vomited. The next morning she felt okay, but the same thing happened again the following Saturday. Max and Penny came up Sunday afternoon for a visit, and I told them that I could not afford these expensive dinners—that Lee Ann kept vomiting them away when we got home. Max insisted that she see Dr. Gannon at Huntington Hospital. He was the doctor that had helped him through medical school. Penny drove Lee Ann to the hospital the next afternoon and I didn't go to school that day. Max came up to keep me company, and I told him that Lee Ann had a good sense of humor and delighted in playing jokes on me. I told Max that when Penny and Lee Ann came back from the hospital, I knew exactly what she would do. She would walk to the coffee table and lay a book there for pregnant women and tell me that she was pregnant. Max and Penny already knew that many doctors had told Lee Ann that she would never be able to have a child.

About an hour later Lee Ann and Penny walked into the room, and Lee Ann placed a brochure on the coffee table that was titled for the pregnant woman. Lee Ann looked at me and said, "Ken, Dr. Gannon says I am pregnant." Max and I looked at each other and broke out laughing. She had followed my script to perfection. Then Penny, in a very sharp voice, said, "What's wrong with you two? This is not funny. Lee Ann is pregnant."

I looked at Lee Ann and she had tears in her eyes. I realized with a shock that Lee

Ann was not joking—she really was pregnant. I got up and apologized and hugged her. Penny told Max to come with her and to leave Ken and Lee Ann alone, for they have a critical decision to make today. I told Lee Ann, "I know what you are thinking, that we already have four children to support, but I would really be happy if we could have our own child."

The next morning we went to see Dr. Gannon to let him know that we wanted Lee Ann to have a child. He explained a new hormone to us and that Lee Ann would have to visit him once a week to monitor the progress of her pregnancy. Since I was in the Military Service, Lee Ann was entitled to have the baby at the Norton Air Base hospital, which would save me several hundred dollars. I called the doctor in command and explained to him the use of this hormone during her pregnancy. The doctor said that the Air Force surgeon had not approved the use of this hormone and that they could not accept Lee Ann as a maternity patient. Dr. Gannon was really pleased when we told him that Lee Ann was his maternity patient, including delivery, at his hospital.

Just a few days after we were told that Lee Ann was pregnant, we had a surprise visit from my father. He had just retired from the U.S. Steel Corporation in Vandergrift, Pennsylvania, and was on his way to visit relatives in Seattle. He let me read a letter he had received from his mistress that he had during the latter days of my mother's life. She now lived in Phoenix, and she asked my dad to come and live with her, that she had a beautiful home and loved him. I asked Dad why was he here rather than in Phoenix. He said that he had stopped for a visit but could not live with her because she was too bossy. I had to leave for school at 4:00 P.M. and told Lee Ann to take Dad to our favorite tavern in Pasadena for dinner. I got home about 10:30, and Dad was asleep on the sofa and Lee Ann was in the bedroom with the door locked. She said that she locked the door because my dad was tipsy from several cocktails.

Come morning I got up and dressed and went out to the living room to wake up my dad. He was gone, bag and baggage. I went back to the bedroom and told Lee Ann that I had news for her, that my dad had sneaked out of the apartment during the night. Kidding her, I told her not to cry. She said if she cried it was because she was happy for me. The following Saturday we went to our favorite tavern for lunch. When we were finished, Lee Ann went to the ladies' room and our friend, the bartender, a very strong athletic type, came over to me and asked if my dad was still with us. I told him no, that he had left without saying goodbye. He asked me if Lee Ann had told me about what happened when the two of them were there for dinner. I shook my head no and he said that he wanted to tell me before Lee Ann came back. He said, "When they finished dinner, your dad started talking sex and pawing her, and she gave me that *help me* look and I went over to your dad and told him to leave her alone or that I would throw him out onto the street. He knew that I was not kidding. He paid the bill and even opened the door for her. I knew that you were due home from school and that I had frightened him enough that Lee Ann was safe on the walk two blocks home." I got up to leave when Lee Ann returned, and I shook my friend's hand and thanked him. Lee Ann gave him a hug and we walked home in silence.

At home I asked Lee Ann why she didn't tell me about my lousy father's treatment of her at the tavern. She said she knew that if she were to tell me about my father's behavior, that I would physically attack him and might get hurt. I told her she was right, and then I would have called the police to have him arrested for trying to rape my pregnant wife. I was really pissed off at him. Then as I calmed down, I realized that my dad was not worth me endangering my life and career just to beat the hell out of him and get myself arrested. I decided that we would eliminate him from our lives, which we did.

In December I received a short letter from my ex-wife telling me that the sewer system was clogging up and that she didn't have the money to have it repaired. I decided that when school was out for the holidays, I would drive to Bellevue and fix the drain, visit with my children, and give them their Christmas presents. Lee Ann would not accompany me since she did not show that she was pregnant and continued to work at Forest Lawn. Ten days before Christmas I drove to my aunt and uncle's home in Federal Way. The next day Mac put some tools in my trunk and said that he was going with me to help fix the sewer line. I was really pleased, for he was an experienced building contractor and would make my repair task much easier. As I suspected, the ex-wife had poured cooking oils down the kitchen sink drain and it had solidified. We replaced the sewer tile and were finished by early evening. Before we left for my uncle's house, Mac wasted no time in telling her what she should and should not do. She didn't argue with him, for she knew that he had never liked her.

The next day I had lunch with my Uncle Ray Hawk and Aunt Mary in Seattle. From there I went to Frederick & Nelson's department store and bought Christmas presents for my children. I told the kids that Santa came early and gave them their presents that evening. The children and I went out for dinner, and then I brought them home and hugged them all goodbye. I had a farewell breakfast the next morning with Uncle Mac and Aunt Rhoda and left for California. I drove all day and decided to spend the night at Medford, Oregon. I checked in at a motel and then drove into town to a restaurant that had been recommended to me. It was dark when I left the restaurant and on the road back, I saw a blinking yellow light at an intersection about a block ahead of me. I slowed down and then I could see a blinking red light pointed at the road entering the intersection on my right. There was no visible traffic, but just as I entered the intersection, a car traveling too fast for a blinking red light, and with no lights on, entered the intersection and crashed into the right side of my Buick, knocking me out of the intersection.

I was able to get out of the car and residents came running out of their houses. I asked one of them to call the police, which he did. They asked if I was hurt and needed an ambulance and I told them no, that I was not hurting anywhere. The driver of the car that hit me came to me. I told him that he did not have his lights on when he went through the flashing red light. He said that his battery was dead and he was hurrying to get home before the engine quit. The police arrived and wrote up the accident report. He was very surprised that after looking at my smashed Buick, I was not hurt. A tow truck arrived and I told him that I had insurance that would pay the toll charge and to take it to the Buick garage. I asked the police officer if he would call me a cab to take me to my motel, and he said that he would drive me there. On the way, the police officer said that the man who hit me was a local dentist. I thanked him and told him that I would be at the Buick dealership the next morning if he needed to see me again.

Before going to bed, I sat down and relived the day and the accident. I thought how fortunate it was that I was in a strongly built Buick that kept me from being injured. Then it came to me; my Guardian Angel was still watching over me, and that explained why I was not hurt. As I crawled into bed, I thanked God and my Guardian Angel for protecting me from injury or even death. The next morning I had coffee and rolls at the motel and took a cab to the Buick dealership. The manager greeted me and took me into his office and had his secretary bring us coffee. He said that he had bad news for me. The man in charge of the repair shop said that the frame of the Buick was badly buckled, which twisted the body, and that my Buick was a total loss. What a blow. I had not even had this car a year and now it was junk. I asked the manager if he had a new Buick on the lot; I would pay the difference from the Blue Book value of my Buick to that of the new Buick. He said that he did not have any new autos on the lot but had a good proposal for me. He had a 1956 Cadillac convertible that was like new. A rancher had traded it for a Buick Roadmaster. The reason he traded was that he discovered that western Oregon was not convertible country with so much damp weather. The manager said that he wanted to move it or he could be stuck with it all winter long. He said that since I lived in southern California, which was great for convertibles, he would give it to me at the price of a new Buick like mine. I agreed to take a look at it, and it was a beautiful light blue and looked like it had never been on the road. I thought, *What a car for Lee Ann with her beautiful blond hair,* and I didn't hesitate and told the manager it was a deal. I really lucked out, for here I was without transportation and Christmas only three days away. I called USAA for insurance coverage while the dealer filled up the tank and prepared the paperwork. By 1:00 P.M., I was on my way to Pasadena in a beautiful Cadillac convertible.

It was still daylight when I arrived at Pasadena and parked the convertible in front of our apartment building. When Lee Ann opened our door, we kissed and hugged like we had been separated for years. It is the greatest thrill in the world to have a beautiful woman in love with you. I told her to come downstairs, that I had a surprise for her. I walked her to the Cadillac and gave her the keys and said, "Here is your Christmas gift." She stood there speechless and finally said, "Ken, this is a beautiful car. What did you do with our Buick?" I had not called her and told her about the accident because

I didn't want to upset her. I related briefly what had happened, and she didn't say anything and put her arms around me and held me tight.

January was a very busy month for the both of us, with me at graduate school and flying weekends, and Lee Ann still working at Forest Lawn and going to the hospital twice a week to be examined by Dr. Gannon. At her eighth and last visit in January, Dr. Gannon had good news for her that her uterus was developing along with the fetus. She also was beginning to show that she was pregnant and submitted her resignation. They were sorry to see her leave and gave her a beautiful farewell dinner.

Now that Lee Ann was not working and I didn't go to school until 2:00 P.M., we were able to spend most of our mornings together. Lee Ann was fortunate that she did not have any morning sickness or any side effects from the hormone treatment. At her last visit to the hospital in March, Dr. Gannon told her that a once-per-week visit was enough since her pregnancy was normal. We had fun selecting names for a boy or a girl. We began with two agreed guidelines. If it was a boy, it was not to be named after me because I was a junior and I had never liked it. If it was a girl, her middle name was to be Ann, the same as her mother's. The baby was due the middle of May, so by the end of April, we reached an agreement on names. A baby girl's name would be Lisa Ann, giving it the same initials as her mother. I finally decided that the boy would be named after my third great-grandfather, Daniel, and after my great-grandfather, William. Lee Ann liked both names because they were masculine and from my Hawk lineage.

May Day came and Lee Ann was ready to have this baby, and so was I. I was scheduled to fly some personnel to Tinker Air Base the next day and return the following day. I asked Max Van Praag, our good downstairs neighbor, that if Lee Ann started to have labor pains while I was gone, would he please take her to the hospital. He said that I didn't have to ask, that Lee Ann was like a daughter to him. I called her the next evening from Oklahoma and she was not having any pains. I told her that I would be back to Pasadena the next day about 4:00 P.M. The next day I got home about 5:00 P.M., and Max and Penny were with her in our apartment. She had started to have labor pains in the afternoon and wanted to wait until I got home. The four of us got into Max's car and went to Huntington Hospital. The nurse put Lee Ann in a private room and said it would be an hour or two because Lee Ann had not dilated enough to have the baby. I stayed with Lee Ann and the Van Praags went to the visitors' room. Lee Ann had still not dilated enough at 9:00 P.M., so Max, Penny, and I decided to go to our favorite tavern and have dinner.

When we finished eating I suggested to Max that he drop me off at the hospital so they could go home. Max said that he would drop Penny off but he was going to stay with me until that baby was born. I asked Max to join me in Lee Ann's room, and she was dilating, but very slowly. Dr. Gannon came into the room and asked me if I had witnessed the birth of any of my previous children and I told him no, that I had not.

He said that he wanted me to witness this birth and that the nurse would prepare me to be in the delivery room. A little after 1:00 A.M., the nurse came in and examined Lee Ann and said that she had dilated enough since the baby was not a large baby. As the nurse wheeled Lee Ann out of the room, we squeezed hands and she said, "Ken, I am glad that you are joining me."

The nurse came back and put me in a sterile gown, cap and a facemask, and led me to the delivery room. Lee Ann was on the table with her legs spread and in stirrups. Dr. Gannon was instructing her on helping push the baby out of its womb, and when I saw the pain that Lee Ann was having, I swore to myself that I would never get her pregnant again. Finally, about a third of the baby's head appeared with hair on it, then it stopped. Dr Gannon called for forceps and when the nurse handed them to him, he saw my worried look and said that this would not hurt the baby and he would gently help the head through the crotch. Dr. Gannon showed his professional skill when he gently eased the head through the crotch, and with a couple of pushes by Lee Ann, the baby was free. The nurse held the baby while the doctor severed the cord. She then held the baby up for Lee Ann to see and said, "Lee Ann, you have a beautiful baby girl."

Then Dr. Gannon said, "Well, look at that!" I was so shaken by his remark that I immediately looked for a malformation and the doctor said, "Her eyes are focused. Usually they don't focus for several hours or even days, and she is looking us over!" The nurse asked me to come with her and watch her clean the baby of blood, etc.

The way she tossed the baby around while cleaning her I feared that she would drop her, but she was an expert at this. She put drops in the baby's eyes, attached a patch to the baby's abdomen, wrapped her in a soft blanket, and said, "Now it goes to its mother." Lee Ann had been moved to a bed in the maternity ward and managed a smile when the nurse placed the baby girl in her left arm. I had seen my first birth of a baby and I was exhausted. Before too long Dr. Gannon came in and looked at the baby and us and said, "Major and Mrs. Slaker, you two have just had a miracle baby. Have you a name for her?"

Lee Ann answered, "Yes, Dr. Gannon, the name of this miracle baby that you brought into this world is Lisa Ann."

I received a copy of orders from the Air Force Institute of Technology in the middle of May that with the completion of my graduate studies I was to report to the Jet Flight Training Headquarters at Randolph Air Base, Texas in July. Lee Ann and I discussed this move and decided that since we had a child, we would buy a house. I finished my classes the first week in June and hitched a ride from Norton Air Base to San Antonio. My brother, who was also an Air Force pilot, met me at Kelly Air Base. I had told him on the phone that I was going to purchase a house in the northern part of San Antonio that had a huge shade tree in the front yard. My brother had laughed at that and said that just a few blocks from the area in which he was living, a new street had been constructed with new houses being built there. He drove us there and entered the new street named Diamond Head. Halfway down the street was a huge cypress tree in front of a house just being built. I told my brother to drive to that house with the tree in front. I went into the house, which was being finished inside, and met the contractor who owned the lot and was building this house. I asked if it were sold and he said not yet, so I decided to sign for it right then. It was a brick rambler with three bedrooms and two baths, and I asked the contractor if he would accept me as a buyer using the GI bill. He said absolutely, and I signed the sales agreement for $15,000. When we got to my brothers house, I called Lee Ann and told her that I had just bought a shade tree. She laughed and then asked if I was teasing her. I described the house to her, and she was really happy that my brother and I had found it.

I spent the rest of June at the USC library searching for a subject for my thesis. Some schools did not require a thesis for a master's degree, just extra classes. The USC Thesis Committee required that the subject for the thesis be original and not covered in any thesis already published. With only a week left in June, I came across a column in a personnel magazine written by a J.K. Gerdel. He stated that the greatest obstacle to better personnel relations was the lack of mutual employer employee confidence posed by the attitude that personnel information was confidential. The employee wants to know where he stands with his supervisor to alleviate the undesirable psychological results caused by secret rating systems. One of the ways in which enlightened employers have met this problem is by adoption of the post appraisal interview.

This was it! I remembered that when I left Continental Division and went into Colonel Beaudry's office to say goodbye, he had asked me to sit down. He had said, "The organizational chart shows your position coming under the division's operations officer, who then makes out your Efficiency Report (ER). Personnel has advised us of a new rating procedure where your rating officer must have an interview with you to discuss the rating. I don't think it will work here where you are both of the same rank. You have a wider experience than the rating officer and both of you are eligible for promotion. I am your endorsing officer, and I assure you that it will be well above average."

I immediately checked the roll of thesis subjects, and there were none on Post Appraisal Interviews. I came up with this thesis title: "A Study of Post Appraisal Interview Practices." I wrote a letter to Professor Mautner of my proposed research and title. He was my thesis advisor and also a member of the Thesis Committee. He called me and said that the title and research area were great and to try and have it ready to present for approval by the Thesis Committee in the fall of 1959.

My reporting date at Randolph Air Base was the 24th of July. I took a month's leave so we would have time for farewell visits with the friends that we had made during our year there. We decided to drive to Texas at night because of the heat and rest during the day at an air-conditioned motel. The daytime temperature was well above 100 degrees all the way to San Antonio. Max and Penny had a farewell dinner for us and helped pack the Cadillac that evening. They really hated to see us leave, and we felt the same sadness because they had been great neighbors. Lee Ann told them that when we had Lisa baptized, we were going to name them as Godparents.

Thank God that our Cadillac had air conditioning, for it was even hot driving at night. Four days later we arrived in San Antonio and stayed at my brother's house until our furniture arrived. Lee Ann was very pleased with our first house and busied herself making one of the bedrooms a nursery for our new baby. I put my desk in the master bedroom, where I would continue to work on my thesis. I signed in at the base on July 23rd and found out that I had been assigned to the office of the inspector general. The year in graduate school at the University of Southern California was very rewarding, but it was good to be back among fellow pilots at an air base.

Chapter 16
BECOMING A JET PILOT

On the 24th of July 1958, I reported to my new boss, Colonel Ross, the inspector general at Randolph Air Base. He said that although I would be given temporary inspector general duties, my primary position in this office was to be the jet flight training inspector. Since I was not then a jet pilot, I would be entered in the next jet training class to prepare me for my primary assignment. Since the next class was a few months away, Colonel Ross assigned me to inspect the officers' club because he had received some complaints about its operation. I had to review the base and ATC (Air Traffic Control) regulations pertaining to the operation of an officers' club. I called Major Dailey, the officer in charge of the officers' club, and made an appointment to see him. I told him that I had been ordered to perform an inspection of the club since it had not been inspected for over a year. He was very cooperative and told his staff to work with me and give me full access to all office records.

I spent one full week going through records, asking questions, and learned of the many problems that exist in operating an officers' club with several hundred members. I had the IG (Inspector General) secretary type my inspection report and met with Major Dailey to brief him and to read my report. My findings were mostly complimentary with a couple of minor discrepancies. I also made a couple of recommendations that I thought would improve the club operation, and he accepted them. He then briefed me on several officers that gave him problems. Some wouldn't pay their club dues for several months, some talked down to the help, and some officers just didn't like him. Then I was surprised when he said that one of them was my boss. I then realized that my boss had a personal grudge against Major Dailey and had asked me to inspect the club operation and find a major discrepancy. I told Major Dailey that if he ever had any question to call me, for I was there to help him. We became good friends.

The first day of November my boss recommended to the wing commander that I be named the base project officer. I was to cooperate with the Air University School of Aviation, located at Randolph, who was hosting the Second International Symposium on Medicine in Space that month. Every day was a long workday, and the base organizations gave me outstanding support to help me provide the symposium with its needs.

I became acquainted with base logistical commanders and the professional medical personnel. I also learned about the research that medical scientists were doing in space medicine. The medical school commander named me in a letter of appreciation to our wing commander. That letter made it all worthwhile to me and the base organizations for our support of the symposium.

The jet fighter class that I was enrolled in started in late February with a graduation date in April. I had already met the school commander who had been informed by Colonel Ross that I was to be the IG Flight Training inspector. I was well received and was told that my flight instructor was one of the top jet pilots. What a difference in flying the jet compared to propeller driven aircraft. I had no difficulty in adjusting to the jet flight characteristics and really enjoyed flying the jet—thanks to my flight instructor, who really was tops.

After several weeks had passed, we took off for my final flight test and after several maneuvers, my instructor said that he wanted me to make an eight point slow roll with no gain or loss in altitude. This was my final test maneuver and I felt that I had done very well. After landing I shook his hand and thanked him for his excellent flight instruction and hoped then that I was a jet pilot. He assured me that I was and was pleased that he had been chosen to be my instructor. A few days later I was in the flight operations office and got permission to look up my record to see how I scored on the final test. He gave me a good score on every test maneuver and added a remark that my eight point slow roll had been one of the best that he had experienced. That remark put me on top of the clouds, for now I knew that I was a qualified jet pilot.

I had no sooner graduated from jet school when Colonel Ross told me that I was the project officer for Armed Forces Day, to be held at Randolph on Sunday, May 17th. The three other officers in the IG office were to work with me. I assigned one to the Army, one to the Navy, and one to the Air Force to coordinate with them on their exhibits, and I would be in contact with the VIP's from the city, state, and military that would be on the speaker's stand. I contacted the Air Installations Officer and told him that I needed a speaker's stand at least eight feet above the ground level so that the visitors could see the VIP speakers. No problem, he would have the stand in place two days before Armed Forces Day. I was really pleased with the cooperation that I received from all the base organizations. My team, plus many of the base personnel, worked long hours every day for two weeks preparing for the big day. Come Sunday the seventeenth, we were blessed with a beautiful weather day. I was the Master of Ceremonies and was on the speaker's stand from daylight to dark. Tallies from the base entrance gates showed that over 50,000 visited the base. When all the visitors had departed, did we have a party? Hell no. We were tired and headed home for that wonderful bed.

Our daughter had become one year old that month, and Lee Ann itched to go back to work. She found an excellent day care center for our daughter and went back to work with the Air Force Security Service in the same department that she was with when we

HEADQUARTERS
SCHOOL OF AVIATION MEDICINE, USAF
Air University
Randolph Air Force Base, Texas

SAMCOMD   14 November 1958

SUBJECT: Letter of Appreciation

TO: Commander
         3510th Flying Training Wing
         Randolph Air Force Base, Texas

    1. At the conclusion of the Second International Symposium on the Physics and Medicine of the Atmosphere and Space, it was clearly evident to me that the success of this international scientific meeting was greatly enhanced by the support which you and your staff freely provided. Your wholehearted cooperation in placing your facilities at our disposal enabled us to arrange and conduct the symposium in a most orderly and effective manner.

    2. Several members of your staff deserve special recognition for the part they played in support of this meeting. Major Kenneth W. Slaker, Jr., 11771A, Project Officer, and Technical Sergeant John W. Carder, AF 39571479, NCOIC, Operations, Base Motor Pool, expended every effort to cooperate with members of my staff in arranging a myriad of details before and during the meeting. I consider their excellent performances to be commendable.

    3. Please express my sincere appreciation to each member of your command who helped to make the Symposium a success.

OTIS O. BENSON, JR.
Major General, USAF (MC)
Commandant

Letter of Appreciation from Maj. Gen. Otis O. Benson, USAF, 14 November 1958.

left San Antonio in May 1957. I bought a used car for her to drop the baby off on her way to work.

What little spare time I had after arriving at Randolph Air Base, I worked on my master's thesis. I had obtained the addresses of 133 corporations spread throughout the States and mailed them a page of questions concerning their use or non-use of the Post Appraisal Interview. By the end of July I had received replies from 113 companies. This gave me enough research information that I would be able to complete my thesis for presentation to the Thesis Committee in October.

Towards the end of summer, the wing commander received a letter from a gentleman who said that he was the publicity agent for Joe DiMaggio, the famous professional baseball player, and that they had a proposal for the commander's consideration.

Mr. DiMaggio would be in San Antonio the following week and would like to honor an outstanding WAF, selected by the commander, to a first class dinner in San Antonio. There would be newsmen and photographers present. The agent could act as the chaperon or the commander could select one. The proposal was approved by the commander and forwarded to our office to make the necessary arrangements.

Colonel Ross called me into the office, handed me the letter, and said that it was my baby. After reading the letter, I called the WAF Squadron Commander and asked her to meet me at the officers' club after working hours because I had a confidential letter that involved her. We met at the club and after treating her to a cocktail of her choice, I handed her the letter. When she finished reading it, she looked at me and said, "You son-of-a-gun, you really had me worried. I think this is great publicity for the squadron and the WAF selected for dinner." She choose the WAF that had been selected as the Queen of Randolph Air Force Base. Her name was Donna Maxson, and she had the looks and personality to be DiMaggio's dinner guest. I contacted the agent and he gave me the time and date that a limousine would arrive at the squadron to pick up Donna and the military chaperon.

The next morning Donna briefed the WAF Commander and me on her evening as a dinner guest of Joe DiMaggio. She said the food was delicious and that he had many questions about her being a WAF. When they finished eating, the hotel manager told DiMaggio there were newsmen that really wanted to ask some questions and get some pictures. DiMaggio nodded his head and the newsmen came swarming in and asking questions like how long they had known each other, etc. She said that she and DiMaggio just laughed at their questions. Donna said it was a dinner that she would never forget.

I took a liking to Donna and suggested to Lee Ann that we invite her to dinner some weekend. Lee Ann agreed, and a couple of weeks later Donna had dinner at our house. When I drove her back to the base, I asked her if she would be interested in babysitting once in a while. She agreed, and we started using her so often that she became a family member.

From the day that I graduated from Jet Flight School, I tried to fly the jet twice a week to build up my jet pilot time and to maintain my jet proficiency. I was lucky if I logged ten hours a month in the jet when I normally logged thirty to fifty hours a month in the prop driven aircraft. I still maintained my proficiency in prop driven C-47s and C-54s.

The first week in October I sent my master's thesis to the University of Southern California's Thesis Committee. I had spent many hours on it and had two other officers with college degrees proofread it. They both thought that it was graduate material. A month later, the Thesis Committee returned my thesis booklet with two suggestions and asked me to resubmit it in the spring of 1960. I was very disappointed and called Professor Mautner, my thesis advisor. He said not to be upset, for rarely did the com-

Military's Might Impresses 50,000

By JOE RUST

Stepping into the future isn't an everyday occurrence. For many of those attending the armed forces open house at Randolph AFB Sunday, today did become a glimpse into tomorrow. Units of the army, air force, marines, national guard, and navy from 11 local commands joined in the exhibiting of America's defense might. More than fifty thousand turned out for the show, Major Kenneth Slaker, Master of Ceremonies, reported. Space exhibits, including the Ajax, Hercules, Thor, Redstone and Snark missiles, drew a large number of attendees. But, amidst the latest in supersonic jets and missiles, the plane stealing attention was a 1936 model Buecker-Jungmeister German bi-plane.

Pilot was Beverly "Bevo" Howard, a World War II ace. Snatching a ribbon placed between two 20-foot poles climaxed an aerial acrobatic show by Howard. Contrasted with Howard's demonstration was a jet acrobatic show by Captain Carl Miller flying a Thunderbird. Miller, a Randolph officer named outstanding serviceman in Texas, by the Texas Society of the Daughters of the American Revolution during the open house ceremonies, presented a spectacular demonstration of low-flying flips at 400 miles per hour.

CROWDS ATTEND ARMED FORCES OPEN HOUSE AT RANDOLPH AFB
More than 50,000 persons turned out to view space exhibits.

Article from San Antonio's *The Light* newspaper about the Randolph Air Base Open House, 18 May 1959.

mittee approve a thesis the first time it was submitted. He said to follow their suggestions and resubmit it, and he felt that it would be approved and published for the USC Library.

The Mexican Government had invited the Air Force to participate in an anniversary celebration of the Mexican Air Force, to be held in Mexico City on the 18th, 19th, and 20th of January 1960. Air Force Headquarters forwarded an approval to the Air Training Command at Randolph since it had the nearest jet operation to Mexico City. I was selected to fly our C-47 to Mexico City loaded with jet maintenance personnel, their supplies, and two jet pilots as backup to the four jet pilots flying the four jets to Mexico City. We departed on the 19th of January and the four jets arrived the next day. The airport at Mexico City is around 8,000 feet above sea level, and I had to use

---

HEADQUARTERS
3510TH FLYING TRAINING WING
UNITED STATES AIR FORCE
RANDOLPH AIR FORCE BASE, TEXAS

REPLY TO
ATTN OF:

22 May 1959

SUBJECT: Letter of Appreciation

TO: Major Kenneth W. Slaker
Wing Inspection
3510 Fly Tng Wg
Randolph AFB, Tex

1. I wish to express my sincere thanks and appreciation for a successful Armed Forces Day, 1959. I have received many complimentary remarks from military officials and our civilian friends who visited Randolph on Sunday, May 17, 1959. It was my good fortune to hear these praiseworthy comments concerning the excellence of the arrangements, appearance of the area, and the interesting program which was presented.

2. I am deeply grateful for the splendid manner in which you carried out your responsibilities and contributed to the successful staging of this event. Only through your efforts were we able to accomplish our task in the best traditions of the military service.

H. F. MUENTER
Colonel, USAF
Commander

Letter of Appreciation from Col. H. F. Muenter, Commander, 22 May 1959.

more engine power than normal to keep from stalling out on the final approach. We were well received and taken in taxis to a fine hotel in the city center.

The 21st of January was the big show day for our jets. The pilots were our flight-training instructors, and they flew a terrific aerial demonstration for the thousands of spectators. After they landed, they stood by their jets and the spectators were permitted to get a close look at the jets. Many asked questions in English to the pilots. The next day the jets returned to Randolph. This being my first visit to Mexico City, I spent the fourth day on two tours of the city and its outskirts. The fifth day we loaded our C-47 and returned to Randolph.

The last week in January was quiet with just routine office work, so I was able to redo my thesis according to the committee suggestions. I mailed the thesis to my advisor, Professor Mautner, the first week in February, hoping that it would be approved in time to receive my MBA at the graduation ceremony in June. I thought it ironic that I completed the subject and class requirements in one year, and it had taken two years to complete my thesis.

The first week in February I received a call from Air Training Command (ATC) Headquarters that the chief of Personnel wanted to see me the next morning. I asked Colonel Ross if he had any idea why the personnel chief wanted to see me and he replied in the negative. The next morning I went to ATC Headquarters and the secretary got clearance for me to enter his office. I saluted him and he held out his hand to shake mine and said that he was pleased to finally meet me. He called his secretary and told her that he didn't want any calls for half an hour. He then said to me that he needed to give me some background as to why I was there.

He said that both the Air Force and the Army were organizing a new operational office to be called Management Engineering. They would be called upon to analyze and recommend solutions to serious problems within a major command. It would be chaired by a Management Engineer supported by three or four highly educated and experienced civilian or military Ph.D.s. He said, "We surveyed the records of all field grade officers in our command, and you are the most qualified. As someone with two years of Engineering at the University of Washington, a graduate of the Army Engineering School at Ft. Belvoir, an associate professor at and a degree from Washburn University, a master's degree in Industrial Management from the University of Southern California, a pilot qualified in both propeller and jet aircraft, and a regular career officer, our staff has selected you to be named our management engineer." He looked at me and smiled, and I was so surprised that I was at a loss for words.

He said, "I see you are surprised!" I found my voice and said that I felt very honored to be selected for such an important position and promised him that I would do my very best.

He said, "We know you will, for you have several letters of commendation in your file and some outstanding ratings from your superiors. You will be housed at Lackland

Air Force Base for both physical and administrative requirements. We have already submitted your name to attend the next Army Management Engineering Course at Rock Island, Illinois."

Orders were published on February 9, 1960 transferring me from Randolph Air Base to Lackland Air Force Base. They also stated that my primary duty was to be military code 7331, Management Engineer. When I told Lee Ann that we would be moving to Lackland on April 1st when quarters would be available on base, she was very pleased because her job was with the Air Force Security, which was located next to Lackland, relieving her of driving completely around the city to get to work. The day care center where Lee Ann dropped off our daughter Lisa was also close to Lackland. I told Lee Ann that we would sell our house on Diamond Head because I didn't have the time to be bothered taking care of a rental. She agreed with me. We sold the house in April for three thousand more than we paid for it.

Chapter 17
A MANAGEMENT ENGINEERING PILOT

I signed in at the Lackland Military Training Headquarters the second week in March 1960, and reported to Major General Robert Stillman, the commander. He was very cordial and already knew about my background and new assignment. I liked him immediately and told him I was a football fan and knew all about his football record while at West Point. That brought a smile to his face and he then told me that my office would be located in the same building as Manpower since it had the space and administrative help. I told him that the commanding general of the Lackland hospital had sent Lt. Colonel Duquette, his executive officer, to request a Management Engineering study of his Material function as soon as I had my team organized. General Stillman then said, "Major Slaker, I also have a serious problem here that I want your team to study. It has caused complaints to the U.S. Congress and time is of the essence to solve the problem." I told him that his request was the number one priority just as soon as we finished with the hospital study.

Two days later, I had just gotten settled in my new office when two civilians reported to me. One was Michael Zaccaria, with a Ph.D. from St. Mary's University, and Richard Flowers, a Ph.D. from San Marcos State. An hour later Master Sergeant Gomez reported to me, a very personable airman with a college degree. We spent the afternoon getting to know one another and discussing our plan of action. I told them our first study was to be the Material function in the Lackland hospital. I had listed four areas that we should concentrate on: the acquisition and storage of medical supplies; the contracting for and storage of food supplies; the manning and experience within the Material department; and the purchasing of physical and housekeeping supplies. Dr. Zaccaria chose the medicine area since his brother was a medical doctor and could be of help. M/Sgt. Gomez selected the food area because he had experience in that area. Dr. Flowers selected the manning and experience of material personnel. I told them to keep detailed notes and that when we were all done with our study, we would meet and build a report containing our recommendations to the commanding general.

We finished our study the afternoon of the fourth day, and as each one of us reported our findings to the team, it was no wonder that they had a Material problem.

The officer in charge was not a supply officer and this was not his primary job, but an additional duty. Our very first recommendation was to have Personnel obtain a career supply officer who had attended the Supply School at Lowery Field. Our second recommendation was to find an officer with experience in the purchasing and storing of medical supplies. If an officer could not be found for this duty, Manpower was to establish a civil service position and hire a qualified civilian to fill this position. We also mechanized the menus and service system to the patients for more accurate food service for the hospital kitchen. There were many more minor recommendations that we presented to the general and his staff the next day. They accepted the majority of our recommendations and the general thanked us for the study.

I was pleased with the study results and that we had worked as a team. I contacted General Stillman's office and his secretary gave us an appointment with the general in three days. I gave the team two days off, and I flew the jet out of Kelly Field for two days. The flight operations at Kelly asked me if I would be available to fly with General Stillman in the jet, for he liked to have a jet pilot with him on his flights. I told them no problem and for the next year, I flew with the general, and on every flight he made me log instructor pilot time.

We met with General Stillman at 10:00 A.M. on the third day. He said that all Air Force enlistees were sent to Lackland for basic training. They came under the jurisdiction of a Training Instructor (TI), and when he felt that one of the enlistees could not adjust to military life, the TI would send the individual to the Mental Hygiene section. The mental hygienist would interview the enlistee, and if he agreed that this individual was unsuitable for the Air Force, he would inform Personnel that this enlistee was to be discharged. Instead of being discharged within a few days, the school commander would retain them for three or four weeks and use them for housecleaning duties. What had happened was some of these unsuitables complained to their parents about the treatment they were receiving, and their parents complained to their congressmen. They, in turn, had asked the Air Force for an explanation.

The general looked at me and said that he wanted my team to study this problem and come up with a solution for the most efficient and quickest way that we could discharge these unsuitables. He said he had informed the school commander that he had asked the Management Engineering team to study this situation, and to give us full access to all records, which he did with a scowl on his face.

I let the team members select the areas that they wanted to become familiar with, which left me with the mental hygienist discharge participation. They were very cooperative, and after explaining to them why my team was there, I asked, "How long after you receive the name of an enlistee from the training instructor do you interview him or her?" The senior hygienist said they interviewed the enlistee within forty-eight hours, but there were exceptions, usually medical—but no longer than four days. I asked if it were possible for me to sit in on an interview of a male and a female enlistee. The senior hygienist said yes, but I had to be in the next room with an open door because the enlistee was not to know that the interview was being monitored. He had three interviews scheduled for the next day and invited me to listen in. Two were males and a female.

The hygienist's first interview was with a male enlistee, and I was out of sight in the next room. He was asked about his family and his education, why he enlisted in the Air Force, etc. His father had died a year ago and he was the only child. His mother was not able to work and he did not have a job. He had decided that he would be less of a burden to her if he joined the Air Force because then he would have some money to send to her. Since then, she had called and cried and wanted him to come home. He said, "I realize I made a mistake and I can't concentrate on being trained to be an airman." The hygienist dismissed him and came into the room I was in. He surprised me by asking me what I thought. I said that the young man was homesick and it would be in the best interest of him, his mother, and the Air Force to discharge him. The hygienist laughed and said that I had read his mind and that he had already made that recommendation to Personnel.

His second interview was with a female enlistee, and I was in the side room when she arrived. I had not been told anything about her as to race, color of hair, appearance, etc. Here again he asked questions about her family, her interests, what she did in her spare time, if she had a boyfriend, etc. Then out of the clear blue sky he asked her how long she had been having sexual relations with her brother. I was really surprised at this question, and she started to cry and said two years. He said, "You really miss him and that is a big part of your problem here." She said yes and he told her that she had to make some changes in her life and dismissed her. I then saw her walk out of the building, and she was a very attractive blond. I asked the hygienist how he knew to ask that question. He said that he had been in this business for a long time, and you get very good at seeing their real problem. I was really impressed, for this mental hygienist was a real professional. I did not spend any more time with them, for they were not contributing to the delay in discharging unsuitables.

We spent two weeks determining why there was a three or four week delay in discharging the unsuitables. My team got together and pooled their findings and came up with an in-house system that would have the unsuitables discharged within seven days or less. I notified the general that we were ready to present our solution to the discharge problem. He had us come in the next morning, and also there were the school commander and two of his staff officers. The general gave me the go ahead signal, and I opened by saying that our system that I would present did not require any additional manpower to the current staff. Then I presented our proposed plan that would have the unsuitables discharged within seven days or less. The general was quiet for a couple of minutes and then he said, "I like it, and there is no need for any further discussion.

Major Slaker and his team will help the administrative staff to adopt this new system and I expect full cooperation from all school personnel."

In the meantime, I had contacted the ex-wife and asked her to let me have my four children for a couple of weeks that summer. She agreed, and when my team finished installing our program for the discharging of unsuitable enlistees, I drove my big Buick Limited to Seattle. I picked up my daughter and three sons, and we had a fun three-day drive to San Antonio. They adored Lee Ann, who took a two-week vacation to be with them.

While I was gone, my office received a request from the commander of the Jet Armament School at Nellis Air Base in Nevada for a few members of the Management Engineering Team to help them solve a problem they were having. This was a classified area, and the two members would have to be cleared for at least the Secret classification. I selected Dr. Zacarria to accompany me, and since I could not get a jet to fly us to Nellis, I was provided a C-47 with copilot and engineer. We arrived at Nellis in early afternoon and met with the commander within an hour. They had come up with two solutions but were having a difficult time selecting the best one. They had agreed that having us study the problem was best because we were unbiased; we could select the better solution or even come up with one of our own.

The problem was a training one, which was Dr. Zacarria's professional field for many years. We spent a few hours studying the problem, and then he explained to me why one solution was better, and he also added a couple of suggestions to it. We met with the commander the next morning and Dr. Zacarria briefed him on our selection, plus a couple of recommendations. The commander and his staff really appreciated our selection and we departed that afternoon. We made a quick stop at Bisbee to cross the border and load up with Mexican vodka at half the Texas price at home. When I checked my in-basket in my office, there was a memo from the hospital commander requesting my team because he had another problem for us to solve.

We spent three days at the hospital, and it became clear to us that too many doctors were tied up with administrative duties. We told the general that the manning tables were out of date for a hospital of this size; they were more for a clinic operation. We suggested that he request the manpower office to come to the hospital and revise the manning table for a thousand-bed hospital. In support of his request, we would send a copy of our findings to the manpower office. One doctor told us that he had been complaining about spending too much of his time on paperwork. The general was pleased with our proposal.

With what little spare time I had, I finished the thesis for my master's degree and submitted it to the Thesis Committee. Two weeks later I was notified that my thesis had been accepted and I would received my master's degree at the graduation ceremony in January 1961.

My team made several studies during the winter of 1960-61. I received notice that

MBA Diploma from the University of Southern California, 27 January 1961.

I had been chosen to attend a top management seminar at the Army Management Engineering School at Rock Island, Illinois in March. The two weeks that I spent there were very rewarding. There were top executives telling of their experiences in various business fields, and our conference leader, Mr. Wallace, was tops. My second week there, Mr. Wallace said that he had good news for a member of the class. He said, "Major Slaker has just been promoted to lieutenant colonel." What a surprise, and the class gave me a hand.

In April I was invited to attend a Management Engineering conference to be held at ATC Headquarters at Randolph Air Base. This new concept for problem solving was approved by Air Force Headquarters by their representative at the meeting. Our Management Engineering Team at Lackland Air Base was voted the most outstanding by the Management Engineers at the conference. I was so proud that I called our office, and Dr. Zacarria answered. I gave him the good news and he said that was no surprise, for he already knew that!

Donna, our babysitter and family friend, told me that her date to re-enlist was coming up. I knew that she could do better and suggested that she enroll at the Santa Rosa Junior College in California. I selected that school because it was not very far from Hamilton Air Base, where we had many single lieutenant pilots and she would be welcome at the officers' club on Saturday evenings. She agreed with me, and went to California. In August I received a letter from her telling me that she had met a pilot who was from her home state in New England and that they had really become serious about their relationship. I wanted to make sure that this pilot was not just playing with her. I flew to Hamilton Air Base in a T-33 and met with them that evening. Any doubts that I had about him were eliminated, and I wished them well and flew home the next day. They got married on my birthday in 1962.

The last week in May, Lee Ann had a surprise for me. After dinner one evening we went outside to sit on our patio to relax and watch Lisa play with a girl her own age from the far end of our apartment building. Lee Ann looked at me and said, "Ken, I visited the maternity ward at the hospital today, and I am pregnant. Remember at your promotion party at the officers' club in March, when we had a ball dancing and drinking vodka tonics? We came home, went straight to bed, made love, and went to sleep. You didn't wear protection, and I didn't get up and take a douche. So, I am pregnant." Lee Ann just looked at me and waited for an answer. I had always said to myself that I would never raise one child, that it would grow up with a brother or sister. I looked at our only daughter playing with the neighbor's daughter. I told Lee Ann that this pregnancy would not be as complicated and painful as with Lisa, and I would like to see Lisa with a brother or sister. However, the final decision was up to her because she was the one who would give birth to the baby, not me.

Lee Ann looked at me with a beautiful smile on her face and said, "Ken, I agree with you and I feel that it is God's doing that I have this child. After all, God gave women

HEADQUARTERS
LACKLAND MILITARY TRAINING CENTER (ATC)
UNITED STATES AIR FORCE
LACKLAND AIR FORCE BASE, TEXAS

REPLY TO
ATTN OF:

15 May 1961

SUBJECT: Appreciation

TO: Lt Colonel Kenneth W Slaker, 11771A
Military Training Center
Lackland Air Force Base, Texas

THRU: Chief, Manpower and Organization Division
Operations, LMTC

1. Upon the occasion of my departure from Lackland Military Training Center, I should like to avail myself of the opportunity to express my thanks and appreciation for the splendid work which you and the Management Engineering Branch have done during my tenure as Operations Officer.

2. I have been most favorably impressed with the manner in which you have organized the projects assigned to you, by your superb delegation of tasks to your subordinates, and by the constant review and follow-up which you personally have carried out. The study aimed at reducing the out-processing time of unsuitable basic airmen dischargees has already paid off handsomely in cutting this time from some two to three weeks down to three days. I think that the estimate of 500,000 dollars in annual savings to the Air Force is most conservative. Another major factor which really cannot be measured is the time and trouble saved by the Basic Military School Commanders concerned by being free of these men in so very short a time. The recently-completed study on the Clothing Sales Division of the Maintenance and Supply Group will result in my opinion, in equally favorable advantages.

3. I desire that this letter be commented upon in your next Officer Effectiveness Report. Further, in the event that your fine work is cited in some other form, I would be most happy to have this letter attached as evidence, if such be appropriate.

4. It has indeed been a pleasure to work with you and I trust that I may again have an opportunity to be associated with you at some time in the future. You are a credit to Operations, LMTC and to this base. I know that you will go far in your Air Force career.

R C BOYS
Colonel, USAF
Operations Officer

Letter of Appreciation from Col. R. C. Boys, Operations Officer, Lackland Army Training Center, 15 May 1961.

the physical structure to give birth to a human being. I remember how disappointed I was when I was eighteen and the doctor told me that I would never be able to have children. It left me with an empty feeling, and then you came along and got me pregnant. I love you and we are going to have this child." I got up and took her into my arms, kissed her, and in my mind thanked God that he had given me a woman that was not only a loving wife, but also soul mate.

May was to be a busy month. General Stillman appointed me the project officer for the Annual United States Payroll Savings Plan for Lackland Air Base. This took up my spare time that I had left after completing two Management Engineering studies. I spoke at squadron and headquarters staff meetings, posted signs at the post exchange, service station, etc. The base newspaper gave me space where I explained to servicemen that the savings plan was actually the loaning of money to the federal government by purchasing bonds. I explained that this way, they would be helping to keep the United States strong and financially solvent. By the end of May the finance office announced that May was a good month for the savings plan.

June, July, and August in San Antonio are very hot and humid, and all base operations seem to slow down then. Many of us would take our monthly vacations at this time. Lee Ann resigned from her job the 30th of July and I took the last three weeks in August off. We drove to Denver and spent one day with her niece. Then to Jackson Hole, Wyoming, where we spent the night. The next morning it was a cool fifty degrees, and we had to use the heater in the car that morning. We arrived late that evening at my Aunt Rhoda's house near Seattle. After a couple of days there, we picked up my kids in Bellevue and drove to the Ocean Shores Resort on the Washington coast. We went fishing, horseback riding, hiking, etc. After a fun week with the kids, we took off for Burbank, California. There we visited with Bob and Rosalie King, the friends we had made when I was at the University of Southern California in 1957-58. They were surprised to see Lee Ann pregnant, for they remembered me saying that I would never get her pregnant again after the tough time she had having Lisa in 1958. After three pleasant days with the Kings, we headed for San Antonio. Thank God we had air conditioning in the car, for every day the temperature was above 100 degrees. Although Lee Ann was completing her fifth month of pregnancy, she was a real trooper. This was to be our last long trip together for a long time. We also spent more evenings at home and did less partying on weekends.

I was getting more jet time during September, but I have to tell about the first time I had to make an emergency landing in the T-33. The last week in October I was scheduled to fly a local training flight with a new jet pilot getting time in the back seat. Take-off time was 1500 hours, and due to the low ceiling and poor visibility with rain, I filed an instrument flight plan with VFR on top, to remain within 100 miles of the Somerset VOR. I performed the standard preflight check of the fuel systems. All was okay and the tower cleared me for takeoff. I taxied out onto the runway, made an eighty percent run up of the engine, and all systems were normal. The tower reported a wet runway and a ceiling at 1,400 feet. I lifted off after a 3,500-foot run. All systems were normal, and I retracted the gear and contacted departure control.

I then noticed that the number two needle was showing fifteen degrees left for the Kelly VOR with the heading indicator showing the runway heading of 330 degrees. A correction this large is unusual for the Kelly VOR on a 330-degree takeoff. At this time I entered the overcast at 700 feet above the ground. Then I noticed the flag drop up and down on the VOR, and the pilot in the rear seat called to me that the generator was out. I decreased speed and dropped speed brakes to descend to VFR conditions. I turned all electrical equipment off except the radio. I informed the tower of my electrical problems, but could not read them. I spotted the airfield on my left side but was not in position to drop my tip tanks in the designated area. I turned and flew over the tower at 400 feet and got the green light. It was raining, causing low visibility but I spotted the tip drop area. I decided to drop the tips because of a wet runway, and not having any flaps to decrease our speed for a landing. Because the low ragged ceiling prevented me from making a long power on approach it required full tips for a landing.

I told the other pilot to drop the tips on my command and I would stand by with the manual release if none or only one dropped. Both tips dropped. I immediately had better stick control and turned 180 degrees to line up with runway 330. I activated the gear control and it lowered slowly. I then placed the flap control in the full down position and they came down very slowly. Just before I touched down on the runway, the flaps came full down. We touched 500 feet down the runway and rolled the entire length of the runway before I got it stopped. The battery had just enough juice to open the canopy very slowly. The ramp crew towed the jet to the ramp, and I filled out the necessary reports for an emergency landing and gave them to the flying safety officer in operations. It turned out to be a real training flight in case of generator failure. I had been flying the T-33 for three years, and this was the first time that I had to drop the tips full of fuel. The other pilot shook my hand and thanked me for a safe landing. As I walked to my car, I looked up and thanked my Guardian Angel for a safe emergency landing.

The first week in November I was surprised that I was being transferred to Germany in December. I was selected by Headquarters Air Force to fill a requisition by Air Force Headquarters in Europe as Director of Operations at Sembach Air Base, located near Kaiserslautern, Germany. I had served as the base operations officer for two years at Furstenfeldbruck, a large air base near Munich, so I knew Germany. Sembach was the headquarters for the 38th Tactical Missile Wing, so before I was to leave for Europe, I was ordered to attend the Tactical Missile Staff Officer Course at Orlando, Florida on the 27th of November. Lee Ann was due to have our baby in December, which really put us into a jam. Also, when an officer transferred and occupied base housing, he had to vacate at the end of the next month. Lee Ann and I discussed our problem, for no way could she have the baby in December and then move out at the end of the month. Her uncle, Oval Stanislaus, had an empty rental in her hometown of Vinita, Oklahoma, so we decided to move right away. I took ten days' leave, and in two days the mover arrived and we moved to Vinita.

My Management Engineering team was as upset as I was about my being transferred to Germany. Before we moved out of quarters, we had a farewell dinner at the officers' club with my team, close friends Lt. Colonel Duquette, the hospital executive officer and his wife, Jim Dawson and his wife Jeannie, etc. We would miss them. There was also Helen, the secretary that did all our typing, etc., an exceptional lady. Lisa and my pet dachshund, Betty, were both excited on our drive to Vinita. We stayed at a motel for two days until our furniture arrived. Two days later I had to leave for Orlando because I had to sign in at the school on the 26th of November. I drove to Orlando so that I would have transportation the two weeks that I would be there. I departed on the 23rd of November and arrived the afternoon of the twenty-fifth. We were housed two to a large bedroom with two double size beds. My roommate was a senior lieutenant colonel who had emphysema. His coughing spells really bothered me, and I spent the last three days there in a motel.

We attended class during the day and then after an early supper, a bus took us to Cape Canaveral to participate in the actual launching of the Mace A and B nuclear missiles. Here they carried dummy warheads, but the missiles already installed in Germany carried nuclear warheads. The Mace A missile is a low level map-matching missile that cannot be traced by radar and is very accurate and destructive. The Mace B is a high altitude missile between twenty and thirty thousand feet. It has a greater range than the Mace A due to its high altitude approach. The last day of school we were tested on what we had learned at Cape Canaveral. We then had a small ceremony where we were awarded the missile badge, which we could wear beneath our pilot's wings. This had been a very interesting week for me since I had never been exposed to our missile warfare. I departed Orlando on the 3rd of December for Lackland Air Base in accordance with my official orders.

I arrived at Lackland Air Base four days later and stayed at the VOQ (Visiting Officers' Quarters). The first thing I did was to go to Personnel and ask them to send a wire to Air Force Personnel requesting a delay en route to Germany due to my wife expecting her baby any day. The Lackland personnel office agreed with me since Christmas was coming up and the wife was expecting any day. The Air Force denied my request, and I quote the partial contents of my orders:

Concurrent travel of dependents is not authorized. In the event of Limited War or if the Continental U.S. is attacked by a foreign military force while you are en route to the port, you will report to the nearest AF install as soon as possible.
Signed William J. Bell, MAJGEN

I got my physical examination and shots updated as required before one goes overseas. I wrote goodbye letters to my children in Bellevue, Washington. I also made out a new will and wanted to name my first daughter, Patricia Elaine, in the will. I got my first wife's address from her mother, and this was the first time I had communicated with her since 1945. I received a friendly letter back with a photo of Patti in her senior year. She was very attractive. My orders said to report to the MATS passenger terminal at McGuire Air Base, New Jersey on the 28th of December. I was authorized seven days' travel time if I went by private vehicle. I decided to drive and ship the Buick to Germany. Lee Ann's cousin lived just a few doors away from our rental house and could drive Lee Ann wherever she needed to go. I departed Lackland the morning of December 21st and drove to Vinita to spend Christmas with Lee Ann and Lisa.

I knew that if I left Vinita Christmas evening and drove straight through, that I could be in New Jersey on the 28th of December. The next three days Lee Ann and I never left each other's side. I never dreamed that I would have to leave Lee Ann pregnant like this. I hoped that she would have the baby sometime during the next three days. Lisa was daddy's girl, and I had to tell her that I was leaving her and her mother for a few months. She had difficulty accepting this, and I told her that after her mother had her baby, they could come to Germany. I knew that was just a guess on my part but it helped to calm her down. I purchased a lot of staples and food for the dog to make it easier for Lee Ann. On Christmas morning I had beautiful presents for Lee Ann and Lisa. Lee Ann prepared a farewell dinner at 4:00 P.M. I put my bags in the Buick and Lee Ann and I hugged one another for a long time. I then took Lisa in my arms and she cried, and so did I. I knew that the sooner I left, the better, so I patted Betty on the head and went out the door. I could hardly see the road to drive from the tears that would not stop. True love is great, but sometimes it can make you sad. This was one of those times.

Chapter 18
CHIEF OF NUCLEAR MISSILE WAR PLANS

I arrived at McGuire Air Force Base the evening of the twenty-seventh really tired of driving. The next morning I received instructions as to where to turn in my Buick for shipment to Germany. Late that evening my flight, a MATS C-54, took off for the non-stop flight to Frankfurt. We arrived at Rhine Main Air Base early in the morning on the 29th of December. I called Sembach Air Base and they sent a staff car to pick me up. We arrived at Sembach early in the afternoon and I signed in and met the executive officer. He said that the base was on skeleton manning for the holidays, so I would find it pretty quiet. Billeting had a suite reserved for me in the BOQ, so I had an early dinner and hit the sack because I had experienced a very demanding week. I slept eleven hours, got up, dressed in uniform, and walked to headquarters where I met the base group commander. He was surprised to see me because he didn't expect me until after the holidays. He suggested that I just look around and become familiar with the base. I told him that I would like to go to Weisbaden to meet the German who had helped me escape through the Iron Curtain in 1948, as I had not seen him since. He agreed and called the motor pool and got a staff car for me to use.

I arrived in Weisbaden in the afternoon and found the apartment building the Schnabel family were living in. I walked up four floors of steps (no elevators) and knocked on a door with Rudolph's name on it. He opened the door and looked hard at me. I knew that he had never seen me in civilian clothes, so I said, "Rudolph, I am Kannath, we escaped together." He then shouted, "Kannath!" and put his arms around me and said, "Mein God!"

Then he shouted his wife's name and said, "It is Kannath!" His wife and three daughters came running and they swarmed around me hugging and kissing me. Rudolph pulled me into their living room, and I saw on the wall the picture of me that was published on the front page of the *Stars and Stripes* in 1948. His wife, Magdalena, brought in wine and snacks and we talked until midnight. They insisted that I stay all night, and I slept on the sofa. The next day was spent greeting the neighbors that lived in the building and drinking and talking. Some of them could speak English and acted as interpreters. I told Rudolph that I would come back to see them whenever I picked up my car. I never in my life had such a great welcome. I left after dinner and made it safely back to Sembach. I went straight to bed because I never had as much wine and food the two days that I spent with Rudolph and his family. Ten hours later I woke up, and it was the first day of 1962. I tried all day to get a call through to the States, but no luck. I spent the day at the officers' club making new friends with fellow pilots. Our conversation was not much about flying, but about tactical nuclear missiles.

I had a business meeting with the base commander on the morning of January 8th and when we finished, he asked about my family. I told him my wife was pregnant and overdue. He was really upset that I was not given a delay en route, and he said to go pack my bag because he was giving me an emergency leave to go back to the States and stay there until the baby was born. What a prince of a man, and I thanked him and headed for the BOQ. I decided to call Lee Ann to give her the good news. I gave the long distance German operator the number, and she said she would call me back when she got through to Lee Ann. About ten minutes later she called back and told me that no one answered the phone. I then told her the wife was pregnant and expecting and to ask the Vinita operator to connect her to the hospital because Lee Ann might be there. Again she said she would call me back. It was not more than three minutes that she called me, and in an excited voice she said, "Colonel Slaker, your wife is in the hospital and you are the father of a new baby. Congratulations. I will let the wife tell you if it's a boy or girl. They are getting a phone to her so don't hang up." In a short minute Lee Ann came on the phone and it was great to hear her voice. She said she had been there about a half hour having labor pains when the doctor and nurse were called to give emergency medical aid to patients that had been injured in an automobile accident on the freeway. She felt the baby coming and gave a big push, and the head appeared. She gave another push and the baby was halfway out when the nurse walked in and immediately paged the doctor, who came in right away and finished the birth. Lee Ann said, "Ken, you are the father of a nine-pound beautiful girl. Both she and I are okay. Don't worry about us because both cousin Joan and her mother are here with me." We had both agreed that if it were a girl, her name would be Laurie Ann. I told her that since she had the baby, I wouldn't get my emergency leave. We confirmed our love for one another and I hung up. I called the adjutant and told him that I would not be taking emergency leave.

The first week in March I told my base operations officer that I needed some time in the T-33, that I had not logged any time in December and January, and only three hours in February. He scheduled me for two and a half hours the first and second weeks in March, and then he told me that one of the jets was being scheduled for a major inspection that could only be done at the depot in Seville, Spain. He had me scheduled to fly the jet to this depot, which would give me about nine hours. That, I liked. I flew the T-33 out of Sembach on the 19th of March and landed at Zaragoza, Spain to refuel. The sky was clear all the way to Seville and the airport was a couple of miles east of the city. After landing, I taxied to the depot and turned the jet over to them. They said the inspection would take a couple of days so I got transportation to the city and stayed at the Princess Hotel. The food was good, the service was excellent, and there was live music for dancing after dinner.

The depot called me the evening of the second day and said that the inspection was complete. The only work it needed was in the fuel system, and that had been repaired. I signed for the jet on the morning of March 22nd and made the usual visual check of the aircraft. I started the engine and checked the electrical, hydraulic, and fuel systems, and all were functioning. I taxied out for a takeoff to the south because there was a

Newspaper welcomes Slaker to Missile Wing, March 1962.

strong wind from the southwest. Takeoff was normal with no problem with the fuselage tank feeding fuel to the engine. I entered the overcast at 1,500 feet and started my climb to get on top of the overcast reported to be 18,000 feet. The takeoff and climb is done with fuel from the fuselage tank, and when it shows a decrease in the fuel level, you turn on the tip tanks, which feed to the fuselage tank. I had not reached the top of the overcast when I turned on the tip tanks. I noticed that the needle in the fuselage tank was not stationary or showing an increase of fuel in the fuselage tank, but rather declining.

Just then I broke out of the overcast, made a couple of hard maneuvers with the wings, turned the switch off and on, and the tips were not feeding. I immediately turned to a southern heading and started to descend. I could not decrease the power too much because I now had a strong headwind. The fuselage needle was now below half a tank and I was able to call the tower and declare an emergency. If the fuselage tank went empty before I landed, I would not have enough speed to keep from stalling and would crash. When I broke out of the overcast, the field was not in sight. The tower did not have radar to give me a heading to the airfield. The needle was getting close to the big E, and then I spotted the city of Seville a few miles about twenty degrees to the right of my current heading. Now I knew where the airfield was and headed a little left of Seville. I spotted the airfield, and the needle was now touching E. Between me and the airfield were green pastures, and I decided that the tips were not as valuable as the aircraft and my life. I jettisoned the tip tanks and immediately had good control of the aircraft and decreased power. I touched down on the runway with the needle on the big E. I was able to taxi to the depot before the engine died. The chief of maintenance was there along with his one American assistant. The rest of the crew were Spaniards. I told him briefly what was wrong and went into operations and wrote up the reason for my emergency requiring dropping the tip tanks. I made two copies, one for the maintenance people there and one for maintenance at Sembach. I went back to the same hotel and relaxed.

The next morning I called the maintenance chief and he said they found the problem and had to order some parts and it would be four or five days before the jet would be ready. I gave him my phone and room number, and he then said that I was to call operations because they had a message for me. I called the operations officer and he said that General Caldara, whose office was at our airfield just outside of Madrid, wanted me to call him. I said that I would come right out to operations to make the call. The operations officer told me that General Caldara asked him if what I did—dropping the tanks—was as directed in the manual. The operations officer said that he didn't know but would have me call him. I asked the operations officer if he had a T-33 flight manual because I wanted to check it just to make sure that I had gone by the manual. He did not have one, so I went to the maintenance chief and got one from him. I found the correct page and I was in the clear. I then placed a call to the number that General

Caldara had asked me to call. He answered the phone and I said, "This is Colonel Slaker returning your call. I hope that you remember me when I flew as your pilot several times when you were commander at Forbes Air Base."

He said that he recalled the name right away, and here was why he called. The farmer would be wanting money for the damage the tips caused to his pasture, and if dropping the tips was proper, then the Air Force would pay him. I then read the paragraph from the flight manual to the general, which supported my dropping the tip tanks. He thanked me and then asked where and what was I doing. I brought him up

Slaker sworn into the Daedalian Society, 9 January 1962.

to date and invited him to stop by Sembach and visit one of our nuclear missile sites. He hoped he could do that, and we said our farewells.

I enjoyed my stay the next few days. The food was good, the service was excellent, and they had live music for dancing after dinner. I think a couple of the Spanish girls that I had talked to in my first stay at the hotel thought I had come to see them. I did dance with a couple of them, but I really enjoyed flirting and dancing with two attractive girls from Australia that were vacationing in Spain. I really had a tough time behaving myself with Lee Ann pregnant and not being with me the past three months. These girls were not teasing; they were ready to make love. It was during this time that I decided I was going to have Lee Ann come to Germany at our expense as tourists, and we would rent a house and live in the German economy.

Four days later I was notified that my T-33 would be ready for its flight to Sembach the next morning. Early the next morning I had breakfast, said goodbye to the waiters, and checked out. I was at the airfield by 9:00 A.M., signed for my jet, and after very thorough system checkouts, I took off for Zaragoza. I was on the ground only long enough to refuel and take off for Sembach. No problem landing at Sembach. I had been gone a week, but it seemed a lot longer.

My annual flight physical was coming up in April and had to be completed by my birthday on April 14th. I made an appointment with the flight surgeon for the first week in April so that I would be finished before Lee Ann arrived from the States. I reported at 8:00 A.M. on the day scheduled, stripped my clothes off, and for a couple of hours had every test one could think of. When all the lab reports and x-rays showed me to be in good health, I was told to get dressed and report to the dental clinic for a dental examination and full mouth x-ray. The dentist in charge was a lieutenant colonel and he examined my teeth and did the full mouth x-ray. He said to relax, that he would be back in a few minutes with the x-ray. When he returned he had a frown on his face. He said that my upper right rear molar had an abscess and would have to be pulled. He made an appointment for me to have it pulled two days later.

Since I had been living on base, I ate most of my meals there. Also eating most of his meals there was Major Scott, a single officer who was a dentist in our clinic. We became friends and would meet at the bar before dinner. I told him that his boss was going to pull one of my teeth, and Scott really got upset. He said all his boss knew about dentistry was to pull teeth. Scott asked me to come to the clinic the next morning because he wanted to x-ray my molar. I arrived at the clinic the next morning and Dr. Scott x-rayed the molar. After the x-ray was developed, he showed me the print and said that the tooth was okay, that the pus at the root of the molar was coming from an infection in the sinus above the tooth. He gave me a prescription for medicine to heal the sinus and told me that he would cancel my appointment with his boss. Thanks to Dr. Scott, I still have that tooth.

I called Lee Ann to make sure that she, Lisa, and the baby could travel the second week in April before I purchased air tickets with Pan American. She already had her passport with the children and was ready. My German secretary had told me of a new commercial building with an apartment on the second floor located in a small village about ten miles from the air base. I drove there and met the owner, and he was pleased to rent it to me. It was in the center of the village with a clear stream running about fifty yards behind the building. The day before my family was to arrive, I went to the base commissary and loaded up with all the food and staples that I hoped would be enough for several days at our new apartment.

I was so excited while driving to the Rhine Main airport at Frankfurt to pick up my family that I don't even remember being on the autobahn to get there. I arrived at the airport just in time to see the Pan American aircraft land and taxi to the ramp. It took me about ten minutes to get to the terminal window to watch the passengers unload. I became worried when all the passengers and the crew got off and I didn't see Lee Ann and the children disembark. I rushed to the Pan American counter and asked if the Slaker family had missed this flight from the States. The clerk said, "No, they didn't. Because of the new baby, we took her off the aircraft before the passengers got off. Your wife went through customs and should be in the waiting room." I rushed there, and standing at the glass exit door was Lisa crying and saying, "Where is my daddy?" I walked up behind her, tapped her on the shoulder, and she turned and shouted "Daddy!" and jumped into my arms and kept saying "Daddy" and crying. I also had tears.

There was not a happier man in the world when I walked over to the bench where my beautiful wife was sitting beside the basket holding our new daughter. She was awake and smiled at me like she knew that I was her father. Lee Ann said that Laurie had slept all the way from Tulsa to New York, where she woke her up to feed her. She then slept all the way to Frankfurt. I picked up the basket and said, "Let's go to your new home." Lisa sat up front with me, and Lee Ann sat in the back seat with the baby.

Fortunately it was a clear and sunny day, and when we drove into Kaiserslautern, Lisa asked if this was our new home. I told her that our new home was just a few miles away and was called Imsweiler. I told Lee Ann that our apartment was on the second floor above a beauty salon and came with a part time housekeeper. Lee Ann liked that, and I told her that her name was Idda and that she had worked for an American family and could speak basic English. She lived in a small house about two blocks away and had a young son. She was waiting in the apartment when we arrived.

I had the next day off to help my family get settled and familiar with their surroundings. Lisa was already taking care of a huge cat sitting on our back deck. In the afternoon the owner of the building came by to welcome us and he spoke very good English. I told Lee Ann that we would go to the base on Saturday so that she would know how to get there and where the commissary and post exchange were located. I worked Friday and met Dr. Scott for our afternoon cocktail. He could not stay at the club for dinner because he was having a dinner party at his condo. I did not tell him that my family had arrived.

Lee Ann made her first drive to the base on Saturday, and we visited the commercial area and then had lunch at the officers' club. After lunch we went to my office and got my mail. There was a letter from Lee Ann's mother and an official letter to me from USAFE Headquarters. I opened the official letter while Lee Ann drove us back to our apartment. It stated that the Secretary of Defense, Mr. McNamara, had developed a new policy for pilots. If your primary assignment was not a rated one, then you were not authorized to fly any aircraft but would receive your flight pay. The letter stated that as of April 14, 1962, I would no longer pilot an aircraft but would continue to receive flight pay. What a blow this was to me. I was a private pilot before I went to aviation cadet training in 1945. This was my life. Even though I had several assignments as a staff officer, I always maintained my proficiency as a pilot. I was a regular officer and planned on staying in the Air Force for thirty years. I had eighteen years' service time, so I decided that when I got my twenty in, I would retire and apply for a pilot's position with one of the airlines.

Lee Ann could see that I was upset and asked what was in the letter that had me upset. I explained it to her and she shook her head in disbelief. She said, "Ken, that is not only going to lower the morale in the Air Force, but hundreds of pilots, both regular and Reserve, will not make the Air Force a career." I told her that she was correct and that her husband was one of them.

I was not the only staff officer unhappy with McNamara's new policy for pilots, for this applied to many of the pilots at Sembach because we were primarily a missile group and not a combat pilot group. Some of the younger Reserve pilots said they were going to resign at the end of their overseas tour and apply for the airlines, where they would be flying for a much better pay than what the Air Force paid.

A week later Lee Ann made arrangements with the housekeeper to stay for the evening with the children so that she could have dinner with me at the officers' club. She drove me to work that morning so that she would have the car to drive to the club that evening. I walked to the club after work, and Dr. Scott was already there so I joined him. He still did not know that my family was there. I asked what was on his mind because he seemed depressed. He said that he was approaching forty and didn't have a family and was wasting his life just playing around. I turned my head just as Lee Ann walked into the bar, and Dr. Scott turned his head to see what had my attention. When he saw Lee Ann walking toward us, he said, "Boy, Ken, that is bedroom stuff."

I stood up to greet Lee Ann and said, "Dr. Scott, I would like you to meet my wife, Lee Ann." I really enjoyed the surprised look on his face, and he got up to meet her. He said that it was a real pleasure to meet her and asked when she had arrived. She told him a week ago, and he looked at me and I gave him a happy smile. He had dinner with us and became a good friend to the both of us.

As director of operations for the air base group, I did business with all the wing staff officers. Colonel Lawrence, the wing commander, had Personnel put me on orders, making me a member of the officers' club board. This was more interesting than the stateside clubs because we had slot machines just like Reno. The club officer was rotating to the States come fall. I talked to the group commander about requesting my friend Major Dailey, the club officer at Randolph Air Base, to be our new club officer. To my surprise, USAFE was able to get Major Dailey transferred to Sembach and he became our new officers' club president.

When I had visited the Schnabel family in Wiesbaden the past December, I had promised Rudolph that I would drive them to his wife's home near the French border come summer. Lee Ann and Lisa decided to come along, and our maid stayed with Laurie. One Saturday morning we drove to Wiesbaden in my big Buick Limited and picked up the Schnabel family, consisting of mom and dad and daughters Karin, Edda, and Christa. I had placed several Hershey chocolate bars in the seat pockets and they enjoyed those. They spent the afternoon with relatives and friends and on the return trip I stopped at our apartment so that Lisa and her mother would not have the drive to Wiesbaden and back. It was near midnight when I dropped the Schnabels off at their residence. The girls hugged and thanked me, and Rudolph and I shook hands. I was really thankful that he was alive and the father of a fine family.

The post engineer and I were good friends since we had both graduated from engineering school at Ft. Belvoir. He lived in a new apartment building in Winnweiler, which was closer to the base and bigger than our building. I found out that he was rotating to the States that fall and asked him if it had been leased. He called me the next day and said that the building owner would be glad to lease it to me. Early that September we moved into a much larger apartment on the first floor, and there were American families in all the other apartments. In October I received a letter from Mr. Atwood, my attorney in Seattle, that my daughter Pamela and her girlfriend had been sexually abused by the mayor of Bellevue. Mr. Atwood felt that this was the right time to go to court and sue for custody of my daughter. I discussed this with Lee Ann since bringing a sixteen-year-old girl into the family would put more pressure on her. Lee Ann strongly agreed with my attorney to sue for custody of Pam. I felt that I could get emergency leave to appear in the court in Seattle.

A few days later Colonel Upson, the director of missile wing operations, asked to see me. He knew that I was not happy being the director of flight operations for the air base group when I was no longer authorized to fly. He said that he would like for me to join the missile wing as Director of Tactical Missile Wing Plans. I quickly agreed, and he said that I would be put on orders to attend the launching of the TM-76B at Cape Canaveral in November, which would bring me up to date on technical and operational improvements.

The third week in October the base loudspeakers announced that there was a commander's call of all officers to the base theatre at 11:00 A.M. The wing intelligence officer briefed us that the base was going on full alert, that the United States was planning to attack Cuba and this had created a critical relationship between Russia and the United States. All leaves and requests for leaves were canceled. Officers that were scheduled to duty in the combat center would be provided quarters on base. I drove the Buick to our apartment and picked up some clothing and toilet articles. I briefed Lee Ann about the tense climate between the United States and Russia and told her that our nuclear missiles were on full red alert.

The combat center was built ninety feet below the surface of the athletic field, to which all hot lines to the missile sites were terminated inside two control decks. The control decks were about twenty-five feet apart so that it took two operators to launch a missile. The one deck operator had to have orders from the President to fire certain missiles. The other deck could not arm a certain missile until ordered by the alert officer on duty. Once a missile was launched, it could not be recalled or destroyed. There were two alert officers: one was the primary alert officer, and the other officer was backup alert. I pulled six-hour alert duty every two days.

The end of the third week in October we received word that the Russians had nuclear missiles in Cuba aimed at the U.S. Also, all dependents were ordered to evacuate their bases and drive to the Air Force Command at Zaragoza in Spain. I hitched a ride to our apartment, and Lee Ann had the minimum amount of clothing and food supplies already packed. A couple in the building that had no children and a sedan invited Lee Ann and girls to go with them. Our big Buick was too much of a gas hog to take it. The girls had tears in their eyes as I kissed them goodbye. As I kissed Lee Ann, I could tell by the look on her face and in her eyes that she knew we might never see one another again. I told her to take care of herself and the girls and not to worry about me because I had a Guardian Angel. This was a terrible moment in my life when I watched them drive away.

On the last Monday in October, we were informed that the alert was over. President Kennedy and Khrushchev had come to a peaceful agreement. Dependents were ordered to return to their respective bases. I had not had any word from Lee Ann, and for all I knew she could be in the States. That same day, orders were published ordering me to report to Cape Canaveral by November 4th to attend the testing of the improved Mace missile. I then sent a wire to Stan Atwood, my attorney in Seattle, that I could be there the second week to appear in court to seek custody of my daughter. My orders authorized a five-day delay on my return to Sembach. My orders contained the departure date and times from Frankfurt to Cape Canaveral for the 2nd of November. I was unhappy that I would leave before I knew where my family was, and I decided to change my departure date to the 3rd of November, which would still put me at the Cape on the third. Fortunately the dispatcher at Rhine Main was able to change my reservation to the third.

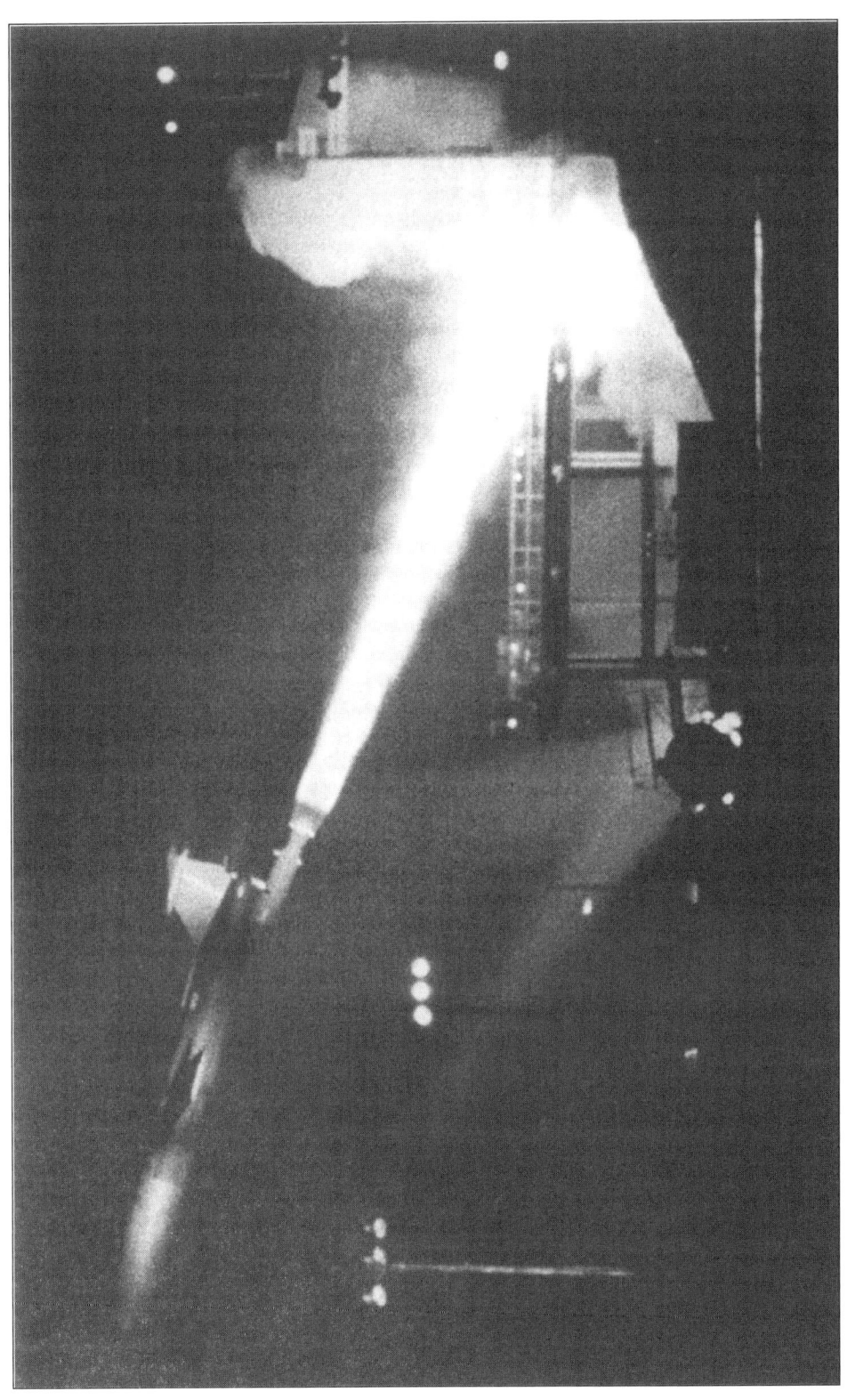

Test firing of the improved B-76 missile, Cape Canaveral, November 1962.

Late in the evening of the 1st of November, there was a call for me from some little town in France. I answered it, and what a thrill to hear Lee Ann's voice. She said they would be back late the next morning. I told her that I would be at the apartment waiting for her and to please arrive no later because I had to leave for the States the next day. The car drove in at noon, and the girls jumped out of the car, screaming and laughing. Seeing Lee Ann coming towards me, I knew that she was a part of me for now I felt whole again. I thanked God and my Guardian Angel for bringing Lee Ann back to me.

I arrived at Cape Canaveral on the 3rd of November and was assigned to the same quarters that I had stayed in one year ago. I had attended and completed the staff course for the introduction of the utilization of the Mace A and B missiles for the deliverance of nuclear weapons. Now I was to learn of the technical and operational improvements of the improved 76-B missile. All the test launchings of the missile were accomplished at night since they were of a classified nature. When this course was completed, I flew to Seattle via commercial air. My aunt Rhoda met me at the airport and I stayed overnight at her residence in Federal Way.

The next day I arrived at the Superior Court in Seattle at 9:00 A.M. and met my attorney, Mr. Atwood. My ex wife was already there with Pamela and her attorney. I spoke to Pam and her mother, and Pam responded verbally with a smile, but her mother ignored me. The judge entered and the court was called to order, and my attorney was called to present his case. He gave several strong basic reasons why the court should give me custody of my daughter. Glenna's attorney did not deny any of my attorney's presentation. He did state that Pam had a good home and would miss her three brothers if custody was granted to her father. The judge then said that he wanted to see both attorneys in his chamber.

Twenty minutes later the attorneys came back into the courtroom, and then the judge appeared and the clerk called the court to order. Judge Meakim then stated that after consulting with the attorneys, Pamela would be in a much better environment, especially at this time, under the custody of her father. He then granted the custody of Pamela to me and said that her mother was to have Pamela ready for her father to pick her up at her mother's residence at 10:00 A.M. the next morning. I also had the court's approval to take Pamela to my base in Germany.

Glenna had tears, but Pamela rushed to me and we embraced and I told her that I would come for her in the morning.

Mr. Atwood and I walked out into the hallway, and I thanked him for getting Pamela under my custody. He then suggested that we go to a first class restaurant that overlooked Lake Union for cocktails. When we got settled and ordered a cocktail, he asked if I realized what we had just accomplished. This was a rare court decision to take a daughter away from her mother. Then he said he had to tell me what happened in the judge's chamber, and it was very confidential. Glenna's attorney told the judge that he had to be honest and that his client was not to know what he was about to say. He said that Pamela would be better off with her father and he should be given custody of his daughter. "Don't ever tell anyone, especially Glenna!" he said. My attorney and I had a few more cocktails celebrating our court victory, and then Mr. Atwood said that I was not going to drive to Federal Way—he had the waiter get a cab for me and he paid the fare!

The next morning before picking up my daughter, I made reservations on British Overseas Airlines to London, then a domestic airline to Frankfurt for the following day. I arrived at the house, for which I had given title to Glenna and the four children, at 10:00 A.M. Pam was ready, and her three brothers were beside her to say goodbye. I drove us to my relative's residence where we stayed until the next morning when my Uncle Mac drove us to the airport. We had a smooth eight and a half hour flight to London, where we boarded a flight to Frankfurt. Lee Ann was waiting at the airport for us and drove us to Winnweiler.

The missile wing personnel published orders on the 14th of November 1962, assigning me as the Chief of Missile Operation Plans. Four officers were assigned to my office, one of whom was Major Gordon Haworth, my assistant and a fine and efficient officer. Shortly into the New Year Colonel Upson called me to his office and talked to me about an officer named Donald Hedges. He felt that this captain would make a good Missile Wing Briefing Officer and would be assigned to my office. He then introduced me to Captain Hedges, and I agreed with Colonel Upson's proposal. Captain Hedges was a tall, well-built, and alert officer with a clear, positive voice, and a pilot still on flying status.

We had a lot of snow in February, and since we were only a few miles from a snow-covered mountain with a road to the top, I purchased a deluxe toboggan with a steering wheel and brakes on the runners that held four people. I would pull the toboggan with Lee Ann, Lisa, Pamela, and our next-door neighbor's young girl up to the top of the mountain and then change places with Lee Ann, and down the hill we went at a fairly good speed. Lee Ann would meet us at the bottom with the car and tow us back up to the top. Then Lee Ann steered the toboggan down the road. The kids screamed and really enjoyed the ride. On one of my trips the road at the bottom was slick, and I lost control and the toboggan ploughed through the snow bank and into the woods. We missed a couple of trees but a big one appeared directly in front of us, and I rolled the toboggan over and we all went flying into the deep snow. I got up and the kids were okay, and Lisa stood up laughing and screamed, "Let's do it again!" When we would return to our apartment, the parents of the young girl would have hot wine waiting for us.

The wing commander received a call in the spring from USAFE that McNamara's team was currently at Wiesbaden and would be arriving at Sembach Air Base the next morning. They wanted to be briefed on the current status of our missile operation. Colonel Upson then called me and suggested I try having a dry run in the briefing room with Captain Hedges that evening. Captain Hedges started immediately on an outline, and my staff was preparing current statistics on all our missile sites for Hedges. I notified the Post Engineer to ensure that electrical and heating systems were operating in the briefing room, and I asked the mess sergeant to have beverage and snack items available in the briefing room. A majority of the missile officers were present for the briefing that evening. Suggestions were made and discussed, and those approved were inserted into Captain Hedges' briefing.

The McNamara team arrived by air at 10:00 A.M. They were greeted by Colonel Lawrence, the missile wing commander, who escorted them to the briefing room where greetings were exchanged. Colonel Lawrence then called the meeting to order and gave a short speech as to how the missile wing was organized to support and operate our various missile sites spread throughout West Germany. He then introduced Captain Hedges, who would brief them on our operational plans with our nuclear missiles.

Captain Hedges gave a clear description of the location and capability of the low altitude Mace A nuclear missile, then the utilization of the high altitude long-range nuclear missile 76-B. This missile was targeted on Russian military sites in East Germany and western Poland. He then gave the total number of nuclear missiles ready to launch. A team member interrupted Hedges and said that was not the same number they had received the day before at USAFE. Before Hedges could try to answer that he was not familiar with the reports submitted by my office, I said that I could explain the number difference. Each morning at 9:00 A.M., my office wired a status report to USAFE Operations giving the number of missiles available for launch at that time. The figures he had received were from yesterday's report. The team member nodded in agreement and Hedges continued with his briefing. When he finished Colonel Upson stood up and asked the team if they had any questions. They did have several, which were answered by the colonel. The team's attitude was not a friendly business one, but more cool like an inspection team. The colonel asked if they would like lunch, but they had a tight schedule and had to leave. The colonel walked with them to their staff cars that took them to their aircraft. They never gave us any reason as to why they were there in Germany.

The following weekend the maid agreed to spend Saturday night with the children so that Lee Ann and I could have a break. We drove the Buick towards the Mosel River, planning to visit one of the wineries. We saw a small village on the river and turned onto the narrow road that led to the town. We got into town and saw a winery to our right. I turned right onto the next street and it kept narrowing and narrowing until it became too narrow for our Buick. I stopped to back up and a horn blew from a small car behind me. I got out of the Buick, went back to the driver behind me, and made him understand that I had to back up this narrow street so that he could get ahead of me. He understood and backed his car to a wide intersection. I got out of the Buick and thanked him, and he laughed and drove off.

We stayed on the main road until we arrived at Trier, where we spent the night. Trier had been the capital of the Roman Empire North and was now a tourist town. The huge black gate which had been the entrance to Trier was still in place. There was also the coliseum where the audience cheered when Christians that had been put into the center of the huge coliseum were attacked and eaten by lions released by the Roman guards. At dinner that night I told Lee Ann that we would not be able to tour and visit many towns in Germany and bordering countries with our big Buick. I suggested that we buy a Volks 1700 sedan for us to use during vacations. She agreed and when we returned to Sembach, I flew to Wiesbaden and purchased a new Volks 1700 sedan for 1,500 American dollars.

In late spring I got a call from the base housing officer stating he had quarters for my family on base. The very next weekend we moved into our new home, which was a large apartment on the third floor of a large apartment building in the base housing area. This move was very timely because Lisa was to start to school that fall and Pamela was to start high school, and both were located on base. A full time maid was also assigned to us. Her name was Erika Gerber. She lived with us most of the time.

We took advantage of having a good full time maid and did a lot of sightseeing the summer of 1963. We drove to Copenhagen, Denmark, where Lee Ann enjoyed shopping. She bought a teak dining room set, pewter coffee and tea set with crystal glasses, etc. The merchant shipped her purchases to our air base without any charge! Two weeks later we took a special tour to Vienna with stops at Munich, Salzburg, and Innsbruck. Captain Hedges and his lovely wife went with us and we really had fun. I could have stayed several days more in my favorite city, Vienna. Before summer ended, we drove to Luzern, Switzerland and stayed in a hotel built in the fourteenth century. When you walked through the hallways, the wooden floor really squeaked. There was only one bathroom that served the entire floor, and you could hear people going to the bathroom all during the night. Again Lee Ann enjoyed shopping here.

During this time, Germany had a visit by a man they really admired, President Kennedy. German TV followed him all over Germany, and when he spoke to a live audience of over one million people in Berlin, he ended his speech with this in German: "I am a Berliner." The audience clapped, roared, and shouted so loud that it could be heard all the way to America! All we service personnel in Germany also admired our President. All of us in Germany were aware of how he stood up to Khrushchev and got us out of the missile crisis the previous year. All of us in the tactical nuclear missile defensive weapons knew that President Kennedy saved not only our lives in Germany, but also thousands of lives in the United States and Russia.

The fall of 1963 was a busy and exciting one for Lee Ann and me. She was elected president of the Sembach Wives' Club. She had the personality and energy for this position and a husband that would be of help to her. I was on the Board of Directors for the officers' club and our good friend, Major Dailey, was the club officer. We arranged for various entertainers, dance bands, buffet dinners, etc. We made it a habit to take one night off a week and go into Kaiserslautern with one or two other couples for dinner. On the third Friday in November, we and the Hedges and Millers met at our apartment to go to a restaurant where I had made reservations for dinner that evening. Just as we were about to leave, the phone rang and I answered it. The duty Officer of the Day told me to turn on the German TV channel right then because there was terrible news. I turned the TV on, and it showed the Capitol in Washington D.C. while the announcer told us that President Kennedy had been murdered in Dallas, Texas. The six of us stood in shock and kept our eyes glued on the TV. It showed the scene that happened in Dallas and the rushing of President Kennedy to the hospital where he died. Just then, our phone rang and it was the manager at the restaurant where I had reservations and he said, "Colonel Slaker, we have closed the restaurant tonight in respect of President Kennedy and will not be serving dinner." I thanked him, and we six just sat and walked and talked, wondering who would do this to our popular President. I then suggested that maybe this had been planned by the Russians. Lee Ann had some food that we nibbled on, and about midnight we bid one another a sad goodnight.

The next morning all the flags on the base were at half mast, and the wing commander announced that there would be no entertainment functions at either the officers' club or the NCO Club for thirty days, only regular meals.

Our children liked this because now they saw more of Lee Ann and me. I gave the maid the next four weeks off. The wives' club had started to plan a Christmas party, but that was too close to the end of the memorial period. Lee Ann and I called a meeting of selected two members of the wives' club and Colonel Keating, the deputy commander, to discuss deleting the plan for the Christmas party and have a New Year's party instead. This suggestion was approved and Lee Ann and I agreed to come up with the outline for the New Year's party within ten days. Lee Ann came up with a suggestion that we have Baby New Year appear at the party, where he would announce that he had brought representatives from the next twelve months to advertise their month. She also said that we should have Colonel Haney's father-in-law, who had been visiting there for a month, to be Baby New Year wearing only a white diaper. She said that she had already talked to him and he was all for it, but since he was in his sixties and a little plump, who was going to pin his diaper on? Lee Ann said she told him she would, and he said it was a deal.

I wrote the skits for each month, and Lee Ann selected the individuals that were to perform in a specific month. The club had a large ballroom with a stage along one wall. Lee Ann spent a lot of time acquiring and making the costumes to be worn for the presentation of each month, and I had several officers helping me with the stage props. Three days before New Year's Eve, we had a trial performance (but not of Baby New Year) of the twelve months. Corrections and adjustments were made and all of us agreed that we were ready.

The Stars and Stripes, 23 November 1963.

The wing commander's father-in-law agreed to be Baby New Year. Only three of us knew it. When he appeared on stage, the audience was stunned . . . then they broke into wild laughter. Lee Ann fitted him with the diaper!

Come New Year's Eve, the club's ballroom opened at 6:00 P.M. for cocktails and dinner. The ballroom was jammed with not an empty table or chair available. We had acquired a professional piano player to provide the background music for each month. At 9:00 P.M. a teenager carrying the U.S. flag came onto the stage, and one of the wives who was a good singer joined the piano player and sang our National Anthem. When she was finished, I walked onto the stage and welcomed everyone to our New Year's Celebration Party. I told them we were very fortunate, for Baby New Year had agreed to join us and had brought individuals who would show us what we could expect from each one of his twelve months. I then said that it was a very rare privilege that I had been given to introduce Baby New Year. The piano played New Year's music, and out came Colonel Haney's father in law dressed in a white diaper and carrying a huge champagne glass half full of wine. The club membership went wild with laughter and clapping of hands. The base photographer got a picture of Baby New Year's arrival. I wish he had gotten a photo of Mrs. Haney's face when she saw her father appear in a diaper, for it was a shocked look. Her father put on quite an act, walking among all the guests and offering them a drink out of his huge glass. When he got to the end of the ballroom, he raised his glass and departed, and the membership was still clapping and shouting their approval.

I then announced that January had arrived, and the piano played appropriate music and two couples came out onto the stage dressed in fur jackets and carrying snowshoes. They did a little dance and departed. February and March were very good, and the membership really liked April. Four officers' wives wearing two-piece bathing suits and carrying umbrellas did a dance while singing "April Showers Bring May Flowers." Just as they walked off the stage, four teenage daughters wearing flowered blouses and skirts and carrying bouquets of flowers danced onto the stage for the month of May. Then came four men dressed in summer shorts, each carrying a bottle of beer and singing "Happy Days Are Here Again," and dancing in a circle representing June. The following months were excellently performed, and when the September group was finished, I announced that the month of October was going to be a contest month. I was going to give selected members the opportunity to guess the identity of Miss Halloween.

A wives' club member helped Lee Ann with her ugly false face, huge black wig, and pantyhose under a black and orange skirt. I called for Miss Halloween, and she came dancing out onto the stage to piano music and then did a curtsy to the audience. I said that each person would have ten seconds to guess the identity of Miss Halloween. Colonel Lawrence, the wing commander, took ten seconds and then gave the wrong name. Lee Ann then did a one-minute dance showing her beautiful legs, and I called on the deputy commander, Colonel Keating, who guessed the wrong name. Lee Ann did another busy leg dance and I called on my boss, Colonel Upson, and he said, "Those beautiful legs belong to Lee Ann Slaker." There were a couple of boos when she took off her mask and wig; some thought I had tipped off Colonel Upson since he was my boss. I handed a large bag of Halloween candy to Lee Ann, and she went to Colonel Upson's table and gave him the bag of candy and a kiss. She then went back onto the stage, did a little dance, and waved to the audience as she left the stage. The audience gave her a great hand, for they knew that she was one of the organizers of the party.

I then told the audience that November was the month that we all, regardless of age or sex, enjoy. During this month, Thanksgiving Day arrives and the men loosen their belts and the ladies take off their pantyhose and gorge themselves with turkey and mashed potatoes—and look what happens. At this time a member walked onstage really padded in flight coveralls with his command pilot's wings pinned on his left chest. He said in a sobbing voice, "I really enjoyed Thanksgiving dinner and the leftovers, but due to my excessive weight, I just flunked my annual flight physical." He then shuffled and sobbed as he left the stage. I said, "That should be a warning to you hungry pilots next Thanksgiving. I suggest you get a cross-country flight that day to Alamogordo for dinner."

I then said, "Now, it is the last month of the year and all of our monthly actors and actresses have a December message for all of you." The entire cast came out onstage, lined up, and with piano playing, sang the Christmas song, "Santa Claus is Coming To Sembach." When they finished we on the stage bowed to the audience and they gave us an ovation that could have brought the ceiling down. We bowed again and walked off stage and then hugged and thanked one another for the time and effort we had used to put on this New Year's party. At midnight there was no shortage of liquid spirits, and then a member in a loud voice shouted, "Three cheers for Sembach!" Three loud cheers erupted, and I am sure that we could be heard all over Germany. Lee Ann and I got to our apartment at 3:00 A.M. Our maid and the girls were asleep, and we very quietly prepared for bed.

Before we crawled into the sack, I looked Lee Ann in the eyes and said, "Honey, the time and work that we put into this party for the club members was worth it." She agreed, and we kissed and crawled into bed and yes, went right to sleep!

With President Kennedy gone, and Johnson now President, we missileers spent the first few weeks of 1964 watching and waiting to see if our relationship with Russia would change. Most of my friends there doubted that Johnson would ever attain the popularity that President Kennedy held.

Lee Ann and I decided to get away from the missile environment for a few days and drive to Holland for the tulip festival. We took my daughter Pamela with us and stayed at a hotel in Rotterdam. We drove to the town where the festival parade was to be seen and it was a cold, foggy day. The Dutch girls that were on the floats in the parade wearing only bathing suits were shivering from the damp cold, but the tulip displays were beautiful. From there we drove to Amsterdam for two days. The first day it was clear and sunny, we boarded a tourist boat and spent the day sailing the river and canals. The next day we visited the city market and it was enjoyable. There were live musicians scattered throughout the market and many variety shops, but the most interesting to us was the cheese market. There were scores of different flavors and colors of cheese that were available. We bought a couple of flats that looked appetizing. By the time we returned to Sembach two days later, one flat of cheese had such a bad smell that we disposed of it.

My best physical sport was tennis, and whenever I had some free time I was on the tennis courts. Most of the time my opponent or partner was Colonel Aundry, Missile Operations Executive Officer. He surprised me when he notified me that he had signed us up as a doubles team in the European Seniors' Tennis Tournament to be held at Bitberg, Germany. Lee Ann decided to go with Aundry and me to Bitberg so that we would have at least one person cheering for us. We were given one day to practice, and I was surprised that we were to play on clay courts. I was used to smooth black top or tight grass courts for my style of play. We were scheduled to meet our opponents the next afternoon and we won the match. This put us into the semifinals. Aundry was a little slower on the courts because of his weight. With my 6'3" height at the net, they would return a hard hit ball to Aundry. Once in a while I would shift to the other side of the net just as they were swinging to return Aundry's serve. They must have been mind readers because they would hit the ball to my alley and, of course, Aundry didn't know that I was going to shift, so they scored a point. We lost that match and were eliminated. I then decided to play in the Senior Singles Tournament. I had trouble with my serve as I was used to grass courts and had a spin that when my serve hit the grass, it would not have much of a bounce and was difficult to return. I lost the match and was pissed off at myself. Lee Ann said to come along with her, and she took me to the local brewery and kept me drinking beer until I was smiling again.

During our tour at Sembach, Germany, the wife and I visited many of the countries that were not a part of the Russian communistic government. Since I was in a Top Secret assignment and had been requested to be returned to Russia to be tried as an American spy, I was prohibited from traveling in any of the Russian Empire. Lee Ann wanted to visit Poland before we left Germany because her ancestors had come from there and she was a descendant of King Stanislaus Leszynski, who was elected King of Poland in 1704. Through several generations the name Leszynski was dropped before coming to America, and the descendants were all born with the last name as Stanislaus. She was able to get a visa to visit Poland and took the train to Berlin, then boarded a train to Warsaw. When she returned to West Germany, she was very depressed at what she had witnessed in Warsaw. Their economy was in very bad shape and the people were poorly clothed and starving. She had taken several goodies with her, like Hershey bars, chewing gum, ink pens, etc. She told me of seeing a poor elderly man sitting against a building begging for food, and she had given him a couple of her Hershey chocolate bars. He said to her, "God bless you Americans." Lee Ann had tears in her eyes as she related this story to me.

This would be our last summer in Germany, and we had visited all of Europe except Italy. Most of my fifty bombing missions in World War II had been on the mainland of Italy and the islands of Sicily and Sardinia. I had been warned that if I visited Italy, I was not to mention that I had been a pilot that bombed Italy because many Italians would not be very receptive to my presence. However, the wife and I decided to visit Italy, and I would be careful not to mention my part in World War II.

I was able to get leave near the end of August 1964, and we left the girls with the maid and took off in our Volks sedan for Italy. We drove through Switzerland, using the St. Gottard Tunnel and Pass as a shortcut to get to Lugano on the Italian border. The next day we toured Lake Como, then went on to the large and busy city of Milano. Our hotel was first class, as was its food and service. The next day we arrived at our hotel located in Livorno, a seaport city on the western coast. We called it Leghorn during World War II when we had dropped bombs on the docks. There was no damage to be seen now because they had been rebuilt. We drove north to a sandy beach the next day to relax and do some swimming. I wanted to stay all day because the Italian girls swam without any tops. I paid for this show because the next day I suffered from sun blisters and could not wear any clothes. Lee Ann had no sympathy for me and spent the next two days in Pisa shopping for marble items. I finally healed enough that we left for Florence. This was a city to see. From there we went to Rome where we spent two days sightseeing. Then we took to most exciting visit to Pompeii. We hired a private guide that spoke English and we learned facts about Pompeii that are not found in the tour book. Then we returned to Sembach, tired but happy.

The Air Force policy for permanent party overseas was to forecast their stateside assignment a minimum of three months before their rotation date. The first week in September, I had a call from the personnel officer that he had just received my stateside assignment. I was to come to his office and he would let me read the wire that he had received. I wasted no time getting to his office and reading the wire. It stated that I was to be assigned to the Air University with station at the University of North Carolina as the professor of Aerospace Studies. Reporting date was the 1st through 5th of December at Chapel Hill, NC.

I was surprised and happy for that assignment because our family could be together and the girls would grow up in the good old United States. I went to our Class 6 store on base and purchased a bottle of chilled champagne. I entered our apartment and told Lee Ann to get two glasses because we were going to make a toast. We sat down at the dining table and I filled the glasses, looked at Lee Ann, and said, "A toast to my new assignment as professor of Aerospace Studies at the University of North Carolina at Chapel Hill." She looked at me and knew that I was not kidding, raised her glass, and said, "Ken, that is great news and you are deserving of that assignment. I am so proud of you and happy to be your wife." We emptied the wine bottle, went to the officers' club, and celebrated the good news with an excellent dinner.

September and October were routine working months, but come November it was a busy month. My orders gave me five days' travel time to Chapel Hill, North Carolina, and we decided that we wanted to visit Lee Ann's mother and relatives in the Midwest, so I requested fifteen days' leave, which meant that we would be leaving Sembach on the 26th of November. We would need our Buick when we arrived at Dover Air Base, so I drove the Buick to the port of Bremerhaven, Germany for shipment to Brooklyn. The Air Force would pay for the Buick's shipment to Brooklyn, but not for our Volkswagen sedan. I decided to ship it to Houston, Texas, for the boat and dock costs were less than shipping it to Brooklyn. Our furniture would be packed on the 26th of November for shipment and should arrive at Chapel Hill by the 15th of December. The day before we departed, Erika Gerber, our maid for two years, said goodbye to Lee Ann and the girls. I drove her in a friend's car to her home in Longsfeld and she cried all the way. She and the girls were going to miss one another.

The officers' club gave us a farewell dinner party the night before we left, and we said goodbye to our many Air Force friends. A staff car picked us up on the morning of the 26th of November and drove us to the Air Force passenger terminal at Frankfurt. We boarded a MATS C-54 aircraft and flew to Iceland, where we spent the night. Lee Ann went shopping at the PX where she purchased beautiful hand made woolen sweaters for all of us at a very reasonable price. The next day we had a long flight to Dover Air Base in Delaware. We were bedded in the transient billets, and the next morning I took the bus to Brooklyn and picked up our Buick. I got back to the base late in the evening so we stayed another night at Dover. The next morning we headed for the Midwest. Although it was wintertime, we had clear skies and highways. We were excited and happy to be back home in the United States.

Chapter 19
PROFESSOR OF AEROSPACE STUDIES AT UNC

The day after Christmas the family and I departed for Chapel Hill, North Carolina, the home of the University of North Carolina. We arrived in Chapel Hill the evening of the twenty-seventh and checked into a motel close to the campus. The next morning I signed in at the registrar's office and received a folder containing a letter of welcome from the chancellor, and a card containing the name of a reputable real estate agent. The following day the motel provided a sitter for the children, and Lee Ann and I called upon the real estate salesman recommended by the university. He was very friendly and good mannered and said that he was a graduate of the university. He was pleased that they had given me his name and said we would need suitable housing befitting my rank and position at the university.

The salesman informed us that he had a beautiful colonial only one year old in a first class area that he wanted to show us. He drove us to an area of attractive homes not far from the campus. He entered the driveway of a large colonial style house located on a big lot with mature trees. When he turned off the engine, I said to him that I was afraid the house was too large for my family. He asked us to please tour the house with him and then we could discuss details. He was very knowledgeable of the house and the area and ended his tour with the statement that a large house is easier to keep clean and orderly than a small house. I looked at Lee Ann, and she said that she liked it but could we afford it? The salesman then said that the owner had built the house, would carry the mortgage, and would agree to any addition or remodeling that we would desire. The asking price was $25,000, and I told the salesman that I had $5,000 that I could deliver to him from a savings account that I had. If I could afford the monthly mortgage payments, I told him that we would really want the house. He excused himself to call the owner, and when he returned he held out his hand and said that he wanted to congratulate the new owner. Lee Ann and I were really excited to finally have a house like this for our family. We returned to his office, signed the paperwork, and picked up the girls at the motel and drove to the house.

I parked on the street in front of the house and said, "Lisa and Laurie, this is your new home. You each have your own bedroom and a large playroom next to the kitchen.

Do you want to see inside the house now or tomorrow?" They both stared at the house for several seconds and then Lisa shouted, "I want to see it now!" I opened the door and she and Laurie were halfway to the house before Lee Ann and I could get out of the car. I unlocked the front door and asked Lee Ann to show the children the house because I was going to a pay phone to make a call about our furniture. All of our belongings had been shipped to a warehouse in Brooklyn until we had a stateside address. I reached them without any problem and gave them our new address and asked if our furniture could be delivered before the end of the year. They promised me that it would be delivered within two days, which would be the 30th of December. It arrived the afternoon of the thirtieth and we moved into our new house that afternoon. Our next door neighbors came over that evening to welcome us and to brief us about the neighborhood and answer our questions.

The first working day after New Year's, I reported to AFROTC Headquarters and met Lt. Colonel Kage, the non rated officer whom I was replacing as the AFROTC Commander. He was very pleased to see me and gave me an excellent briefing on the working environment there at the university. The following weekend Colonel Kage and wife gave a cocktail party at their residence for the wife and me to meet the staff officers and their wives that would be working with me. My executive officer was Major Klinker, a rated pilot, also an instructor of upper class cadets. Captain Garrison, a rated pilot and a full time instructor, was also in charge of our drill team. Captain Buchor, a non rated officer, was a full time instructor and highly experienced in Educational Plans and Programming.

I was assigned to flight operations at Pope Air Base to maintain my flight records and to schedule me for the annual flight physical. I was still being paid not to fly, and McNamara was still on my shit list. He was not aware of the camaraderie that existed between pilots which helped me get some unrecorded jet time at Pope.

My daughter Pamela, now sixteen years old, arrived in Chapel Hill after spending Christmas and New Year's at her grandmother's in Lincoln, Nebraska. Lee Ann got her enrolled in high school and Lisa started grade school, located just four blocks from our house. Lee Ann was not alone in the house because Laurie, just three years old, was at home all day every day.

The second week that I was at my new assignment, Colonel Kage had made an appointment for me, as a professor, to meet my university boss, Chancellor Sharp. I was very impressed with him because he had a warm professional attitude and was very sincere in his discussion with me. I felt at ease and knew that I could ask him if he could enlighten me as to why he selected me from the three names submitted to him by the Air University. He said that the other two officers had obtained their graduate degrees at the same school and could be too inbred. When he saw that I had attended three different universities for my graduate degrees, he selected me. I thanked him and told him that my staff and I would work hard to make the AFROTC at the University of North

Carolina one of the best in the country. He told me that I did not need an appointment to see him, for the door was always open for me.

The Navy ROTC had their own large brick building on the campus. They had a larger staff and more students enrolled in their program than we did. After I had been on the campus a couple of weeks and knew that we were an important activity within this university, I went to the Navy building to meet the commander, Captain Rex Warner. He was very pleased to meet me, and we spent a couple of hours briefing each other on our military backgrounds and our respective ROTC programs. We met often as the months passed and became good friends. Both the AFROTC and NROTC had

In West Berlin, Slaker was interviewed by a newspaper reporter and his story was published in the *Berliner Morgenpost* the next day, 29 September 1989.

always held separate graduation ceremonies in the spring. When the 1965 graduation ceremonies were over, I met with Captain Warner and suggested that at the next graduation in the spring of 1966, we have a joint ROTC ceremony and invite the Navy and Air Force Secretaries as guests. Captain Warner agreed and, with the approval of the university chancellor, it happened for the first time at the 1966 graduation.

I received a call from Air University Personnel in early spring of 1965 that I had been selected to attend the AFROTC Training Encampment in July and August at Keesler Air Force Base, Mississippi. Since I had two years as the associate professor of AFROTC at Washburn University, I would be the commander of a large group of AFROTC cadets. I took this assignment very seriously and performed to the best of my ability. I received excellent military performance from my seven tactical officers, which helped me to receive an outstanding report from the camp executive officer.

During the fall of 1965, there were many demonstrations in the United States by private and public organizations, especially college students, against our fighting a war in Vietnam. The negative feeling of the majority of students on our campus was so intense that they spit at our ROTC personnel who were in uniform. I called my military boss at the Air University and requested permission for the ROTC personnel to wear civilian clothes on campus during this tense situation. He informed me that my request was denied by higher authority.

A few days later I was in my office when I heard loud shouting from students in front of our building. My executive officer, Major Klinker, informed me that there was a large number of students shouting for the PAS (Professor of Aerospace Studies). I walked outside onto our balcony and gave the signal to let me speak. They quieted down and I spoke loudly to them: "I do not have any authority to cease this fighting in Vietnam, for we military personnel take orders from the President and Congress. I suggest that you contact your congressman and tell him to use his position to end this conflict in Vietnam. Personally, I would like to see it end because I have a very tough task that saddens me. When an Air Force member from this area loses his life, I am notified to visit his family with the bad news. "It is a very sad situation and difficult to control one's emotions during this meeting with the family. This young lady holding a sign down here in front of you is certainly a part of my philosophy. For those of you that can't see the sign, it reads: *Make Love, Not War.* So be it."

I clasped my hands together, waved to the students, and returned to my office. The students never demonstrated in front of our building again. From that day on the wife and I received invitations to the students' social gatherings to represent the faculty, which we did.

A wonderful and supportive organization of our ROTC cadets was the Angel Flight, consisting of very personable and attractive UNC co-eds. In early 1965, I attended one of their meetings and was very impressed by their enthusiasm—except I was not happy with their dress. They wore World War II WAF uniforms, which the Air Force had provided originally. I wrote to the commander of Air University explaining the need for more appropriate dress for the morale of both the Angels and the cadets. I received a negative reply that funds were unavailable for the new Angel Flight uniforms. I decided to talk to Chancellor Sharp about my problem.

After one of the weekly faculty meetings, Chancellor Sharp asked me how I was doing, and I told him about the Angel Flight and their outdated dress for a great university like ours. He told me to hire a good seamstress to work with the Angel Flight and

---

HEADQUARTERS
AIR FORCE ROTC FIELD TRAINING
Keesler Technical Training Center
Keesler Air Force Base, Mississippi 39534

REPLY TO
ATTN OF: ROTC-E

11 SEP 1965

SUBJECT: Performance of Duty (LtColonel Kenneth W. Slaker, Jr.)

TO: Commander
Air Force ROTC Field Training
Keesler AFB, Mississippi

1. During the period 26 July through 4 September 1965, LtColonel Slaker was assigned duty as Commandant of Students of Group III for this Six Weeks AFROTC Field Training. In this capacity he was in command of seven tactical officers, one NCO, and one hundred and seventy-five AFROTC students. Through his excellent management abilities the Tactical Officers were assigned students, in-processing completed in a most efficient manner and students assigned to quarters without delay. This officer briefed his assigned personnel on their duties and continually supervised the entire training program for his group. His outstanding job knowledge, individual room standardization and personal interest in the welfare of all personnel contributed immeasureably to the high esprit de corps and morale of all his students and the success of this encampment.

2. Colonel Slaker's military bearing and behavior were exemplary at all times. The personal hygiene of students, cleanliness of barracks and appearance of rooms in his building were consistently among the highest. This was directly attributed to his outstanding supervisory ability. Colonel Slaker delegated both responsibility and authority to the Tactical Officers which improved morale and efficiency. His constructive suggestions helped to improve the overall operation of the camp. He established and maintained high standards of conduct for students and tactical officers.

3. I found him to be completely dependable, extremely loyal, an outstandingly clear thinker and planner, to possess exceptional leadership qualities, to have a high degree of initiative, eager to accept additional reponsibilities and the quality and quantity of his work to be superior.

4. The overall evaluation of Colonel Slaker's duty performance is outstanding. He was a very definite asset to this training program and one of the finest Air Force Officers it has been my pleasure to work with. This officer's broad experience would make a valuable asset to ROTC Headquarters.

RUSSELL P. STRANGE
Colonel, USAF
Executive Officer

Performance of Duty letter from Col. Russell P. Strange, Executive Officer, 11 September 1965.

fit them with the dress that they wanted, and that the university would pick up the tab. What a wonderful surprise for me, and when I told the Angels the good news, they gave three cheers for Chancellor Sharp. He was idolized by not only them, but by the cadets as well.

I received a notice from the War Department in early 1966 that a young man from the Chapel Hill Durham area had been killed in combat and that I would receive the official notice to be delivered to his wife the next morning. I arrived at the house just before lunch and rang the doorbell. When she opened the door and saw me in uniform, she knew why I was there. I told her that I was very sorry to have to deliver this wire to her. While she was reading the wire, her little daughter, about two years old, came running to the open doorway and seeing me in uniform, started shouting, "Daddy . . . Daddy." I picked her up and told her that I was not her father, and the little girl started to cry. I gave her to her mother, and when the mother regained her composure, I told her that if she wanted a military service for her husband, to call me. I left with tears in my eyes. Having a young wife with two young daughters, I would try not to ever put them through what this wife just experienced. My test was soon to come.

The last week in April 1966, I had just finished teaching a class of senior ROTC cadets when I had a phone call from a colonel friend of mine in the Pentagon. We spent a couple of minutes talking about our families and current military tasks, and then he said, "Ken, the reason that I have called you is that our computer system has been searching for pilots who have flown jet fighter aircraft. We are short scores of fighter aircraft since the Air Reserve Pilots are resigning and being hired by the commercial airlines and many of the regular pilots are retiring. The computer has listed your name as a jet fighter pilot who is still on active duty. You will be scheduled to attend the jet fighter F-105 School for one month and then ordered to Vietnam."

This shocked me, and I told him that I had not flown in a jet fighter for four years due to McNamara's mistake in paying many of us pilots not to fly. I doubted that I could be a jet fighter pilot qualified for combat in four weeks. I said, "This is suicide and I can't do this to my family, so I will request retirement."

He then said, "Ken, that is why I called you, for you have done more than your share for our country and the Air Force. If you wish to retire, I can get you a retirement number, but I have to have a report from your flight surgeon that you have taken a retirement physical. Time is of the essence since there is serious talk about freezing regular officers, and you would then not be able to retire." I thanked him for calling me and said that I wished to retire and would request a physical from the hospital at Pope Air Base.

I called the flight surgeon and told him of my need for a retirement physical. He saw in his records that I had passed my flight physical two weeks ago and asked me if I had any health problems. I told him that I felt fine and had no problems that I knew of. He then said that I had just passed my retirement physical and he would send me the paperwork with a current date. The next morning I called my friend at the Pentagon, and he said that he should have my retirement number for me in a couple of days.

I had always said that when I retired I was going to live in western Washington. I immediately wrote a one-page résumé of my pilot experience and my education and mailed it to The Boeing Company. One week later I received a letter from the personnel office at Boeing that they were interested in interviewing me. They had enclosed a commercial air ticket and made a reservation for me at the Hilton Hotel in Seattle.

Before I left for Seattle, I met with Chancellor Sharp to inform him that I was going to retire. I thanked him for the outstanding cooperation that I had received from him, and he then said that he had news for me. He also was leaving the university to accept the position of President of Drake University in Iowa. If I was interested in a civilian

---

DEPARTMENT OF THE AIR FORCE
OFFICE OF THE SECRETARY
WASHINGTON

March 8, 1966

Dear Colonel Slaker:

It was with much pleasure and profit that I read the article in Sunday's issue of the News & Observer on "'Angel Flight' Boosts Cadet Morale".

This was an excellent article prepared by Harry D. Hollingsworth, Jr., and I want to commend you and your ROTC Detachment on such an informative article for public consumption in North Carolina. It is articles of this type which will boost greater public interest in our ROTC Program on the campuses throughout the United States.

With best wishes to you and your AFROTC Detachment at Chapel Hill, I am

Sincerely,

JOHN A. LANG, JR.
Administrative Assistant

Lt Colonel Kenneth W. Slaker, Jr.
Professor of Aerospace Studies
University of North Carolina
Chapel Hill, North Carolina

Congratulations letter from John A. Lang, Department of the Air Force, 8 March 1966.

teaching position, I was to let him know. I was very lucky to have met and worked for such an outstanding educator.

I called three uncles that were in the construction business in the Seattle area to inform them that I was coming to Seattle to be interviewed for a job with the Boeing Company. I had not seen them since the fifties and wished to visit with them before returning to Chapel Hill. I arrived at the Sea Tac airport in the late afternoon and was met by Mr. Derr, a Boeing manager, who drove me to the hotel and hosted me for dinner. He briefed me on the interviewing schedule for the next day. He also was going to pick me up the next morning and be my escort to the various division managers.

I had three interviews in the morning and three in the afternoon. Flight operations really wanted me because of my experience as a pilot, but here again, as in the Air Force, I would be spending much of my time in other countries away from home. Flying had always been my first priority, but now my wife and two daughters were my primary reason for my living. The Commercial Aviation Division asked me to join them because with my teaching experience at Washburn and North Carolina universities, I could help them to organize an in-house sales program that was currently very expensive. The next morning I met with the manager of the Commercial Aviation Division and told him that I would like to be a member of his organization. He was very pleased, and the next morning I signed an employment contract, reporting for work on July 1, 1966.

I called Lee Ann that evening, Friday, to tell her of the good news. I asked her to make up a *For Sale* sign and install it on the front lawn Sunday morning. If an individual wanted to purchase it before I got back, she was to give him the price that I told her before I left for Seattle and tell him and that she wanted $5,000 down before she would sign a sales agreement. I spent Saturday visiting with my relatives and stayed with my aunt and uncle that night in Federal Way. My flight back to North Carolina was scheduled to leave Seattle at 11:00 A.M.

I was enjoying breakfast with my aunt and uncle when at 9:00 A.M., the phone rang and my aunt answered it and said it was for me. It was from Lee Ann and she said, "Ken, I hope you were not kidding about your job at Boeing because I just sold the house. I put the *For Sale* sign in the front yard at 8:30, and at 11:30 a man knocked at the door and asked if the house was sold yet. I told him no and he then said, 'You just have. My wife and I have always wanted this house. I am a professor at the university and can afford a house in this area.' He came back an hour later with earnest money and a sales agreement." I congratulated her and told her that I would be home about 11:00 P.M.

On Monday I met with the professor who had purchased our house and he wanted to move into it as soon as possible. He offered us his house at no expense until July 1st, at which time he would list it for sale. Lee Ann and I agreed to move out at the end of the week, which we did. I called Gordon Smith, the contractor who was to build us a house in Federal Way, Washington and asked if the house could be ready to move into the first of July. He assured me that it would be, so I called Mayflower Movers and made a reservation to have our furniture picked up the 25th of June. During the middle of June, Lee Ann and I were given a farewell party by my AFROTC staff, the cadet officers, the Angel Flight, and some of our close friends. I was really going to miss these exceptional people. This assignment at the University of North Carolina was one of the most enjoyable of my military career. The furniture was picked up early in the morning and we departed that afternoon for a new life in western Washington.

Arnold Air Society

HONORARY  MEMBER

This is to Certify that

LT COLONEL KENNETH W. SLAKER, JR. USAF

was duly initiated into the

JESSE J. MOORHEAD SQUADRON
University of North Carolina, Chapel Hill, N. C.

of the Arnold Air Society affiliated with the Air Force Association

on

22 MARCH 1966

In witness whereof we hereunto affix
our signatures and official seal.

Robert B. Wesson
NATIONAL COMMANDER

Charles W. Finch
SQUADRON COMMANDER

Certificate of Initiation, Arnold Air Society Honorary Member, 22 March 1966.

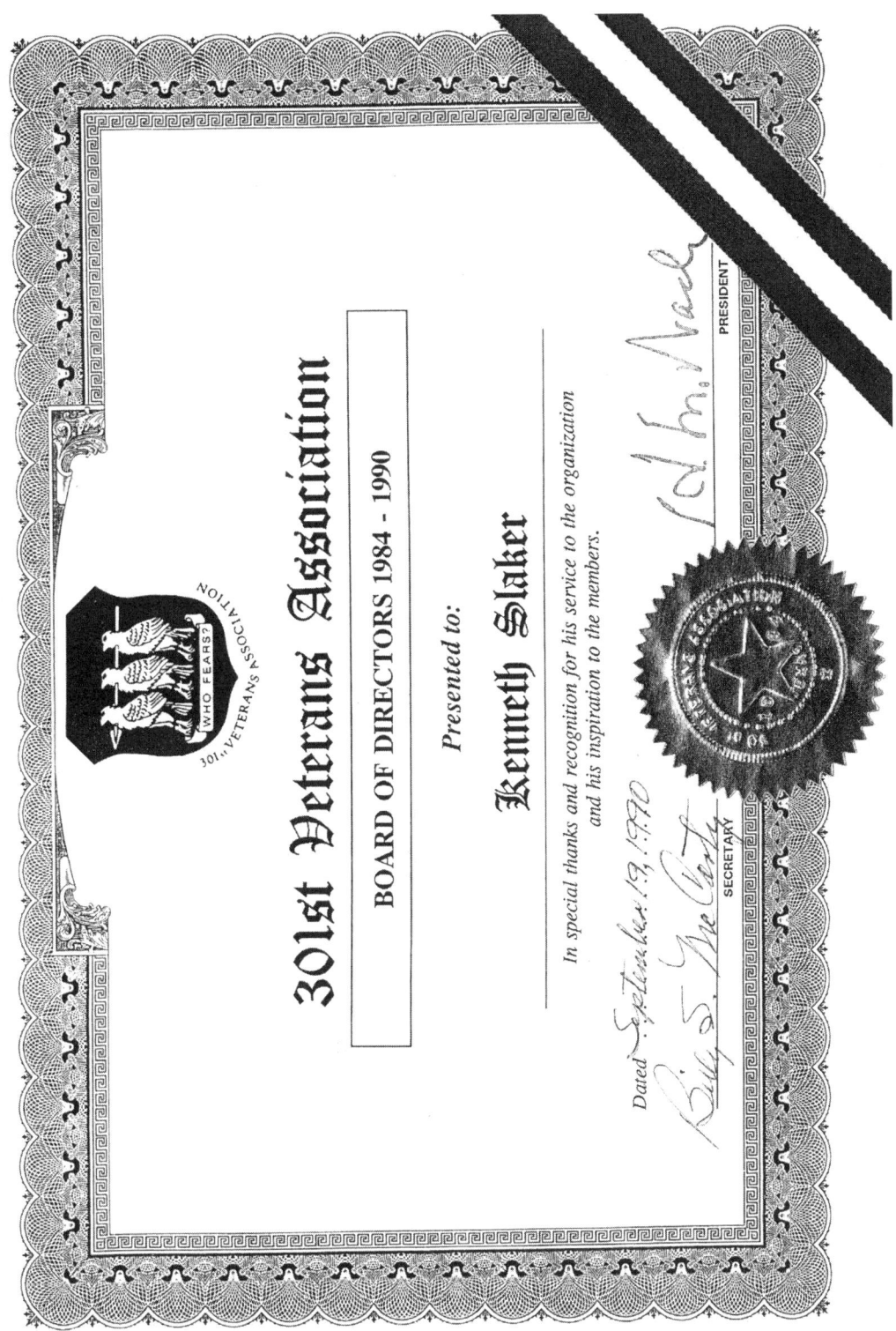

Slaker served on the Board of Directors for the 301st Veterans Association for six years and was presented with this certificate at his last Board meeting in Dayton, Ohio, 19 September 1990.

Chapter 20
BOEING HIRES A MANAGEMENT ENGINEER

On our drive to Seattle, we stopped for a day at Wichita to visit Lee Ann's mother, Gladys Stanislaus. Our next stop was Fort Collins to visit daughter Pamela's grandmother, Mildred Buck, my former mother-in-law. We finally arrived at my Aunt Rhoda and Uncle Herman McMillian's house on the 1st of July. Our furniture arrived on the 3rd of July and we spent that night in our new home in Federal Way, Washington.

I reported to the commercial division of the Boeing Company on the 6th of July for my first day as a civilian employee. My immediate supervisor was Mr. Buroughs, whom I liked and respected from our very first meeting. The primary mission of his division was to improve Boeing managers to the highest level of professional management. The next week I was scheduled to sit in on a class in Good Management conducted by Dr. Zoll, an excellent and knowledgeable instructor. I then had a meeting with my boss, who briefed me on what the commercial division had planned for me.

A professor at Harvard had developed a psychological program for the selling of ideas, physical items, etc. to potential recipients. Boeing had a contract with a teacher who was a graduate of this special course to teach the sales personnel this new approach developed by Harbridge House. Top management at the commercial division had decided that, rather than paying an outside instructor several thousand dollars per attendee at the two-week seminar, they would teach this skill in house. My boss said that since I had a master's degree in Industrial Management, and had been a professor at two universities, that I was to attend the Harbridge House School now at Barrington, Illinois to become a Boeing manager with this skill. It was a three-month course, but Boeing would pay for visits home with my family every other weekend.

The Harbridge House School at Barrington had several classes of students receiving instruction on the new sales technique, but only three of us were there to become instructors: myself, Mr. Vansenus from the Kodak Company, and Mr. Elf from a large industrial corporation in New York. We three became good friends and stayed in touch with one another for several years. Vansenus visited me in Seattle, and I hosted him to his first deep-sea fishing in the Pacific Ocean.

Our instructors were exceptional, and I had never been exposed to the subject matter that we were being taught. I became more and more convinced as to the psychological power of the unusual material and procedures being presented to us. The last two weeks the school assigned us as instructors to students attending the two-week course. Our final test was to make a sales pitch to the top staff of the school. The three of us received top grades and the school gave us a graduation dinner. The three of us verbally praised our instructors at the dinner, for they were smart and professional.

The week after I returned from being awarded an Instructor's Certificate for the Psychological Approach to Sales of Items or Ideas from Harbridge House, I briefed the president of the commercial division and his staff on my confidence and approval in the sales system that I was to teach Boeing managers. I outlined the equipment and a suitable classroom that I would need to perform my duty as the instructor. A short two weeks later my classroom was ready with the photographic and recording equipment that I had requested to support the instruction of fifteen managers for a two-week period.

While I was at Harbridge House, Boeing had received approval for several of our sales managers to make a presentation to the president of a growing commercial airline that flew our top selling commercial aircraft. They hoped to receive an order for these aircraft from the airline's president. The sales team returned to Seattle very disappointed and without an order. When I learned of this failure to obtain a sale from this meeting, I made a request to the division president that this sales team attend my first class. My request was approved and they, with four other managers, made up my first class to be instructed in the Harbridge House new approach in the successful method of sales.

The president of the commercial aircraft division welcomed the managers to the first in house class of the Harbridge House System for the Sale of Ideas and Items. He was proud to introduce our own Boeing Instructor, Kenneth Slaker, a command pilot, a World War II B-17 pilot with a master's degree in Industrial Management, and a just retired professor of Aerospace Studies at the University of North Carolina. They surprised me with their applause, and I thanked the president as he departed.

I then asked each manager to introduce himself and give his position and duty with Boeing. I explained our objective and that they would find our classroom work very new and exciting. That afternoon I asked each manager that had been a member of the sales team that returned without an order for our aircraft to make the same pitch to the class that he had made to the airline president. What each member of the class didn't know was that I had remote cameras and recorders making copies of their presentations.

The next day I gave the class two basic rules that our new approach to sales required. "First, don't talk about yourself or the Boeing Company. He is not interested in the new rivet developed by Boeing; his interest is in his company. Research his company and compliment your client on his successes. Your remarks must be honest when you tell him how our product can increase his success with his business. Second, do not disagree with your client or cut him off. He may make a negative remark about your product that may be correct. Don't get into an argument—agree or be ignorant."

The next two days I taught the sales managers the basic structure of a psychological system developed by professors at Columbia and Harvard Universities. It was an outstanding system in selling ideas or items, and this gave birth to Harbridge House to teach this approach to business personnel in the sale of their products. I presented actual examples of how to utilize the system symbols befitting the product and goals of a customer's profession. By the end of the sixth day, the class was excited and ready to organize the symbols presented by the new sales method. I asked each manager to prepare a sales plan to be given to the president of the airline that had declined to order our aircraft. The morning of the eighth day I had each manager give his sales pitch to the class. The class then made suggestions that they felt would improve his presentation. The next morning I really surprised the class. I told them that I was going to show some sales presentations that were made by our sales team to an airline president. With the screen showing the very first pitch that I had filmed without their knowledge, the room was filled with moans and groans. They did not need any comments from me, and a couple of the managers looked at me and shook their heads in the negative. I told them to polish their sales presentations to be shown on the morning of our last day of the seminar.

In the meantime Boeing's top management had contacted the president of the airline that had declined to place the order. He was told that we had some new ideas that would be of benefit to his airline and would not be a waste of his time. He agreed to host the sales team again, and a date was selected. On the morning of the last day of our sales seminar, I surprised the class when I informed them that they were going to make another sales presentation to the airline president that same day. We spent the entire day creating an honest and true sales presentation, and I was very confident in its outcome. At 4:00 P.M. I presented each manager with his graduation certificate and expressed my confidence in their new sales approach. When I finished, they surprised me with a certificate.

The commercial division sales team made their trip to the meeting with the president and staff of the subject airline and returned to Seattle with an order for over forty of our commercial aircraft. Needless to say, I was very pleased to know that not only was it the quality of our Boeing aircraft that resulted in the order, but that my instruction of the Harbridge House Sales System to the sales team had added to their success. This gave additional prestige to my Harbridge House Seminar, and I had no trouble meeting the attendance quota in future seminars. I was even ordered to give this seminar to selected personnel in the Aerospace Division. This was very rewarding for me since I met some very highly educated and intelligent Aerospace personnel.

The first year I was with the Boeing Company, my family lived in our new house in Federal Way. I had purchased a lot one block from a new elementary school so that

KEN –

THE
* MM-B-B-B-GQ-B-B

AND

‡ AP-AP-AP-MM-B-B-GQ-B

ARE SINCERELY APPRECIATED

Y'all Gonna Rise Again

* FINE COURSE
‡ YOUR EXCELLENT PRESENTATION

A card from Slaker's Sales Analysis class that he instructed at the Boeing Aerospace Center, Kent, Washington.

our young girls could walk to school. When Lee Ann went to enroll the girls she was informed that the school was full and that our girls would have to ride a bus six miles to another school. To add to this disappointment, a couple of weeks later I discovered why I had not felt comfortable in this new house. I thought that it was because I had always lived in a two-story house and this was a new rambler. However, one morning I got out of bed and walked into the living room and stretched. I saw that my fingertips almost touched the ceiling. I immediately got a tape measure, and the distance from the floor to the ceiling was seven and one-half feet. The plans that I had given to the contractor called for nine-foot ceilings. I was really upset because I am 6" 3" and need high ceilings. I immediately called the contractor, and he said he lowered the height of my rambler so that it would not interfere with the view of Mt. Rainier from the lot next door. My first thought was to sue him for damages, but a better thought came to my mind.

I suggested that he build my house on the lot next to me and sell this one. He said that was not possible because the lot was already sold to another customer. I decided to sue him and met with my uncle, Mr. McMillian, who had recommended this contractor to me. He listened to my house and location problems. He was quiet for a few minutes and then recommended that I do the following. There was the possibility that I could get a negative decision from the court, which would cost me hundreds of dollars for attorney and court costs—and I would still have the house and location problems. I should locate a house in a better location and sell the one I currently owned. Problems solved. In the early summer of 1967, Lee Ann found a house that solved all our problems which was located in the city of Normandy Park. It had high ceilings, was only five miles to my office, and the kids could walk to school. The lady who owned he house was the widow of a Boeing engineer and would only sell to a Boeing manager. We signed the papers in a very short time, and I listed the problem house for sale. It sold within a week, and I made $3,000 more than what I had paid the contractor for it. I heard he was upset that I had made more on the house than he had made.

The following Sunday we took the children to see the house. They were thrilled with the view of Puget Sound and the Olympic Mountains and the fact that they could walk to school. My daughter Lisa, who had lived in four different houses since her dad was a military pilot, rushed up to me and asked, "Daddy, is this house going to be our real home?"

I said, "Lisa, this is going to be your real home even after you graduate from high school." She screamed with delight, gave me a hug and a kiss, and then grabbed her sister Laurie. They ran outside to go look for their school building.

At a monthly staff meeting of the management development section, the decision was made to present motivational seminars to select managerial positions. Dr. Zoll and I were selected to research and come up with the material to be presented at the seminars. One of our leads came from a distant relative of mine, Dr. Hawk, at the Univer-

March 13, 1969

To: K. W. Slaker 6-1800 89-21

cc: R. J. Boroughs 6-1800 89-21

Subject: "Motivation" - Presentation for Leads

The above subject given to my leads March 10, 1969, after work hours, certainly has had some very nice reactions and compliments. For example: "I could have listened for many more hours, Mr. Slaker's presentation certainly impressed me." Another: "Mr. Slaker made an excellent presentation on motivation." Also: "We were very fortunate to have Mr. Slaker give the Dr. Hershberg Motivation presentation, it was different."

Ken, I could give you more compliments on your presentation- mine, you were very good, and I enjoyed the film. I know the group absorbed the material. Thanks again.

N. H. Martin
6-1200 8W-16

Letter of appreciation from N. H. Martin, 13 March 1969.

sity of California at Berkeley. I had called him concerning my research of the Hawk family and mentioned that I was going to conduct motivational seminars at Boeing. He said that one of the most successful professors in the field was a Dr. Hershberg. I was able to view a motivational film credited to him and integrated much of his material into my lesson plan. The motivational seminars were well received, and I received many letters of praise from the managers who had attended a seminar.

One of the most exciting meetings at the Boeing Company in the late sixties occurred when all the middle and top managers were ordered to meet at the Boeing plant in Auburn, Washington. We enjoyed a good dinner, and then the president of Boeing walked to the center of the large curtain covering the entire wall on one side of the room. He told us that the company was planning on building a new and very large passenger aircraft, but only if the managers voted to approve this project and would work hard to make it a success. He then gave a signal with his hand and the curtain opened to expose a model of a really large aircraft. The size of the model really took all of us by surprise and being a pilot, I wondered if it would be too big to fly. He said that it would be designated the 747 and that we would have to sell close to 200 of the 747s to break even because it would cost the company millions and millions of dollars. He answered a few questions and then said that the final decision to build the 747 was up to us. He asked us to use the pad in front of us and write yes or no. The votes were collected and when counted, almost 100 percent said YES! Almost all of us rose to our feet, clapping our hands and shouting, "Build It! Build It!"

Once each year the management development section presented a seminar for the senior managers titled Fundamentals of Management. The seminar for 1969 was held in May and Philip Swain, the director of this section, asked me to assist in the presentation. When the seminar was finished, the class gave us applause. When they finished, a Boeing executive entered the room, introduced himself, and told us that he had some bad news for us. The company did not have enough orders to continue the current production of aircraft and would have to decrease the labor force for 1970. Layoffs would begin that fall and continue into the next year. By the middle of September, half of the employees in our section had been let go. The managers remaining were all senior to me, and I knew that it was just a matter of time before my boss would be forced to give me my walking papers. I decided to save him this task and submitted my resignation to Mr. Boroughs, who did not want to accept it. I was not happy to do this because Boeing had been good to me, and I had really enjoyed working there.

PRIDE IN EXCELLENCE

MAY 1969

CERTIFICATE OF OUTSTANDING PERFORMANCE
PRESENTED TO

KENNETH W. SLAKER

THIS CERTIFICATE IS BEING PRESENTED TO YOU IN
APPRECIATION OF THE EXCELLENT MANNER IN WHICH YOU
ASSISTED IN TEACHING THE "FUNDAMENTALS OF MANAGE-
MENT" COURSE.

YOUR ASSISTANCE HELPED TO MAINTAIN A HIGH LEVEL
OF INTEREST AND CLASS PARTICIPATION, CREATING A
GOOD ATMOSPHERE FOR LEARNING. THIS HAS BEEN ONE
OF THE BETTER CLASSES WE HAVE HAD THE OPPORTUNITY
TO ATTEND.

THANK YOU FOR A JOB WELL DONE.

BOEING COMMERCIAL AIRPLANE DIVISION

Certificate of Outstanding Performance from students in Slaker's Fundamentals of Management class, May 1969.

Chapter 21
A New Career

During a discussion with Brian Smith, a neighbor friend of mine, I mentioned that I had resigned from the Boeing Company. He worked for the Feige Design & Construction Company and said that they needed an estimator. He said that with my Civil Engineering education he would like to arrange a meeting for me with Mr. Feige, his employer, to be considered for the estimator position. I agreed to his suggestion and met with Mr. Feige in late September. We discussed my education background and Civil Engineering experience, and he informed me that we were both Huskie classmates, for he had graduated from the University of Washington with a degree in Architecture. He then briefed me on the work required in the position he had in mind, and if that was agreeable to me, the estimator position was mine. I accepted, and we shook hands and became good friends.

Over the next couple of months the Feige Company was very busy. Project costs were based on my estimates of labor hours, building materials required, and miscellaneous costs such as construction permits, temporary site utilities, broker fees, etc. I was alarmed at the high brokerage fees we were paying for either selling or purchasing commercial property. I mentioned this to my uncle who was in the construction business, and he suggested that I get a broker's license, which would provide the Feige Company with in-house capability and control.

My uncle got me a sales position with Jackson & Berg, a solid commercial real estate company in Seattle. Before I made this move, I discussed it with Mr. Feige and he agreed that I could wear both hats with his company. Jackson & Berg were very receptive and taught me the required knowledge in the buying and selling of commercial properties. While working there, I came across a commercially zoned tract of land in eastern Tacoma for sale by the owner. I visited the area, which was having an increase in population. K-Mart had just built a huge new retail store on the eastern border of this tract that was for sale. I convinced Mr. Feige to purchase this tract of land, and we drew up plans for the construction of a regional shopping center.

The month of December completed one year as a salesman, and I took the test to be a broker and passed. I obtained the license for my office located with the Feige Con-name for the hotel shop rather than the same name of our lingerie store. We agreed to do that, and he said that the gift shop was ours come the 1st of January.

I then called my attorney, Stanley Atwood, and asked him to have lunch with me at the College Club in Seattle. I briefed him on the possible growth of our business and asked if we should form a partnership, remain a single proprietorship, etc. After many questions and answers, Stan suggested that we form a family corporation naming Lee Ann the president, me the treasurer, and naming our two daughters on the board of directors. I asked him if he would agree to serve on the board for at least a year and he agreed to that. He said that he would take care of the paperwork, but we had to give him a name for the corporation.

I returned home and briefed Lee Ann about my meeting with our attorney and his recommendation. She agreed with it and we came up with several names, but we didn't like any of them. Then Lee Ann's face lit up and she said, "Ken, I think I have the name that we both will agree to. Remember the name of the private club that we belonged to in San Antonio? The name was *Algo Diferente*, which is Spanish for *Something Different*. We are going to have gift shops that are different!" I agreed with her, and she called Mr. McClasky and he liked and approved the name for the gift shop. Our attorney submitted the paperwork, and the license for the Algo Diferente Corporation was issued in 1975.

The lease for our Feminique shop would expire the end of 1975, and we gave notice to Mr. Feige that we would not be renewing it. We had a buyer for our lingerie inventory, and I had located a company that expressed an interest in the space to be vacated. All of our Feminique employees agreed to work in our gift shop except one. Our daughter Lisa, now eighteen years old, was put on the payroll to fill the vacancy.

A couple of years later Mr. McClasky asked us to purchase the gift shop in the Thunderbird Inn located at the west end of the I-5 highway bridge crossing the Columbia River to Portland. We had no trouble agreeing to the purchase price from the current owners and immediately had the shop remodeled to give it exposure from the lobby. We also removed the counters and decorated the interior to match our shop in the Red Lion at Sea-Tac. We kept the same employees except for the manager, who we replaced with our daughter Lisa, who now had two years gift shop experience. Lee Ann and I traveled to Dallas and Los Angeles, visiting wholesale markets to find new items suitable for our gift shops.

I became so busy with the gift shops that I no longer had time to operate my real estate broker's business. I closed my office and established the Algo Diferente corporate office at our residence in Normandy Park. Mr. McClasky then notified us that he was going to build a new motel in Bellevue and wanted us to work with the architect in drawing up the plans for the gift shop. The architect was very cooperative, and we had

Corporation License for Algo Diferente from the State of Washington.

a fine shop when the new Red Lion Inn opened for business in Bellevue, Washington in 1981.

My cousin, Cherie Hawk Storm, lived in Renton and was forming a horseracing club called Stable Old Bunch. She owned a couple of racehorses and was experienced in the horseracing business. She asked Lee Ann and me to join the club and we accepted. The club consisted of five couples, and at the first meeting, my cousin was elected president and I was elected treasurer. My cousin submitted the name of a horse called "I Don't Lie" that we should purchase. We all agreed and I collected the required funds. We now owned our first racehorse.

What an exciting day that was when our horse was listed in the Longacres racing schedule. "I Don't Lie" was not a large muscular horse. He was of medium build but a fast horse. He came in third place, which pleased us. A few days later he was listed in the racing schedule, which ended in a disaster. In the final turn to the finish line, he stumbled, fell down, and was carried off the track with a broken leg. The vet declared the leg damaged beyond repair, and "I Don't Lie" was put to sleep.

A few weeks later our trainer gave us a lead on a horse with thoroughbred history named "Soft Schuman." I charged our members for enough money to claim this horse, and it gave us several good years, including first place wins at Longacres and the track at Portland. One of our members passed away, one became very ill, and another couple moved a far distance away. We entered "Soft Schuman" in a claim race, which resulted in a new owner east of the Cascade Mountains. I did learn that in this business the best return is to the trainer, not the owner.

My World War II B-17 combat crew had not had a reunion since the end of the war, and I decided to contact them for a reunion in 1982. I was able to contact George O'Hoppe, the bombardier; James Passmore, the navigator; and I called the air freight company that my copilot, Leo Flowers, worked for. They informed me that he had died in the late seventies from lung cancer. My flight engineer, John Jaranson, assumed the task of finding the enlisted crewmembers. He found Frank Laky, our tail gunner, and William Nick, my ball turret gunner. I also advertised our reunion plans in military and civilian magazines. From this source I received a letter from a Master Sergeant Tucker in Oklahoma. He proposed that we work together for a 301st reunion to be held in the fall of 1982. I liked his suggestion, and we spent many hours contacting 301st Bomb Group members that were still alive. When we had 100 members that promised to attend the reunion, Sgt. Tucker made arrangements with the Sheraton Hotel in Bossier City, Louisiana to host our reunion in September 1982. I was able to locate Colonel Gormly, who was our group commander in 1943. I reserved a flight for him from Tucson to attend the reunion as our guest of honor. Seven of the *Elaine*'s combat crew were able to attend with their wives except O'Hoppe, whose wife had passed away.

Shortly after the opening of our gift shop in the new Red Lion Inn at Bellevue, another new Red Lion Inn was finished just east of the south end of the I-5 bridge into Portland. Here again we helped design the gift shop and get it into operation. By this time our corporation was listed in Dunn & Bradstreet with an excellent rating, which opened the door for us at the top wholesale markets.

Mr. McClasky, on one of his surprise visits to the Red Lion Inn at Sea-Tac, invited Lee Ann to have coffee with him. He surprised her with a proposal that our corporation own and operate all the Red Lion Inn gift shops in California. He gave no deadline for a decision but asked us to study the proposal and let him know. We obtained the location of all the Red Lion Inns in California from the Red Lion Inn headquarters and studied the supply, employee, and transportation problems.

We realized that with our corporate headquarters located in the Seattle area, to operate all the gift shops in California, Oregon, and western Washington would require constant traveling. Since I was a pilot it could save a lot of hours on the highways by use of a corporate aircraft. I previewed several types and settled on the Lear jet. I made arrangements to have it hangared at Boeing Field and contacted a flight instructor to help me renew my private license. We became good friends since he was dating Pat Kassner, a longtime friend of ours.

One Friday evening the four of us were enjoying a swimming party at the Kassner residence when my check pilot told me that he had a flight to make Sunday night and that I could fly the aircraft back to Seattle, which he would use as my renewal check. I called him the day he was to depart that evening and thanked him, but I could not make the flight with him due to a tight schedule. On his takeoff from Kitsap airport that evening, he lost power from one of the engines just after takeoff. He was not able to maintain enough altitude to return to the airport and crashed into the trees, killing all on board.

This aircraft accident was very sad news, and then I realized how close I had come again to losing my life in an aircraft. Then I realized that my Guardian Angel was still watching over me as she had promised when I was three months old. I discussed this with Lee Ann and told her that we were doing very well without expanding to California. Also, it would steal time away from us from being together during our senior years. Lee Ann had never expressed any negative feelings about my flying career but surprised me when she said that she didn't want me flying again. She put her arms around me, kissed me, and said, "Ken, I love you and you are my life, and I want you alive and your Guardian Angel knows this." I canceled the purchase of the Lear jet and notified Mr. McClasky that we were not interested in owning the shops in California.

One afternoon I was taking inventory at our shop in Bellevue and noticed a gentleman looking at items in our main display window. The store clerk was busy with a customer, and I asked him if I could be of any help. He said he was interested in our scrimshaw, and I told him that it came from Alaska since stateside scrimshaw was scarce due to the import restrictions of elephant tusks from Africa. I asked if he were a traveler and a registered guest of the Red Lion Inn, and he said no, that he lived in Seattle and was a retired Navy Medical Officer. I told him that I was a retired Air Force pilot and lived in Normandy Park. We shook hands and he said that he still contributed some time to the Navy by giving new recruits their acceptance physicals. He said that he also was a member of the Medical Committee for the Sons of the American Revolution. I was not familiar with this organization, and he was pleased to answer my questions. He asked if I had any ancestors that fought in the American Revolution and I told him that my uncle, Ray Hawk, mentioned that we had Hawk ancestors that had fought against the British for our freedom. Dr. Senter then said that he would like to sponsor me to become a member. He gave me the name of the Seattle chapter genealogist, Ralph Taylor, who would help me in my research. Ralph worked constantly with me and before the year 1984 was over, I became a member of the Seattle Chapter of the Sons of the American Revolution.

The Boeing Company planned a huge celebration in the summer of 1985 for the fiftieth anniversary of the famous World War II bomber, the B-17. I visited the Boeing Anniversary Committee to register our 301st Bomb Group that had flown the B-17s in combat during World War II. Since I had organized the first two reunions of our bomb group and was now on the board of directors created by General Wade, a postwar 301st Group Commander, I was confident that he would approve our group's participation in this related event. I called the general and briefed him that I had registered our bomb group with the Boeing B-17 Celebration Committee and that they were pleased to have us on board. The general disagreed and said that we would not divert from our two-year schedule.

I was really upset and decided that I should resign from the board of directors. I visited the Boeing Committee and told them to dismiss our bomb group from the register and why. They were upset, and one of the members suggested that I have the 419th Squadron reunion independent of the group. I agreed and registered the 419th to attend the celebration. I called upon the manager of the Red Lion at Sea-Tac, told him that I was having a squadron reunion, and would like the Red Lion to be our host. He agreed to block enough rooms and a banquet room for their stay here. He even agreed to give our squadron special room and banquet rates in appreciation for helping the United States win World War II.

I sent scores of invitations to 419th members who had flown B-17s with the 301st Bomb Group during World War II, and to the staff officers who had served in the bomb group at the same time. Several of them attended, including Colonel Gormly. I then got in touch with my daughter, Patti Elaine Reed, for whom my B-17 was named *Elaine*. She was in Norway with her husband Ron, who was a petroleum engineer whose company had the contract to design and install oil well derricks in the North Sea. Patti had never met with any of the *Elaine* aircrew and this was a wonderful opportunity for her to do so. I used the carrot approach and told her that I would provide her with a round trip ticket from Oslo to Seattle to attend the B-17 celebration, and it worked—she came!

I had an outdoor cocktail party catered on our lawn for my squadron and aircrew members the afternoon before the big day. What a pleasure it was to see Patti greet each *Elaine* aircrew member for the first time in her life with a hug and a kiss. They had not seen her since she was three months old at her baptism at Topeka, Kansas. It was also the first time that Patti met her half brothers and sisters, and Lee Ann and I were pleased to see how happy and excited they were to finally get together.

I received an invitation for the wife and I to attend a reception given by the Boeing president for a member from each of the B-17 registered units. I had always been invited to various functions to represent the crew of the *Elaine* but I decided that they were just as important as I was and I selected Frank Laky, the tail gunner, for he was the ranking enlisted crew members. His wife was very charming and sophisticated and would certainly help them mix with other attendants. I got Laky and his wife aside and told him that I had selected him and his wife to attend the reception on behalf of the 419th Bomb Squadron. I would drive them to the reception, and when it was over they were to take a taxi back to my house at my expense.

The morning of the day programmed for the B-17 celebration, I hosted my aircrew at breakfast. I informed them that Laky and his wife were representing our squadron at the Boeing reception and that Vic Carpine, one of our squadron pilots, had offered to drive them to the reception, thus freeing me to attend other program activities. The banquet for the squadron was scheduled at the Red Lion Inn for 7:00 P.M. The dining room for our banquet was very first class with our seating on the outside of a large square table so that we all looked at one another. I had reserved the seating for Colonel Gormly with Elaine on his right and Lee Ann on his left. When we were finished eating, I introduced Colonel Gormly, who gave us a very complimentary speech. Farewells were made since many were leaving the next morning. Daughter Elaine and Lt. Passmore and wife stayed at our house until the end of the week.

When I was accepted as a member of the Sons of the American Revolution, I became interested in their goals and programs. The Seattle chapter met once a month at the Sand Point Navy Officers' Club, and I was made an assistant to the club secretary. This increased my workload, for in addition to my work with our gift shops in 1980 I started to research the genealogy of my Hawk ancestors who settled in Pennsylvania in 1742. I spent three or four weeks each summer back East researching church records and cemeteries, wills, deeds, etc. Then to really keep me busy, I was elected to be the Chapter president for the year 1987.

Another milestone in my life was achieved when the court, at the beginning of 1987, approved a change in my name. My father had always been upset when my mother gave me his name at my birth. I never liked being his junior either. After six years of research of my Hawk ancestors, I realized I was more of a Hawk than a Slaker, Jr. I had my attorney petition the court to change my middle name from Waverly to Hawk. This eliminated the Waverly and Junior, and in January 1987, I became Kenneth Hawk Slaker.

The chapter president that I replaced was of the old school and didn't approve of the wives attending the chapter meetings which were business meetings, not social meetings. At the second meeting I asked the members if they would mind if I and some of our members brought our wives to the monthly meetings, and the answer was a loud clapping of hands and shouts of approval.

The chapter lacked current bylaws so I assumed the task of drafting the bylaws. A compatriot's wife, Jackie Daniels, a DAR member, was of great help in proofreading and finalizing the draft, a copy of which was given to each chapter officer for their approval. After some minor changes, enough copies were made for distribution to each chapter member.

I also made myself known by the Daughters of the American Revolution by attending a couple of their meetings and even being invited as a guest speaker. We organized joint patriot programs which were very successful. I attended two Children of the American Revolution (CAR) meetings, which was a rewarding exposure. I suggested to the Seattle chapter members that we make an annual contribution to the Washington State CAR, which they started. My accomplishments as the chapter president were recognized by the state officers, and I was nominated and elected to be the President of the Washington State SAR for 1988. This was to be a year of many experiences, mostly good ones.

The first five months as the state president were spent getting to know the state officers and their duties, updating the state bylaws, and visiting our three chapters of Spokane, Seattle, and Alexander Hamilton at Tacoma to meet and know their officers. I also invited the president general of the Sons of the American Revolution, Nolan Carson and wife Nancy, to visit our Washington SAR chapter's spring meeting in Seattle. They accepted and arrived there in late spring, and I took them to the Red Lion Inn where I had the presidential suite reserved for them. We then took them sightseeing the next day with lunch at the Space Needle. The banquet that night at the Red Lion Inn was superb. When we were finished dining, President Carson gave an interesting speech concerning the accomplishments of our organization, and then he turned to Lee Ann and asked her to join him on the podium. He told the members that as a businesswoman, she had been of great help to both the DAR and CAR with their programs and therefore he was very pleased to present her with the Martha Washington Medal. She received a standing ovation as he pinned the medal on her dress. She rewarded him with a hug and kiss and he escorted her back to her chair.

There were no meetings for the SAR chapters during the summer months so I drove back East to finish the research on my Hawk ancestors. On the way I stopped at Tyson

Corners, Virginia to attend the Sons of the American Revolution Annual Congress. I finished my research in August and then had the task of writing a 500-page book with data extracted from 2,000 pages of research. I made contact with Anne Hughes, a publishing manager at Gateway Press in Baltimore. Words cannot begin to give her credit for the professional help she gave to me in preparing the Hawk book for publication.

I returned to Seattle in August to be informed of an event that was to change Lee Ann's life and mine. Mr. McClasky had sold the Red Lion Inn chain for close to a billion dollars to a company out of our state. A representative from the new owners notified us that it was their policy to own and operate their gift shops. We were to prepare the inventory of our shops for transfer on a date to be provided. This date completed fifty years of work for me, so it was time to enjoy the remaining years and give my Guardian Angel some rest.

A primary goal of the state president of the SAR is to increase the membership by qualified friends or relatives or by organizing new chapters. The towns east of Lake Washington were growing and I decided that we needed a new chapter there after I had cased the area and found several SAR members living here. I submitted the request for a charter for a new chapter along with the seven names of SAR members at large required by the national headquarters. I received the charter for a new chapter from the national headquarters in October 1988. I immediately called for a meeting in Bellevue where we named it the "Cascade Centennial." We elected Maurice Greiner president; he had moved there from Idaho where he had been the Idaho State SAR President. I was not eligible for any chapter office since the state bylaws prohibited the state president from holding any office within a chapter.

When I stopped in Louisville the past summer to visit the library of the SAR headquarters, I discovered that all the states had their state seals displayed on the wall except for the state of Washington. I asked the librarian why Washington State's seal was not shown, and he said that the only reason was that the state officials never made it available. As soon as I arrived in Seattle, I called my good SAR friend, Judge Goodloe, a member of the Washington State Supreme Court, and informed him of the absence of our state seal in the National Headquarters of the Sons of the American Revolution. I asked if he could be of help to correct this oversight. He arranged for us to have lunch with Mr. Monroe, the State Secretary, who was very cooperative and got us permission to construct the state seal. Since Washington is known as the Evergreen State, Judge Goodloe and I decided the seal should be carved from wood. Fred Kiser, a SAR member known for his wood carving skill, agreed to carve the seal out of Western Hybrid timber. When it was completed, it was officially delivered to the Sons of the American Revolution Headquarters Library.

Two more important events took place that would result in a change in my life pattern and beliefs. In November, the Washington SAR members re-elected me to remain as state president for the year 1989. This would make me eligible to be selected to fill the national office as Vice President General of the Western District in later years. Since I was no longer in the retail business, I would have more time to devote to the growth of our State Society of the Sons of the American Revolution.

The second event happened as a result of our youngest daughter getting married in February 1989. She and her husband-to-be decided to have their honeymoon at the resort city of Puerto Vallarta, Mexico. Lee Ann and I had never been there and were worried about their stay there. We decided to make a reservation at the same hotel the first week in December to ensure that it would be suitable for our newlyweds. We flew Mexicana Airlines non-stop from Seattle to Puerto Vallarta, and the meal and drinks were complimentary. We received a royal welcome at the hotel, especially when I informed the manager why we were there. He said that he would show us the honeymoon suite the next morning after the present occupants departed. The dinner was delicious and our suite had a great view of the large bay and the mountains. The surf did not keep us awake but rather lulled us to sleep.

The next morning we had a very enjoyable breakfast on the warm beach veranda and decided to tour the city. Our hotel was located on the beach in the area known as Old Town. It was several blocks south of the Cuale River, which flowed from the mountains through the city into Banderas Bay. We walked north across the river to city center, then took a bus to the marina.

The marina was very large with several hundred boats moored there. New condos were being constructed on the shoreline, and we toured one of them and had lunch at a new Mexican restaurant. We struck up a conversation with an American tourist couple from Minnesota, and they liked the warm winter months, the reasonable prices, and the friendly attitude of the natives. They were thinking of buying a condo and spending the winter months there. After they left, Lee Ann and I discussed the pros and cons of owning a condo there. We then took a taxi back to our hotel and had the tour of the honeymoon suite where our daughter and new husband would be staying.

At 4:00 P.M. we went to the hotel lounge to have a margarita. While waiting at the table for our drinks, an American came in and sat down at the table next to ours. I assumed that he was a tourist and asked him if he had anyone joining him. He said no and I invited him to join us. I gave him our names and that we were tourists from Seattle. He said that he was from Michigan and had been there working as a real estate salesman for several years. I told him that we had just come back after looking at condos at the marina. He wasted no time in telling us that he could do better for us because he was the agent for a wealthy Mexican who was planning on building a first class condominium right there on the beach. He asked us to please have breakfast with him in the morning, and he would also have the Mexican and his American business partner there. I looked at Lee Ann and she nodded her head in agreement.

The next morning Big John escorted us to the El Dorado Restaurant and introduced us to Mr. Wolff, and to his American partner, Dr. Inglehorn. They asked some questions about my background and I gave them a brief résumé on my career as a pilot and as a retailer. When I mentioned that I had obtained my master's degree from the University of Southern California, Dr. Inglehorn became very interested and asked when I had been at USC. When I told him, he said that he had been there about the same time getting his doctorate degree in Medicine and that we were both Trojans! I no longer had any qualms about dealing with the Wolff Inglehorn team.

Dr. Inglehorn opened a large blueprint showing the condominium to be built and gave us a briefing on the units still available for sale. Lee Ann and I liked the corner units and were impressed with the entire building. Mr. Wolff said that they needed to sell one more unit so they could start building it immediately. He said that if we would purchase a unit that day, he would give us a $20,000 discount. I looked at Lee Ann and she said, "Let's buy one." We selected a unit, signed the papers, and shook hands. I told them that we would have the funds transferred to the bank as soon as we got back to Seattle. We were one happy couple on our flight back to cold and wet Seattle, knowing that next winter we would be in warm Puerto Vallarta, Mexico.

We decided that since we were no longer in business in King County and the kids were no longer living with us, that we were going to look for a new place to live. Come July we had not found anything we liked in Washington State, so we decided to tour the States. We departed in our beautiful Lincoln for a sightseeing trip through Canada to Pennsylvania. Upon our arrival there, I spent several days doing some final research on my Hawk ancestors for my genealogy book. We enjoyed a visit with Jack and Betty Foster, my high school classmates that I had kept in touch with since our graduation in 1938. We then drove to Chapel Hill, North Carolina to visit friends that I had made when I was a professor at the university. It was very rewarding to renew our friendship with these dedicated educators. Atlanta, Georgia was our next destination to visit Bob Bullay and his wife Helen. He had been the manager of the Red Lion Inn at Sea-Tac, where we operated one of our gift shops. After a week of fun with them and my cousin Barbara Wilson from Snellville, we pointed the Lincoln west to Texas.

Our visit to Texas was a nostalgic one since Lee Ann and I had lived five of our first marital years in San Antonio. We were very excited to drive to the first house that we had ever owned, but we were very disappointed when we arrived. The landscaping was in shambles and the great view that we had of the hills was now scores of houses. We had a fine dinner with Dr. Michael Zaccaria and his wife. He had been an outstanding member of my Air Force Management Team that I had in the late sixties. The next day was an enjoyable one with our longtime friends, Jim and Jeannie Dawson. He was a well-known weather forecaster on a local TV station. We left San Antonio for Phoenix with an empty feeling in our bodies. In fact, during our long drive to Phoenix, we had a serious discussion of buying a retirement home in San Antonio.

Don and Dot Hedges were our hosts at their retirement home a few miles north of Phoenix. Don had worked for me in Germany and the four of us had become close friends. We had fun playing golf and bridge, and they almost talked us into buying a retirement home there. The next and last stop was Northridge, California to visit my former boss in Germany, Colonel Upson and his wife Betty. He was the best officer that I had ever worked for. They were also parents of an outstanding family. We could use more families like the Upsons in our country. After a very rewarding visit, we drove the long trip to Seattle without any trouble.

The winter of 1989-90 gave me enough time to finish my manuscript for my Hawk book. I typed every page with my Canon AP-740, which gave me a variety of print sizes for the manuscript. I was in constant communication with Anne Hughes, a top manager at Gateway Press in Baltimore. She advised me on all the variables in publishing my book. I sent her my final manuscript in April, and a few days later she sent me a draft with some suggestions. I accepted her advice and returned the final format the first of May. That month several hundred copies were printed with an embossed title on the hard cover: *Early German Hawk Families of Westmoreland County, PA*. During the next two years I received many letters of praise from Hawk descendants that had purchased the book.

We received exciting news from Puerto Vallarta in February 1992 that the condo building we owned a unit in was finished. All owners were urged to attend the dedication to the building on March 27th. Many notables would be there, including the U.S. Consulate to the State of Jalisco, the city mayor, the Jalisco state representative, etc. Lee Ann and I flew non stop on Mexicana Airlines to Puerto Vallarta, really happy to know that we were going to spend that night in our beautiful condominium.

The next afternoon the building's sunroof was jammed with owners, guests, Mexican food and beverages, and a very enjoyable ten-piece mariachi orchestra. The majority of the owners stayed on the sunroof until dusk to enjoy a very beautiful sunset. We enjoyed living in our condo until the end of May and getting to know other condo owners, the business district of Puerto Vallarta, and its suburbs. I enjoyed the climate with temperatures between seventy-five and eighty-five degrees. I didn't wear underwear—a pair of shorts and a sun cap and you were ready for the day. Our flight back to Seattle with Mexicana was very enjoyable with complimentary food and drinks.

We returned to our Mexican condo in the fall of '91 and stayed until a week before Christmas. We had invited some of our friends from the bike and ski clubs that we belonged to. They really enjoyed themselves and had many complimentary remarks about our condo. We decided to drive to Puerto Vallarta in the fall of '92 in our station wagon, which we loaded with kitchen utensils, paints, tools, etc. that would make our condo more livable. We cleared through Mexican Customs at Nogales on the border and drove on a good four-lane highway all the way to our overnight stop at a AAA listed hotel at Los Mochis. We left early the next morning for Mazatlan where we stopped for brunch. We no longer had a four-lane highway and took the two-lane to the city of Setif. About twenty miles from Setif, the engine died. I was able to coast to a clear area on the right

Top: Our 4th-floor condo. Bottom: Participants at the Grand Opening, L-R: Hardy Setzer, owner from Sacramento; Ken Slaker, owner from Seattle; Hardy's wife, Cheryl; and Jennie, the U. S. Consul.

THE STATE OF WASHINGTON

To all to Whom These Presents Shall Come, Greetings:
Know Ye, That

Kenneth Slaker
Is Commissioned A

WASHINGTON GENERAL

In the Association of Washington Generals with all the rights, privileges and responsibilities thereunto appertaining.

In Testimony Whereof, we have hereunto set our hands and caused the Great Seal of The State of Washington to be affixed at Olympia, this **10** day of **Nov** A.D. one thousand nine hundred **87**.

Booth Gardner
GOVERNOR

John A. Cherberg
LIEUTENANT GOVERNOR

SECRETARY of STATE

Washington 5 Star General

Slaker commissioned a Washington State General, 10 November 1987.

side of the road and checked the fuel, oil, water lines, and the wiring around the engine and could not find any problem. I waited for the engine to cool and turned the key and starter on. The engine turned over but would not start.

In Mexico they have what they call the Green Angel who monitors the main highways to help drivers in trouble. About two hours after our engine died, a Green Angel pulled in beside us and I told him of our trouble with the engine. He did a very thorough check of the engine and its connections but could not get it started. He said that he would push me to a Ford garage in Setif. I didn't know whether to accept his offer but I knew that we could not stay there overnight. He was very good at pushing us and I never felt one bump against my car. We arrived at the Ford garage and they promised to have the car ready the next day. He then drove us to a good hotel and would not accept any money from me, saying that he was doing his job.

We had been in our condo a short week when Lee Ann told me that she had been having pains in the vaginal area for several weeks that were now very severe. We immediately drove back to Seattle where the doctors found that Lee Ann had ovarian cancer. She was operated on and the surgeon said that the cancer had not spread from the area. Two weeks later she had a post-operative examination along with x-rays of her lungs, and they found growths in both lungs. Tests verified that they were cancer growths. There was no doubt that her cancer growths were a result of her addiction to cigarettes. Chemo and radiation treatments followed and slowed the growth, but it did not eliminate them. She was able to travel and spend the winter months at our condo in Mexico.

I was notified in January 1993 that the Washington State SAR President was submitting my name to the SAR National Headquarters to be accepted as the Vice President General of the Pacific District effective July 1993. This was quite an honor, and I was to be sworn in at the National Congress that would be held the first week in July. Lee Ann was losing her hair and not feeling well from the chemo treatments and could not accompany me. I contacted my daughter Patti Elaine in Houston to see if she could attend the meeting and be my companion at the swearing in ceremony. She agreed and it was a very memorable event.

The Pacific district consisted of the states of Oregon, Washington, and Alaska. As the vice president general I was to hold a district meeting each year at a different location to help increase membership in the SAR, to organize new chapters, and to perform such duties as assigned by the president general. I was to visit each SAR chapter in the Pacific district, which required a lot of traveling. I discovered that Alaska did not have enough members to form a chapter and met once a year in Anchorage. I contacted Rev. Richard Miller, the president of the Alaskan SAR, and he informed me that there never had been a district meeting there nor an official visit by a president general. I asked him if he would support my having a district meeting there in the spring of '95, and he was delighted and promised me full support from all of his members scattered throughout the huge state of Alaska.

At our SAR Congress in July 1994, our new president general, Stewart McCarty, was sworn in to serve until July 1995. That evening I was able to get his attention for a few minutes and briefed him on my plans for a district meeting in Alaska in May 1995. When I told him that there had never been an official visit by a president general nor a district meeting, he thought for a moment, then held out his hand and said, "I will attend that meeting in Anchorage in May, that is a promise." We shook hands and I had never left an annual congress feeling as good as I did that time. I called President Miller in Anchorage and told him that the SAR President General would be there and he was delighted. The cooperation that he and other Alaskan members gave me the following months until the meeting in May was outstanding.

President General McCarty, his wife, Lee Ann, and I arrived at Anchorage, Friday, May 26th and had reserved suites at the same hotel. We had dinner together and then Mr. McCarty and I polished the agenda that I had prepared for the district meeting. The next morning just before I called for order, Rev. Miller informed me that all Alaskan SAR members were present except one, and that we had several Washington and Oregon SAR officers present. The meeting was very interesting with pro and con discussions on the agenda topics, plus new ideas for the improvement of the National Society of the Sons of the American Revolution.

I have no adjective that can describe the wonderful food and Alaskan cocktails that we had for dinner. When our plates were clean, Rev. Miller introduced our guest speaker, the Director of Commerce for the state of Alaska. He welcomed us to Alaska and wanted us to know that the biggest problem his office was having was the U.S. Federal Government. It was preventing the utilization of many of the natural resources of Alaska based on damage to the environment. "We have already proven that our drilling of oil on the North Slope has not harmed the animal and plant life, and yet the government denies us the right to drill for oil in the discovery of a much larger oil reserve. We Alaskans made a mistake in becoming a state, and we have the right to withdraw from the United States by the vote of its citizens. Ladies and gentlemen, it could and may happen." He received a standing ovation from the Alaskans there, and I sat amazed at what I had just heard.

Rev. Miller, who was the pastor of a large Baptist congregation in Anchorage, invited us to attend the service Sunday morning, which we did. Prior to the service, he introduced us to the hundreds of church members, telling them why we were there. He was an exceptional host to the SAR visitors from the lower forty-eight, and we all left with great admiration for our Alaskan compatriots. I also had great pride in myself for having held a successful district meeting in Alaska.

My assignment as Vice President General of the NSSAR terminated in July 1995. This was the first time in seven years that I did not hold an elected office, and it gave

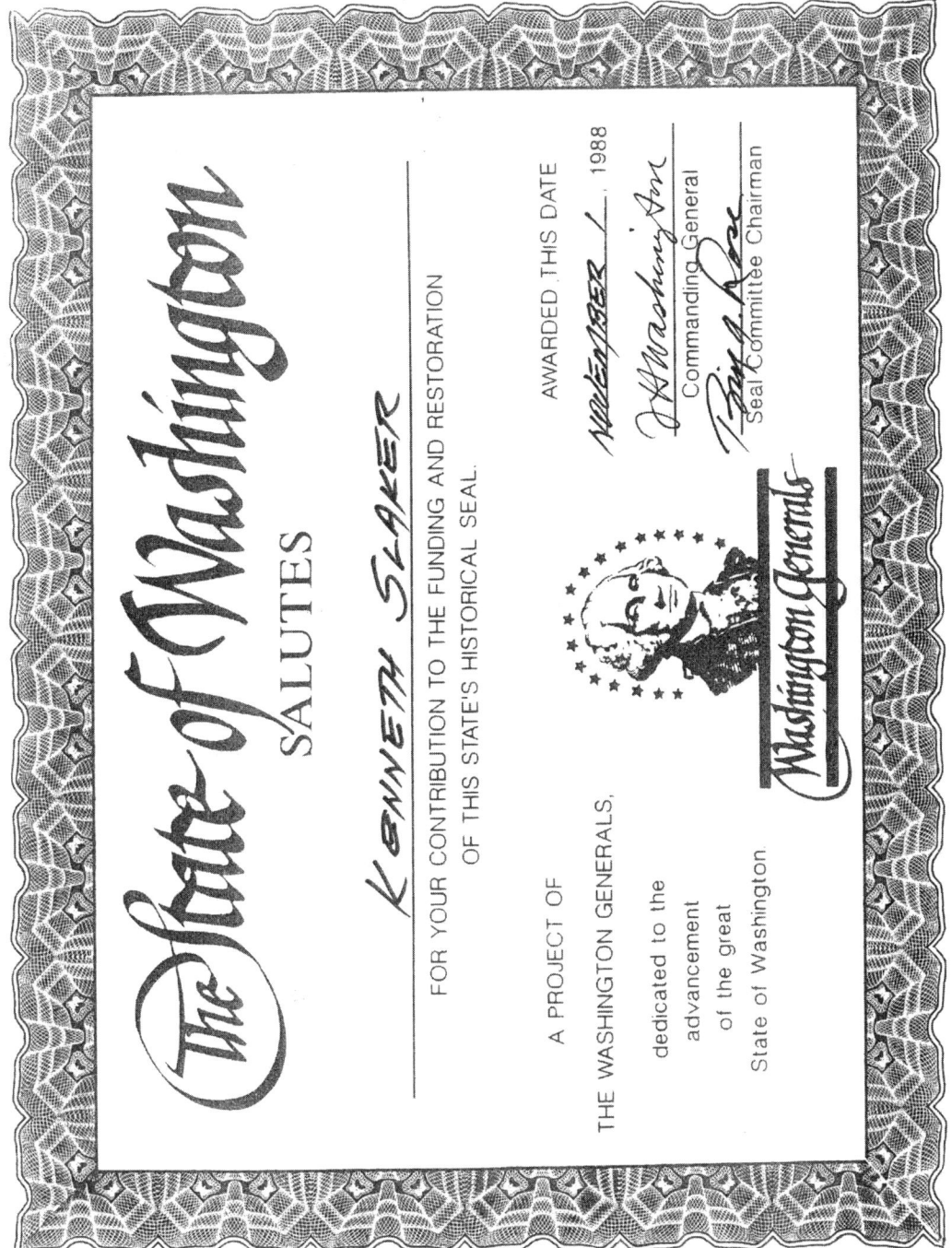

Certificate for contribution to the funding and restoration of the state of Washington's historical seal, 1 November 1988.

me more time to attend the meetings of other organizations that I belonged to. That fall I attended the 301st Bomb Group reunion at St. Louis, along with Lt. Passmore, my aircrew navigator, and Frank Laky, my tail gunner. We were enjoying dinner together the first evening when a stranger walked to our table and introduced himself. His name was John Souther, a retired army lieutenant colonel. He said that I had been pointed out to him as a B-17 pilot that had flown combat in North Africa. I told him that was correct and he asked me if I had been there in February 1943. I answered in the affirmative and he said that maybe I could give him some information about a B-17 pilot that all his life he had been hoping to meet. I said that I hoped that I could and I quote his reply: "I was a First Lt. in the First Armored Division fighting against General Rommel's Africa Korp that had defeated us at Kasserine Pass. We retreated some miles west of the Pass, and then Rommel returned to the Pass and remained there. On the 23rd of February we were attempting to regroup after a terrible loss of personnel to make an attempt to drive Rommel out of the Pass. We were being bombed continually by German JU 88s that morning. Early in the afternoon I heard aircraft engines and I shouted to the men to take cover that it was another JU-88. I looked up and recognized that it was a B-17 and shouted that it was a B-17, a high altitude bomber and what the hell is it doing down here? Then it opened its bomb bay doors, entered the Pass at a low altitude, and flew directly over Rommel's Panzer outfit, dropping fragmentation bombs and strafing the German troops with its guns, killing and wounding scores of the Africa Korp. It gave us great support and we were able to force General Rommel out of Kasserine Pass." I guess it was the look on my face and then he said: "Were you the pilot of that B-17?" I said yes I was, got up and we embraced and shook hands. I told him the difficulty that we had with the weather and how lucky we were to find the Pass. He said that he had published a book about the First Armored Division in Africa and would send me a copy. I received the book titled, *War Not Forgotten* and on the first page he had endorsed it: "To Ken Slaker, the B-17 pilot who gave me life support at Kasserine Pass, Tunisia, North Africa. I wish you health and happiness. Signed John Souther." This means more to me than most medals.

Early in the spring of 1996, we were enjoying our condo in Puerto Vallarta when Lee Ann started suffering from severe pains in her back and head. We immediately returned to Seattle where x-rays showed that her lung cancer had spread to her spine. I spent the summer taking Lee Ann to the hospital for chemo treatments a few times a week. By October she was not able to walk, and I had a hospital bed delivered to the house for her comfort. Dr. Davidson declared her terminal, and she was registered with the Seattle Hospice. They were outstanding with their nursing, feeding, and cleaning help.

I was given the task of administering her daily Morphine shot. I also had a very powerful shot to be given to her if the pain became really bad, but only when approved by the doctor. Lee Ann knew of this heavy dose, and one night in November she asked me to give her the shot with a couple of daily Morphine shots so that she could terminate her pain and her life. I called Dr. Davidson, and he said to give her one regular Morphine shot only. Up until this time I had prayed to God to cure her of this cancer, but from this time on, seeing her suffer from this terrible disease, I prayed to God to take her.

The day before Thanksgiving, the Hospice nurse who visited with Lee Ann every Monday and Wednesday broke into tears as she was leaving, telling me that Lee Ann would not live until her next appointment. Our daughter Laurie and I stayed at Lee Ann's side all Thanksgiving Day when she was awake. Laurie left at 6:00 P.M. to have dinner with her family. I stayed at Lee Ann's side and kept talking to her, hoping that she could understand what I was saying to her. About 8:00 P.M., she started having trouble breathing and I took hold of her hands, looked into her eyes, and told her that I loved her. She looked at me and in a rasping voice said, "Ken, thank you for giving me a wonderful life, and I love you." She stopped breathing. I sat there, sadly realizing that my beautiful wife had died . . . and I cried.

I called Laurie to tell her that mother had died, and Laurie arrived in a few minutes. We sat at Lee Ann's side all night knowing that we were suffering a great loss. In the morning I called the funeral home to advise them of her death. As they carried her body away, I cursed the killer that had taken her life . . . those damn cigarettes.

The National Society of the Sons of the American Revolution

Certificate of Appreciation

KENNETH H. SLAKER

has been awarded the Certificate of Appreciation in recognition of outstanding support given to the ideals of the Sons of the American Revolution.

June 1994
Date

Vice President General
1993-1994

President General

Certificate of Appreciation for Slaker's service as Vice-President General for the Sons of the American Revolution, June 1994.

THE NATIONAL SOCIETY of the SONS OF THE AMERICAN REVOLUTION
PACIFIC DIVISION

Regal Alaskan Hotel
May 27, 1995
7:00 P.M.

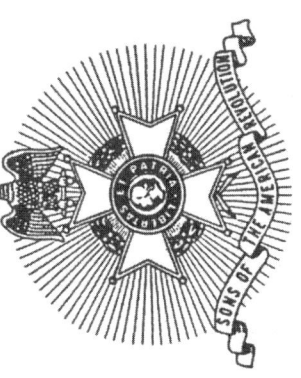

Honoring
STEWART B. McGARTY
PRESIDENT GENERAL
THE NATIONAL SOCIETY OF THE
SONS OF THE AMERICAN REVOLUTION

on the occasion of the first formal visit by
a President General to the
State of Alaska

Persons on the program

Theresa Diemer	Guest Singer Anchorage, Alaska
John Haynes	Past-President, AKSAR Anchorage, Alaska
Wilfie Hensley	Commissioner of Commerce and Economic Development State of Alaska
Stewart B. McCarty	President General, NSSAR Fairfax, Virginia
Richard A. Miller	President, AKSAR Anchorage, Alaska
Kenneth H. Slaker	Vice President General Pacific District, NSSAR Normandy Park, Wash.

Officers
Alaska Society SAR

Richard A. Miller	President, Anchorage
Harvey E. Rookus	Vice-President, Anchorage
Joe A. Clapp	Sec./Treasurer, Wasilla
John L. Haynes	Registrar/Past President, Anchorage
Jack Easley	Trustee/Immediate Past President, Palmer

Record of the Pacific District meeting of the SAR at Anchorage, Alaska, 27 May 1995.

Chapter 22
A Visit from the Hereafter

With the death of my wife, the sale of our retail stores, the publication of my Hawk book, and no longer holding office in the Sons of the American Revolution, I now had more time to search for the relationship between God and mankind.

I had done some reading in the fifties and sixties concerning the history of Christianity, Judaism, and Hinduism, but my interest was permanently aroused when I was accepted (one had to have a master's or doctorate degree) to attend a theological seminar in the late seventies. The instructor was a Theology professor, and he wasted no time informing us that we were educated individuals, "but you are only using fifteen to twenty percent of the brainpower that God gave you. Just because I am the seminar leader, don't accept every statement that I make. Challenge me, and let's use that brain of yours to come up with new and more sensible beliefs."

The professor then held up his hand with the palm facing us and said that according to many scientists, we were looking at the end of the universe. He then pointed to the back of his hand and said, "What then, is this?" The class was silent and then he said, "Gentlemen, it is the universe, for it is infinite." This brought the class to life, and after positive and negative discussions were completed, the instructor then supported his statement with the fact that Carl Sagan, a brilliant scientist in Astronomy, and others have proven that our solar system is not alone, that there are millions of galaxies, some leaving us at an increasing rate of speed. This could not happen in a closed universe.

A discussion followed on the possibility of some type of life existing within the galaxy and whether they have our God or one of their own. The professor then told us that we were to draw a slip of paper containing a question out of the basket on his desk, and we had fifteen minutes to write our answer. The question on my paper was: *If God exists and is our prime mover, where did he come from?* I came up with a couple of ideas like he was from a family of gods from another galaxy, or a traveling god visiting a designated planet within a galaxy—and then my brain gave me the answer. During the past centuries here on Earth there were scores of individual tribes and communities that existed and never communicated with one another, yet they all had one very strong drive: they had to worship something, be it fire or the sun, for the spirit of God is in everything alive. Now to answer the second part of the question, *where did God come from?* Several possible answers came to mind, and then I had the answer. We are very narrow in our view of the universe and all living things, for everything we see has a beginning and an ending. God has no beginning, God has always been. The more I thought about this, the more convinced I was, and I wrote that answer on my test paper.

A month later I received a letter from the seminar professor, which said: *I have given you an A for your answer to the question, not because you may be correct, but you used that brain of yours and did some exceptional thinking.*

I had a short conversation with the seminar professor when I turned in my paper. I told him that I had been seeking the truth about our current religious beliefs, and he asked me if I had come across Mithraism. I replied in the negative, and he said that I would understand the Christian religion much better if I were to read some of the existing history concerning the popularity of this religion over thirty centuries ago.

I had no trouble finding documented information on Mithraism, which existed in many Asian and European areas more than one thousand years before the birth of Jesus. The Mithraism faith was named after the god Mithra, who was born from a huge rock. His birth was witnessed by shepherds who brought gifts and declared him a holy infant. His date of birth was identified as occurring on the sanctified December 25th. The exact date of Jesus' birth was not on record, and it was almost 500 years after his arrival that it was decided that Jesus was born on the same sanctified date as the god Mithra.

Mithra became recognized as the creator of all life, and Mithraism spread throughout middle Asia. A claim was made and recorded that he had saved all life and land from a terrible drought by striking a rock from which great waves of water flowed. Women were not recognized as equals and were never accepted into the Mithraism cult. It was the number one faith in the Roman Empire until Emperor Constantine eliminated it, but it was the forerunner of Christianity.

I found it very difficult to separate the truth from the many assumptions made by the so called prophets for many hundreds of years after the birth of Jesus. The majority of the humans born during this time accepted the cult that they were born and raised into. They were illiterate and never used the greater part of their brain to challenge these fairy tales. For example, many of the religious cults supported the claim that the Earth was flat and that the sun rotated around the Earth, which was the center of the universe. Along came Copernicus and Galileo, who used the greater parts of their brains to prove the current beliefs wrong and were condemned by their own cult leaders.

I do not accept the fear approach that has been used by many cult leaders to control the non-thinkers to believe that we are all sinners and must seek God's forgiveness, that if not, you could end up with the devil, you could be denied entrance to heaven, etc. I believe in a God that is at a much higher level than man and whose spirit exists in every living thing. I don't have to go through a cult leader to talk to God; I can talk to him directly, for he is my savior.

After the death of Lee Ann, I spent the winter months at our condo in Puerto Vallarta, Mexico. I enjoyed the warm climate and the friendship of other owners and my guests. In November 2002, I experienced the most exciting and theological happening in my entire life. I have never walked in my sleep nor had nightmares or hallucinations. I went to bed at 10:00 P.M., watched the CNN news on TV, and then went to sleep. I awoke about 3:00 A.M., and a feeling came over me that there was someone in my bedroom. The room had filtered light from outside, and I could see the outline of the furniture and the walls. I decided to get out of bed and case the inside of the condo and the terrace. Just as I threw the bed sheet off of me, Lee Ann's clear voice came to me from a dark area of one wall and I stood frozen. She said, "Ken, this is Lee Ann, and it is good to see that you are enjoying the condo and our friends in Mexico."

I said, "Lee Ann, is this really your voice?"

She replied, "Yes it is, and I am pleased that you have not sold the condo so that the children and grandchildren can enjoy it."

I asked, "How did you get here?"

She said, "I can't answer that question but . . ." I made the mistake of turning on the bedside lamp and she was gone.

I walked out onto the terrace, and although this was my first experience hearing the voice from a person deceased for six years, I knew that it was not a nightmare. The most important result of Lee Ann's visit was that it proved there is a hereafter where our spirit (Soul) departs after the physical body dies. I knew that I had to keep Lee Ann's visit a secret because very few people would believe me. I was so shaken by her visit that I left for Seattle the same day. The last week in January I received a call from our youngest daughter, Laurie, that she had something to tell me.

We met for lunch at a local restaurant and when we were finished, she looked at me and said, "Dad, the reason that I called you to meet with me is that I had to tell you that Mother visited me. I have not told anyone, not even my husband. I awoke the middle of the night and had the feeling that there was someone in the room. I could see that both our boys were in their room, and my husband Nick was snoring in his sleep. Then Mother's voice called my name, she said that she was here to visit the family and was pleased to see that I was living in the house that I had grown up in. Then she said that Normandy Park was a good city for the boys also to grow up in. I then turned on the lamp by the bed and Mother was gone." I had not told my daughter about Lee Ann's visit to me so I asked her whether her mother's visit was before or after I returned early from Mexico. What a surprise when she said that it was the night before I came home. I then told her about Lee Ann's visit to me. There we were, a couple of a thousand miles apart, and her mother had visited us both on the same night. We held hands, shed tears, and agreed to keep these two meetings to ourselves.

A couple of weeks passed and I began to feel that as a father I was not doing right by not telling our oldest daughter about her mother's visit. I called her and she agreed to have lunch with me the next day. We had lunch at a small restaurant in the city of Burien and when we finished, I asked her to be quiet and not to ask questions until I finished what I had to tell her. As I related her mother's visit to me, her body stiffened and her hands started to shake. I then told her that her mother had also visited her sister, and she started to cry and shake and I tried to calm her down. She said, "Dad, mother visited me the same night! I have not told anyone for fear that they would not believe me." I then asked her to tell me about her mother's visit.

"Dad, I awoke during the night and I could not go back to sleep because I had a feeling that there was someone in our bedroom. Elmer was sound asleep and son Tommy was in his bedroom. Then from a vague shadow on the wall opposite our bed, came mother's voice: 'Lisa, this is your mother and I am visiting you to see how you and your family are doing.' I then asked, 'Mother is it really you?'

"She replied, 'Yes, I am your mother and I have been given permission to visit my family once.' Mother and I then had a short chat about my family, and then I turned on the lamp by the bed and Mother was gone."

What a miracle! All three of us were visited by Lee Ann's spirit during the same night even though we were hundreds of miles apart. The most important remark made by Lee Ann's spirit was that she had been given permission to visit her family once. Was it from a higher spiritual level, or is there one spiritual level with various levels of authority?

The visits our Earth had in the 1950s by spacecraft far superior to our own—operated by individuals with human configuration, but much smaller—proved that we are not alone in this universe. They were from another planet within our Milky Way, another galaxy in the infinite universe. Since they were alive, the Prime Mover's spirit is within them. When we die physically, the spirit within us transfers to a higher level within the universe (the Hereafter).

I believe in the Prime Mover and if you do, there are many paths to Heaven. I look forward to my visits with my mother's spirit, my Guardian Angel's spirit, and hopefully the greatest spirit in this universe . . . GOD.

Randolph Site For Jet Study

RANDOLPH AFB, Texas — The 3510th Flying Training Group's jet qualification course Class 59-D, currently in training here will graduate April 22.

Purpose of the jet qualification course is to train pilots of conventional aircraft in the jet. Both classroom work and many hours of jet flight with competent jet instructor pilots, are part of the course.

The 47 pilots comprising 59-D are from all the major USAF commands and from bases from Washington, D.C. to California.

They are:

Cols. Richard S. Nye, Hq. USAF; and Wright J. Sherrard, Hq. Comd;

Lt. Cols. Berry D. Brazile, SAC; Chandler B. Estes, Hq. USAF; Floyd E. Slipp, Hq. Comd; and Richard D. Stowell, MATS.

Also Lt. Cols. Billie J. Barry, SAC; Joseph F. Davis, Hq. USAF; Harry C. Henry, ARDC; Ray C. Staley, AU; and Robert L. Weniger, SAC.

Majs. Ray L. Barry, Hq. USAF; William J. Beach, TAC; Phillip E. Everett, ARDC; Ralph W. Everett, ARDC; Edgar W. Headley, SAC; Walter A. Keils, MATS; Kenneth N. Libby, SAC; and Kenneth W. Slaker, ATC.

Also Majs. John R. Blunk, SAC; Harry D. Immel, Jr., Hq. Comd; Harris Y. Lauterbach, ConAC; Clayton F. McDaniel, AMC; Merritt A. Reeves, AMC; Young A. Tucker, Hq. USAF; and Howard E. Weinhuff, Hq. USAF.

Goodbye propellers . . . Hello jets. Graduation photo from Jet Aircraft Flying School at Randolph Air Base, Texas in April 1959.

BIBLIOGRAPHY

The author's diary and library.

Adventure in Analysis of the Holy Bible, Edmund W. Gaugnier, Philosophical Library, 1954.

Cosmos, Carl Sagan, Random House, New York, New York, 1980.

Galileo's Daughter, Dava Sobel, Walker and Company, New York, New York, 1999.